FORMULARIES OF
FAITH

Articles About Religion, 1536
The Institution of a Christian Man, 1537
A Necessary Doctrine and Erudition for Any Christian Man, 1543

SEMINARY STREET PRESS
The Library of Anglican Theology
Number 8

Published by Seminary Street Press, the Library of Anglican Theology seeks to provide newly typeset editions of important works from the Anglican tradition for a wide array of contemporary readers—Christian laypeople, historians of the Church, seminary students, bishops, priests, deacons, catechists, and theologians. The Library will provide a rich foundation on which to build as Anglicans continue to theologically engage with the pressing questions of our time.

Series Editor
CHRISTOPHER POORE

Formularies of Faith

Confessional Documents Issued by Henry VIII & Thomas Cranmer

Articles About Religion • The Institution of a Christian Man • A Necessary Doctrine and Erudition for Any Christian Man

Edited by
Charles Lloyd
and Andrew Raines

SEMINARY STREET PRESS
GALESBURG, ILLINOIS

SEMINARY
STREET PRESS

Galesburg, Illinois

2022 Paperback Edition
ISBN: 979-8-84-837565-7

facebook.com/SeminaryStreetPress
Twitter: @SeminaryStPress
Instagram: @SeminaryStreetPress
seminarystreetpress@gmail.com

Contents

The Bishops' Book, Also Known as the Institution of a Christian Man

The King's Book, Also Known as a Necessary Doctrine and Erudition for Any Christian Man

Appendices

Preface of the Editor

The volume here reprinted is published with the design of putting into the hands of the Clergy treatises valuable for their matter, and of such rare occurrence as to be found only in public libraries, or in the private collections of the curious. It contains, as is stated in the title-page, the Formularies of Faith, which were put forth in the reign of Henry VIII, after the secession of that monarch from the church of Rome. To this secession, indeed, the original publication of these formularies was altogether owing. The promulgation of the scriptures to the people, for the first time, in their native language; the irruption of the new opinions; the rejection of that infallible authority, to which all men had hitherto been accustomed to appeal for the relief of their consciences, and the satisfaction of their doubts; these and other circumstances of a similar nature, all bearing upon one and the same point, gave rise to a variety of opinions, which, if unchecked, might degenerate into licentiousness, and to alarms, which it became expedient without delay to quiet and assuage.

Accordingly, the first *Articles about Religion* were devised and set forth with the intent of *establishing Christian quietness and unity among us, and avoiding contentious opinions;* and some of them were inserted with the express purpose of giving comfort to the wounded spirit, and of declaring publicly that the *bishop of Rome's pardons* were not necessary for obtaining everlasting life, or for *delivering the souls of men out of purgatory and the pains of it.* At the same time it was intended to convey to the people such instruction as the circumstances of the times admitted, and which might prepare the way gradually for a more ample explanation of the principles of the Christian faith.

It is needless to observe that these documents cannot pretend to any authority in the present day. Nothing antecedent to the reign of Edward VI has any title to that character. It was then only that the errors of Popery were formally renounced, and the pure doctrines of Protestantism authoritatively established in this kingdom. In these formularies, accordingly, many of the tenets of Romanism are to be found, which, in the succeeding reign, on a closer examination of scripture, and under the exercise of an unfettered liberty of judgment afforded by the more fortunate circumstances of that reign, were discarded as erroneous. The attentive reader, however, will not fail to observe, that, in many points, the name only of the doctrine appears to be retained, while the principle is, in fact, surrendered; and every portion of those doctrines which had been found by experience to be productive of evil, and of dangerous influence on the moral or religious practice of mankind, is mitigated and explained away.

Still, however, these documents, though they carry no authority along with them as formularies of faith, are of great importance to all, who are anxious to acquaint themselves with the rise and progress of the Protestant opinions in this country, or who would examine critically into the history and intention of those formularies which were afterwards established, and are still of primary authority in the Church of England. It is in these works too that they may trace the last departure of that darkness, which had so long obscured the genuine form of Christianity, that they may hail the reappearance of the pure light of the gospel, and mark the first dawnings of a brighter day.

Nor must it be forgotten that these treatises were all composed and published under the immediate inspection and superintendence of that illustrious prelate to whom, under Providence, the Church of England is indebted for the first volume of her Homilies, her Articles, and her Liturgy; and that they may be considered as representing the deliberate opinions of Cranmer on all those points in which the positive doctrines of Popery were not immediately concerned; for on these points, undoubtedly, the free expression of his sentiments was impeded and overruled.

It remains only to give some account of the formularies themselves: they are in number three.

1. The *Articles about Religion set out by the Convocation, and published by the King's Authority* in the year 1536. Under this title, but without date, they were originally printed by Bishop Burnet, from a MS. in the Cotton Library, in the Addenda to the first volume of his History of the Reformation. They have, of course, been reprinted in every subsequent edition of that work. But it was not under this title that these Articles were given to the world. The title of the volume which was edited by Thomas Berthelet in 1536, was, *Articles devised by the kinges highnes majestie, to stablyshe Christen quietnes,* &c. It was not till after the Articles had been worked off according to Burnet, that I discovered a copy of this original edition in Bishop Tanner's valuable collection now preserved in the Bodleian Library; when, finding that it differed in many particulars, though of no essential importance, from the Cotton MS., I thought it advisable to subjoin an exact reprint of it to the Preface, without cancelling the other.[1] The Articles are to be found also in Collyer's Eccles. Hist. II. p. 122; Fuller's Church Hist. Cent. XVI. book 5. sect. 3; but it is observable that none of these copies coincide exactly with each other. The most material differences occur in the king's Declaration prefixed to the Articles, in which the Cotton MS. varies from all the rest. There can be no doubt however that Berthelet's edition contains the most authentic record of the Articles; as may be concluded from the correction of many errors which are to be found in the Cotton MS. and from the incorporation of the Articles as they stand in the printed volume, into the *Institution of a Christian Man*, it seems reasonable to suppose that the Cotton MS. contains the Articles, as they were prepared by Convocation, before they were finally submitted to the king; an hypothesis confirmed by the observation which has been already made, that the principal variations occur in the king's Declaration, and more especially by a remarkable difference at the conclusion of the Article *of praying to Saints,* where the Cotton MS. has *by the commandment of the supreme head;* the printed volume *by the commandment of us, the supreme head;* the word *us* having, in all probability, been inserted by the king's own hand. Collyer's copy of the Articles, taken from a MS. in the Paper-Office, appears to be the earliest and most imperfect of the

---

[1] [In the current edition, the Berthelet-Bodleian MS. of the *Articles devised by the kinges highnes majestie* begin on pg. 1, while the Cotton MS. of the *Articles about Religion set out by Convocation* begin on pg. 19.]

whole; the king's Declaration he has adopted from Fuller, as it is not found in his MS.

These articles the Clergy were enjoined to explain to the people in their discourses.[2]

2. *The Institution of a Christian Man,* published in 1537, both in 4to and 8vo. I have seen no other edition. This work contains a great part of the former Articles, together with large additions on the Creed, the Ten Commandments, &c. It was called *the Bishops book.*[3]

3. The *Necessary Doctrine and Erudition for any Christian Man,* printed first in 1543, and again in 1545, both in 4to and 8vo. The editions in 8vo, some copies of them at least, seem to carry the date 1534 in the title-page. This date however belongs not to the book itself, but to the or- namented compartment which surrounds the letter-press of the title-page, and which was employed to embellish other books in a similar way. The true date is to be gathered from the colophon at the end.[4] A free translation of this book in Latin appeared in 1544, under the title of *Pia et Catholica Christiani Hominis Institutio.*

This work is, in fact, nothing more than the *Institution* in a varied form, with some additional articles on the subject of Free-will, Good- works, &c. It was called *the King's Book,* in contradistinction to the work last mentioned. I think it is truly said by Collyer, that it "manages with less latitude than the Institution, bends to the six Articles, and in some points of controversy drives farther into the doctrines of the Roman Commun- ion." It is probable that Gardiner had greater influence in the preparation of this work than in either of the former.

It is evident from the account which has here been given of these trea- tises, that if the object of the Editor had been merely to put the reader in possession of the matter contained in them, it would have been sufficient to reprint the *Necessary Doctrine* only, and to mark the differences and ad- ditions which have been just described. But, as the critical history of these

---

[2] See Appendix A.

[3] See Appendix B.

[4] Thus, in a volume in the Bodleian Library printed by Berthelet. which has the same compartment in the title-page bearing the date 1534, the letter-press within the compartment is as follows: "The boke named the Governour, devised by sir Thomas Elyot, knt. Londini, ann. 1546." thus evidently distinguishing the date of the book from the date of the compartment.

treatises has been the subject of much mistake and controversy, and as it is matter of extreme difficulty for any one who is removed from the use of public libraries to obtain an opportunity of collating them for himself, it appeared advisable to place them separate and unmutilated under the eyes of the reader.

A more detailed account of these works may be found in Strype's Memorials of Cranmer, I. c. 11, 13. and 20; in his Ecclesiastical Memorials, I. c. 41. and 48; in Lord Herbert's History of Henry VIII. p. 465. and 557; in Fuller, book V. sect. 3; Collyer, book II. p. 122, 127, and 128; and Wilkins' Concilia, III. p. 817; and more especially in Dr. Laurence's Bampton Lectures, p. 14. and 189, who has corrected the extraordinary mistakes and inaccuracies of Burnet; in Mr. Todd's Introduction to the *Declarations of our Reformers;* and Dr. Burrow's Introduction to his *Summary of Christian Faith and Practice.*

As it did not appear that any sufficient advantage would be derived from the retention of the ancient orthography, the modern mode has been adopted. Besides, the original editions are so inconsistent with each other, that it is not easy for an editor of the present day to find any certain rule to guide him in his decisions. I have now before me three copies of the *Necessary Erudition*, all professing to be printed by Berthelet on the 29th of May, 1543; but all differing in their mode of spelling the most ordinary words.[5] No other change, however, has been made: and it is hoped that the reader, with the exception of the orthography, will here have an exact and accurate reprint of the original volumes.

CHARLES LLOYD.
Ch. Ch. Feb. 18, 1825.

---

[5] See Appendix C.

Articles

Devised By

The Kinges Highnes Majestie,

To Stablyshe Christen Quietnes
and Unitie Amonge Us,

and

To Avoyde Contentious Opinions,

Which Articles Be Also Approved

By the Consent and Determination
of the Hole Clergie of this Realme.

ANNO M.D.XXXVI.

Articles Devised by the Kinges Highnes Majestie

The Preface

Henry the VIII, by the grace of God king of England and of France, defensor of the faith, lord of Ireland, and in earth supreme head of the Church of England, to all and singular our most loving, faithful, and obedient subjects, greeting.

Among other cures appertaining unto this our princely office, whereunto it hath pleased Almighty God of his infinite mercy and goodness to call us, we have always esteemed and thought, like as we also yet esteem and think, that it most chiefly belongeth unto our said charge diligently to foresee and cause, that not only the most holy word and commandments of God should most sincerely be believed, and most reverently be observed and kept of our subjects, but also that unity and concord in opinion, namely in such things as doth concern our religion, may increase and go forthward, and all occasion of dissent and discord touching the same be repressed and utterly extinguished.

For the which cause, we being of late, to our great regret, credibly advertised of such diversity in opinions, as have grown and sprung in this our realm, as well concerning certain articles necessary to our salvation, as also touching certain other honest and commendable ceremonies, rites, and usages now of long time used and accustomed in our churches, for conservation of an honest policy and decent and seemly order to be had therein, minding to have that unity and agreement established through our said Church concerning the premises, and being very desirous to eschew not only the dangers of souls, but also the outward unquietness which by occasion of the said diversity in opinions (if remedy were not provided) might perchance have ensued, have not only in our own person at many times taken great pains, study, labours, and travails, but also have caused our bishops, and other the most discreet and best learned men of our clergy of this our whole realm, to be assembled in our convocation, for the full debatement and quiet determination of the same. Where, after long and mature deliberation, and disputations had of and upon the premises, finally they have concluded and agreed upon the most special points and articles, as well such as be commanded of God, and are necessary to our salvation, as also divers other matters touching the honest ceremonies and good and politic orders, as is aforesaid, which their determination, debatement, and agreement, for so much as we think to have proceeded of a good, right, and true judgment, and to be agreeable to the laws and ordinances of God, and much profitable for the establishment of that charitable concord and unity in our Church of England, which we most desire, we have caused the same to be published, willing, requiring, and commanding you, to accept, repute, and take them accordingly. And further we most heartily desire and pray Almighty God, that it may please him so to illumine your hearts, that you and every of you may have no less desire, zeal, and love to the said unity and concord, in reading, divulging, and following the same, than we have had, and have in causing them to be thus devised, set forth, and published.

And, for because we would the said Articles and every of them should be taken and understanden of you after such sort, order, and degree, as appertaineth accordingly, we have caused, by the like assent and agreement of our said bishops and other learned men, the said Articles to be divided into two sorts; whereof the one part containeth such as be commanded expressly by God, and be necessary to our salvation; and the other containeth such things as have been of a long continuance for a decent order and honest policy, prudently instituted and used in the churches of our realm, and be for that same purpose and end to be observed and kept accordingly, although they be not expressly commanded of God, nor necessary to our salvation. Wherefore we will and require you to accept the same, after such sort as we have here prescribed them unto you, and to conform yourselves obediently unto the same. Whereby you shall not only attain that most charitable unity and loving concord, whereof shall ensue your incomparable commodity, profit, and lucre, as well spiritual as other, but also you shall not a little encourage us to take further travails, pains, and labours for your commodities, in all such other matters as in time to come may happen to occur, and as it shall be most to the honour of God, the profit, tranquillity, and quietness of all you our most loving subjects.

The Principal Articles Concerning Our Faith

First, as touching the chief and principal articles of our faith, sith it is thus agreed as hereafter followeth by the whole clergy of this our realm, we will that all bishops and preachers shall instruct and teach our people, by us committed to their spiritual charge, that they ought and must most constantly believe and defend all those things to be true, which be comprehended in the whole body and canon of the Bible, and also in the three Creeds or symbols, whereof one was made by the apostles, and is the common creed, which every man useth; the second was made by the holy council of Nice, and is said daily in the mass; and the third was made by Athanasius, and is comprehended in the Psalm *Quicunque vult:* and that they ought and must take and interpret all the same things according to the selfsame sentence and interpretation, which the words of the selfsame creeds or symbols do purport, and the holy approved doctors of the church do entreat and defend the same.

Item, That they ought and must repute, hold, and take all the same things for the most holy, most sure, and most certain, and infallible words of God, and such as neither ought, ne can be altered or convelled, by any contrary opinion or authority.

Item, That they ought and must believe, repute, and take all the articles of our faith contained in the said creeds to be so necessary to be believed for man's salvation, that whosoever being taught will not believe them as is aforesaid, or will obstinately affirm the contrary of them, he or they cannot be the very members of Christ and his espouse the church, but be very infidels or heretics, and members of the Devil, with whom they shall perpetually be damned.

Item, That they ought and must most reverently and religiously observe and keep the selfsame words, according to the very same form and manner of speaking, as the articles of our faith be already contained and expressed in the said creeds, without altering in any wise, or varying from the same.

Item, That they ought and must utterly refuse and condemn all those opinions contrary to the said articles, which were of long time past condemned in the four holy councils, that is to say, in the council of Nice, Constantinople, Ephesus, and Chalcedonense, and all other sith that time in any point consonant to the same.

The Sacrament of Baptism

Secondly, as touching the holy sacrament of baptism, we will that all bishops and preachers shall instruct and teach our people committed by us unto their spiritual charge, that they ought and must of necessity believe certainly all those things, which hath been always by the whole consent of the church approved, received, and used in the sacrament of baptism; that is to say, that the sacrament of baptism was instituted and ordained in the New Testament by our Saviour Jesu Christ, as a thing necessary for the attaining of everlasting life, according to the saying of Christ, *Nisi quis renatus fuerit ex aqua et Spirttu Sancto, non potest intrare in regnum cœlorum:* that is to say, No man can enter into the kingdom of heaven, except he be born again of water and the Holy Ghost (John 3:5).

Item, That it is offered unto all men, as well infants as such as have the use of reason, that by baptism they shall have remission of sins, and the grace and favour of God, according to the saying of Christ, *Qui crediderit et baptizatus fuerit, salvus erit:* that is to say, Whosoever believeth and is baptized shall be saved (Mark 16:16).

Item, That the promise of grace and everlasting life (which promise is adjoined unto this sacrament of baptism) pertaineth not only unto such as have the use of reason, but also to infants, innocents, and children; and that they ought therefore and must needs be baptized: and that by the sacrament of baptism they do also obtain remission of their sins, the grace and favour of God, and be made thereby the very sons and children of

God. Insomuch as infants and children dying in their infancy shall undoubtedly be saved thereby, and else not.

Item, That infants must needs be christened because they be born in original sin, which sin must needs be remitted; which cannot be done but by the sacrament of baptism, whereby they receive the Holy Ghost, which exerciseth his grace and efficacy in them, and cleanseth and purifieth them from sin by his most secret virtue and operation.

Item, That children or men once baptized, can, ne ought ever to be baptized again.

Item, That they ought to repute and take all the anabaptists' and the Pelagians' opinions contrary to the premises, and every other man's opinion agreeable unto the said anabaptists' or the Pelagians' opinions in this behalf, for detestable heresies, and utterly to be condemned.

Item, That men or children having the use of reason, and willing and desiring to be baptized, shall, by the virtue of that holy sacrament, obtain the grace and remission of all their sins, if they shall come thereunto perfectly and truly repentant and contrite of all their sins before committed, and also perfectly and constantly confessing and believing all the articles of our faith, according as it was mentioned in the first article.

And finally, if they shall also have firm credence and trust in the promise of God adjoined to the said sacrament, that is to say, that in and by this said sacrament, which they shall receive, God the Father giveth unto them, for his son Jesu Christ's sake, remission of all their sins, and the grace of the Holy Ghost, whereby they be newly regenerated and made the very children of God, according to the saying of saint John and the apostle saint Peter, *Delictorum pœnitentiam agite, et baptizetur unusquisque vestrum in nomen Jesu Christi in remissionem peccatorum, et accipietis donum Spiritus Sancti;* that is to say, Do penance for your sins, and be each of you baptized in the name of Jesu Christ, and you shall obtain remission of your sins, and shall receive the gift of the Holy Ghost (Acts 2:38). And according also to the saying of saint Paul, *Non ex operibus justitiæ quæ fecimus nos, sed secundum suam misericordiam, salvos nos fecit per lavacrum regenerationis et renovationis Spiritus Sancti, quem effudit in nos opulente per Jesum Christum Servatorem nostrum, ut justificati illius gratia hæredes efficiamur juxta spem vitæ æternæ;* that is to say, God hath not saved us for the works of justice which we have done, but of his mercy by baptism, and renovation of the Holy Ghost, whom he hath poured out upon us most plentifully, for the love of Jesu Christ our Saviour, to the intent that we, being justified by his grace, should be made the inheritors of everlasting life, according to our hope (Titus 3:5-7).

The Sacrament of Penance

Thirdly, concerning the sacrament of penance, we will that all bishops and preachers shall instruct and teach our people committed by us unto their spiritual charge, that they ought and must most constantly believe, that that sacrament was institute of Christ in the New Testament as a thing so necessary for man's salvation, that no man, which after his baptism is fallen again, and hath committed deadly sin, can, without the same, be saved, or attain everlasting life.

Item, That like as such men which after baptism do fall again into sin, if they do not penance in this life, shall undoubtedly be damned; even so whensoever the same men shall convert themselves from their naughty life, and do such penance for the same as Christ requireth of them, they shall without doubt attain remission of their sins, and shall be saved.

Item, That the sacrament of perfect penance which Christ requireth of such manner persons consisteth of three parts, that is to say, contrition, confession, and the amendment of the former life, and a new obedient reconciliation unto the laws and will of God, that is to say, exterior acts in works of charity according as they be commanded of God, which be called in scripture, *fructus digni pœnitentia*, the worthy fruits of penance.

Furthermore, as touching contrition, which is the first part, we will that all bishops and preachers shall instruct and teach our people committed by us unto their spiritual charge, that the said contrition consisteth in two special parts, which must always be conjoined together, and cannot be dissevered; that is to say, the penitent and contrite man must first knowledge the filthiness and abomination of his own sin, (unto which knowledge he is brought by hearing and considering of the will of God declared in his laws,) and feeling and perceiving in his own conscience that God is angry and displeased with him for the same; he must also conceive not only great sorrow and inward shame that he hath so grievously offended God, but also great fear of God's displeasure towards him, considering he hath no works or merits of his own which he may worthily lay before God, as sufficient satisfaction for his sins; which done, then afterward with this fear, shame, and sorrow must needs succeed and be conjoined the second part, that is to wit, a certain faith, trust, and confidence of the mercy and goodness of God, whereby the penitent must conceive certain hope and faith that God will forgive him his sins, and repute him justified, and of the number of his elect children, not for the worthiness of any merit or work done by the penitent, but for the only merits of the blood and passion of our Saviour Jesu Christ.

Item, That this certain faith and hope is gotten and also confirmed, and made more strong by the applying of Christ's words and promises of his grace and favour, contained in his gospel, and the sacraments instituted by him in the New Testament; and therefore to attain this certain faith, the second part of penance is necessary, that is to say, confession to a priest, if it may be had; for the absolution given by the priest was institute of Christ to apply the promises of God's grace and favour to the penitent.

Wherefore as touching confession, we will that all bishops and preachers shall instruct and teach our people committed by us to their spiritual charge, that they ought and must certainly believe that the words of absolution pronounced by the priest, be spoken by authority given to him by Christ in the gospel.

Item, That they ought and must give no less faith and credence to the same words of absolution so pronounced by the ministers of the church, than they would give unto the very words and voice of God himself if he should speak unto us out of heaven, according to the saying of Christ, *Quorumcunque remiseritis peccata, remittuntur eis: quorumcunque retinueritis retenta sunt:* that is to say, Whose sins soever ye do forgive, shall be forgiven; whose sins soever ye do retain, shall be retained (John 20:23). And again in another place Christ saith, *Qui vos audit me audit,* &c.; that is to say, Whosoever heareth you heareth me, &c. (Luke 10:16).

Item, That in no wise they do contemn this auricular confession which is made unto the ministers of the church, but that they ought to repute the same as a very expedient and necessary mean, whereby they may require and ask this absolution at the priest's hands, at such time as they shall find their consciences grieved with mortal sin, and have occasion so to do, to the intent they may thereby attain certain comfort and consolation of their consciences.

As touching the third part of penance, we will that all bishops and preachers shall instruct and teach our people committed by us to their spiritual charge, that although Christ and his death be the sufficient oblation, sacrifice, satisfaction, and recompense, for the which God the Father forgiveth and remitteth to all sinners not only their sin, but also eternal pain due for the same; yet all men truly penitent, contrite, and confessed, must needs also bring forth the fruits of penance, that is to say, prayer, fasting, almsdeeds, and must make restitution or satisfaction in will and deed to their neighbours, in such things as they have done them wrong and injury in, and also must do all other good works of mercy and charity, and express their obedient will in the executing and fulfilling of God's commandment outwardly, when time, power, and occasion shall be ministered unto them, or else they shall never be saved; for this is the express precept and commandment of God, *Agite fructus dignos pœnitentiæ;* that is to say, Do you the worthy fruits of penance (Luke 3:8): and saint Paul saith, *Quemadmodum præbuistis membra vestra serva immunditiæ et iniquitati ad aliam atque aliam iniquitatem; sic et nunc præbete membra vestra serva justitiæ ad sanctificationem,* &c.; that is to say, Like as in times past you have given and applied yourself and all the members of your body to all filthy living and wickedness, continually increasing the same, in like manner now you must give and apply yourself wholly to justice, increasing continually in purity and cleanness of life (Rom 6:19): and in another place he saith, *Castigo corpus meum, et in servitutem redigo;* that is to say, I chastise and subdue my carnal body and the affections of the same, and make them obedient unto the spirit (1 Cor 9:27).

Item, That these precepts and works of charity be necessary works to our salvation, and God necessarily requireth that every penitent man shall perform the same, whensoever time, power, and occasion shall be ministered unto him so to do.

Item, That by penance and such good works of the same, we shall not only obtain everlasting life, but also we shall deserve remission or mitigation of these present pains and afflictions in this world, according to the saying of St. Paul, *Si nos ipsi judicaremus, non judicaremur a Domino;* that is to say, If we would correct and take punishment of ourselves, we should not be so grievously corrected of God (1 Cor 11:31): and Zacharias the prophet saith, *Convertimini ad me, ei ego convertar ad vos;* that is to say, Turn yourselves unto me, and I will turn again unto you (Zech 1:3): and the prophet Esay saith, *Frange esurienti panem tuum, et egenos vagosque induc in domum tuam. Cum videris nudum, operi eum, et carnem tuam ne despexeris: tunc erumpet quasi mane lumen tuum, et sanitas tua citius orietur, et anteibit faciem tuam justitia tua, et gloria Dei colliget te: tunc invocabis et Dominus exaudiet te, clamabis, et dicet: Ecce adsum. Tunc orietur in tenebris lux tua et tenebræ tuæ erunt sicut meridies, et requiem tibi dabit Dominus semper, et implebit splendoribus animam tuam, et ossa tua liberabit, et eris quas hortus irriguus et sicut fons aquarum, cujus non deficient aquæ,* &c.; that is to say, Break and deal thy bread unto the hungry, bring into thy house the poor man, and such as want harborough; when thou seest a naked man, give him clothes to cover him with, and refuse not to succour and help the poor and needy, for he is thine own flesh. And if thou wilt thus do, then shall thy light glister out as bright as the sun in the morning, and thy health shall sooner arise unto thee, and thy justice shall go before thy face, and the glory of God shall gather thee up, that thou shalt not fall: and whensoever thou shalt call upon God, God shalt hear thee; and whensoever thou shalt cry unto God, God shall say, Lo, here I am, ready to help thee. Then shall thy light overcome all darkness, and thy darkness shall be as bright as the sun at noon days: and then God shall give unto thee continual rest, and shall fulfil thy soul with brightness, and shall deliver thy body from adversity: and then thou shalt be like a garden, that most plentifully bringeth forth all kind of fruits, and like the well-spring that never shall want water (Isa 58:7-11).

These things, and such other, should be continually taught and inculked into the ears of our people, to the intent to stir and provoke them unto good works: and by the selfsame good works to exercise and confirm their faith and hope, and look for to receive at God's hand mitigation and remission of the miseries, calamities, and grievous punishments, which God sendeth to men in this world for their sins.

The Sacrament of the Altar

Fourthly, as touching the sacrament of the altar, we will that all bishops and preachers shall instruct and teach our people committed by us unto their spiritual charge, that they ought and must constantly believe, that under the form and figure of bread and wine, which we there presently do see and perceive by outward senses, is verily, substantially, and really contained and comprehended the very selfsame body and blood of our Saviour Jesus Christ, which was born of the Virgin Mary, and suffered upon the cross for our redemption; and that under the same form and figure of bread and wine the very selfsame body and blood of Christ is corporally, really, and in the very substance exhibited, distributed, and received unto and of all them which receive the said sacrament; and that therefore the said sacrament is to be used with all due reverence and honour, and that every man ought first to prove and examine himself, and religiously to try and search his own conscience, before he shall receive the same; according to the saying of St. Paul, *Quisquis ederit partem hunc aut biberit de poculo Domini indigne, reus erit corporis et sanguinis Domini; probet igitur seipsum homo, et sic de pane illo edat et de poculo illo bibat: nam qui edit aut bibit indigne judicium sibi ipsi manducat et bibit, non dijudicans corpus Domini;* that is to say, Whosoever eateth this body of Christ unworthily, or drinketh of this blood of Christ unworthily, shall be guilty of the very body and blood of Christ: wherefore let every man first prove himself, and so let him eat of this bread, and drink of this drink. For whosoever eateth it or drinketh it unworthily, he eateth and drinketh it to his own damnation: because he putteth no difference between the very body of Christ and other kinds of meat (1 Cor 11:27-29).

Justification

Fifthly, as touching the order and cause of our justification, we will that all bishops and preachers shall instruct and teach our people committed by us to their spiritual charge, that this word Justification signifieth remission of our sins, and our acceptation or reconciliation into the grace and favour of God, that is to say, our perfect renovation in Christ.

Item, That sinners attain this justification by contrition and faith joined with charity, after such sort and manner as we before mentioned and declared; not as though our contrition, or faith, or any works proceeding thereof, can worthily merit or deserve to attain the said justification; for the only mercy and grace of the Father, promised freely unto us for his Son's sake Jesu Christ, and the merits of his blood and passion, be the only sufficient and worthy causes thereof: and yet that notwithstanding, to the attaining of the same justification, God requireth to be in us not only inward contrition, perfect faith and charity, certain hope and confidence, with all other spiritual graces and motions, which, as we said before, must necessarily concur in remission of our sins, that is to say, our justification; but also he requireth and commandeth us, that after we be justified we must also have good works of charity and obedience towards God, in the observing and fulfilling outwardly of his laws and commandments: for although acceptation to everlasting life be conjoined with justification, yet our good works be necessarily required to the attaining of everlasting life; and we being justified, be necessarily bound, and it is our necessary duty to do good works, according to the saying of saint Paul, *Debitores sumus non carni, ut secundum carnem vivamus. Nam si secundum carnem vixerimus, moriemur: sin autem spiritu facta corporis mortificaverimus, vivemus; etenim quicunque spiritu Dei ducuntur, hi sunt filii Dei;* that is to say, We be bound not to live according to the flesh and to fleshly appetites; for if we live so, we shall undoubtedly be damned. And contrary, if we will mortify the deeds of our flesh, and live according to the Spirit, we shall be saved. For whosoever be led by the Spirit of God, they be the children of God (Rom 8:12-14). And Christ saith, *Si vis ad vitam ingredi, serva mandata;* that is to say, If ye will come to heaven, keep the commandments (Matt 19:17). And saint Paul, speaking of evil works, saith, *Qui talia agunt regnum Dei non possidebunt; that* is to say, Whosoever commit sinful deeds, shall never come to heaven (Gal 5:21). Wherefore we will that all bishops and preachers shall instruct and teach our people committed by us unto their spiritual charge, that God necessarily requireth of us to do good works commanded by him; and that not only outward and civil works, but also the inward spiritual motions and graces of the Holy Ghost; that is to say, to dread and fear God, to love God, to have firm confidence and trust in God, to invocate and call upon God, to have patience in all adversities, to hate sin, and to have certain purpose and will not to sin again, and such other like motions and virtues: for Christ saith, *Nisi abundamrit justitia vestra plusquam Scribarum et Pharisceorum, non intrabitis in regnum cælorum* (Matt 5:20);[1] that is to say, we must not only

---

[1] [For I tell you, unless your righteousness exceeds that of the scribes and Pharisees, you will never enter the kingdom of heaven.]

do outward civil good works, but also we must have these foresaid inward spiritual motions, consenting and agreeable to the law of God.

Articles Concerning the Laudable Ceremonies Used in the Church

And First of Images

As touching images, truth it is that the same have been used in the Old Testament, and also for the great abuses of them sometime destroyed and put down; and in the New Testament they have been also allowed, as good authors do declare. Wherefore we will that all bishops and preachers shall instruct and teach our people committed by us to their spiritual charge, how they ought and may use them. And first, that there may be attributed unto them, that they be representors of virtue and good example, and that they also be by occasion the kindlers and stirrers of men's minds, and make men oft to remember and lament their sins and offences, especially the images of Christ and our lady; and that therefore it is meet that they should stand in the churches, and none otherwise to be esteemed: and to the intent the rude people should not from henceforth take such superstition, as in time past it is thought that the same hath used to do, we will that our bishops and preachers diligently shall teach them, and according to this doctrine reform their abuses, for else there might fortune idolatry to ensue, which God forbid. And as for censing of them, and kneeling and offering unto them, with other like worshippings, although the same hath entered by devotion, and fallen to custom; yet the people ought to be diligently taught that they in nowise do it, nor think it meet to be done to the same images, but only to be done to God, and in his honour, although it be done before the images, whether it be of Christ, of the cross, of our lady, or of any other saint beside.

Of Honouring of Saints

As touching the honouring of saints, we will that all bishops and preachers shall instruct and teach our people committed by us unto their spiritual charges, that saints now being with Christ in heaven be to be honoured of Christian people in earth; but not with that confidence and honour which are only due unto God, trusting to attain at their hands that which must be had only of God: but that they be thus to be honoured, because they be known the elect persons of Christ, because they be passed in godly life out of this transitory world, because they already do reign in glory with Christ; and most specially to laud and praise Christ in them for their excellent virtues which he planted in them, for example, of and by them to such as yet are in this world to live in virtue and goodness, and also not to fear to die for Christ and his cause, as some of them did; and finally to take them, in that they may, to be advancers of our prayers and demands unto Christ. By these ways, and such like, be saints to be honoured and had in reverence, and by none other.

Of Praying to Saints

As touching praying to saints, we will that all bishops and preachers shall instruct and teach our people committed by us unto their spiritual charge, that albeit grace, remission of sin, and salvation, cannot be obtained but of God only by the mediation of our Saviour Christ, which is only sufficient Mediator for our sins; yet it is very laudable to pray to saints in heaven everlastingly living, whose charity is ever permanent, to be intercessors, and to pray for us and with us, unto Almighty God after this manner: All holy angels and saints in heaven pray for us and with us unto the Father, that for his dear Son Jesu Christ's sake, we may have grace of him and remission of our sins, with an earnest purpose, (not wanting ghostly strength,) to observe and keep his holy commandments, and never to decline from the same again unto our lives' end: and in this manner we may pray to our blessed lady, to St. John Baptist, to all and every of the apostles or any other saint particularly, as our devotion doth serve us; so that it be done without any vain superstition, as to think that any saint is more merciful, or will hear us sooner than Christ, or that any saint doth serve for one thing more than another, or is patron of the same. And likewise we must keep holydays unto God, in memory of him and his saints, upon such days as the church hath ordained their memories to be celebrated; except they be mitigated and moderated by the assent and commandment of us, the supreme head, to the ordinaries, and then the subjects ought to obey it.

Of Rites and Ceremonies

As concerning the rites and ceremonies of Christ's church, as to have such vestments in doing God's service, as be and have been most part used, as sprinkling of holy water to put us in remembrance of our baptism, and the blood of Christ sprinkled for our redemption upon the cross: giving of holy bread, to put us in remembrance of the sacrament of the altar, that all Christian men be one body mystical of Christ, as the bread is made of many grains, and yet but one loaf, and to put us in remembrance of the receiving of the holy sacrament and body of Christ, the which we ought to receive in right charity; which in the beginning of Christ's church men did more often receive than they use nowadays to do: bearing of candles on Candlemas-day, in memory of Christ the spiritual Light, of whom Simeon did prophesy, as is read in the church that day: giving of ashes on Ash Wednesday, to put in remembrance every Christian man in the beginning of Lent and penance, that he is but ashes and earth, and thereto shall return; which is right necessary to be uttered from henceforth in our mother tongue always on the same day: bearing of palms on Palm-Sunday, in memory of the receiving of Christ into Jerusalem, a little before his death, that we may have the same desire to receive him into our hearts: creeping to the cross, and humbling ourselves to Christ on Good Friday before the cross, and there offering unto Christ before the same, and kissing of it in memory of our redemption by Christ made upon the cross; setting up the sepulture of Christ, whose body after his death was buried; the hallowing of the font, and other like exorcisms and benedictions by the ministers of Christ's church: and all other like laudable customs, rites, and ceremonies be not to be contemned and cast away, but to be used and continued as things good and laudable, to put us in remembrance of those spiritual things that they do signify; not suffering them to be forgot, or to be put in oblivion, but renewing them in our memories from time to time: but none of these ceremonies have power to remit sin, but only to stir and lift up our minds unto God, by whom only our sins be forgiven.

Of Purgatory

Forasmuch as due order of charity requireth, and the Book of Maccabees, and divers ancient doctors plainly shew, that it is a very good and a charitable deed to pray for souls departed, and forasmuch also as such usage hath continued in the church so many years, even from the beginning, we will that all bishops and preachers shall instruct and teach our people committed by us unto their spiritual charge, that no man ought to be grieved with the continuance of the same, and that it standeth with the very due order of charity, a Christian man to pray for souls departed, and to commit them in our prayers to God's mercy, and also to cause other to pray for them in masses and exequies, and to give alms to other to pray for them, whereby they may be relieved and holpen of some part of their pain: but forasmuch as the place where they be, the name thereof, and kind of pains there, also be to us uncertain by scripture; therefore this with all other things we remit to Almighty God, unto whose mercy it is meet and convenient for us to commend them, trusting that God accepteth our prayers for them, referring the rest wholly to God, to whom is known their estate and condition; wherefore it is much necessary that such abuses be clearly put away, which under the name of purgatory hath been advanced, as to make men believe that through the bishop of Rome's pardons souls might clearly be delivered out of purgatory, and all the pains of it, or that masses said at *scala cœli,* or otherwhere, in any place, or before any image, might likewise deliver them from all their pain, and send them straight to heaven: and other like abuses.

———————————

LONDINI IN ÆDIBUS
THOMÆ BERTHELETI REGII IMPRESSORIS.

Articles About Religion

Set Out by the Convocation,

and

Published by the King's Authority

Articles About Religion

Henry the Eighth, by the grace of God, king of England and of France, defender of the faith, and lord of Ireland, and in earth supreme head of the church of England, to all and singular our most loving, faithful, and obedient subjects, greeting. Amongst other cures committed unto this our princely office, whereunto it hath pleased God of his infinite mercy and goodness to call us, we have always esteemed and thought (as we also yet esteem and think) this to be most chief, most ponderous, and of most weight, that his holy word and commandments may sincerely, without let or hinderance, be of our subjects truly believed, and reverently kept and observed; and that unity and concord in opinions, namely in such things as doth concern our religion, may increase and go forthward, and all occasion of dissent and discord touching the same be repressed, and utterly extinguished; for the which cause we being of late, to our great regret, credibly advertised of such diversity in opinions as have grown and sprongen in this our realm, as well concerning certain articles necessary to our salvation, as also touching certain honest and commendable ceremonies, rites, and usages in our said church, for an honest policy, and decent order heretofore of long time used and accustomed; minding to have that unity and agreement established through our said church concerning the premises; and being very desirous to eschew not only the dangers of souls, but also the outward inquietness which by occasion of the said diversity in opinions (if remedy had not been provided) might perchance have ensued;

21

have not only in our own person many times taken great pain, study, labour and travails, but also have caused our bishops, and other the most discreet and best learned men of our clergy of this our whole realm, to be assembled in our convocation, for the full debatement and quiet determination of the same: where, after long and mature deliberation and disputations, had of and upon the premises, finally they have concluded and agreed upon the said matters, as well those which be commanded of God, and are necessary to our salvation, as also the other touching the honest ceremonies, and good and politic order, as is aforesaid; which their determination, debatement, and agreement, forasmuch as we think to have proceeded of a good, right, and true judgment, and to be agreeable to the laws and ordinances of God, and much profitable for the establishment of that charitable concord and unity in our church of England, which we most desire, we have caused the same to be published, willing, requiring, and commanding you to accept, repute, and take them accordingly; most heartily desiring and praying Almighty God, that it may please him so to illumine your hearts, that you, and every of you, may have no less desire, zeal, and love to the said unity and concord, in reading, divulging, and following the same, than we have had and have, causing them to be thus devised, set forth, and published. And, for because we would the said articles, and every of them, to be taken and understanden of you after such sort, order, and degree as appertaineth accordingly; we have caused, by the like assent and agreement of our said bishops and other learned men, the said articles to be divided into two sorts, that is to say, such as are commanded expressly by God, and are necessary to our salvation, and such other, as, although they be not expressly commanded of God, nor necessary to our salvation, yet being of a long continuance, for a decent order and honest policy, prudently instituted, are for that same purpose and end to be observed in like manner; which ye following, after such sort as we have prescribed unto you, shall not only attain that most charitable unity and loving concord, whereof shall ensue your incomparable commodity, profit, and lucre, as well spiritual as other; but also ye conforming yourselves, and using these our said articles as is aforesaid, shall not a little encourage us to take further travail, pains and labours for your commodities in all such other matters, as in time to come may happen to occur, and as it shall be most to the honour of God and ours, the profit, tranquillity, and quietness of all you our most loving subjects.

The Articles of Our Faith

First, as touching the chief and principal articles of our faith, sith it is thus agreed as hereafter followeth by the whole clergy of this our realm, we will, that all bishops and preachers shall instruct and teach our people, by us committed to their spiritual charge, that they ought and must most constantly believe and defend all those things to be true, which be comprehended in the whole body and canon of the Bible, and also in the three Creeds or symbols, whereof one was made by the apostles, and is the common creed which every man useth; the second was made in the holy council of Nice, and is said daily in the mass; and the third was made by Athanasius, and is comprehended in the Psalm *Quicunque vult:* and that they ought and must take and interpret all the same things according to the selfsame sentence and interpretation, which the words of the selfsame creeds or symbols do purport, and the holy approved doctors of the church do entreat and defend the same.

Item, That they ought and must repute, hold, and take all the same things for the most holy, most sure, and most certain, and infallible words of God, and such as neither ought, ne can be altered or convelled by any contrary opinion or authority.

Item, That they ought and must believe, repute, and take all the articles of our faith contained in the said creeds to be so necessary to be believed for man's salvation, that whosoever being taught will not believe them as is aforesaid, or will obstinately affirm the contrary of them, he or they cannot be the very members of Christ and his spouse the church, but be very infidels or heretics, and members of the Devil, with whom they shall perpetually be damned.

Item, That they ought and must most reverently and religiously observe and keep the selfsame words, according to the very same form and manner of speaking, as the articles of our faith be already conceived and expressed in the said creeds, without altering in any wise, or varying from the same.

Item, That they ought and must utterly refuse and condemn all those opinions contrary to the said articles, which were of long time past condemned in the four holy councils, that is to say, in the council of Nice, Constantinople, Ephesus, and Chalcedonense, and all other sith that time in any point consonant to the same.

The Sacrament of Baptism

Secondly, as touching the holy sacrament of baptism, we will that all bishops and preachers shall instruct and teach our people committed by us unto their spiritual charge, that they ought and must of necessity believe certainly all those things, which hath been always by the whole consent of the church approved, received, and used in the sacrament of baptism; that is to say, that the sacrament of baptism was instituted and ordained in the New Testament by our Saviour Jesus Christ, as a thing necessary for the attaining of everlasting life, according to the saying of Christ, *Nisi quis renatus fuerit ex aqua et Spiritu Sancto, non potest intrare in regnum cœlorum* (John 3:5).[1]

Item, That it is offered unto all men, as well infants as such as have the use of reason, that by baptism they shall have remission of sins, and the grace and favour of God, according to the saying of John, *Qui crediderit et baptizatus fuerit salvus erit* (Mark 16:16).[2]

Item, That the promise of grace and everlasting life, which promise is adjoined unto the sacrament of baptism, pertaineth not only unto such as have the use of reason, but also to infants, innocents, and children; and they ought therefore and must needs be baptized: and that by the sacrament of baptism they do also obtain remission of their sins, the grace and favour of God, and be made thereby the very sons and children of God, insomuch as infants and children dying in their infancy shall undoubtedly be saved thereby, or else not.

Item, That infants must needs be christened because they be born in original sin, which sin must needs be remitted; which cannot be done but by the sacrament of baptism, whereby they receive the Holy Ghost, which exerciseth his grace and efficacy in them, and cleanseth and purifieth them from sin by his most secret virtue and operation.

Item, That children or men once baptized, can, ne ought ever to be baptized again.

Item, That they ought to repute and take all the anabaptists' and the Pelagians' opinions contrary to the premises, and every other man's opinion agreeable unto the said anabaptists' or the Pelagians' opinions in this behalf, for detestable heresies, and utterly to be condemned.

---

[1] [No one can enter the kingdom of God without being born of water and Spirit.]

[2] [The one who believes and is baptized will be saved.]

Item, That men or children having the use of reason, and willing and desiring to be baptized, shall, by the virtue of that holy sacrament, obtain the grace and remission of all their sins, if they shall come thereunto perfectly and truly repentant and contrite of all their sins before committed, and also perfectly and constantly confessing and believing all the articles of our faith, according as it was mentioned in the article before, or else not.

And finally, if they shall also have firm credence and trust in the promise of God adjoined to the said sacrament, that is to say, that in and by this said sacrament, which they shall receive, God the Father giveth unto them, for his Son Jesus Christ's sake, remission of all their sins, and the grace of the Holy Ghost, whereby they be newly regenerated and made the very children of God, according to the saying of Christ and his apostle St. Peter, *Pœnitentiam agite et baptizetur unusquisque vestrum in nomine Jesu Christi in remissionem peccatorum, et accipietis donum Spiritus Sancti* (Acts 2:38);[3] and according also to the saying of St. Paul *ad Titum 3. Non ex operibus justitiæ quæ fecimus nos, sed secundum suam misericordiam, salvos nos fecit per lavacrum regenerationis et renovationis Spiritus Sanctis quem effudit in nos opulenter per Jesum Christum Servatorem nostrum, ut justificati illius gratia hæredes efficiamur juxta spem vitæ æternæ* (Titus 3:5-7).[4]

The Sacrament of Penance

Thirdly, concerning the sacrament of penance, we will that all bishops and preachers shall instruct and teach our people committed by us unto their spiritual charge, that they ought and must most constantly believe, that that sacrament was instituted of Christ in the New Testament as a thing so necessary to man's salvation, that no man which after his baptism is fallen again, and hath committed deadly sin, can, without the same, be saved, or attain everlasting life.

---

[3] [Repent, and be baptized every one of you in the name of Jesus Christ so that your sins may be forgiven; and you will receive the gift of the Holy Spirit.]

[4] [He saved us, not because of any works of righteousness that we had done, but according to his mercy, through the water of rebirth and renewal by the Holy Spirit. This Spirit he poured out on us richly through Jesus Christ our Savior, so that, having been justified by his grace, we might become heirs according to the hope of eternal life.]

Item, That like as such men which after baptism do fall again into sin, if they do not penance in this life, shall undoubtedly be damned; even so whensoever the same men shall convert themselves from the said naughty life, and do such penance for the same as Christ requireth of them, they shall without doubt attain remission of their sins, and shall be saved.

Item, That this sacrament of perfect penance which Christ requireth of such manner of persons, consisteth of three parts, that is to say, contrition, confession, with the amendment of the former life, and a new obedient reconciliation unto the laws and will of God, that is to say, exterior acts in works of charity according as they be commanded of God, which be called in scripture, *fructus digni pœnitentia.*[5]

Furthermore, as touching contrition, which is the first part, we will that all bishops and preachers shall instruct and teach our people committed by us unto their spiritual charge, that the said contrition consisteth in two special parts, which must always be conjoined together, and cannot be dissevered; that is to say, the penitent and contrite man must first knowledge the filthiness and abomination of his own sin, whereunto he is brought by hearing and considering of the will of God declared in his laws, and feeling and perceiving in his own conscience that God is angry and displeased with him for the same; he must also conceive not only great sorrow and inward shame that he hath so grievously offended God, but also great fear of God's displeasure towards him, considering he hath no works or merits of his own, which he may worthily lay before God, as sufficient satisfaction for his sins; which done, then afterwards with this fear, shame and sorrow must needs succeed and be conjoined, the second part, viz. a certain faith, trust and confidence of the mercy and goodness of God, whereby the penitent must conceive certain hope and faith that God will forgive him his sins, and repute him justified, and of the number of his elect children, not for the worthiness of any merit or work done by the penitent, but for the only merits of the blood and passion of our Saviour Jesus Christ.

Item, That this certain faith and hope is gotten and also confirmed, and made more strong by the applying of Christ's words and promise, of his grace and favour contained in his gospel, and the sacraments instituted by him in the New Testament; and therefore to attain this certain faith,

---

[5] [Fruits worthy of repentance; cf. Matthew 3:8 and Luke 3:8.]

the second part of penance is necessary, that is to say, confession to a priest, if it may be had; for the absolution given by the priest was instituted of Christ to apply the promises of God's grace and favours to the penitent.

Wherefore as touching confession, we will that all bishops and preachers shall instruct and teach our people committed by us to their spiritual charge, that they ought and must certainly believe that the words of absolution pronounced by the priest, be spoken by the authority given to him by Christ in the gospel.

Item, That they ought and must give no less faith and credence to the same words of absolution so pronounced by the ministers of the church, than they would give unto the very words and voice of God himself if he should speak unto us out of heaven, according to the saying of Christ, *Quorum remiseritis peccata,* &c. (John 20:23);[6] *et qui vos audit me audit* (Luke 10:16).[7]

Item, That in no ways they do contemn this auricular confession which is made unto the ministers of the church, but that they ought to repute the same as a very expedient and necessary mean, whereby they may require and ask this absolution at the priest's hands, at such time as they shall find their consciences grieved with mortal sin, and have occasion so to do, to the intent they may thereby attain certain comfort and consolation of their consciences.

As touching the third part of penance, we will that all bishops and preachers shall instruct and teach our people committed by us to their spiritual charge, that although Christ and his death be the sufficient oblation, sacrifice, satisfaction, and recompense, for the which God the Father forgiveth and remitteth to all sinners not only their sin, but also eternal pain due for the same; yet all men truly penitent, contrite, and confessed, must needs also bring forth the fruits of penance, that is to say, prayer, fasting, almsdeeds, and must make restitution or satisfaction in will and deed to their neighbour, in such things as they have done them wrong and injury in, and also must do all other good works of mercy and charity, and express their obedient will in the executing and fulfilling of God's

---

[6] [If you forgive the sins of any, they are forgiven them; if you retain the sins of any, they are retained.]

[7] [Whoever listens to you listens to me, and whoever rejects you rejects me, and whoever rejects me rejects the one who sent me.]

commandments outwardly, when time, power, and occasion shall be ministered unto them, or else they shall never be saved; for this is the express precept and commandment of God, *Agite fructus dignos pœnitentiæ* (Luke 3:8);[8] and St. Paul saith, *Debitores sumus* (Rom 8:12);[9] and in another place he saith, *Castigo corpus meum et in servitutem redigo* (1 Cor 9:27).[10]

Item, That these precepts and works of charity be necessary works to our salvation, and God necessarily requireth that every penitent man shall perform the same, whensoever time, power, and occasion shall be ministered unto him so to do.

Item, That by penance and such good works of the same, we shall not only obtain everlasting life, but also we shall deserve remission or mitigation of these present pains and afflictions in this world, according to the saying of St. Paul, *Si nos ipsi judicaremus, non judicaremur a Domino* (1 Cor 11:31);[11] and Zacharias, *Convertimini ad me, et ego convertar ad vos* (Zech 1:3);[12] et Esaias 58. *Frange esurienti panem tuum, &c. tunc eris velut hortus irriguus.*[13] *Hæc sunt inculcanda ecclesiis et ut exercitentur ad bene operandum, et in hiis ipsis operibus exerceant et confirment fidem, petentes et expectantes a Deo mitigationem præsentium calamitatum.*[14]

The Sacrament of the Altar

Fourthly, as touching the sacrament of the altar, we will that all bishops and preachers shall instruct and teach our people committed by us unto their spiritual charge, that they ought and must constantly believe, that under the form and figure of bread and wine, which we there presently do see and perceive by outward senses, is verily, substantially, and really contained and comprehended the very selfsame body and blood of our

---

[8] [Bear fruits worthy of repentance.]

[9] [We are debtors . . .]

[10] [I punish my body and enslave it . . .]

[11] [But if we judged ourselves, we would not be judged.]

[12] [Return to me, and I will return to you.]

[13] [Share your bread with the hungry . . . and you shall be like a watered garden.]

[14] [This must be inculcated in the churches so that they may be stirred to good works, and may exercise and confirm their faith in these works, by seeking and waiting for God's mitigation of the present calamities.]

Saviour Jesus Christ, which was born of the Virgin Mary, and suffered upon the cross for our redemption; and that under the same form and figure of bread and wine the very selfsame body and blood of Christ is corporally, really, and in the very substance exhibited, distributed, and received of all them which receive the said sacrament; and that therefore the said sacrament is to be used with all due reverence and honour, and that every man ought first to prove and examine himself, and religiously to try and search his own conscience, before he shall receive the same; according to the saying of St. Paul, *Quisquis ederit panem hunc aut biberit de poculo Domini indigne, reus erit corporis et sanguinis Domini; probet autem seipsum homo, et sic de pane illo edat et de poculo illo bibat; nam qui edit aut bibit indigne, judicium sibi ipsi manducat et bibit, non dijudicans corpus Domini* (1 Cor 11:27-29).[15]

Justification

Fifthly, as touching the order and cause of our justification, we will that all bishops and preachers shall instruct and teach our people committed by us unto their spiritual charge, that this word Justification signifieth remission of our sins, and our acceptation or reconciliation into the grace and favour of God, that is to say, our perfect renovation in Christ.

Item, That sinners attain this justification by contrition and faith joined with charity, after such sort and manner as we before mentioned and declared; not as though our contrition, or faith, or any works proceeding thereof, can worthily merit or deserve to attain the said justification; for the only mercy and grace of the Father, promised freely unto us for his Son's sake Jesus Christ, and the merits of his blood and his passion, be the only sufficient and worthy causes thereof; and yet that notwithstanding, to the attaining of the said justification, God requireth to be in us not only inward contrition, perfect faith, and charity, certain hope and confidence, with all other spiritual graces and motions, which, as we said before, must necessarily concur in remission of our sins, that is to say, our justification;

---

[15] [Whoever, therefore, eats the bread or drinks the cup of the Lord in an unworthy manner will be answerable for the body and blood of the Lord. Examine yourselves, and only then eat of the bread and drink of the cup. For all who eat and drink without discerning the body, eat and drink judgment against themselves.]

but also he requireth and commandeth us, that after we be justified we must also have good works of charity, and obedience towards God, in the observing and fulfilling outwardly of his laws and commandments: for although acceptation to everlasting life be conjoined with justification, yet our good works be necessarily required to the attaining of everlasting life; and we being justified, be necessarily bound, and it is our necessary duty to do good works, according to the saying of St. Paul, *Debitores sumus non carni, ut secundum carnem vivamus. Nam si secundum carnem vixerimus, moriemur: sin autem spiritu facta corporis mortificaverimus, vivemus; etenim quicunque spiritu Dei ducuntur, hi sunt filii Dei* (Rom 8:12-14):[16] and Christ saith, *Si vis ad vitam ingredi, serva mandata* (Matt 19:17);[17] and St. Paul, *de malis operibus,* saith, *Qui talia agunt regnum Dei non possidebunt* (Gal 5:21).[18] Wherefore we will that all bishops and preachers shall instruct and teach our people committed by us unto their spiritual charge, that God necessarily requireth of us to do good works commanded by him; and that not only outward and civil works, but also the inward spiritual motions and graces of the Holy Ghost; that is to say, to dread and fear God, to love God, to have firm confidence and trust in God, to invocate and call upon God, to have patience in all adversities, to hate sin, and to have certain purpose and will not to sin again, and such other like motions and virtues: for Christ saith, *Nisi abundaverit justitia vestra plusquam Scribarum et Pharisæorum, non intrabitis in regnum cœlorum* (Matt 5:20);[19] that is to say, we must not only do outward civil good works, but also we must have these foresaid inward spiritual motions, consenting and agreeable to the law of God.

---

[16] [So then, brothers and sisters, we are debtors, not to the flesh, to live according to the flesh—for if you live according to the flesh, you will die; but if by the Spirit you put to death the deeds of the body, you will live. For all who are led by the Spirit of God are children of God.]

[17] [If you wish to enter into life, keep the commandments.]

[18] [. . . and St. Paul, of evil works, saith, "Those who do such things will not inherit the kingdom of God."]

[19] [Unless your righteousness exceeds that of the scribes and Pharisees, you will never enter the kingdom of heaven.]

Of Images

As touching images, truth it is that the same have been used in the Old Testament, and also for the great abuses of them sometimes destroyed and put down; and in the New Testament they have been also allowed, as good authors do declare. Wherefore we will that all bishops and preachers shall instruct and teach our people committed by us to their spiritual charge, how they ought and may use them. And first, that there may be attributed unto them, that they be representers of virtue and good example, and that they also be by occasion the kindlers and stirrers of men's minds, and make men often remember and lament their sins and offences, especially the images of Christ and our lady; and that therefore it is meet that they should stand in the churches, and none otherwise to be esteemed: and to the intent the rude people should not from henceforth take such superstition, as in time past it is thought that the same hath used to do, we will that our bishops and preachers diligently shall teach them, and according to this doctrine reform their abuses, for else there might fortune idolatry to ensue, which God forbid. And as for censing of them, and kneeling and offering unto them, with other like worshippings, although the same hath entered by devotion, and fallen to custom; yet the people ought to be diligently taught that they in no ways do it, nor think it meet to be done to the same images, but only to be done to God, and in his honour, although it be done before the images, whether it be of Christ, of the cross, or of our lady, or of any other saint beside.

Of Honouring of Saints

As touching the honouring of saints, we will that all bishops and preachers shall instruct and teach our people committed by us unto their spiritual charge, that saints now being with Christ in heaven be to be honoured of Christian people in earth; but not with that confidence and honour which are only due unto God, trusting to attain at their hands that which must be had only of God; but that they be thus to be honoured, because they be known the elect persons of Christ, because they be passed in godly life out of this transitory world, because they already do reign in glory with Christ; and most specially to laud and praise Christ in them for their excellent virtues which he planted in them, for example, of and by them to such as are yet in this world to live in virtue and goodness, and also not to fear to die for Christ and his cause, as some of them did; and finally to take them, in that they may, to be the advancers of our prayers and demands unto Christ. By these ways, and such like, be saints to be honoured and had in reverence, and by none other.

Of Praying to Saints

As touching praying to saints, we will that all bishops and preachers shall instruct and teach our people committed by us unto their spiritual charge, that albeit grace, remission of sin, and salvation, cannot be obtained but of God only by the mediation of our Saviour Christ, which is only sufficient Mediator for our sins; yet it is very laudable to pray to saints in heaven everlastingly living, whose charity is ever permanent, to be intercessors, and to pray for us and with us, unto Almighty God after this manner: All holy angels and saints in heaven pray for us and with us unto the Father, that for his dear Son Jesus Christ's sake we may have grace of him, and remission of our sins, with an earnest purpose, not wanting ghostly strength, to observe and keep his holy commandments, and never to decline from the same again unto our lives' end: and in this manner we may pray to our blessed lady, to St. John Baptist, to all and every of the apostles or any other saint particularly, as our devotion doth serve us; so that it be done without any vain superstition, as to think that any saint is more merciful, or will hear us sooner than Christ, or that any saint doth serve for one thing more than other, or is patron of the same. And likewise we must keep holydays unto God, in memory of him and his saints, upon such days as the church hath ordained their memories to be celebrated; except they be mitigated and moderated by the assent or commandment of the supreme head, to the ordinaries, and then the subjects ought to obey it.

Of Rites and Ceremonies

As concerning the rites and ceremonies of Christ's church, as to have such vestments in doing God service as be and have been most part used, as sprinkling of holy water to put us in remembrance of our baptism, and the blood of Christ sprinkled for our redemption upon the cross: giving of holy bread, to put us in remembrance of the sacrament of the altar, that all Christian men be one body mystical of Christ, as the bread is made of many grains, and yet but one loaf, and to put us in remembrance of the receiving the holy sacrament and body of Christ, the which we ought to receive in right charity; which in the beginning of Christ's church men did more often receive than they use nowadays to do: bearing of candles on Candlemas-day, in memory of Christ the spiritual Light, of whom Simeon did prophesy, as is read in the church that day: giving of ashes on Ash Wednesday, to put in remembrance every Christian man in the beginning of Lent and penance, that he is but ashes and earth, and thereto shall return; which is right necessary to be uttered from henceforth in our mother tongue always on the same day: bearing of palms on Palm Sunday, in memory of receiving of Christ into Jerusalem, a little before his death, that we may have the same desire to receive him into our hearts: creeping to the cross, and humbling ourselves to Christ on Good Friday before the cross, and offering thereunto Christ before the same, and kissing of it in memory of our redemption by Christ made upon the cross; setting up the sepulture of Christ, whose body after his death was buried; the hallowing of the font, and other like exorcisms and benedictions by the ministers of Christ's church: and all other like laudable customs, rites, and ceremonies be not to be contemned and cast away, but to be used and continued as things good and laudable, to put us in remembrance of those spiritual things that they do signify; not suffering them to be forgotten, or to be put in oblivion, but renewing them in our memories from time to time: but none of these ceremonies have power to remit sin, but only to stir and lift up our minds unto God, by whom only our sins be forgiven.

Of Purgatory

Forasmuch as due order of charity requireth, and the Book of Maccabees, and divers ancient doctors plainly shewen, that it is a very good and charitable deed to pray for souls departed, and forasmuch also as such usage hath continued in the church so many years, even from the beginning, we will that all bishops and preachers shall instruct and teach our people committed by us unto their spiritual charge, that no man ought to be grieved with the continuance of the same, and that it standeth with the very due order of charity, a Christian man to pray for souls departed, and to commit them in our prayers to God's mercy, and also to cause others to pray for them in masses and exequies, and to give alms to others to pray for them, whereby they may be relieved, and holpen, of some part of their pain: but forasmuch as the place where they be, the name thereof, and kind of pains there, also be to us uncertain by scripture; therefore this with all other things we remit to God Almighty, unto whose mercy it is meet and convenient for us to commend them, trusting that God accepteth our prayers for them, referring the rest wholly to God, to whom is known their estate and condition; wherefore it is much necessary that such abuses be clearly put away, which under the name of purgatory hath been advanced, as to make men believe that through the bishop of Rome's pardon souls might clearly be delivered out of purgatory, and all the pains of it, or that masses said at *scala cœli,* or otherwhere, in any place, or before any image, might likewise deliver them from all their pain, and send them straight to heaven; and other like abuses.

Signed,
Thomas Cromwell

T. Cantuarien.	Joannes Bangoren.
Edwardus Ebor.	Nicholaus Sarisburiens.
Joannes London.	Edvardus Hereforden.
Cuthbertus Dunelmens.	Willielmus Norwicensis.
Joannes Lincoln.	Willielmus Meneven.
Joannes Lincoln. nomine	Robertus Assaphen.
procuratorio pro dom.	Robertus abbas sancti Albani.
Joan. Exon.	Willielmus ab. Westmonaster.
Joannes Bathonien.	Joannes ab. Burien.
Hugo Wygornen.	Richardus ab. Glasconiæ.
Joannes Roffen.	Hugo ab. de Redying.
Rich. Cicestren.	Robertus ab. Malmesbur.
Thomas Elien.	Clemens ab. Eveshamen.
Joannes Lincoln. nomine	Johannes ab. de Bello.
procuratorio pro dom.	Willielmus ab. S. Petri Glocest.
Rowlando Coven. et	Richardus ab. Winchel-
Lichfielden.	combens.

Joannes ab. de Croyland.
Robertus ab. de Thorney.
Robertus ab. de Walntham.
Joannes ab. Cirencest.
Joannes ab. Texber.
Thomas prior Coventr.

———————

Joannes ab. de Osney.
Henricus ab. de Gratiis.
Anthonius ab. de Eynsam.
Robertus prior Elien.
Robertus prior sive magister
    ordinis de Sempringham.
Richardus ab. de Notteley.
Hugo prior de Huntyngdon.
Willielmus ab. de Stratford.

Gabriel ab. de Buckfestria.
Henricus ab. de Wardenor.
Joannes prior de Merton.
Richardus pr. de Walsingham.
Thomas ab. de Gerendon.
Thomas ab. de Stanley.
Richardus ab. de Bytlesden.
Richardus pr. de Lanthoni.
Robertus ab. de Thame.
Joannes prior de Neweham.
Radulphus prior de Kyme.
Richardus ab. de Bruera.
Robertus ab. de Welhows.
Bartholamaus pr. de Overey.
Willielmus pr. de Burgaveni.
Thomas ab. de Abendon.

———————

Inferior Domus.

Ri. Gwent archidiaconus
    London, et Breck.
Robertus Aldrydgearchid.
    Colecest.
Thomas Bedyll archid.
    Cornub.
Richardus Strete archid.
    Derbiæ.
David Pole ar. Salop.
Richardus Doke archid.
    Sarum.
Edmundus Bonner archid.
    Leycestriæ.
Thomas Baghe archid. Surr.
Gamaliel Gyfton decanus
    Hereford. et proc. capit.

Joannes London decanus
    Wallingford.
Nicholas Metcalf. archid.
    Roffens.
Richardus Layton archid.
    Bucks.
Hugo Coren proc. cleri
    Hereford.
Richardus Sparcheford proc.
    cleri Hereford.
Mauritius Griffith proc. cleri
    Roffen.
Gulielmus Buckmastre
    procurator cleri London.
Richardus Rawson archid.
    Essex.

Edmundus Cranmer archid.
Cant.

Polidorus Vergilius archid.
Wellen.

Richardus Coren archid.
Oxon.

Henricus Morgan procurator
cleri Lincoln.

Petrus Vannes archid.
Wygornen.

Georgius Hennage decanus
Lincoln.

Nilo Spencer procurator cleri
Norwicen.

Willmus Knyght archid.
Cestriæ.

Nicolaus Metcalf archid.
Roffen.

Willmus Hedge procurator
cleri Norwicen.

Adam Traves archid. Exon.

Richardus Woleman dec.
Wellen.

Tho. Brerewood archidiacon.
bar. procur. capituli et
cleri Exon.

Georgius Carew archid.
Totton proc. capituli et
cleri Exon.

Thomas Bennet proc. cleri. et
capit. Sarum.

Richardus Arche proc. cleri et
capit. Sarum.

Petrus Ligham pr. cleri Cant.

Edmundus Steward proc. cleri
Winton.

Joannes Rayne pr. cleri
Lincoln.

Leonardus Savile proc. cleri
archid. Lewen.

Simon Matthew pr. cleri
London.

Lanfrid Ogle archid. Salop.

Gulielmus Maye proc. cleri
Elien.

Rolandus Phylips proc.
capituli eccles. St. Pauli
London.

Joannes Bell ar. Glocest.

Richardus Shelton Mag.
colleg. de Metyngham.

Per me Willielmum Glyn.
archi. Anglessem.

Robertus Evans decan.
Bangoren

Walterus Cretyng ar.
Bathonien.

Thomas Bagard procurator
cleri Wygornen.

Joannes Nase proc. cleri
Bathon. et Wellen.

Georgius Wyndam archid.
Norwicen.

Joannes Chambre dec. St.
Stephani archid. Bedford.

Nicolaus Wilson.

The Bishops' Book

Also Known As

The Institution of a Christian Man

Containing

The Exposition or Interpretation

Of

The Common Creed,

Of

The Seven Sacraments,

Of

The Ten Commandments,

And of

The Pater Noster

And the

Ave Maria, Justification, and Purgatory

*To the most high and most excellent prince, our most gracious and most re-
doubted sovereign lord and king, Henry the VIII, by the grace of God king
of England and of France, defender of the faith, lord of Ireland, and supreme head in earth immediately under Christ of the church of England,
Thomas archbishop of Canterbury, Edward archbishop of York, and all
other the bishops, prelates, and archdeacons of this your realm, wish all
grace, peace, and felicity from Almighty God the Father and our Lord Jesu
Christ.*

Pleaseth it your most royal majesty to understand, that whereas of your
most godly disposition and tender zeal, which is impressed in your most
noble heart, towards the advancement of God's glory, and the right institution and education of your people in the knowledge of Christ's true
religion, your highness commanded us now of late to assemble ourselves
together, and upon the diligent search and perusing of holy scripture, to
set forth a plain and sincere doctrine, concerning the whole sum of all
those things which appertain unto the profession of a Christian man, that
by the same all errors, doubts, superstitions, and abuses might be sup-
pressed, removed, and utterly taken away, to the honour of Almighty God,
and to the perfect establishing of your said subjects in good unity and concord, and perfect quietness both in their souls and bodies: we, considering
the godly effect and intent of this your highness' most virtuous and gracious commandment, do not only rejoice and give thanks unto Almighty

God with all our hearts, that it hath pleased him to send such a king to reign over us, which so earnestly mindeth to set forth among his subjects the light of holy scripture, which alone sheweth men the right path to come to God, to see him, to know him, to love him, to serve him, and so to serve him as he most desireth; but have also, according to our most bounden duties, endeavoured ourselves, with all our wit, learning, and power, to satisfy your highness' said desired most godly purpose. And thereupon calling to our remembrance how the whole pith and sum of all those things which be at great length contained in the whole canon of the Bible, and be of necessity required to the attaining of everlasting life, was sufficiently, exactly, and therewith shortly and compendiously comprehended in the twelve articles of the common creed, called the Apostles' Creed, in the Seven Sacraments of the church, in the Ten Commandments, and in the prayer of our Lord, called the Pater noster: and considering therefore, that if your highness' people were perfectly instructed and learned in the right knowledge and understanding of the same, they should not only be able easily to perceive and understand, and also to learn by heart and bear away the whole effect and substance of all those things, which do appertain and be necessary for a Christian man, either to believe or to do, but also that all occasions might thereby be removed, which by any colour or visage have caused any of them to fall or to be offended: we have, after long and mature consultation had amongst us, compiled a certain treatise, wherein we have employed our whole study, and have therein truly and purely set forth and declared in our mother tongue the very sense and meaning, and the very right use, virtue, and efficacy of all the said four parts. And forasmuch as faith is that singular gift of God, whereby our hearts, that is to say, our natural reason and judgment, (obscured and almost extincted by original and actual sins,) is lightened, purified, and made able to know and discern what things be indeed acceptable and what be displeasant in the sight of God; and for because also that faith is the very fountain and chief ground of our religion, and of all goodness and virtues exercised in the same, and is the first gate whereby we enter and be received and admitted, not only into the family or household of our Lord God, but also into the knowledge of his majesty and deity, and of his inestimable power, wisdom, righteousness, mercy, and goodness; we have first of all begun with the Creed, and have declared by way of a paraphrasis, that is, a kind, mere, and true exposition of the right understanding of every article of the same. And afterward we have entreated of the institution, the virtue, and right use of the Seven Sacraments. And thirdly, we have declared the Ten Commandments, and what is contained in every one of them. And fourthly, we have shewed the interpretation of the Pater noster, whereunto we have also added the declaration of the Ave Maria. And to the intent we would omit nothing contained in the book of articles, devised and set forth this last year by your highness' like commandment, we have also added, in the end of this treatise, the article of Justification, and the article of Purgatory, as they be in the said book expressed. And thus having determined our sentence in all things contained in the said treatise, according to the very true meaning of scripture, we do offer the same herewith unto your most excellent majesty, most humbly beseeching the same to permit and suffer it, in case it shall be so thought meet to your most excellent wisdom, to be printed, and so with your supreme power set forth, and commanded to be by us and all other your subjects of the clergy of this your most noble realm, as well religious as other, taught to your highness' people; without the which power and license of your majesty, we knowledge and confess that we have none authority, either to assemble ourselves together for any pretence or purpose, or to publish any thing that might be by us agreed on and compiled. And albeit, most dread and benign sovereign lord, we do affirm by our learnings with one assent, that the said treatise is in all points so concordant and agreeable to holy scripture, as we trust your majesty shall receive the same as a thing most sincerely and purely handled, to the glory of God, your grace's honour, the unity of your people, the which things your highness, we may well see and perceive, doth chiefly in the same desire: yet we do most humbly submit it to the most excellent wisdom and exact judgment of your majesty, to be recognised, overseen, and corrected, if your grace shall find any word or sentence in it meet to be changed, qualified, or further expounded, for the plain setting forth of your highness' most virtuous desire and purpose in that behalf. Whereunto we shall in that case conform ourselves, as to our most bounden duties to God and to your highness appertaineth.

Your highness' most humble subjects
and daily beadsmen,

Thomas Cantuarien.   Edouardus Ebor.

Joannes London.

Cuthbertus Dunelmen.

Stephanus Winton.

Robertus Carliolen.

Joannes Exon.

Joannes Lincoln.

Joannes Bathonien.

Rolandus Coven. et Lich.

Thomas Elien.

Nicolaus Saris.

Joannes Bangor.

Edouardus Hereforden.

Hugo Wigornien.

Joannes Roffen.

Ricardus Cicestren.

Guilielmus Norwicen.

Guilielmus Meneven.

Robertus Assaven.

Robertus Landaven.

Ricardus Wolman
   archidiaconus Sudbur.

Gulielmus Knight arch.
   Richemond.

Joannes Belle arch. Gloucestr.

Edmundus Boner arch.
   Laicestr.

Gulielmus Skippe arch.
   Dorset.

Nicolaus Heeth arch. Stafford.

Cuthbertus Marshal arch.
   Notingham.

Ricardus Curren arch. Oxon.

Gulielmus Cliffe.

Galfridus Downes.

Robertus Oking.

Radulphus Bradforde.

Ricardus Smith.

Symon Mathewe.

Joannes Pryn.

Gulielmus Buckmaster.

Gulielmus May.

Nicolaus Wotton.

Ricardus Coxe.

Joannes Edmundes.

Thomas Robertson.

Joannes Baker.

Thomas Baret.

Joannes Hase.

Joannes Tyson.

Sacræ theologiæ, juris ecclesiastici et civilis professors.

Exposition of the Creed

The Creed, Called the Apostles' Creed

1. I believe in God the Father, and that he is Almighty, and Creator of heaven and earth.

2. And I believe in Jesu Christ, and that he is his only begotten Son, and our Lord.

3. And that he was conceived by the Holy Ghost, and born of the Virgin Mary.

4. And suffered passion for our redemption under a certain judge, whose name was Pontius Pilatus, and so was crucified, dead, and buried.

5. And that he descended into hell, and rose again the third day from death to life.

6. And that he ascended afterward up into heaven, and sitteth there upon the right hand of Almighty God his Father.

7. And that he shall come from thence at doomsday to judge the quick and dead.

8. And I believe in the Holy Ghost.

9. And I believe that there is one holy catholic and universal church.

10. And I believe that there is in the same church communion of saints, and remission of sins.

11. And I believe that at doomsday all the people of the world that ever was or ever shall be unto that day, shall then arise again in the selfsame flesh and body, which they had while they lived here in earth.

12. And I believe that all the elect people of God shall have and enjoy everlasting life for their reward.

The Sense and Interpretation of the First Article

I believe in God the Father, and that he is Almighty, and Creator of heaven and earth.

In my heart I believe assuredly, and steadfastly with my mouth I profess and knowledge, that there is but one very God, and three Persons in Trinity, the Father, the Son, and the Holy Ghost, and that these three Persons be not three Gods, but all one God, all of one nature, and of one substance, and all of one everlasting essence or being, and all like and equal in might, power, wisdom, knowledge, rightwiseness, and all other things belonging unto the Deity. And that beside or without this God, there is no other God.

And I believe also and profess, that God the Father, which is the first Person in Trinity, is not only the God, the Lord, and the Father of heaven and earth, and all things contained therein, by creation and governance; but also that he is the Father of his only begotten Son, the second Person in Trinity, and that he did beget him of his own substance by eternal generation, that is to say, by generation that never had beginning.

And I believe also and profess, that all and singular the words and sayings of this God the Father, (be they laws, precepts, promises, prophecies, or threatenings,) and all that ever was spoken of him or by him in the whole body and canon of the New and the Old Testament, is most certainly true, and of such infallible verity and truth, that the same cannot be altered or convelled by any contrary opinion, power, or authority. And I promise and profess, that I do and will not only hope and look surely and without all doubt to attain and enjoy all those things, which God promiseth in holy scripture unto the elect children of God; but also that I do and will fear lest those punishments and afflictions which God in holy scripture threateneth to cast upon those persons which do transgress his will and commandments, shall fall upon me, if I shall not, like an obedient servant and child, study to fulfil and accomplish the same.

And I believe also and profess, that this God and this Father is almighty, that is to say, that his power and might excelleth incomparably all the other powers in heaven and earth. And that all other powers, which be in heaven, earth, or hell, be nothing as of themselves, but have all their might, force, and strength of him only, and be all subject unto his power, and be ruled and governed thereby, and cannot resist or let the same.

And I believe also and profess, that this Almighty God and Almighty Father did, at the beginning, create, form, and make of nought heaven and earth, and all things contained in this world, as well angels and man's soul, and all other things invisible, as also all other visible creatures; and that he did give unto them all the power and might which they have.

And I believe also and profess, that among his other creatures he did create and make me, and did give unto me this my soul, my life, my body, with all the members that I have, great and small, and all the wit, reason, knowledge, and understanding that I have; and finally, all the other outward substance, possessions, and things that I have or can have in this world.

And I believe also and profess, that he is my very God, my Lord, and my Father, and that I am his servant and his own son, by adoption and grace, and the right inheritor of his kingdom; and that it proceedeth and cometh of his mere goodness only, without all my desert, that I am in this life preserved and kept from dangers and perils, and that I am sustained, nourished, fed, clothed, and that I have health, tranquillity, rest, peace, or any other thing necessary for this corporal life. I knowledge also and confess, that he suffereth and causeth the sun, the moon, the stars, the day, the night, the air, the fire, the water, the land, the sea, the fowls, the fishes, the beasts, and all the fruits of the earth, to serve me for my profit and my necessity.

And in like manner I confess and knowledge, that all bodily sickness and adversity, which do fortune unto me in this world, be sent unto me by his hand and his visitation, and that he punisheth me not to destroy me, but only to save me, and to reduce me again by penance unto the right way of his laws and his religion, and so thereby to prove me, and to exercise me in patience and other virtues, and also to signify unto me the great care, and fatherly love, and goodness, which he beareth towards me. And therefore I will have none other God, but only this God, which by his almighty power hath created and made heaven and earth, and all things contained in the same. Neither will I glory or put my trust and confidence in mine own power, force, strength, riches, learning, science, wisdom, or any thing else whatsoever I have, or shall have, and possess in this world. Neither will I glory or put my confidence in any other man or creature of this world, be it in heaven, hell, or in earth, nor in any craft of magic, sorcery, charms, witchcrafts, or any other false arts, subtiled and invented by the Devil; but I will put my whole hope, my whole trust and confidence in God only, and in him only will I glory, and give all honour and glory unto him, and unto him only, and unto his governance will I commit and submit myself, my goods, and all that ever I have, without fearing or regarding the malice, the craft, or power of the Devil, or any of his members, which might induce me to the contrary. Neither will I desire any sign to tempt God, but I will trust firmly and faithfully unto him. And although he shall send any adversity unto me, or shall defer and tarry his pleasure in granting such request and petition as I shall make unto him, yet will not I murmur or grudge thereat, nor go about to prescribe or appoint unto him any end, any time, any measure, or season; but I will commit all to his will, with a pure and a steadfast faith, and will patiently abide the time which unto him shall be thought most expedient for me.

This faith I retain steadfastly engraved in my heart, and I promise, by the grace and help of God, never to swerve or decline from the same, for any argument, persuasion, or authority, that may be objected; nor for any worldly affection, or respect of pleasure, pain, persecution, or torment, whatsoever shall fortune unto me. From this trust and confidence will I never be brought, although all the men in the world should forsake me, and persecute me. Neither will I the less trust in God, for that I am a man of great power, force, and authority, endued with all sufficiencies in this world; ne yet because I want the possessions of this world, and am but wretched and poor, rude and unlearned, and despised of all men; nor, finally, because I am a wretched sinner. For sith this God is the Almighty Lord and Maker of all things, and hath all things under his hands and governance, what can I lack that he cannot give or do unto me, if it be his will so to do? And sith he is my Father, I am assured, that for the fatherly love and pity which he hath and beareth unto me, he will not only care for me, but he will be also continually present with me by his grace and favour, and will continually govern and direct me, aid and assist me, and provide that that shall be best for me, and will also forgive me all the sins that I ever committed or have done, contrary to his commandment, so oft as I shall by true and unfeigned penance return unto him with all my heart, and shall apply my whole mind, purpose, and endeavour, to amend my naughty life, and to observe his commandments.

The Sense and Interpretation of the Second Article

I believe constantly in my heart, and with my mouth I do profess and knowledge, that Jesu Christ is the only begotten Son of Almighty God the Father, and that he was begotten of his godly nature and substance eternally before the world was made or formed, and that he is very God, equal with God the Father and the Holy Ghost in substance, and all other things belonging unto the Godhead.

And I believe in Jesu Christ, and that he is his only begotten Son, and our Lord.

And I believe likewise, that this Jesu Christ was eternally preordained, and appointed by the decree of the holy Trinity, to be our Lord, that is to say, to be the only Redeemer and Saviour of mankind, and to reduce and bring the same from under the dominion of the devil and sin, unto his only dominion, kingdom, lordship, and governance.

And I believe likewise, that this Jesu Christ is true in all his words and promises, or rather that he is very truth itself. And that all things which be spoken of him or by him, in holy scripture, be certainly and infallibly true.

And I believe also and profess, that Jesu Christ is not only Jesus, and Lord to all men that believe in him, but also that he is my Jesus, my God, and my Lord. For whereas of my nature I was born in sin, and in the indignation and displeasure of God, and was the very child of wrath, condemned to everlasting death, subject and thrall to the power of the Devil and sin, having all the principal parts or portions of my soul, as my reason and understanding, and my free will, and all the other powers of my soul and body, not only so destituted and deprived of the gifts of God, wherewith they were first endued, but also so blinded, corrupted, and poisoned with error, ignorance, and carnal concupiscence, that neither my said powers could exercise the natural function and office for the which they were ordained by God at the first creation, nor I by them could do or think any thing which might be acceptable to God, but was utterly dead to God and all godly things, and utterly unable and insufficient of mine own self to observe the least part of God's commandments, and utterly inclined and ready to run headlong into all kinds of sin and mischief; I believe, I say, that I being in this case, Jesu Christ, by suffering of most painful and shameful death upon the cross, and by shedding of his most precious blood, and by that glorious victory which he had, when he descending into hell, and there overcoming both the Devil and death, rose again the third day from death to life, and so ascended into heaven, hath now pacified his Father's indignation towards me, and hath reconciled me again into his favour, and that he hath loosed and delivered me from the yoke and tyranny of death, of the Devil, and of sin, and hath made me so free from them, that they shall not finally hurt or annoy me, and that he hath poured out plentifully his holy Spirit and his graces upon me, specially faith, to illumine and direct my reason and judgment, and charity, to direct my will and affections towards God, whereby I am so perfectly restored to the light and knowledge of God, to the spiritual fear and dread of God, and unto the love of him and mine neighbour, that with his grace I am now ready to obey, and able to fulfil and accomplish his will and commandments. Besides all this, he hath brought and delivered me from darkness and blindness to light, from death to life, and from sin to justice, and he hath taken me into his protection, and made me as his own peculiar possession, and he hath planted and grafted me into his own body, and made me a member of the same, and he hath communicated and made me participant of his justice, his power, his life, his felicity, and of all his goods; so that now I may boldly say and believe, as indeed I do perfectly believe, that by his passion, his death, his blood, and his conquering of death, of sin, and of the Devil, by his resurrection and ascension, he hath made a sufficient expiation or propitiation towards God, that is to say, a sufficient satisfaction and recompense as well for my original sin, as also for all the actual sins that ever I have committed, and that I am so clearly rid from all the guilt of my said offences, and from the everlasting pain due for the same, that neither sin, nor death, nor hell, shall be able, or have any power, to hurt me, or to let me, but that after this transitory life I shall ascend into heaven, there to reign with my Saviour Christ perpetually in glory and felicity.

All which things considered, I may worthily call him my Jesus, that is to say, my Saviour and my Christ, that is to say, mine anointed King and Priest, and my Lord, that is to say, my Redeemer and Governor. For he hath done and fulfilled the very office both of a Priest, and of a King, and of a Lord. Of a Priest, in that he hath offered up his blessed body and blood, in the altar of the cross, for the satisfaction of my sins. And of a King and Lord, in that he hath, like a most mighty conqueror, overcome and utterly oppressed his enemies, (which were also mine enemies,) and hath spoiled them of the possession of mankind, which they won before by fraud and deceit, by lying and blasphemy, and hath brought us now into his possession and dominion, to reign over us in mercy and love, like a most loving Lord and Governor.

Finally, I believe assuredly, and also profess, that this redemption and justification of mankind could not have been wrought nor brought to pass by any other means in the world, but by the means of this Jesu Christ, God's only Son, and that never man could yet, nor never shall be able to come unto God the Father, or to believe in him , or to attain his favour by his own wit or reason, or by his own science and learning, or by any his own works, or by whatsoever may be named in heaven or in earth, but by the faith in the name and power of Jesu Christ, and by the gifts and graces of his holy Spirit. And therefore, sith he is my Jesu Christ and my Lord, I will put my whole trust and confidence in him, and will have the selfsame faith and affiance in him in all points which I have in God the Father. And I will knowledge him for my only Lord, and will obey all his commandments during my life, without any grudging. And I am sure that while he is my Lord and Governor, and I under his protection, neither sin, neither the devil, nor yet death, nor hell, can do me any hurt.

The Sense and Interpretation of the Third Article

I believe in my heart assuredly, and constantly do profess, that when the time was come, in the which it was before ordained and appointed by the decree of the holy Trinity, that mankind should be saved and redeemed, this Jesu Christ, the second Person in Trinity, and very God, descended from heaven into earth, to take upon him the very habit, form,

And that he was conceived by the Holy Ghost, and born of the Virgin Mary.

and nature of man, and in the same nature to work, to suffer, and fulfil all those things which were necessary for our redemption.

And I believe also and profess, that he so descending from heaven, did light down into the womb of a most blessed virgin called Mary, and that he did there take upon him our nature, and was conceived, begotten, and born of her very flesh, nature, and substance; and so did unite and conjoin together the same nature of man with his Godhead in one person, with such an indissoluble and inseparable knot and bond, that he being one person Jesu Christ, was then and ever shall be in the same person, very perfect God and very perfect man.

And I believe also and profess, that this most blessed virgin conceived this her child Jesu Christ, without spot, or blot of sin, or carnal concupiscence, and without any commixtion or conjunction had between her and any mortal man, or any other creature in heaven or earth. And that the Holy Ghost, the third Person in Trinity, descending also from heaven, lighted down into this most blessed virgin, and there of her flesh and substance wrought this ineffable and incomprehensible work of the incarnation of this child Jesu Christ.

And I believe also and profess, that this work and operation of the Holy Ghost was all holy, without any sin or impurity, and that it was done without any violation or detriment unto the virginity of that blessed virgin saint Mary.

And I believe also, that this child Jesu Christ was not only thus conceived without sin, but also that he was born in like manner of his said most blessed mother, and that she, both in the conception, and also in the birth and nativity of this her child, and ever after, retained still her virginity pure and immaculate, and as clear without blot, as she was at the time that she was first born.

And I believe, that this conception and nativity of our said Saviour was ordained to be thus pure, holy, and undefiled, to the intent that all filthiness and malediction, wherewith the conception and birth of me, and of all other men that ever were sith Adam, or shall be, and all the filthiness and malice of the sins of the whole world, as well original as actual, should thereby be purified, purged, and made clean.

The Sense and Interpretation of the Fourth Article

I believe assuredly in my heart, and with my mouth I do profess, that this Christ, very God and man, after he was thus conceived and born of his blessed mother, waxed and lived forth here in the world, until he came unto the age of thirty-two years and above, and that in all this time of his life he suffered and endured for our sakes, and for our wealth, much bodily affliction, much labour and travail, much hunger, thirst, and poverty, much injury and ignominy, and many other the miseries and infirmities, whereunto all mortal men be subject.

And suffered passion for our redemption under a certain judge, whose name was Pontius Pilatus, and so was crucified, dead, and buried.

And I believe that although this our Saviour Jesu Christ passed over all the whole course of his said life, even from his nativity until his death, in such perfect obedience unto the laws of God and man, and in such perfect innocency of living, that neither any man in the world, nor the devil himself, could ever find in him suspicion of any the least crime or offence that might be devised: yet the blind, ignorant Jews, replete with envy and malice, and the very members of the Devil, by whom they were provoked and induced thereunto, laboured continually, by all craft and means they could, to destroy him; and at length conspiring together, and subornating false witness, they took him, and after they had beat him, and spit in his face, and used all the villainy they could unto him, they bound and brought him before one Pontius Pilatus, being then the chief judge in Jerusalem, under the emperor of Rome, and there they most falsely accused him, as a subverter of the laws of God, and as a person that seduced the people, and moved sedition among them, and as a traitor against the emperor of Rome.

And I believe, that our Saviour Jesu Christ, being thus most falsely and wrongfully accused, and brought before the said judge, was at length in public and open judgment condemned, by the sentence of the said judge, to be nailed unto a cross, and to be hanged upon the same, to the intent he should so suffer that kind of death, which among the Jews was ever most abhorred and detested, and accounted to be the most shameful and cursed of all others.

And I believe, that after this sentence and judgment thus pronounced and given contrary to all justice and equity, the Jews did take this innocent

Jesu Christ our Saviour, and first of all binding him fast to a pillar, and pressing with great violence a crown of thorn upon his head, they did not only most spitefully mock him, and scorn him, but they also most cruelly scourged, tormented, and afflicted him, and finally they crucified him, that is to say, they nailed him through hands and feet unto a cross, and so hanged him up upon the same, on a certain hill called Calvary.

And I believe also and profess, that he hanged there upon the same cross between two thieves, which were malefactors, until he was dead, and his soul departed from his body. And that after he was thus dead, one Joseph ab Arimathea, being one of Christ's disciples, and certain other devout men and women, which also believed in Christ, obtained license of the said judge to take down this blessed body of our Saviour Jesu Christ from the said cross. And that when they had so done, they wrapped and folded the same body in a clean syndone, and so laid it and buried it in a new grave or sepulchre, which the said Joseph had made of stone, wherein there was never man buried before.

And I believe that our Saviour Jesu Christ, in all the time of his most bitter and grievous passion, and in suffering this most vile and shameful death, not only endured and sustained all the pains and injuries, and all the opprobries and ignominies, which were done unto him therein, most patiently, without resistance, and like an innocent lamb not opening once his mouth to the contrary, but also that he did willingly and gladly, without force or constraint of any power, suffer this cross, and this kind of death, and his soul also to depart from his body.

And I believe that by this passion and death of our Saviour Jesu Christ, not only my corporal death is so destroyed that it shall never have power to hurt me, but rather it is made wholesome and profitable unto me, but also that all my sins, and the sins also of all them that do believe in him and follow him, be mortified and dead, that is to say, all the guilt and offence thereof, and also the damnation and pain due for the same, is clearly extincted, abolished, and washed away, so that the same shall not afterward be imputed or inflicted unto me. And therefore will I have this passion and this death in my daily remembrance. And I will not only glory and rejoice continually therein, and give all the thanks I can unto God for the same, considering I have and shall assuredly attain thereby my redemption, my justification, my reconciliation unto God's favour, and life everlasting; but I will also endeavour myself to my possible power, and by the help of God, to follow this my Saviour Jesu Christ, in the bearing of mine own cross, according to the will and commandment of God, that is to say, I will daily labour and study to mortify and kill my carnal affections, and to subdue them unto the Spirit, and I will patiently bear all the adversities, afflictions, and punishments that God shall send unto me in this world, and I will in my heart hate, abhor, and detest all sin, considering that the same was ever so odious and displeasant unto God, that nothing in the world could worthily satisfy and content him for the same, but only the death and the blood of his only and most dear beloved Son Jesu Christ.

The Sense and Interpretation of the Fifth Article

I believe assuredly in my heart, and with my mouth I do profess, that this our Saviour Jesu Christ, after he was thus dead upon the cross, he descended immediately in his soul down into hell, leaving his most blessed body here in earth, and that at his coming thither, by the incomparable might and force of his Godhead, he entered *And that he descended into hell, and rose again the third day from death to life.*
into hell. And like as that mighty man, of whom St. Luke speaketh, which entering into the house of another strong man, first overcame him, and bound him hand and foot, and afterward spoiling him of all his armour and strength, wherein he trusted, took also away from him all the goods and substance he had (Luke 11:21-22); and like as strong Samson slew the mighty lion, and took out of his mouth the sweet honey (Judges 14): even so our Saviour Jesu Christ, at his said entry into hell, first he conquered and oppressed both the devil and hell, and also death itself, whereunto all mankind was condemned, and so bound them fast, that is to say, restrained the power and tyranny which they had before, and exercised over all mankind, that they never had sith that time, nor never shall have any power finally to hurt or annoy any of them that do faithfully believe in Jesu Christ; and afterward he spoiled hell, and delivered and brought with him from thence all the souls of those righteous and good men, which from the fall of Adam died in the favour of God, and in the faith and belief of this our Saviour Jesu Christ, which was then to come. And I believe that by this descending of our Saviour Jesu Christ into hell, not only his elect people, which were holden there as captives, were delivered from thence,

but also that the sentence and judgment of the malediction and of eternal damnation (which God himself most rightfully pronounced upon Adam and all his posterity, and so consequently upon me) was clearly dissolved, satisfied, released, and discharged, and that the devil and hell both have utterly lost and be deprived of all the right, claim and interest which they might have pretended to have had in me by the authority of that sentence, or by reason of any sin that ever I had or have committed, be it original or actual. And that the devil, with all his power, craft, subtilty, and malice, is now subdued and made captive, not only unto me, but also unto all the other faithful people and right believers in Jesu Christ that ever was or shall be sith the time of Christ's said descending into hell. And that our Saviour Jesu Christ hath also, by this his passion and this his descending into hell, paid my ransom, and hath merited and deserved that neither my soul, neither the souls of any such as be right believers in Christ, shall come therein, or shall finally be encumbered with any title or accusation that the devil can object against us, or lay unto our charge.

And I believe that this our Saviour Jesu Christ, after he had thus in soul conquered and spoiled the devil and hell of all their force, power, and tyranny, and made them subject unto me, and all true Christian men, in like case as they were unto Adam before his fall, he returned again from hell, like a most mighty king and conqueror, in triumph and glory, and came unto the sepulchre, where his blessed body lay buried, and so resuming and taking again the very same body upon him, the third day after his said death he lived again, and so rose out of that sepulchre in his natural and perfect manhood, that is to say, in his soul, and in the selfsame body which was born of the virgin Mary, and did hang upon the cross.

And I believe also and profess, that after lie had so done, he lived in the world by the space of forty days, in the which time he was conversant, and did eat and drink with his apostles and his disciples, and preached unto them, and authorized them to go forth into the world, to manifest and declare that he was the very Christ, the very Messias, and the very God and man, which was promised in scripture to come and save, and to redeem all those that would believe in him.

And I believe assuredly, that by this descending of Christ into hell, and this his resurrection again from death to life, Christ hath merited and deserved for me and all true and faithful Christian men, not only that our souls shall never come into hell, but also that we shall here in this life be perfectly justified in the sight and acceptation of God, and shall have such grace, might, and power given unto us by him, that we shall be made able thereby to subdue, to mortify, and to extinguish our old Adam, and all our carnal and fleshly concupiscences, in such sort, that sin shall never afterward reign in our mortal bodies, but that we shall be wholly delivered from the kingdom of sin, and from spiritual death, and shall be resuscitated and regenerated into the new life of the Spirit and grace.

And whereas I and all other Christian men should have been the most miserable of all other creatures in the world, and should have died like heathens and pagans, without all hope of everlasting life, or of rising again after our death, if Christ our Head and Saviour had not risen again to life after his death; I believe and trust now assuredly, that by the virtue and efficacy of this descending of Christ into hell, and of his resurrection again from death to life, not only our corporal death and all the afflictions which we may sustain in this world shall not annoy us, but shall rather turn unto our profit, and be as entries and occasions of our greater glory; but also that we shall after our corporal death be preserved from the captivity of hell, and shall be made partakers of Christ's resurrection, that is to say, that we shall arise and live again in the selfsame bodies and souls that we now have, and so shall utterly overcome death, in like manner as our Head and our Saviour Jesu Christ hath done before us, and shall finally live with him immortally in joy and felicity.

The Sense and Interpretation of the Sixth Article

I believe assuredly, and constantly do profess, that this our Saviour Jesu Christ, after he had perfectly accomplished and performed the whole mystery of the redemption of mankind by his incarnation, his birth, his passion, his death, his burial, his descending into hell, and rising again from death to life, and after he had been here in earth conversant with his apostles and disciples by the space of forty days after his said resurrection; the same

And that he ascended afterward up into heaven, and sitteth there upon the right hand of Almighty God his Father.

fortieth day, when he was among his said apostles, he in their sight ascended up again into heaven, in the very same his natural body, which was born of the blessed virgin his mother, and was crucified upon the cross.

And so did withdraw his corporal presence from the sight of his apostles, and from the sight of all other creatures here in earth, to the intent they should from thenceforth elevate and lift up their whole hearts, their minds, their desires, and all their affections from earthly things, and from all carnal and worldly cares, towards heaven and heavenly things, and so should prepare their hearts, and make themselves meet and apt to receive the Holy Ghost and his spiritual gifts, which he would send down into the world soon after his said ascension.

And I believe in like manner, that this our Saviour Jesu Christ, after he was returned into heaven, being very God and very man in one person, Almighty God his Father did constitute and set him upon his right hand, and that ever sith that time he hath so sat, and so shall sit eternally, that is to say, Almighty God his Father did communicate and give unto him glory, honour, felicity, power, and everlasting monarchy, governance, rule, and dominion over all the principates, potestates, powers, dominations, and over all creatures that can be named, either in this world or in the world to come (Eph 1:20-23). And so ordained, that he should be King of all kings, and Lord of all lords, and that all things in heaven and earth should be cast under his feet, and made subject unto him. And that he should be the only head of the catholic church, and that the same church should be the body under that head. And likewise, as the head alway excelleth all the other members; so Christ should excel incomparably in honour and dignity all the members of his said body the church, and that he should be the only perfection and consummation of the same.

And I believe also and profess, that this our Saviour Jesu Christ, being thus constituted and set upon the right hand of his Father, was and is also constituted to be not only the eternal King, the Head, the Lord, and Governor of his body the catholic church, but also to be the only eternal priest and bishop of his said church, that is to say, to be the only patron and advocate, and the only mediator between God and mankind, and the only intercessor for the sins of all them that rightfully believe in him.

And I believe, that according thereunto, our Saviour Jesu Christ is of his own goodness not only more ready always than any other creature in the world is, to help me by his mediation and intercession, but also that whensoever I do invocate and call upon him in right faith and hope, with full intent and purpose to amend and return from my naughty life, he presenteth and exhibiteth unto the sight of his Father his most blessed body, as it was wounded, crucified, and offered up in sacrifice for the redemption of mankind, and so from time to time maketh continual request and intercession unto God his Father for the remission of all my sins, and for my reconciliation unto his favour, and finally doth obtain, that God, so reconciled, will vouchsafe to send down his holy Spirit to dwell within my heart, there to rule, to govern, and to sanctify me with all my thoughts and deeds, and to comfort and strength me with all spiritual gifts necessary to the attaining of everlasting life.

And therefore, sith my Head and my Saviour Jesu Christ ascended up into heaven, and sitteth there upon the right hand of his Father, and maketh there continual intercession for me; I shall never from henceforth, by the grace of God, seek nor set my felicity in any worldly thing, but shall always use the creatures and ordinances of this world, and all worldly things, as a passenger or a pilgrim useth the commodities of a strange country, wherein he intendeth not to tarry, but to pass forth, until he shall come unto his own dwelling-place. And I shall convert my whole care, desire, and study from these earthly pleasures to the attaining of that heavenly and everlasting life, which is prepared and ordained for me. And being assured of so good, so loving, and therewith so mighty a governor, mediator, and advocate in heaven as Christ is, I will by the help of his grace, from henceforth continue still, and persevere under his kingdom, his tuition, and his governance, and so being, I will account myself safe and sure in all manner adversities, and against all manner adversaries and enemies. And I will never, by the help and grace of God, seek other governor or mediator; nor all the displeasures, injuries, or adversities in the world, nor all the malice, craft, and subtilty of the Devil, nor all the multitude or burden of my sins, shall cause me to distrust or despair of help at his hands, nor yet shall make me afraid to prosecute this my said desire and purpose, or cause me to desist from the same.

The Sense and Interpretation of the Seventh Article

I believe assuredly, and constantly do profess, that our Saviour Jesu Christ, being thus ascended into heaven, and set there on the right hand of Almighty God his Father, shall at the last end of the world, which we call

And that he shall come from thence at doomsday to judge the quick and dead. doomsday, return once again, and come from heaven, and appear unto all the people of the world, both quick and dead, in his perfect manhood, and in the selfsame body wherein he ascended, to the inestimable comfort and rejoice of the good, and to the extreme terror and confusion of the wicked.

And although our Saviour Jesu Christ, at his first advent or coming into the world, (which was when he came to be incarnate,) appeared in the habit and form of a very low servant, and of an abject person, in all humbleness, poverty, affliction, and misery, and suffered himself to be unjustly judged and condemned to death by others, and although he hath ever sith that time, and ever shall until doomsday, use his mercy, and long patience, and sufferance towards the wretched sinners of the world, inviting always and calling them from time to time to repentance; yet I believe assuredly, that at his second advent or coming, he shall appear in the high and almighty power, glory, and majesty of his kingdom, and being accompanied with all the orders of angels, waiting upon him as his ministers, he shall sit openly in the clouds of the air, and shall judge all the world, quick and dead, and that straitly, according to truth and justice, and according as he hath promised and threatened to do by his holy word, expressed in scripture, that is to say, according to every man's own works and deeds done by him while he lived in the world, without sparing, or favouring, or shewing of mercy unto any, which have not deserved the same in their lifetime (Matt 25, Rev 1).

And I believe assuredly, that at this day, when Christ shall thus sit in the seat or throne of his judgment, all the people of the world, quick and dead, that is to say, as well all those which shall be found on life in the world, at the day of this second advent or coming of Christ, as also all those which ever sith the creation of Adam lived here in this world, and died before that day, shall come and appear before the presence of Christ, in their very bodies and souls. And when they shall be so gathered and assembled together, our Saviour Jesu Christ shall pronounce the extreme or final sentence and judgment of everlasting salvation upon all those persons, which in their lifetime obeyed and conformed themselves unto the will of God, and exercised the works of right belief and charity, and so persevering in well-doing, sought in their hearts and deeds the honour and glory of God, and life immortal (Rom 2). And contrary upon all those, which in their lifetime were contentious, and did repugn against the will of God, and followed injustice and iniquity rather than truth and virtue, our Saviour Christ shall then and there pronounce the sentence of everlasting punishment and damnation.

And I believe that our Saviour Jesu Christ shall also then and there call apart, and make a perfect separation or division between these two sorts of people, that is to say, between the sheep and the goats, the corn and the chaff, the good and the bad, the blessed and the cursed, the members of his body and the members of the devil. And so setting the good and the blessed upon his right hand, he shall clearly and perfectly rid, deliver, and redeem them for ever from the power and malice of the wicked, and from all pains and evil, and so take them all up with him into heaven, there to be crowned and rewarded in body and soul with honour, glory, and everlasting joy and peace, which was prepared for them from the beginning of the world. And contrary he shall set all the other, which shall be judged to everlasting pain and death, upon his left hand, and so shall send them down into hell, there to be punished in body and soul eternally with fire that never shall have end, which was prepared from the beginning of the world for the devil and his angels, and the cursed members of his body.

The Sense and Interpretation of the Eighth Article

I believe assuredly in my heart, and constantly do profess and knowledge, that the Holy Ghost is the third Person in Trinity, and that he is very God and Lord, author and *And I believe in the Holy Ghost.* former of all things created, and that he proceedeth both from God the Father and from God the Son, and is of the selfsame nature and substance, and of the same everlasting essence or being, which the Father and the Son be of, and that he is equal unto them both in almightiness of power, and in the work of creation, and all other things appertaining unto the Deity or Godhead, and that he is to be honoured and glorified equally with them both.

And I believe that this Holy Spirit of God is, of his nature all holy, or rather holiness itself, that is to say, that he is the only Ghost or Spirit, which, with the Father and the Son, ever was and ever shall be the only author, causer, and worker of all holiness, purity, and sanctimony, and of all the grace, comfort, and spiritual life, which is wrought and cometh into the hearts of all true Christian men. Insomuch that neither it is possible that the devil or any of those evil spirits, which do possess and reign in such persons as be subject unto sin, can be expelled or put out of them but by the power of this finger of God, that is to say, of this Holy Spirit, which is called in scripture the finger of God; neither it is possible that the heart of any man, being once corrupted, and made as profane by sin, can be purged, purified, sanctified, or justified, without the special work and operation of this Holy Spirit; neither it is possible for any man to come unto the Father by Christ, that is to say, to be reconciled into the favour of God, and to be made and adopted into the number of his children, or to obtain any part of that incomparable treasure which our Saviour Jesu Christ, by his nativity, his passion, his death, his resurrection, and his ascension, have merited for mankind, unless this Holy Spirit shall first illumine and inspire into his heart the right knowledge and faith of Christ, with due contrition and penance for his sins, and shall also afterward instruct him, govern him, aid him, direct him, and endue him with such special gifts and graces, as shall be requisite and necessary to that end and purpose.

And I believe also assuredly, that this Holy Spirit of God is of his own nature full of all goodness and benignity, or rather that he is goodness itself. Forasmuch as he is the only Ghost or Spirit, which with the Father by Christ instilleth and infoundeth into the hearts of mortal men (after they be once purified from sin by faith, and delivered from the power of the

Timoris.
Sapien.
Intellectus.
Concilii.
Fortitudinis.
Pietas.
Scientia.

devil) divers and manifold most noble and excellent gifts and graces; as, the gift of holy fear and dread of God; the gift of fervent love and charity towards God and our neighbour; the gift of spiritual wisdom and understanding; the gift of free will and desire, and also of very fortitude and strength to contemn this world, to subdue and mortify all carnal concupiscence, and to walk in the ways of God; the gift of perseverance to continue in the same; the gift of pity and mercy, of patience and benignity, of science and cunning, of prophesying, of curing and healing, and of all other virtues necessary for Christian men to have, either for the attaining of their own salvation, or for the edifying and profit of their neighbours. All and singular which gifts and graces I knowledge and profess that they proceed from this Holy Spirit, and that they be given, conferred, and distributed unto us mortal men here in earth, at his own godly will, arbitre, and dispensation, and that no man can purchase or obtain, ne yet receive, retain, or use any one of them, without the special operation of this Holy Spirit. And although he giveth not nor dispenseth the same equally and unto every man in like, yet he giveth always some portion thereof unto all persons, which be accepted in the sight of God, and that not only freely, and without all their deservings, but also in such plenty and measure, as unto his godly knowledge is thought to be most beneficial and expedient.

And I believe that this Holy Spirit of God is of his own nature author of charity and holy love, or rather that he is charity itself. First, because that he is that ineffable and incomprehensible love or concord, wherewith the Father and the Son be conjoined inseparably the one with the other. Second, because he is the bond and knot wherewith our Saviour Jesu Christ and his most dear beloved espouse the church, (which is also his very mystical body,) and all and singular the very members of the same church and body, be united, knit, and conjoined together in such perfect and everlasting love and charity, that the same cannot be dissolved or separated. Thirdly, because he is also the very bond and knot whereby all and every one of the members of Christ's said church and body be united, coupled, and conjoined the one of them with the other, in perfect mutual love and charity. For I believe assuredly, that like as the members of our mortal bodies be, by the spiritual operation and virtue of our souls, not only preserved wholly together in one body, and be endued with life and power to exercise such natural functions and offices as be deputed unto them, but also be contained in mutual affection and desire each to help and conserve the other; even so the members of this mystical body of Christ be, by the only and special operation and work of this Holy Spirit, not only congregated, united, and incorporated into this one body of Christ, and so do consist and endure wholly and perfectly in the same body, every one in his own peculiar function; but also that they be knitted, combined, and conglutinated all together, and every one of them with other, in perfect and indissoluble love, and in the communion of all their gifts and graces, and of all other things wherewith the one of them may help, succour, or comfort the other.

And I believe that this Holy Spirit of God is the Spirit of truth, and the author of all holy scripture, contained in the whole canon of the Bible. And that this Spirit did not only inspire and instruct all the holy patriarchs and prophets, with all the other members of the catholic church that ever was from the beginning of the world, in all the truths and verities that ever they did know, speak, or write; but also that the same Holy Spirit did once descend down from heaven in the similitude and likeness of fiery tongues, and did light down upon all the apostles and disciples of Christ, and inspired them also with the knowledge of all truth, and replenished them with all heavenly gifts and graces (Acts 2). And that from that day unto the world's end, he hath been and shall be continually present, and also chief president in the catholic church of Christ, that is to say, that he hath and shall continually dwell in the hearts of all those people which shall be the very members of the same church, and shall teach and reveal unto them the secrets and mysteries of all truth, which is necessary for them to know, and that he shall also continually from time to time rule them, direct them, govern them, sanctify them, and give unto them remission of their sins, and all spiritual comfort, as well inwardly by faith, and other his secret operations, as also outwardly by the open ministration and efficacy of the word of God and of his holy sacraments; and that he shall endue them with all such spiritual graces and gifts as shall be necessary for them to have, and so finally shall reward them with the gift of everlasting life and joy in heaven.

The Sense and Interpretation of the Ninth Article

And I believe that there is one holy catholic and universal church.

I believe assuredly in my heart, and with my mouth I do profess and knowledge, that there is and hath been ever from the beginning of the world, and so shall endure and continue for ever, one certain number, society, communion, or company of the elect and faithful people of God; of which number our Saviour Jesu Christ is the only head and governor, and the members of the same be all those holy saints which be now in heaven, and also all the faithful people of God which be now on life, or that ever heretofore have lived, or shall live here in this world, from the beginning unto the end of the same, and be ordained for their true faith, and obedience unto the will of God, to be saved, and to enjoy everlasting life in heaven.

And I believe assuredly that this congregation, according as it is called in scripture, so it is in very deed the city of heavenly Jerusalem, the mother of all the elect people of God, the only dove, and the only beloved of God, *Gal 4, Song 6, Jer 13, Rom 8, 1 Cor 3, 2 Cor 6, Eph 5.* in perfect and everlasting charity, the holy catholic church, the temple or habitacle of God, the pure and undefiled espouse of Christ, the very mystical body of Christ. All and singular which names and appellations, and certain such other rehearsed in holy scripture, I believe and profess that they be most worthily attributed unto this holy church or congregation. And like as citizens assembled in one city do live there under common laws, and in common society, and there do consult, study, and labour, each man in his room and office, and according unto his calling, for their common wealth, and finally be made participant or partakers of all and singular such benefits and commodities as do arise unto them thereby; even so I believe, that the members of this holy catholic church or congregation be collected and gathered together within the same church as within one city or fold, and that they be therein all united and incorporated by the Holy Spirit of Christ into one body, and that they do live there all in one faith, one hope, one charity, and one perfect unity, consent, and agreement, not only in the true doctrine of Christ, but also in the right use and ministration of his sacraments; and so living in this perfect unity, sweet harmony, and concord, I believe that they do labour continually, every one in his vocation, for the common wealth of this whole body, and of every part and member of the same. And that all the prayers, good works, and merits, yea and all the gifts, graces, and goods which be conferred, done, or wrought in or unto this whole body, or any member of the same, shall be applied unto every one of them, and shall redound commonly unto the benefit of them all.

And I believe that this whole congregation is all holy, that is to say, that this church and all the parts and members of the same, be so purified and mundified, as well by Christ's most precious blood, as also by the godly presence, governance, and assistance of his Holy Spirit, (which dwelleth and inhabiteth continually within the said congregation, and governeth and sanctifieth the same,) that neither the lepry of heresy, or false and perverse doctrine, neither the filthiness of sin, neither the gates of hell, shall be able finally to prevail against them, or to pull any of them out of the hands and possession of Christ. And although God doth ofttimes suffer not only sin, error, and iniquity so to abound here in the world, and the congregation of the wicked to exercise such tyranny, cruelty, and persecution over this holy church, and the members of the same, that it might seem the said church to be utterly oppressed and extinguished, but also suffereth many and sundry of the members of the same holy church to fall out from this body for a season, and to commit many grievous and horrible offences and crimes, for the which they deserve to be precided and excluded for a season from the communion of this holy church; yet I believe assuredly, that God will never utterly abject this holy church, nor any of the members thereof, but that the same doth and shall perpetually continue and endure here in this world, and that God shall at all times (yea when persecution is greatest and most fervent) be present with his Holy Spirit in the same church, and preserve it all holy and undefiled, and shall keep, ratify, and hold sure all his promises made unto the same church or congregation. And finally, that all such members as be fallen out from the same by sin, shall at length rise again by penance, and shall be restored and united again unto the same holy body.

And I believe assuredly, that in this holy church, and with the members of the same, (so long as they be militant and living here in earth,) there have been ever, and yet be, and ever shall be joined and mingled together an infinite number of the evil and wicked people, which, although they be indeed the very members of the congregation of the wicked, and, as the gospel calleth them, very weeds and chaff, evil fish and goats, and shall finally be judged to everlasting damnation (Matt 13; 3:12; 13:47-8; 25); yet forasmuch as they do live in the common society or company of those which be the very quick and living members of Christ's mystical body, and outwardly do profess, receive, and consent with them for a season in the doctrine of the gospel, and in the right using of the sacraments, yea and ofttimes be endued with right excellent gifts of the Holy Ghost, they be to be accounted and reputed here in this world to be in the number of the said very members of Christ's mystical body, so long as they be not by open sentence of excommunication precided and excluded from the same. Not because they be such members in very deed, but because the certain judgment and knowledge of that their state is by God's ordinance hidden and kept secret from all men's knowledge, and shall not be revealed until the time that Christ himself shall come at the world's end, and there shall manifest and declare his very kingdom, and who be the very true members of his body, and who be not.

And I believe that this holy church is catholic, that is to say, that it cannot be coarcted or restrained within the limits or bonds of any one town, city, province, region, or country; but that it is dispersed and spread universally throughout all the whole world. Insomuch that in what part soever of the world, be it in Africa, Asia, or Europe, there may be found any number of people, of what sort, state, or condition soever they be, which do believe in one God the Father, Creator of all things, and in one Lord Jesu Christ his Son, and in one Holy Ghost, and do also profess and have all one faith, one hope, and one charity, according as is prescribed in holy scripture, and do all consent in the true interpretation of the same scripture, and in the right use of the sacraments of Christ; we may boldly pronounce and say, that there is this holy church, the very espouse and body of Christ, the very kingdom of Christ, and the very temple of God.

And I believe that these particular churches, in what place of the world soever they be congregated, be the very parts, portions, or members of this catholic and universal church. And that between them there is indeed no difference in superiority, preeminence, or authority, neither that any one of them is head or sovereign over the other; but that they be all equal in power and dignity, and be all grounded and builded upon one foundation, and be all called unto like and unto the same purity, cleanness, honour, and glory, and be all subject unto one God, one Lord, one Head Jesu Christ, and be all governed with one Holy Spirit. And therefore I do believe that the church of Rome is not, nor cannot worthily be called the catholic church, but only a particular member thereof, and cannot challenge or vindicate of right, and by the word of God, to be head of this universal church, or to have any superiority over the other churches of Christ which be in England, France, Spain, or in any other realm, but that they be all free from any subjection unto the said church of Rome, or unto the minister or bishop of the same.

And I believe also that the said church of Rome, with all the other particular churches in the world, compacted and united together, do make and constitute but one catholic church or body. And that like as our Saviour Christ is one person, and the only head of his mystical body, so this whole catholic church, Christ's mystical body, is but one body under this one head Christ. And that the unity of this one catholic church is a mere spiritual unity, consisting in the points before rehearsed, that is to say, in the unity of Christ's faith, hope, and charity, and in the unity of the right doctrine of Christ, and in the unity and uniform using of the sacraments consonant unto the same doctrine. And therefore although the said particular churches and the members of the same do much differ, and be discrepant the one from the other, not only in the diversity of nations and countries, and in the diversity, dignity, and excellency of certain such gifts of the Holy Ghost as they be endued with, but also in the divers using and observation of such outward rites, ceremonies, traditions, and ordinances, as be instituted by their governors, and received and approved among them; yet I believe assuredly, that the unity of this catholic church cannot therefore, or for that cause, be any thing hurted, impeached, or infringed in any point, but that all the said churches do and shall continue still in the unity of this catholic church, notwithstanding any such diversity; nor that any of them ought to be reputed as a member divided or precided from the same, for any such cause of diversity or difference used by them or any of them in the said points.

And I believe that all the particular churches in the world, which be members of this catholic church, may all be called apostolical churches, as well as the church of Rome, or any other church, wherein the apostles themselves were sometime resident: forasmuch as they have received and be all founded upon the same faith and doctrine that the true apostles of Christ did teach and profess.

And I believe and trust assuredly, that I am one of the members of this catholic church, and that God of his only mercy hath not only chosen and called me thereunto by his Holy Spirit, and by the efficacy of his word and sacraments, and hath inserted and united me into this universal body or flock, and hath made me his son and inheritor of his kingdom; but also that he shall of his like goodness, and by the operation of the Holy Ghost, justify me here in this world, and finally glorify me in heaven. And therefore I protest and knowledge, that in my heart I abhor and detest all heresies and schisms, whereby the true interpretation and sense of scripture is or may be perverted. And do promise, by the help of God, to endure unto my life's end in the right profession of the faith and doctrine of the catholic church.

The Sense and Interpretation of the Tenth Article

I believe assuredly in my heart, and with my mouth I profess, that between and among all and singular the saints, that is to say, the quick and living members of the catholic church of Christ, which is his mystical body, there is a perfect communion and participation of all and singular the graces of the Holy Ghost, and the spiritual *And I believe that there is in the same church communion of saints, and remission of sins.* goods and treasure which do belong unto the said whole body, or unto any part or member of the same. And like as all the parts and members which be living in the natural body of a man do naturally communicate and minister each to other the use, commodity, and benefit of all their forces, nutriment, and perfection, (insomuch that it lieth not in the power of any man to say that the meat which he putteth in at his own mouth shall nourish one particular member of his body and not another, but that all and every one particularly shall receive of the said nutriment, and of the virtue and benefit thereof, more or less, according to that natural disposition, portion, and place which it hath within the same body,) even so I believe, that whatsoever spiritual gift or treasure is given by God unto any one part or member of this mystical body of Christ, although the same be given particularly unto this member, and not unto another, yet the fruit and merit thereof shall by reason of that incomprehensible union and band of charity which is between them, redound necessarily unto the profit, edifying, and increase in Christ's body of all the other members particularly; insomuch that there shall need no man's authority to dispense and distribute the same, or to apply it unto this member or that, (like as the bishop of Rome pretended to do by virtue of his pardons,) but if the member which shall receive this treasure be a living member in this mystical body, and not putrified or cut off from the same, I believe assuredly that he shall be made participant of the said treasure, and shall have and enjoy the fruit and benefit of the same, and that in such quantity and measure as for the rate, proportion, and quality of the spiritual life, faith, and charity, which he hath in the same body, shall be expedient and necessary for him to have.

And I believe, that I being united and corporated as a living member into this catholic church, (as undoubtedly I trust that I am,) not only Christ himself, being head of this body, and the infinite treasure of all goodness, and all the holy saints and members of the same body, do and shall necessarily help me, love me, pray for me, care for me, weigh on my side, comfort me, and assist me in all my necessities here in this world; but also that I shall be made partaker of the fruit, benefit, and treasure of Christ's most blessed life and his bitter passion, and of all the holy life, passions, and patience, and of all the prayers and other good works of faith and charity, which have been or shall be done or sustained by any and every one of all those faithful and righteous people, which ever have been or shall be members of this catholic church.

And I believe that in this catholic church I, and all the lively and quick members of the same, shall continually and from time to time, so long as we shall live here on earth, obtain remission and forgiveness of all our sins, as well original as actual, by the merits of Christ's blood and his passion, and by the virtue and efficacy of Christ's sacraments, instituted by him for that purpose, so oft as we shall worthily receive the same.

And like as it is not in the power of any man to dispense, minister, or distribute any part of that nutriment which he receiveth in at his mouth unto any member which either is mortified and dead in his body, or that is cut off from the same; even so I believe assuredly, that neither Christ's blood, nor his sacraments, nor any of the graces of the Holy Ghost, nor any good work in the world, do or can any thing profit to remission and forgiveness of sin, or salvation unto any person, which is in very deed out of the catholic church, as long as he shall so stand, and continue out of the same. For I believe assuredly, that out of this catholic church, there neither is nor can be any such communion of saints, or remission of sins, as is before rehearsed; but that like as all the people and beasts, which at the time of Noah's flood were out of his ark or ship, were all drowned and perished, even so all the people of the world, be they Jews, Turks, Saracens, or of any other nation, whatsoever it be, which, either for their infidelity, heresy, or schism, or for their indurateness, and obstinate persevering in mortal sin, be separated and divided from the members of the said catholic church, and so shall finally be found either to be out of the same church, or else to be as dead members therein, shall utterly perish, and be damned for ever.

The Sense and Interpretation
of the Eleventh and Twelfth Articles

I believe steadfastly in my heart, and with my mouth I do profess, that at the day of the general doom, or judgment, when Christ shall come, and sit to judge both quick and dead, Almighty God shall, by the operation of his Holy Spirit, stir and raise up again the very flesh and bodies of all men, women, and children, both good and bad, christened and heathen, that ever lived here in this world, from the beginning of the same, and died before that day. And although the said flesh and bodies were dead before and buried, yea and consumed by fire or water, or by any other means destroyed, yet I believe that God shall, of his infinite power, make them all at that day whole and perfect again, and so every man generally shall resume and take again the very selfsame body and flesh which they had while they lived here on earth, and so shall rise from death, and live again in the very selfsame body and soul which they had before.

And I believe that at dooms-day all the people of the world that ever was or ever shall be unto that day, shall then arise again in the selfsame flesh and body, which they had while they lived here in earth.

And I believe that every man, being thus made perfect man in body and soul, shall at that day appear before the high Judge, our Saviour Jesu Christ, and there shall make a strait account of his own proper works and deeds, such as he did, good or evil, while he lived here in the world: and according thereunto shall be judged to receive, both in body and soul together, either everlasting joy and bliss, or else everlasting pain and wo. And I believe that I myself shall the same day rise again in this very flesh and body which I now have, and in none other; even like as our Saviour Jesu Christ (of whose mystical body I am a portion or member) did arise from death to life, in the selfsame natural body which he had when he was born of his mother, and crucified upon the cross. And after that I shall be so risen again from death to life, I believe that I, and all true penitent sinners that ever died or shall die in the faith of Christ, shall then be perfectly sanctified, purified, and delivered from all contagion of sin, and from all corruption and mortality of the flesh, and shall have everlasting life in glory with God in his kingdom (1 Cor 15), not for, by, nor through the works of

And I believe that all the elect people of God shall have and enjoy everlasting life for their reward.

righteousness which we shall have done (Titus 3:5),—for all passions and martyrdoms that may be suffered in this world be nothing comparable to the glory which we shall then receive and shall be shewed unto us (Rom 8:18)—but by the only grace, goodness, and mercy of God, and by and for the redemption which is in Christ Jesu, that is to say, for and by his most precious death and most painful passion. For I believe that the guerdon, reward, and stipend of sin (wherewith we be all manifold ways polluted, bespotted, and defiled) is death, yea, and that everlasting (Rom 6:23). And that it is by the only grace and mercy of God, that we, repenting us of our sins, and believing steadfastly in his promises, shall have everlasting life, in Jesu Christ our Lord. Amen.

Here follow certain Notes and Observations necessary to be taught unto the people, for the better inducing of them unto the right understanding of the foresaid Creed.

First, it is to be noted, that all and singular the twelve articles, contained in this Creed, be so necessary to be believed for man's salvation, that whosoever being once taught will not constantly believe them, or will obstinately affirm the contrary of them, he or they cannot be the very members of Christ and his espouse the church, but be very infidels or heretics, and members of the devil, with whom they shall perpetually be damned.

Second, it is to be noted, that all true Christian men ought and must most constantly believe, maintain, and defend all those things to be true, not only which be comprehended in this Creed, and in the other two symbols or creeds, whereof the one was made in the council of Nice, the other was made by that holy man Athanasius; but also all other things which be comprehended in the whole body and canon of the Bible.

Thirdly, that all true Christian men ought and must not only repute, take, and hold all the same things for the most holy, most sure, and most certain and infallible words of God, and such as neither ought ne can be altered or convelled by any contrary opinion or authority; but also must take and interpretate all the same things according to the selfsame sentence and interpretation which the words of scripture do purport and signify, and the holy approved doctors of the church do entreat and defend the same.

Fourthly, that all true Christian men ought and must utterly refuse and condemn all those opinions contrary to the said twelve articles of our Creed, which were of long time past condemned in the four holy councils, that is to say, in the council of Nice, Constantinople, Ephesus, and Chalcedonense, and all other sith that time in any point consonant to the same.

In the first article of this Creed two things be also specially to be noted. The first is, that herein is declared the infinite goodness of God towards mankind, in that he created this whole world for man's sake only, and thereby *The notes of the first article.* distributed such part of his felicity unto man as was convenient for him to receive. The belief and knowledge whereof is the first entry to know that God is a spiritual and an invisible substance or nature, of infinite power, and eternal, without beginning or ending, and of incomprehensible knowledge, wisdom, goodness, justice, and mercy, &c. For surely that work of creation is so marvellous, that nothing in the world, neither man nor angel, could perform or accomplish the same; but only such a substance or nature as is before rehearsed, which is God himself. By this belief also and knowledge, we be stirred to fear and dread God, and to love and praise God with all our hearts: considering that he did create us even like unto his own image and similitude, and endued us with all perfections, both in soul and body, which were necessary for us to have, and did put us in the most excellent state of being, having all other creatures subject and obedient unto us. And so by this article we be taught, not only what is the divine essence and being of God the Father, what is his will, what is his power, and what is his work and operation, (the knowledge whereof destroyeth infinite errors and heresies,) but also what faith, love, dread, honour, laud, praise, and thanks he requireth, that all Christian men should at all times, as well in prosperity as in adversity, give unto him for the manifold and excellent gifts which they receive daily and hourly at his hands. And surely if all Christian men would ofttimes call this article to their remembrance, and would busily exercise their meditations therein, and would unfeignedly and with all their hearts profess the same, no doubt but their hearts would wax warm, and would be inflamed to love God, and would be prompt, ready, glad, and willing to serve him, and to fulfil his will and commandments, to their possible powers, and would take in good part, without grudging or maligning, all sickness and adversities, and whatsoever state of life God sendeth unto them, and would give him thanks and praise therefore, and would use all God's creatures, and spend the gifts which he hath given unto them, to his honour and glory. And finally, they would abhor and detest in their hearts all superstition and idolatry, all charms, witchcrafts, and sorceries, all blasphemy and desperation, pride and arrogancy, all covetousness and ambition, all desire of revenging, and malice, and all other vices, which reign now in the world. For surely whosoever believeth inwardly and with his heart that God is his Father, and reputeth him as his son, and that the same God is of infinite might and power, of infinite knowledge and wisdom, of infinite mercy and goodness, of infinite truth and justice, as he is indeed; no doubt that person will be very loath and afraid to contrary or resist his will in any thing, or to have any thing for his God and his Father beside or without him, or to love or prefer money or any thing else in the world before him, or to put affiance, trust, delectation, or pleasure in any thing more than in him or beside him. Neither will he gladly seek help at the devil's hands, by any means of witchcrafts, or sorcery, or any such other crafts invented by the devil. Neither will he commit those things in the sight of God, which he is ashamed to commit in the presence of men. Neither will he murmur against God, nor muse for that he sendeth to some one man health, children, riches, and other the felicities of this world; and unto him, or some other man, he sendeth sickness, poverty, and other adversities. Neither will he despair of remission of his sins, and so go (peradventure) and murder himself. Neither will he rejoice, delight, or glory in his malice and evil living: but will rather live in fear and dread of everlasting death, which is due unto all them, which, serving the devil, the world, and the flesh, live in security without fear and repentance. And finally, to conclude, surely whosoever believeth in his heart that God did create this whole world, and all things that be therein, only for man's sake and for his use and commodity; no doubt he could turn his eyes nowhere, but he should incontinently be stirred and ravished in his heart, to honour, to praise, and to laud the infinite goodness of Almighty God, shewed unto him and all mankind in that party, and should also be afraid to use the things created by God, otherwise than unto his glory. But it is to be feared, lest the most part of them which pronounce and speak daily this article with their mouth, do not believe the same with their hearts, or if they do believe it, that their belief is but faint, and a cold belief. For we see, no doubt, the most part of Christian people live in marvellous darkness and blindness, declaring by their outward facts and deeds that they have no respect in the world to God, nor that they knowledge him to be their Creator, or at the least they give unto him no such fear and reverence as is due unto a Lord and Maker, nor no such honour and obedience as is due unto a Father, nor no such praise and thanks as his sundry benefits and goodness towards us do require (Mal 1:6). All which things no doubt proceed, for that we have not the right and hearty faith in God the Father, which is required in this first article of our Creed.

The second thing to be noted in this first article is this manner of speaking, *I believe in God*. For thereby no doubt is signified, that we must not only believe steadfastly that God is, and that he is true in all his words and promises, and that he is omnipotent, and Creator of heaven and earth, and so forth; but we must also with this belief go into God by love, and adhere only unto him, and that with all our heart and power, and so continue and dwell still in him by love. It signifieth also that we must obey unto his will, and express the same our obedience, as well in all our inward thoughts and affections, as also in all our outward acts and deeds; and that we must abhor all tyranny and vice, and wish or desire of God no vain or ungodly thing. It signifieth also that we must constantly and boldly betake and commit ourselves and all ours wholly unto God, and fix all our whole hope, trust, and confidence in him, and quiet ourselves in him, believing perfectly and assuredly that he will indeed shew no less goodness, love, mercy, and favour unto us, than he promiseth by his word to do; and knowing also for certain that we and all the creatures in the world be conserved by his only goodness and high providence, and that without his special grace we should not be able to continue on life the space of one minute of an hour.

This manner of belief we ought to have in no creature of God, be it never so excellent, but in God only: and therefore in this Creed the said manner of speaking is used only in the three articles which concern the three Persons in Trinity, that is to say, the Father, the Son, and the Holy Ghost.

In the third article it is to be noted, that the cause why it was ordained by God that our Saviour Jesu Christ should be born of a virgin, and conceived by the only operation of the Holy Ghost, (whose work is ever without all manner of sin,) was, for that he was ordained and appointed by God to come and deliver mankind from the captivity of the devil and the

The notes of the third article.

malediction which man was in, and to redeem him clear from all sin, death, and damnation, and to restore him again to the very blessing of God, that is to say, to justice, righteousness, health, life everlasting, and all other the gifts and graces of the Holy Ghost. And forasmuch as it was necessary that he which should work this effect should be himself all blessed, all innocent, all righteous, all void and pure from sin, and utterly free and clear from the yoke and power of the devil; therefore was it ordained by God that this child Jesu Christ should so be conceived and born as was said before. For surely if Christ should have been otherwise born or conceived, that is to say, of the seed of man and woman, and by the act of generation, which is done between them, he should have been born in like sin, in like filthiness and iniquity, as all other the children of men that ever was sith Adam, or ever shall be, be born and conceived. But surely neither was it convenient, neither the will of God, that Christ should by such generation contract any spot of sin, or should be subject to any part of that malediction which was inflicted unto Adam.

The notes of the fourth article. In the fourth article it is to be noted, that the same doth follow upon the second and the third articles. For surely the cause why Christ was thus made man, and born of his mother, was for that he should in the same nature of man not only be conversant in the world with other people, and so, partly by the example of his most godly and most innocent and perfect life, and partly by his marvellous works and miracles, and partly by the heavenly doctrine of his gospel, should induce the world unto the right knowledge of the will of God his Father, and should declare unto them his infinite mercy and goodness towards mankind; but also that he might in the same nature, which was mortal, suffer death, and so offer up the same his corporal death and his blood in sacrifice unto God his Father, as the sufficient host, oblation, or expiation, and as the very just price and valure for the which God the Father should hold himself satisfied for all our sins and offences, and should remit and forgive us the same, and receive us again into his grace and favour; which sacrifice and oblation Christ could not have made by his death and by his blood, if he should have continued still only God, and should not have taken also this our nature of man upon him.

In the fourth article it is also to be noted, that it is the will of God our Father, that we his sons and his children should in this world follow our head Christ in patience and humility, and that we should bear our own cross, as Christ did his: and that we should also hate and abhor all sin, knowing for surety that whosoever doth not in his heart hate and abhor sin, but rather accounteth the breach and violation of God's commandment but as a light matter, and of small weight and importance; he esteemeth not the price and valure of this passion of Christ according to the dignity and worthiness thereof, but rather seemeth to consent, and, as much as in him is, to go about to cause Christ to be crucified again.

In the fifth article it is to be noted, that therein is included and contained the grounds and foundations of the greatest part of all the mysteries of our catholic faith. *The notes of the fifth article.* Insomuch that St. Paul saith, that whosoever believeth in his heart that God the Father did resuscitate and raise up his Son Christ from death to life, he shall be saved (Rom 10:9). And in another place he saith, that whosoever believeth not that Christ is risen from death to life, it is not possible his sins should be remitted (1 Cor 15:17).

It is also to be noted in this article, that the victory and conquest which Christ had over death, hell, and the devil himself, with all their power and tyranny, beside that it proceeded of the infinite mercy and goodness of God towards us, it was also founded upon very justice. For surely like as the sin of man and his disobedience was the only mean and cause wherefore God ordained and suffered that death and the devil should have and occupy such dominion and tyranny over all mankind as they had; even so was it contrary to the will and ordinance of God, that death, hell, or the devil should have or exercise any power or authority where as no sin reigned. Insomuch that if man had never sinned, he should never have died, but should have been immortal; nor never should have descended into hell, but should ever have had the superiority over the devil, death, and hell, and should have had them always subdued unto him. And therefore, sith the devil himself did perfectly know that our Saviour Jesu Christ expressed in all his life most exact and most perfect obedience unto the laws and will of God, and so fulfilled and satisfied the same in every point to the uttermost, that there could never be found untruth or deceit in his mouth, nor any spot or blot of filthiness or impurity in any part of all his living, and yet that notwithstanding, (knowing him to be a very natural man,) laboured, procured, and caused the Jews to kill this innocent Christ, and to put him unto most sharp and bitter death, contrary to all equity and justice, and all to the intent that he might, after his said death, have Christ with him down into hell, as one of his captives, and so there to exercise his tyranny upon him, like as he had done over all other men from the beginning of the world until that time: no doubt but the devil, in this doing, did extreme and manifest wrong, and utterly exceeded the limits of the power given unto him. And therefore God, considering this high presumption and malice of the devil, and this intolerable abuse of his said power, did send his only begotten Son down into hell, there to condemn the devil of this extreme iniquity, and to conquer, to spoil, and deprive him, not only of the possession of all the souls of the righteous men, which by his craft and subtilty he had before reduced and brought under his dominion; but also restrained him of the power and authority which he by death and hell had over mankind. All which things Christ did not by the might of his godly power only, but for and upon this just and reasonable cause given unto him on the behalf of the devil, which for the causes aforesaid most worthily deserved to be served so.

The notes of the sixth article.   In the sixth article three things be specially to be noted and remembered. First, that in the person of Jesu Christ there was and is conjoined and united together inseparably both the nature of God and the nature of man. And that by reason of this indissoluble unity of these two natures, holy scripture useth sometimes to attribute and give unto the same person of Christ those things which do appertain unto his humanity, although the same cannot be verified in him, as touching his Godhead. And therefore, although Christ, as touching his Godhead, was ever present in heaven, and was ever equal in glory with his Father; yet forasmuch as concerning his manhood he was never in heaven, nor did never sit there endued with such power and glory before this his ascension, therefore it is said truly in this Creed, that Christ ascended into heaven, and that Almighty God the Father did, at his said coming thither, set him there upon his right hand.

Secondly, it is to be noted, that this ascension of Christ into heaven was not only very necessary, but also much profitable for all true Christian men, and that for many causes. One is, for that Christ declared thereby very manifestly, that he was not only man, but that he was also very God. And therefore it followeth in this article, he sitteth on the right hand of his Father, not as inferior in Godhead, but as equal unto him. Another is, for that he hath been ever sith that time our continual advocate and solicitor unto God his Father, according to the saying of St. Paul, writing unto the

Hebrews, where he saith in this manner: Christ ascended into heaven, to the intent he should ever appear and ever be present in the sight of God, as a mediator and intercessor for us (Heb 4:14). And in another place also he saith, Jesus the Son of God did penetrate and ascend above all the heavens, to be our great Bishop: wherefore let us firmly and steadfastly believe that we have a great Bishop in heaven, that is to say, a great and a perpetual mediator and intercessor for us; and that the same our Bishop is not only of such infinite might and power, that he is fully able to save all them that will invocate and believe in God the Father by him, but also that he having perfect knowledge of all the infirmities of our flesh and mortality, and having tasted by experience in his own body all the temptations of the same, (sin only excepted,) he will also gladly and willingly have pity and compassion of us, and will be always ready to save us: wherefore let us put our whole trust and confidence in him. And so let us boldly go by prayer and invocation unto the throne of grace, that we may obtain mercy, and find grace and favour, help, succour, and comfort in time of our need and necessity. And St. John the apostle also writeth conformly hereunto in his first epistle, where he saith, I exhort and pray you, good Christian people, flee from sin, and sin no more (1 John 2:1). Notwithstanding, if any of you shall fortune to commit any deadly sin, yet let him consider and remember, that Jesu Christ, which fulfilled all justice for us, and, by the sacrificing and offering up of his precious blood, made due satisfaction and propitiation unto God his Father, not only for all our sins, but also for the sins of all the world, is now our continual and perpetual advocate, our patron and defender before the throne of his Father, and maketh continual intercession and prayer for the remission of all our sins.

Another cause is, for that if Christ had not ascended, we should have lacked all the graces and gifts of the Holy Ghost, which be necessary for the passing of this transitory life, to the pleasure of God, and to the attaining of everlasting life in another world, according to the saying of Christ, speaking unto his apostles, in this manner: I tell you truth, it is expedient and necessary for you that I shall ascend up into heaven. For surely if I should not ascend, the Holy Ghost shall never come unto you: and contrary, if I do ascend into heaven, then will I send him immediately unto you. And when the said Holy Ghost shall come, then shall he reprove and condemn the world and the devil for their sin and iniquity, and he shall fully instruct and teach you all truth, &c.

Thirdly, it is to be noted, that although it be said in this article that Christ is our only mediator and intercessor, yet thereby is not excluded the intercession of the holy saints which be now in heaven, or hereafter shall be; neither yet the intercession of the ministers of Christ's church, or of any the holy members of the same, which be living here in this world. But we must know for certain, that all the members of Christ's church, whether they be departed this life, or yet living here in the world, be all knit and united together in perfect charity, and each doth care and pray for other continually unto Almighty God, and that Christ, being head of the same body, is advocate and intercessor for them all, like as it is more at large declared in the tenth article of this Creed.

The notes of the seventh article. In the seventh article it is to be noted, that like as the world had once a beginning, so shall it once also have an ending. And that upon the same extreme or last day of the world, Christ shall come with glory, as the supreme and highest Judge, and shall hold an universal or general judgment, in the which all the people of the world that ever was, or ever shall be, shall appear before him, there to receive their final sentence and judgment, some of everlasting salvation, and some of perpetual damnation.

It is also to be noted, that this article was for great considerations added immediately, and conjoined unto the former articles, specially to the intent that no man should in his lifetime presume upon the said benefits of Christ, or take occasion of carnal liberty or security, and so live without having any fear to transgress, or regard to observe the commandments of God; but rather that every good Christian man should in every part of his life have a continual remembrance and respect unto that last day of judgment, and so be in continual fear to commit any thing contrary to the will of God, for the which he might deserve to have the sentence of everlasting damnation pronounced upon him. For this is certainly true, that at that day every man shall be called to make a strait account of his life, and shall be then finally judged even according to his own proper works, good or bad, done in his lifetime. That is to say, if in his lifetime he did believe in his heart and profess with his mouth the right belief and faith of Christ, and according unto the same faith did express in his outward works such obedience unto the laws of God as he requireth; he shall be judged to have everlasting life for his reward. And contrary, if in his lifetime he had not this right faith and belief in Christ, or having opportunity did not express this obedience, but transgressed the laws of God, and so died without repentance, although he pretended and said that he believed never so much, and trusted in Christ's benefits never so much, yet shall he be judged and condemned to the everlasting pains of hell.

In this article it is further to be noted, that like as there is nothing more certain unto us than that we be all mortal, and shall once die, and yet no man living knoweth the time when he shall die; even so there is nothing more certain than that this day of judgment shall once come, and yet the hour and the time when it shall be is hidden and kept secret from the knowledge of all men and angels, and is reserved to the only knowledge of God; which thing proceedeth of his only goodness towards us, and is done to the intent we should always here in our lifetime flee from sin, and employ all our whole study and endeavour to walk in the ways of God, that is to say, in such faith, hope, and charity, as God requireth of us, and so prepare ourself, and order our living towards God, that we may be in a readiness at all times, whensoever it shall please God to call and summon us to appear before him in the said general judgment, there by his mercy and goodness to receive the crown and reward, which be promised unto all them that do fear him, and love him, and walk in his ways.

It is also to be noted in this article, that like as the lightning cometh from heaven suddenly, unlooked for, and in one instant or moment casteth light over all; even so this second advent or coming of Christ, and his general judgment, shall come suddenly, and at such time as the greatest part of the people of the world shall fear or look for nothing less than for that day (Matt 24; Mark 13; Luke 17). Truth it is that God shall send many great and evident signs and tokens before the said coming of Christ, to admonish and warn thereby his elect people of his said advent or coming; notwithstanding the same signs shall not be so evident, but that the greatest part of the people of the world shall take and repute them for no such signs. But like as in the time of Noe, that holy patriarch, the people of the world, which then were, would not be induced to believe or think that God would ever send any such general flood to drown up all the world, as the said patriarch shewed them of before and so upon trust thereof continued forth still after their old accustomed manner and fashion, living in all filthiness and abomination, until the said flood came indeed, and so oppressed them suddenly, when they were in the midst of all their belly joy, and drowned them all that ever was, except only the said patriarch, and seven others, which somewhat before the coming of the said flood entered into the ship made for that purpose, and so saved their lives; even so at doomsday, and long before, the greatest part of the people of the world shall little or nothing regard the said signs, which God shall send as tokens before doomsday, but shall rather mock them, and attribute them unto other causes, and so building their faith and trust thereupon, shall give themselves wholly unto carnal and bodily lusts, to covetousness and fraud, to vainglory and ambition, and to all other the works of the flesh, and so shall continue therein without repentance, or thinking of the said last day, until the selfsame hour that Christ shall come himself in person, and call them suddenly to come and appear before his presence to receive their judgment.

The notes of the eighth article.

In the eighth article it is specially to be noted, that notwithstanding any thing contained or mentioned therein, yet we must constantly believe in the second Person in Trinity, according as it is declared in the former articles in all points, that is to say, that our Saviour Jesu Christ hath merited abundantly, and at the full, not only clean remission of all our sins, but also our perfect redemption and deliverance from all the captivity and thraldom of our spiritual enemies, and also our perfect reconciliation unto the favour of God, and our perfect justification and salvation, and that his death and his blood is the only and sufficient price and valure, and the just satisfaction for all the sins of the world. And that he is the only mean and highway whereby Christian men do and must come unto the Father, and that he is our only advocate and patron in heaven, by whom all the heavenly gifts of the Holy Ghost, and whatsoever else is or can be necessary or requisite to the attaining of everlasting life, is conferred and given unto us. And therefore whereas in this eighth article our sanctification, our justification, our incorporation into the body of Christ, our governance, and all the other gifts and graces wherewith Christian men be endued, be attributed unto the work of this Holy Spirit, it is to be understood, first, that like as Christ is the author, the mean, and the very highway to come unto God the Father, so is this Holy Spirit the very conductor, the guide, the director, and the governor, to bring us into the same highway, and to minister unto us not only alacrity and strength to walk and run therein, but also perseverance to continue in the same, until we shall come unto our journey's end.

Second, that the peculiar office and operation of this Holy Spirit is to reveal and teach us the mysteries of Christ's blood and his passion, and how he is our only Lord, our Saviour, and Redeemer; and so to bring us into the right knowledge of all these benefits that Christ hath done for us. For surely if this Holy Spirit should not by his work illumine and light our hearts with the knowledge of this truths all the merits and benefits of Christ should be perpetually hidden from our knowledge, and we should never believe in Christ, but should be like Jews and Turks, which know not Christ, and so we should never be made participant of Christ's merits, nor they should never be applied unto us.

Thirdly, that it is also the peculiar function or office of this Holy Spirit, (after we be inspired, and perfectly instructed in the said knowledge,) first to purge and purify our hearts by this faith and knowledge from the malice and filthiness of sin, and afterward to stir, inflame, and ravish our hearts, and to make us able gladly and thankfully to embrace and receive the said benefits, and so to keep them, to use them, and to dispose them to our own wealth, and to the edifying and profit of our neighbours. And finally, to comfort us, and to be unto us in manner as a certain pledge or an earnest penny, to assure and warrant us, by true and infallible tokens, that we be in the favour of God, and his own children by grace and adoption, and the right inheritors of heaven. And forasmuch as this Holy Spirit, being sent and proceeding from the Father and the Son to dwell and inhabit in our hearts, worketh in us all these effects; holy scripture doth worthily attribute unto him our sanctification, our justification, and all the other benefits which Christ by his passion hath merited and deserved for us, which nevertheless be also the works of the whole Trinity, and be not to be separated in any wise, although scripture commonly doth attribute them unto the Holy Ghost, as it doth attribute power unto the Father, and wisdom unto the Son, which nevertheless be common unto all three.

In the ninth article many things be to be noted. First, that this word *church*, in scripture, is taken sometime generally for the whole congregation of them that be christened and profess Christ's gospel: and sometime it is taken for the catholic congregation, or number of them only which be chosen, called, and ordained to reign with Christ in everlasting life.

The notes of the ninth article.

Second, it is to be noted, that the church, in the first signification, is in scripture compared sometime unto a field full of good corn and naughty weeds mingled together (Matt 13:24-30); and sometimes unto a net full of good fish and bad (13:47-50); and sometimes unto a flock of sheep and goats gathered together in one fold (25:31-46); and sometimes unto the threshing-floor of Almighty God, wherein is contained corn and chaff both together (Matt 3:12; Luke 3:17); and sometimes unto a great man's house, in the which be some vessels or instruments of gold, some of silver, some of tree, some of earth, some to be had in honour and price, and such as will never be corrupted and putrified, and some to be had in contempt, and to serve only for vile uses (2 Tim 2:20).

Thirdly, it is to be noted, that by these parables, and certain such other, rehearsed in scripture, is signified, that among them which be christened, and do profess Christ's gospel, and live in the common society and communion of the sacraments of the church, divers be indeed the very quick and living members of Christ's mystical body, and shall reign with him everlastingly in honour. And that the congregation or society of them is the very field, and they be the very good corn or seed, which Christ himself did sow. And divers be indeed chaff, or stinking and naughty weeds, sown by the devil; naughty fishes, stinking and barren goats, vessels despised, or instruments prepared to everlasting fire, that is to say, they be the very members of the synagogue of the devil, and not the living members of Christ's mystical body.

By these parables also it is signified, that in this present life these two sorts of people, good and bad, be continually mixed and mingled together in the church, as it is taken in the first signification. And that the said members of the synagogue of the devil, so long as they grow in the same field wherein the good corn groweth, that is to say, so long as they do in outward appearance profess the same faith of Christ which the very members of Christ's church do profess, and do consent and agree with them outwardly in the doctrine of the gospel, and in all other things appertaining unto Christ's religion; they must be accepted and reputed here in the world for the very members of Christ's mystical body; and that they ought not ne can be dissevered from them, until the day of judgment. At which time the Shepherd shall divide the sheep from the goats, and the mowers shall try and cleanse the corn from the weeds and chaff, and so shall bring the corn into the barn, and cast the chaff and the weeds into the fire, there to burn perpetually.

Of the church also, in this first manner of signification, scripture meaneth, where it saith that abomination shall sit in the holy place, and that there shall arise in the church horrible errors and false prophets, which shall work such wonders that the elect people of God shall be almost seduced with them (Dan 9; Matt 24). For surely not only the wicked people which be mingled with the good in the church, as it is taken in this first manner of signification, do and shall commit infinite errors and impieties, but also the good people, and such as be the very members of Christ, do and shall err ofttimes as men, and ofttimes do and shall decline for a season from the right way.

Fourthly, it is to be noted, that of the church, as it is taken in the second manner of signification, it is said in scripture that she is the heavenly Jerusalem, the city of God, the temple or habitacle of God, the house of God builded upon a stone, the only dove, the only beloved of God, the garden mured round about, the fountain enclosed, the well of lively water, the paradise full of fruit, *Heb 12; Rev 21; 2 Cor 6; 1 Timothy 2; Matt 5; 1 Pet 2; Eph 2; Song 6, 4; Gal 4; Eph 5; 1 Timothy 3; 2 Timothy 2.* our holy mother, the glorious espouse of Christ full of all beauty, without spot or wrinkle, the mystical body of Christ, the seat or pillar of truth, the golden vessel in the nobleman's house, which shall never corrupt or putrify. All which sentences, and divers such other, spoken in scripture of the church, be to be referred and verified of the church in the second signification. And finally, in this signification also the ninth article of our Creed is to be understanded. For surely it is necessary for our salvation to believe that that church or congregation, which containeth the very quick and living members of Christ's mystical body, and which shall reign everlastingly with him in heaven, is all holy and catholic: and that like as it hath been ever in the world, and yet is, so it shall continue for ever; and for ever is, and shall be unto the world's end, spiritually and inwardly renewed, quickened, governed, justified, and sanctified with the presence, and spiritual assistance, and graces of the Holy Ghost, and inwardly shall be connected and united together in one godly consent in charity, and in the true doctrine of Christ.

And for confirmation hereof, it is also further to be noted and considered, that it is not only very necessary for all true Christian men to learn and know the certain notes and marks whereby the very true church of Christ is discerned from the church or congregation of the wicked, which

God hateth, and also what is the principal cause whereby they be made to be the very quick members of the church of Christ; but it is also one of the greatest comforts that any Christian man can have, to believe and trust for certain that there is such a congregation, which containeth the very lively members of Christ's mystical body, and that he is a member of the same congregation: specially considering the great and excellent promises which Christ himself hath made unto the said congregation, being his own mystical body, and his own most dear and tenderly beloved espouse.

And for these causes and considerations, and such other, it is (no doubt) to be thought, that this ninth article was added and put into this Creed, specially and principally to describe and declare the church, as it is taken in the said second manner of signification.

Fifthly, it is to be noted, that after the mind of certain interpreters of scripture, the quick and living members of the holy and catholic church or congregation be of two sorts, whereof the one part is already departed this life in the state of grace, and is called the church triumphant, forasmuch as after their victory they do or shall triumph in joy and felicity in heaven. The other is all those true Christian people which do and shall live here in this world, daily and continually fighting in Christ's battle, and for Christ's sake, against their spiritual enemies, the world, the devil, and the flesh; and for that cause is called the militant or fighting church.

Sixthly, it is to be noted, that although the lively members of this militant church be subject to the infirmities of their flesh, and fall ofttimes into error and sin, as was said before; yet they always in scripture be called holy, as well because they be sanctified in the blood of Christ, and professing in their baptism to believe in God, and to forsake the devil and all his works, they be consecrated and dedicated unto Christ; as also for that they be from time to time purged by the word of God, and by faith, hope, and charity, and by the exercise of other virtues; and finally shall be endued with such grace of the Holy Ghost, that they shall be clearly sanctified and purified from all filthiness, and shall be made the glorious espouse of Christ, shining in all cleanness, without having any spot, or wrinkle, or any other thing worthy to be reprehended.

The notes of the tenth article.

In the tenth article it is to be noted, that divers interpreters of holy scripture do diversely interpretate the first part thereof, that is to say, communion of saints. For some of them do refer it unto the ninth article, and do take it as a clause added to declare and explain what is signified by these words, *the catholic church;* and so they do conjoin this clause with that that went before in this sense: I believe that this catholic church is the communion, that is to say, the multitude, or the commonalty, or the commonwealth of saints only, that is to say, of those which be under the kingdom of Christ, and be governed and sanctified with his Holy Spirit, and be prepared to come to everlasting life. And some interpreters do divide the said clause from the ninth article, and do conjoin it with the article that followeth, that is to say, *remission of sins.* Now these doctors which be of this opinion do also diversely expound the said clause of communion of saints. For some of them do take it to signify the common utility and profit which all the members of Christ's body do receive by the common merits, suffrages, and prayers of the whole church. And some do expound and take it for the communion of the sacraments of the church, which be common unto all men, be they rich or poor, free or bond, young or old, if they be contained within the unity of this church. And some do take and expound it to signify that unity which is between Christ and all true Christian men, that is to say, between the head and his mystical body. And forasmuch as by the communion and participation of the sacrament of the altar we be inserted into the body of Christ, and so we be incorporated in Christ, and Christ in us; therefore some interpreters do take, that by this clause is signified the sacrament of the altar. And some doctors do expound it to signify that treasure of the church which is common equally unto all the members of the same. And those doctors which be of this opinion do interpretate that treasure to be nothing else but the grace, that is to say, the mercy, the goodness, and the favour of God in this world, and glory in the world to come. They say also, that this grace of God is the common treasure of all the elect people of God, and that our poverty is so extreme, that of ourselves, without this grace, we should be utterly nothing. They say further, that the effect and virtue of this grace is to make us able to rise from sin and flee from sin, to work good works, to receive the reward of everlasting glory, to have and retain the true sense and understanding of holy scripture, and to endue us with Christian faith, hope, and charity. Finally, they say, that this grace worketh all those effects in the elect people of God, by two special instruments, which be, the word of God and his sacraments. And forasmuch as both the word and the sacraments have all their efficacy by and through the might and operation of the Holy Ghost, and forasmuch also as this Holy Ghost dwelleth and abideth only in the catholic church, and in the members of the same, and worketh none of these effects out of the church; they think that by this clause, *communion of saints,* is meant here the treasure of the church: and that this treasure is nothing else but the Holy Ghost himself, and his graces, whereby, and by the word of God and his sacraments, we attain remission of sins, life, light, truth, justice, eternal peace, rest, tranquillity, and health, so long as we be not dissevered from the unity of this catholic church, but do remain therein as lively members of the same.

In this article it is also to be noted, that remission of sins is the final cause of all the whole history of Christ, and of all the works that ever he did or suffered for our sakes and our redemption, and also the special fruit and profit which true Christian men do receive thereby. For surely Christ became man, and was born, crucified, dead, and rose again to life, and ascended to heaven, to the end and intent to merit and deserve for us remission of all our sins, forasmuch as it was impossible for us to have obtained the same by any other means. And the truth is, that we can by no means be made partakers of this merit of Christ, unless we shall first firmly and steadfastly believe in Christ, and that he is the only sufficient author, causer, and worker of remission of all our sins. To the attaining of which faith, it is also to be noted, that Christ hath instituted and ordained in the world but only two means and instruments, whereof the one is the ministration of his word, and the other is the administration of his sacraments instituted by him; so that it is not possible to attain this faith, but by one or both of these two means, as shall be hereafter declared.

The Declaration
of the Seven Sacraments

And First, of the Sacrament of Matrimony

As touching the sacrament of matrimony, we think it convenient that all bishops and preachers shall instruct and teach the people committed unto their spiritual charge, first, how that Almighty God, at the first creation of man in paradise, considering of his infinite wisdom and goodness how necessary it was to couple and conjoin man and woman together in marriage, as well for their mutual aid and comfort, and for the preservation and continuance of mankind in lawful succession, as also that the same generation might after the fall of man be exercised perpetually unto the world's end without sin or offence towards God, did not only then and there conjoin Adam and Eve together in marriage, and instituted the said sacrament of matrimony, and consecrated and blessed it by his holy word; but also described the virtue and efficacy of the said sacrament by the mouth of Adam; who, being inspired with the Holy Ghost, when he was by God conjoined in marriage with Eve, spake these words following: Lo now these bones and flesh of Eve my wife be formed and made of my bones and flesh. And therefore every married man hereafter shall for his wife's sake utterly leave and forsake his father and mother, and shall adhere and cleave unto his wife only, and the husband and the wife shall be two in one flesh and in one body (Gen 2:23-24).

By which words it is meant, that by the virtue and efficacy of matrimony, rightfully and by the authority of God contracted, the man and woman, which were before two bodies, be now united, and made to be one body during their lives; so that the husband hath no power of his own body to use the same as him lust, and with whom him liketh; but it is his wife's, and with her only he may use the act of matrimony: nor the wife hath any power of her own body, to use it at her lust, or with whom her liketh; but her body is her husband's body, and with him only may she use the act of matrimony. And therefore the said two persons, so conjoined, may not be afterward divided for any affection to father or mother, or for any earthly thing in the world; but each must adhere and cleave together, forasmuch as they be now two persons in one flesh and in one body.

Second, how that Almighty God repeated and renewed again his said institution of matrimony, and sanctified and blessed it with his holy word immediately after Noe's flood. At which time being all the people of the world perished and destroyed with the general deluge, (except the said holy patriarch Noe, his children, and their wives, which were then only by God's high providence and goodness towards mankind preserved and left on life,) God calling them out of the ark, said unto them these words: Grow you forth now, and increase by continual generation, and be you multiplied in continual succession, and fulfil you the earth again with your seed lawfully procreated in matrimony, according as I have instituted the same. This law and commandment of matrimony, thus repeated and given again by God unto Noe and his children, although it was sufficient commandment and instruction unto them and all their posterity how to use the same in all purity and cleanness to God's pleasure and his good contentation; yet God, perceiving the natural inclination of man to malice and sin, did afterward further explicate and establish the same by his other laws written; whereby God prohibited that any matrimony should be made between the father and the daughter, the mother and the son, the brother and the sister, and between divers other persons, being in certain degrees of consanguinity and affinity (Lev 18, 20): which laws of prohibition in marriage, although they were not by express words of God declared at the first institution of matrimony, ne yet at this second repetition of the same, made unto Noe; yet undoubtedly God had engraved and enprinted the same laws in the heart of man at his first creation. And forasmuch as in long continuance and process of time the natural light and knowledge of man was almost by sin and malice extincted, or at the least so corrupted and obscured in the most part of men, that they could not perceive and judge what things were of their own nature naughty and detestable in the sight of God, ne yet how far that natural honesty and reverence which we owe unto such persons as be near of blood, or of near alliance unto us, was extended; God commanded his prophet Moses to promulgate and to declare by his word unto the people of Israel the said laws of prohibition of matrimony in certain degrees of consanguinity and affinity, which be specially mentioned in the Book of Leviticus: and commanded also Moses to declare unto his said people, that not only they, but also all other the people of the world, were as much and as straitly bounden to the continual observation of the same laws, as they were unto the other moral laws of the Ten Commandments.

Thirdly, that this conjunction between man and woman in matrimony was instituted by God to the intent thereby should be signified and represented, or rather prefigurated and prophesied before, not only the perfect and indissoluble conjunction and union of the nature of God with the nature of man, (which was fulfilled, when the second Person in Trinity, descending from his Father, did take upon him the very form and substance of our nature, and so those two natures were united and knit together in one person,) but also to the intent there should thereby be signified and represented the like conjunction or society, in perfect and indissoluble love and charity, between Christ and his church, that is to say, the congregation of all Christian people, which be the very mystical body of Christ, and Christ the only head of the same. And this to be true, St. Paul himself confirmeth, in the 5th chapter of his Epistle unto the Ephesians. In which place the apostle, minding to prove and persuade that all women, being married, ought to love, to reverence, to honour, to obey, and to be subject unto their husbands in all things, even as the church is subject unto Christ; and likewise that all husbands ought and be bound to love their wives, even as they love their own selves and their own bodies, and even as Christ loveth the church, his espouse and his own body: he bringeth in the first institution of matrimony, as it was ordained by God in paradise, and allegeth the words of God, pronounced by our first father Adam, as they be before rehearsed. Upon which words the apostle inferreth and saith, This conjunction of man and woman together in marriage, whereby they are knitted, united, and made all one flesh and one body, is the sacrament, that is to say, the figure, the signification, the mystery, or the prophesying before of that great and marvellous conjunction which is between Christ and his church. For like as by the virtue and efficacy of this first institution of matrimony, the husband and the wife be made to be but one body, whereof the husband is the head; even so the love and charity of Christ towards his espouse the church doth knit, unite, conglutinate, and make Christ and his church to be but one body, whereof Christ is the very head. By the which words of St. Paul it appeareth, not only what is the virtue and efficacy of matrimony in the uniting and incorporating of two bodies in one, but also that is was instituted by God to signify this other conjunction which is between Christ and his church; and that this conjunction between Christ and the church is the very self thing which was prophesied, signified, and represented by the other conjunction of man and woman in marriage. For though St. Paul used in this place other arguments and persuasions, taken of the law of nature, to induce married persons the one to love the other, (saying, that men naturally do love and nourish their own bodies and their own flesh, and that it is against nature that a man should hate his own flesh,) yet surely he thought that this was the reason of most efficacy to persuade his said purpose; that is to say, that all husbands and wives ought so to use themselves, the one unto the other, that their matrimony, and all their works and affections in the same, might and should correspond, and be conformable and like in all points unto that most holy thing which is signified and represented thereby, that is to say, unto that spiritual conjunction which is between Christ and his espouse the church. And that therefore specially the man ought and is bound to love his wife, and the wife to love and obey her husband in all things, lest by doing the contrary they should alter and subvert the institution of God, and make the figure all unlike unto the thing that is signified thereby.

And so by these words and reasons of St. Paul it is evident, that concerning the sacrament of matrimony, his sentence and doctrine was, that the same was instituted by God at the first creation of man, to signify that inseparable conjunction and union which is between Christ and his church.

Item, We think it convenient, that all bishops and preachers shall instruct and teach the people committed to their spiritual charge, that although this sacrament of matrimony be no new sacrament instituted in the New Testament, but instituted by God, and consecrated by his word, and dignified by his laws even from the beginning of the world, and before any other of the sacraments were instituted in the New Testament, as was said before; yet the truth is, that Christ himself did also accept, approve, and allow the said institution, as well by his word, as also by his sundry works and deeds, testifying the same. Insomuch that being once invited to come unto a certain marriage, made in Cana, a town of Galilee, Christ vouchsafed not only to come thither, and there to honour the said marriage with his corporal presence, and with the presence also of his blessed mother and his holy apostles; but there he began also, by turning of water into wine, first to work miracles, and to manifest his glory unto the world (John 2). And afterward, in one other place, when the Pharisees came unto Christ, and demanded of him whether a man might lawfully be divorced from his wife for any cause, Christ, calling the said Pharisees unto the remembrance of the first institution of matrimony, as it was made at the first beginning, said unto them, Remember you not, you Pharisees, how that God, which created all things in the beginning, did also form and create man and woman? And when he had conjoined them together in marriage, he said unto them these words: *Propter hoc relinquet homo patrem et matrem, et adhærebit uxori suæ, et erunt duo in carne una?*[1] Wherefore understand you, ye Pharisees, that sith man and woman conjoined in matrimony be by God's ordinance but one flesh and one body, it is not possible that they should afterward be separated or divorced one from the other. And understand you also, that it is not lawful for any man to separate and to divide those persons asunder, which be by God's word and his will and power conjoined together. And when the Pharisees, replying thereunto, said, And why then did Moses command us to make a libel of divorce against our wives, for what cause soever we would, and so depart and separate ourselves from them? Christ answered them again, and said, Moses, considering the indurateness and obstinacy of your hearts, was content to permit and suffer you so to do, for avoiding of greater mischief and inconvenience, which might else have ensued thereof: albeit I say unto you, that it was not so at the beginning, that is to say, it is clean contrary to the godly institution and natural order and laws of matrimony, as it was instituted by God at the beginning, that any man married should divorce himself from his lawful wife. And therefore I say again unto you, that whosoever

---

[1] ["Therefore shall a man leave his father and his mother, and shall cleave unto his wife: and they shall be one flesh" (Gen 2:24; Mark 10:7-8).]

doth forsake his lawful wife, unless it be for adultery committed by her, and doth marry another, I say he committeth adultery in his so doing. And likewise, what woman soever doth forsake her lawful husband, and marry another, she also committeth adultery. And the man also that marrieth her offendeth in like manner. And the cause hereof is, for that the bond of lawful marriage is of such sort, that it cannot be dissolved or broken, but by death only (Mark 10).

These words of Christ evidently declare Christ's sentence in the approbation of the institution of matrimony, made at the beginning of the world: and that it was Christ's will and commandment that all the people of God should follow and conform their doings unto the laws of matrimony then made, and should observe the same in such purity and sanctimony as it was first ordained, without separation or divorce, and that under the pain of damnation.

And here also two things specially be to be noted. The one is, in that Christ saith, *Whom God conjoineth man cannot separate.* By the which words he declareth the infinite benignity and goodness of God towards us, in that, that he hath not only conjoined our first progenitors Adam and Eve together in marriage, whereby he gave unto us the original beginning of our procreation; but that he doth also ever sith that time continually assist man and woman, and worketh with them in this conjunction of marriage, and, as you would say, is the very author, causer, and doer of all matrimonies, which be lawfully contracted between man and woman. The other thing to be noted is, in that Christ saith here unto his disciples, *Non omnes capiunt verbum hoc: sed quibus datum est, qui potest capere capiat* (Matt 19:11).[2] By the which words Christ seemeth to exhort such as he shall endue with the grace and virtue of continence, whereby they shall be able to abstain from the works of matrimony, to continue sole and unmarried.

Item, We think it convenient, that all bishops and preachers shall instruct and teach the people committed unto their spiritual charge, that the sacrament of matrimony doth consist of two parts, like as the other sacraments do, that is to say, of an outward and a visible sign, and of an inward and an invisible grace. The outward sign is that outward contract, made by express words, or other signs equivalent, declaring the consent

---

[2] [Not everyone can accept this teaching, but only those to whom it is given.]

between such persons as may lawfully and by the order of God's law be joined together in marriage, when the same persons do consent and promise each to other to company together continually during their lives, without separation, and to communicate each to other the use and office of their bodies, and all other their faculties and substance. The spiritual and invisible graces which the elect people of God (as well in the time of the law of nature, as in the time of Moses' law, and also in the time of the New Testament) did always and yet do receive by virtue of this sacrament, be divers and sundry; whereof one is the dispensation or grace of God, whereby the act of procreation between man and woman, which is, as of itself and of his own nature, damnable, is sanctified by the word of God and this sacrament, that is to say, is made pure, clean, without spot of sin, and honourable, according to the saying of St. Paul, *Honorabile conjugium in omnibus, et thorus immaculatus* (Heb 13:4). That is to say, the act of procreation between man and woman in matrimony is honourable, and acceptable afore God, and their bed is undefiled. Another is the grace whereby the persons conjoined in matrimony do attain everlasting life, if they bring up their children in the true faith and observance of Christ's religion according to the words of St. Paul, where he saith, The woman was seduced and blinded by the serpent, and so sinned deadly: but she shall be saved by procreation and bringing forth of children, if the same do persevere and continue in faith and love towards God, and in holiness, and in temperance in their outward acts and deeds (1 Tim 2:14-15). And as this is spoken of the woman, so it is also to be verified in the man, he doing likewise as is required of the woman.

Finally, we think it convenient, that all bishops and preachers shall diligently and from time to time exhort and admonish the people committed unto their spiritual charge, to consider the three special benefits or offices which belong unto the sacrament of matrimony. And first of all to consider the thing self, which is signified thereby, which (as was said before) is the high, the mighty, and the incomprehensible work of God, in the conjunction of Christ and the church together, wrought by him to our singular benefit and everlasting salvation. And that therefore the man and wife ought not only to live together in perfect unity and concord, but also they ought to love each other as their own bodies, and to use the same in all cleanness, purity, and honour, and not to defile the same with the rages and lusts of any beastly or filthy concupiscence of the flesh, even as Christ himself loved, and doth love his espouse the church, and suffered all afflictions and pains to make her glorious, and void from all manner of spot or wrinkle of uncleanness. And in this part also it shall be well done, that the bishops and preachers do repeat ofttimes, and lay before the eyes of the people, as well the sayings of St. Paul, before rehearsed, as also the godly exhortation which he maketh in his Epistle unto the Thessalonians, where he writeth in this manner: I pray you, brethren, and instantly desire you for our Lord Jesu Christ's sake, that like as you have heard heretofore of us how and in what manner you should go forward and please God; so ye do proceed in the same, and that after such sort and manner, that you may continually profit and increase therein (1 Thess 4). You remember, I doubt not, what precepts and commandments I have given unto you in times past, in the name of our Lord Jesu Christ. And now in like manner, and in his name also, I say again unto you, that the will and commandment of God is, that you should sanctify yourselves, that is to say, that you should abstain from all manner of fornication, and that every one of you should use and keep the vessel of his body in holiness and in honour, and not in desire of carnal concupiscence, like as the Gentiles do, which know not God. And that no man should craftily compass or circumvent his brother in fleshly lusts. For Almighty God taketh vengeance upon all such people as do commit any of those things. Know you also, that God hath not called us unto uncleanness and filthiness of life, but unto holiness and sanctimony. And therefore I do exhort you all, and in the name of God command you, to eschew all fornication and adultery, all unclean desires and carnal concupiscence, all filthiness and unpure living in fleshly lusts of the body. And I say further, that whosoever despiseth and breaketh these my commandments, doth not despise me, but he despiseth God, for they be his commandments, whose Spirit both you and I have received.

These words of St. Paul be necessary to be declared ofttimes to the people, to the intent they may the better know the will and commandment of God, and also consider and fear the great danger of God's wrath and vengeance, due unto such people as do transgress the godly institution and laws of this holy sacrament of matrimony.

The second special gift or benefit to be considered in the said sacrament, is the faith and mutual promise made between the husband and the wife joined in lawful matrimony, whereby, and by virtue of the said sacrament, the persons so lawfully conjoined be bound to conceive certain trust and confidence, and certainly to believe, not only that their said state and manner of living in wedlock (being the same virtuously and religiously, according to the law of God, by them contracted and observed) is honourable, acceptable, and meritorious before God; but also that the knot and bond of matrimony contracted between the said persons is made thereby to be indissoluble.

Truth it is, that if in any marriage it may appear and be duly proved, that there is such lawful impediment that the same might not at the beginning be contracted by the order of the laws of God and holy church; in that case the church ought and may divorce the said persons so contracted, and declare that such matrimony is unlawful, and the bond thereof to be of no strength or efficacy, because it was never good from the beginning. Notwithstanding in marriages lawfully made, and according to the ordinance of matrimony prescribed by God and holy church, the bond thereof can by no means be dissolved during the lives of the parties between whom such matrimony is contracted.

And in this part also the people be to be taught, that whosoever goeth about to dissever himself from the bond of lawful marriage, he goeth about, so much as in him lieth, to divorce Christ from his church.

The third special gift or office to be considered and observed in matrimony, is the good and virtuous education and bringing up of the children begotten in the same; whereunto all married men and women ought to have a special regard, and to follow therein the example of Tobit, which taught his son, even from his infancy, to love, to dread, and to fear God, and to flee and abstain from all manner of sin, even for God's sake (Tob 4:5). For surely if the fathers and mothers be negligent in the good bringing up of their children in their youth, and so suffer them to fall into follies and sin, in default of due correction and chastisement of them for the same, no doubt they shall answer unto God for it: as it appeareth by the great stroke and punishment of God, when he did suddenly strike Eli the priest unto death, because that he, knowing his children to do amiss, did not punish them therefore (1 Sam 4). And therefore let all parents employ their diligence and busy care to educate and instruct their children by all means in virtue and goodness, and to restrain them from vices by convenient discipline and castigation, according to the saying of the Wise Man, Withdraw not the just discipline from thy child. For if thou do so, he will fall into sundry inconveniences, and so finally shall be but lost and undone. Wherefore spare not to chastise thy child with the rod, and so doing thou shalt deliver his soul from hell (Prov 23:14).

The Sacrament of Baptism

As touching the holy sacrament of baptism, we think it convenient, that all bishops and preachers shall instruct and teach the people committed unto their spiritual charge, that they ought and must of necessity believe certainly all those things which have been always by the whole consent of the church approved, received, and used in the sacrament of baptism. And first that the sacrament of baptism was instituted and ordained by God in the New Testament as a thing necessary for the attaining of everlasting life, according to the saying of our Saviour Jesu Christ, where he saith, that no man can enter into the kingdom heaven, except he be born again of water and the Holy Ghost (John 3:5).

Item, That it is offered unto all men, as well infants as such as have the use of reason, that by baptism they shall have remission of all their sins, the grace and favour of God, and everlasting life, according to the saying of Christ, Whosoever believeth and is baptized shall be saved (Mark 16:16).

Item, That the promise of grace and everlasting life (which promise is adjoined unto this sacrament of baptism) pertaineth not only unto such as have the use of reason, but also to infants, innocents, and children; and that they ought therefore and must needs be baptized; and that by the sacrament of baptism they do also obtain remission of their sins, the grace and favour of God, and be made thereby the very sons and children of God. Insomuch as infants and children dying in their infancy, shall undoubtedly be saved thereby, and else not.

Item, That infants must needs be christened, because they be born in original sin, which sin must needs be remitted, which cannot be done but by the sacrament of baptism, whereby they receive the Holy Ghost, which exerciseth his grace and efficacy in them, and cleanseth and purifieth them from sin by his most secret virtue and operation.

Item, That children or men once baptized ought never to be baptized again.

Item, That all good Christian men ought and must repute and take all the anabaptists' and the Pelagians' opinions, which be contrary to the premises, and every other man's opinion, agreeable unto the said anabaptists' or the Pelagians' opinions in that behalf, for detestable heresies, and utterly to be condemned.

Item, That men or children, which, having the use of reason, and being not christened already, desire to be baptized, shall, by virtue of that holy sacrament, obtain the grace and remission of all their sins, if they shall come thereunto not only perfectly and truly repentant and contrite of all their sins before committed, but also perfectly and constantly confessing and believing all the articles of our faith, according as is mentioned in the Creed, called the Apostles' Creed. And finally, if they shall also have firm credence and trust in the promise of God, adjoined to the said sacrament, that is to say, that in and by this said sacrament, which they shall receive, God the Father giveth unto them, for his Son Jesu Christ's sake, remission of all their sins, and the grace of the Holy Ghost, whereby they be newly regenerated, and made the very children of God, according to the saying of St. John, and the apostle St. Peter, where they say, Do you penance for your sins, and be each of you baptized in the name of Jesu Christ, and you shall obtain remission of your sins, and shall receive the gift of the Holy Ghost (Matt 3; Luke 3; Acts 2). And according to the saying also of St. Paul, where he saith, God hath not saved us for the works of justice which we have done, but of his mercy by baptism, and renovation of the Holy Ghost, whom he hath poured out upon us most plentifully, for the love of Jesu Christ our Saviour, to the intent that we being justified by his grace, should be made the inheritors of everlasting life, according to our hope (Titus 3).

The Sacrament of Confirmation

As touching the sacrament of confirmation, we think it convenient, that all bishops and preachers shall instruct and teach the people committed unto their spiritual charge, how the apostles, in the beginning of Christ's church, although they did certainly know and believe that all such as had duly received the sacrament of baptism were, by virtue and efficacy thereof, perfectly regenerated in Christ, perfectly incorporated and made the very members of his body, and had received full remission of their sins, and were replenished with abundance and plentifulness of the graces and gifts of the Holy Ghost; yet they used to go unto the people after they were baptized, and so by their prayer, and laying of their hands upon them, did give and confer unto them the Holy Ghost (Acts 8, 19). And the said people did speak divers languages, and prophesied, to the intent that the consciences not only of them that had received baptism, and professed Christ, should be thereby the better ascertained, confirmed, and established in Christ's religion, and so more constantly profess the same; but also that the consciences of other, which were out of the church, and unbelievers, should the sooner be reduced thereby from their errors, and be brought into the right belief of Christ and his gospel.

Item, How the holy fathers of the primitive church, taking occasion, and founding themselves upon the said acts and deeds of the apostles, and considering also that such as had once received the gifts and benefits of the Holy Ghost by the sacrament of baptism might and oftentimes did indeed by temptation, frailty, or otherwise by their own sin and malice, lose and fall from the same again; thought it very expedient to ordain, that all Christian people should, after their baptism, be presented to their bishops, to the intent that by their prayers, and laying of their hands upon them, and consigning of them with the holy chrism, they should be confirmed, that is to say, they should receive such gifts of the Holy Ghost, as whereby they should not only be so corroborated and established in the gifts and graces before received in baptism, that they should not lightly fall again from the same, but should constantly retain them, and persevere therein, and should also be made strong and hardy, as well to confess boldly and manfully their faith before all the persecutors of the same, and to resist and fight against their ghostly enemies, the world, the devil, and the flesh, as also to bear the cross of Christ, that is, to suffer and sustain patiently all the afflictions and adversities of this world; but also that they should attain increase and abundance of the other virtues and graces of the Holy Ghost.

Item, We think it convenient that all bishops and preachers shall instruct and teach the people committed unto their spiritual charge, that although it be well done that men do present their children unto the bishop, to receive at his hands the sacrament of confirmation, when they be of so tender age, as commonly they be wont to do; yet it is not to be thought that there is any such necessity of confirmation of infants, but that they being baptized, and dying innocent before they be confirmed, shall be assured to attain everlasting life and salvation by the effect of the sacrament of baptism before received.

The Sacrament of Penance

As concerning the sacrament of penance, we think it convenient, that all bishops and preachers shall instruct and teach the people committed unto their spiritual charge, that they ought and must most constantly believe that the said sacrament was instituted by God in the New Testament, as a thing so necessary for man's salvation, that no man, which after his baptism is fallen again, and hath committed deadly sin, can without the same be saved, or attain everlasting life.

Item, That like as such men, which after baptism do fall again into sin, if they do not penance in this life, shall undoubtedly be damned; even so, whensoever the same men shall convert themselves from their naughty life, and do such penance for the same as Christ requireth of them, they shall without doubt attain remission of their sins, and shall be saved.

Item, That the sacrament of perfect penance, which Christ requireth of such manner persons, consisteth of three parts; whereof the one is contrition, the other is confession, and the third is the amendment of the former life, or the new obedient reconciliation unto the laws and will of God, that is to say, exterior acts and works of charity, according as they be commanded of God, which be called in scripture, *fructus digni pœnitentia*, the worthy fruits of penance.

Furthermore, as touching contrition, which is the first part, we think it convenient, that all bishops and preachers shall instruct the people committed unto their spiritual charge, that the said contrition consisteth in two special parts, which must always be conjoined together, and cannot be dissevered, that is to say, the penitent and contrite man must first knowledge the filthiness and abomination of his own sin, (unto which knowledge he is brought by hearing and considering of the will of God, declared in his laws,) and feeling and perceiving in his own conscience that God is angry and displeased with him for the same: he must also conceive not only great sorrow and inward shame that he hath so grievously offended God, but also great fear of God's displeasure towards him, considering he hath no works or merits of his own, which he may worthily lay before God, as sufficient satisfaction for his sins: which done, then afterward with this fear, shame, and sorrow must needs succeed and be conjoined the second part, that is to wit, a certain faith, trust, and confidence of the mercy and goodness of God, whereby the penitent must conceive certain hope and faith that God will forgive him his sins, and repute him justified, and of the number of his elect children, not for the worthiness of any merit or work done by the penitent, but for the only merits of the blood and passion of our Saviour Jesu Christ.

Item, That this certain faith and hope is gotten, and also confirmed, and made more strong, by the applying of Christ's words and promises of his grace and favour contained in his gospel, and the sacraments instituted by him in the New Testament. And therefore to attain this certain faith, the second part of penance is necessary, that is to say, confession to a priest, if it may be had. For the absolution given by the priest was instituted of Christ to apply the promises of God's grace and favour to the penitent.

Wherefore, as touching confession, we think it convenient, that all bishops and preachers shall instruct and teach the people committed unto their spiritual charge, that they ought and must certainly believe, that the words of absolution pronounced by the priest be spoken by the authority given to him by Christ in the gospel. And that they ought and must give no less faith and credence to the same words of absolution, so pronounced by the ministers of the church, than they would give unto the very words and voice of God himself, if he should speak unto us out of heaven, according to the saying of Christ, Whose sins soever you do forgive, shall be forgiven: whose sins soever you do retain, shall be retained (John 20:23). And again, in another place, Christ saith, Whosoever heareth you heareth me (Luke 10:16).

Item, That the people may in no wise contemn this auricular confession, which is made unto the ministers of the church; but that they ought to repute the same as a very expedient and necessary mean, whereby they may require and ask this absolution at the priest's hands, at such time as they shall find their consciences grieved with mortal sin, and have occasion so to do, to the intent they may thereby attain certain comfort and consolation of their consciences.

As touching the third part of penance, we think it convenient, that all bishops and preachers shall instruct and teach the people committed unto their spiritual charge, that although Christ and his death be the sufficient oblation, sacrifice, satisfaction, and recompense, for the which God the Father forgiveth and remitteth to all sinners not only their sins, but also eternal pain due for the same; yet all men truly penitent, contrite, and confessed, must needs also bring forth the fruits of penance, that is to say, prayer, fasting, and almsdeed, with much mourning and lamenting for their sins before committed. And they must also make restitution or satisfaction in will and deed to their neighbours, in such things as they have done them wrong and injury in. And finally they must do all other good works of mercy and charity, and express their obedient will in the executing and fulfilling of God's commandment outwardly, when time, power, and occasion shall be ministered unto them, or else they shall never be saved. For this is the express precept and commandment of God, Do you the worthy fruits of penance (Luke 3:8). And St. Paul saith, Like as in times past you have given and applied yourselves, and all the members of your bodies, to all filthy living and wickedness, continually increasing in the same; in like manner you be now bound, and must give and apply yourselves wholly to justice, increasing continually in purity and cleanness of life (Rom 6:13). And in another place he saith, I chastise and subdue my carnal body, and the affections of the same, and make them obedient unto the spirit (1 Cor 9:27).

Item, That these precepts and works of charity be necessary works to our salvation; and God necessarily requireth that every penitent man shall perform the same, whensoever time, power, and occasion shall be ministered unto him so to do.

Item, That by penance, and such good works of the same, we shall not only obtain everlasting life, but also we shall deserve remission or mitigation of the present pains and afflictions, which we sustain here in this world. For St. Paul saith, That if we would correct and take punishment of ourselves in this world, we should not be so grievously corrected of God (1 Cor 11:32). And God by his prophet Zacharye saith, Turn yourselves unto me, and I will turn again unto you (Zech 1:3). And the prophet Esai saith, Break and deal thy bread unto the hungry, bring into thy house the poor man, and such as want harborough; when thou seest a naked man, give him clothes to cover him with, and refuse not to succour and help the poor and needy, for he is thine own flesh. And if thou wilt thus do, then shall thy light glister out as bright as the sun in the morning, and thy health shall sooner arise unto thee, and thy justice shall go before thy face, and

the glory of God shall gather thee up, that thou shalt not fall; and whensoever thou shalt call upon God, God shall hear thee; and whensoever thou
shalt cry unto God, God shall say, Lo, here I am ready to help thee. Then
shall thy light overcome all darkness, and thy darkness shall be as bright as
the sun at noon days: and then God shall give unto thee continual rest, and
shall fulfil thy soul with brightness, and shall deliver thy body from adversity; and then thou shalt be like a garden, that most plentifully bringeth
forth all kind of fruits, and like the well-spring, that never shall want water
(Isa 58:7-11).

These things, and such other, should be continually taught and inculked into the ears of all true Christian people, to the intent to stir and
provoke them unto good works: and by the selfsame good works to exercise and confirm their faith and hope, and to ascertain them, that they shall
for the same good works receive at God's hand mitigation and remission
of the miseries, calamities, and grievous punishments, which God sendeth
to men in this world for their sins.

The Sacrament of the Altar

As touching the sacrament of the altar, we think it convenient, that all
bishops and preachers shall instruct and teach the people committed unto
their spiritual charge, that they ought and must constantly believe, that
under the form and figure of bread and wine, which we there presently do
see and perceive by outward senses, is verily, substantially, and really contained and comprehended the very selfsame body and blood of our Saviour Jesu Christ, which was born of the virgin Mary, and suffered upon
the cross for our redemption. And that under the same form and figure of
bread and wine, the very selfsame body and blood of Christ is corporally,
really, and in the very same substance exhibited, distributed, and received
unto and of all them which receive the said sacrament. And that therefore
the said sacrament is to be used with all due reverence and honour; and
that every man ought first to prove and examine himself, and religiously
to try and search his own conscience, before he shall receive the same, according to the saying of St. Paul, Whosoever eateth this body of Christ
unworthily, or drinketh of this blood of Christ unworthily, shall be guilty
of the very body and blood of Christ: wherefore let every man first prove

himself, and so let him eat of this bread, and drink of this drink. For whosoever eateth it or drinketh it unworthily, he eateth and drinketh it to his own damnation: because he putteth no difference between the very body of Christ and other kinds of meat (1 Cor 11:27-29).

The Sacrament of Orders

As touching the sacrament of holy orders, we think it convenient, that all bishops and preachers shall instruct and teach the people committed unto their spiritual charge, first, how that Christ and his apostles did institute and ordain in the New Testament, that besides the civil powers and governance of kings and princes, (which is called *potestas gladii*, the power of the sword,) there should also be continually in the church militant certain other ministers or officers, which should have special power, authority, and commission, under Christ, to preach and teach the word of God unto his people; to dispense and administer the sacraments of God unto them, and by the same to confer and give the graces of the Holy Ghost; to consecrate the blessed body of Christ in the sacrament of the altar; to loose and absolve from sin all persons which be duly penitent and sorry for the same; to bind and to excommunicate such as be guilty in manifest crimes and sins, and will not amend their defaults; to order and consecrate others in the same room, order, and office, whereunto they be called and admitted themselves; and finally, to feed Christ's people, like good pastors and rectors, (as the apostle calleth them,) with their wholesome doctrine; and by their continual exhortations and admonitions, to reduce them from sin and iniquity, so much as in them lieth, and to bring them unto the perfect knowledge, the perfect love and dread of God, and unto the perfect charity of their neighbours.

Item, That this office, this ministration, this power and authority, is no tyrannical power, having no certain laws or limits within the which it ought to be contained, nor yet none absolute power; but it is a moderate power, subject, determined, and restrained unto those certain ends and limits, for the which the same was appointed by God's ordinance; which, as was said before, is only to administer and distribute unto the members of Christ's mystical body spiritual and everlasting things, that is to say, the pure and heavenly doctrine of Christ's gospel, and the graces conferred in his sacraments; and further to do and execute such other things appertaining unto their office, as were before rehearsed. And therefore this said power and administration is called in some places of scripture, *donum et gratia*, a gift and a grace; and in some places it is called, *claves, sive potestas clavium*, that is to say, the keys, or the power of the keys; whereby is signified a certain limited office, restrained unto the execution of a special function or ministration; according to the saying of St. Paul, in the first chapter of his Epistle to the Romans, and in the fourth chapter of his first Epistle unto Timothy, and also in the fourth chapter of his Epistle unto the Ephesians, where he writeth in this sentence: When Christ ascended into heaven, he subdued and vanquished very captivity herself, and led or made her thrall and captive, and distributed and gave divers heavenly gifts and graces unto men here in earth. And among all he made some apostles, some priests, some evangelists, some pastors and doctors, to the intent they should execute the work and office of their administration, to the instauration, instruction, and edifying of the members of Christ's mystical body. And that they should also not cease from the execution of their said office, until all the said members were not only reduced and brought unto the unity of the faith, and the knowledge of the Son of God; but also that they were come unto a perfect state and full age therein, that is to say, until they were so established and confirmed in the same, that they could no more afterward be wavering therein, and be led or carried like children into any contrary doctrine or opinion, by the craft and subtil persuasion of the false pastors and teachers, which go about by craft to bring them into erroneous opinions: but that they should constantly follow the true doctrine of Christ's gospel, growing and increasing continually by charity unto a perfect member of that body, whereof Christ is the very head. In whom, if the whole body, that is to say, if every part and member be grown and come unto his perfect estate, (not all in like, but every one according to the gift and quality which is deputed unto it,) and so be compacted, united, and corporated together in the said body; no doubt but that the whole body, and every part thereof, shall thereby be made the more perfect and the more strong, by reason of that natural love and charity, which one member so united in the body hath unto the other.

By these words it appeareth evidently, not only that St. Paul accounted and numbered this said power and office of the pastors and doctors among the proper and special gifts of the Holy Ghost; but also it appeareth, that the same was a limited power and office, ordained specially and only for the causes and purposes before rehearsed.

Item, That this power, office, and administration is necessary to be preserved here in earth for three special and principal causes. First, for that it is the commandment of God it should so be, as it appeareth in sundry places of scripture. Second, for that God hath instituted and ordained none other ordinary mean or instrument whereby he will make us partakers of the reconciliation which is by Christ, and confer and give the graces of his holy Spirit unto us, and make us the right inheritors of everlasting life, there to reign with him for ever in glory; but only his word and sacraments. And therefore the office and power to minister the said word and sacraments may in no wise be suffered to perish, or to be abolished; according to the saying of St. Paul, How can men invocate and call upon the name of him, in whom they believe not? And how can men believe in him, of whom they never heard tell? And how should men hear tell of God, unless there be some men to shew and preach unto them of him? And how shall men dare take upon them to preach and shew of God, unless they be first sent with authority and commission from God so to do (Rom 10:14-15)? And therefore it is said by the prophet Esai, Blessed be the feet of those preachers, which, being authorized and sent by God, do preach and shew unto us the peace and benefits which we receive by Christ (Isa 52:7; Nah 1:15).

Thirdly, because the said power and office, or function, hath annexed unto it assured promises of excellent and inestimable things. For thereby is conferred and given the Holy Ghost, with all his graces, and finally our justification and everlasting life; according to the saying of St. Paul, where he saith, I am not ashamed of the room and office which I have given unto me by Christ, to preach his gospel (Rom 1:16). For it is the power of God, that is to say, the elect organ or instrument ordained by God, and endued with such virtue and efficacy, that it is able to give and minister effectually everlasting life unto all those that will believe and obey the same.

Item, That this office, this power, and authority was committed and given by Christ and his apostles unto certain persons only, that is to say, unto priests or bishops, whom they did elect, call, and admit thereunto, by their prayer and imposition of their hands.

Second, we think it convenient that all bishops and preachers shall instruct and teach the people committed unto their spiritual charge, that the sacrament of orders may worthily be called a sacrament, because it is a holy rite or ceremony instituted by Christ and his apostles in the New Testament, and doth consist of two parts, like as the other sacraments of the church do, that is to say, of a spiritual and an invisible grace, and also of an outward and a visible sign. The invisible gift or grace conferred in this sacrament is nothing else but the power, the office, and the authority before mentioned. The visible and outward sign is the prayer and imposition of the bishop's hands upon the person which receiveth the said gift or grace. And to the intent the church of Christ should never be destituted of such ministers, as should have and execute the said power of the keys, it was also ordained and commanded by the apostles, that the same sacrament should be applied and administered by the bishop from time to time unto such other persons as had the qualities necessarily required thereunto; which said qualities the apostles did also very diligently describe, as it appeareth evidently in the third chapter of the first Epistle of St. Paul to Timothy, and the first chapter of his Epistle unto Titus. And surely this is the whole virtue and efficacy, and the cause also of the institution of this sacrament, as it is founded in the New Testament. For albeit the holy fathers of the church, which succeeded the apostles, (minding to beautify and ornate the church of Christ with all those things which were commendable in the temple of the Jews,) did devise not only certain other ceremonies than be before rehearsed, as tonsures, rasures, unctions, and such other observances, to be used in the ministration of the said sacrament; but did also institute certain inferior orders or degrees, as janitors, lectors, exorcists, acolytes, and subdeacons, and deputed to every one of those certain offices to execute in the church, (wherein they followed undoubtedly the example and rites used in the Old Testament,) yet the truth is, that in the New Testament there is no mention made of any degrees or distinctions in orders, but only of deacons or ministers, and of priests or bishops. Nor there is any word spoken of any other ceremony used in the conferring of this sacrament; but only of prayer, and the imposition of the bishop's hands.

Thirdly, forasmuch as it is an old heresy of the Donatists, condemned in general councils, to think that the word of God and his sacraments should lose and be of none efficacy, strength, or virtue, when they be ministered by men of evil, vicious, and filthy living: we think it convenient that all bishops and preachers shall instruct and teach the people committed unto their spiritual charge, that according to the saying of St. Gregory

Nazianzene, Like as there is no difference between the selfsame image or figure of any thing imprinted with a signet of gold and with a signet made of iron or wood, or any other viler matter; even so the word and sacraments of God, ministered by any evil and naughty man, be of the same self vigour, strength, and efficacy, as when they be ministered by a man of excellent virtue and goodness. The cause and reason whereof is, for that the priests and bishops, although in the execution of their office and ministration they do use and exercise the power and authority of God committed unto them, and do supply and represent his room and place; yet they be not the principal nor the sufficient or efficient causers or givers of grace, or of any other spiritual gift, which proceedeth and is given of God by his word and his sacraments. But God is the only principal, sufficient, and perfect cause of all the efficacy of his word and sacraments; and by his only power, grace, and benefit it is that we receive the Holy Ghost and his graces by the office and ministration of the said priests or bishops. And the said priests or bishops be but only as his instruments or officers, to execute and minister with their hands and tongues the outward and corporal things, whereby God worketh and giveth grace, according to his pact and covenant made with and unto his espouse the church. And this to be true Chrysostom affirmeth, in his 85th Homily upon St. John, where he saith in this manner, What speak I of priests? I say, that neither angel nor archangel can of his own power give us any of those things which be given unto us from God; but it is the Father, the Son, and the Holy Ghost, which is the effectual cause of all those things; the priest doth only put to his hand and his tongue. And in this point St. Ambrose also agreeth with the said opinion of Chrysostom. For in his book, *De Dignitate Sacerdotali,* he saith these words: The priest layeth his hands upon us; but it is God that giveth the grace. The priest layeth upon us his beseeching hand; but God blesseth us with his mighty hand. The bishop consecrateth another bishop; but it is God that giveth the dignity. Wherefore we must always think and believe that the virtue and efficacy of the word of God and his sacraments consist and depend in and upon the commandment, ordinance, power, and authority of God only. And that neither the merits and worthiness of the ministers, (be they never of such excellency,) do give them their authority, strength, or efficacy: neither yet the malice or corrupt living of them, (be it never so evil, unless they be open blasphemers of the gospel, as the Jews and the Turks be,) can frustrate or take away from the said word or sacraments their said power, authority, strength, or virtue. For as Chrysostom saith in the said Homily, if God made not only an ass to speak, but also gave his benediction and blessing upon the Jews by Balaam, that false and wicked prophet, and so wrought these spiritual graces by such unclean and impure instruments, and that for the love only which he had unto the Jews, which nevertheless were great offenders against God; no doubt but that God will much rather send down unto us, his faithful people, the graces of his holy Spirit, and will work all other things necessary for us by our priests and bishops, although they be never so evil of their living.

Fourthly, forasmuch as after the mind of certain doctors of the church, this whole power and authority belonging unto priests and bishops is divided in two parts, whereof the one is called *potestas ordinis,* and the other is called *potestas jurisdictionis;* and forasmuch also as good consent and agreement hath alway been in the church concerning the said first part, and contrary, much controversy for this other part of jurisdiction: we think it convenient, that all bishops and preachers shall instruct and teach the people committed unto their spiritual charge, that the jurisdiction committed unto priests and bishops, by the authority of God's law, consisteth in three special points.

The first is, to rebuke and reprehend sin, and to excommunicate the manifest and obstinate sinners, that is to say, to separate, exclude, and repel from the communion and perception of the sacraments, and to reject and cast out of the congregation and company of Christ's people, such persons as have manifestly committed mortal sin, and do obstinately persevere in the same; and to absolve and receive them again, whensoever they shall return unto the church by condign penance. And forasmuch as such persons as do commit manifest and open sin, do thereby offend not only God, but also some other of the multitude and congregation which they be of; although the said persons so offending publicly do not obstinately persevere in their sin so committed, yet the priests and bishops, by the authority of their said jurisdiction, may, in some cases, upon consideration of the crime and quality of the person so offending, suspend and inhibit them for a time from the receiving of the sacraments, to the intent the same may be, not only a medicine to the offenders themselves, but also an example and satisfaction unto those persons which were before with their said manifest sins offended.

And in this part also two things be to be noted. The first is, that all punishment which priests or bishops may, by the authority of the gospel, inflict or put to any person, is by word only, and not by any violence or constraint corporal. The second is, that although priests and bishops have the power and jurisdiction to excommunicate, as is aforesaid; yet they be not bound so precisely by any commandment of God, but that they ought and may attemper, moderate, or forbear the execution of their said jurisdiction in that part at all times, whensoever they shall perceive and think that by doing the contrary they should not cure or help the offenders, or else give such occasion of further trouble and unquietness in the church, that the peace and tranquility thereof might thereby be impeached, troubled, or otherwise interrupted or broken.

The second point, wherein consisteth the jurisdiction committed unto priests and bishops, by the authority of God's law, is to approve and admit such persons as (being nominated, elected, and presented unto them to exercise the office and room of preaching the gospel, and of ministering the sacraments, and to have the cure of jurisdiction over these certain people within this parish or within this diocese) shall be thought unto them meet and worthy to exercise the same; and to reject and repel from the said room such as they shall judge to be unmeet therefore. And in this part we must know and understand, that the said presentation and nomination is of man's ordinance, and appertaineth unto the founders and patrons, or other persons, according to the laws and ordinances of men provided for the same. As for an example, within this realm the presentation and nomination of the bishoprics appertaineth unto the kings of this realm; and of other lesser cures and personages some unto the king's highness, some unto other noble men, some unto bishops, and some unto other persons, whom we call the patrons of the benefices, according as it is provided by the order of the laws and ordinances of this realm. And unto the priests or bishops belongeth, by the authority of the gospel, to approve and confirm the person which shall be, by the king's highness or the other patrons, so nominated, elected, and presented unto them to have the cure of these certain people, within this certain parish or diocese, or else to reject him, as was said before, from the same, for his demerits or unworthiness. For surely the office of preaching is the chief and most principal office, whereunto priests or bishops be called by the authority of the gospel, and they be also called bishops or archbishops, that is to say, superattendants or overseers, specially to signify, that it is their office to oversee, to watch, and to look diligently upon their flock, and to cause that Christ's doctrine and his religion may be truly and sincerely conserved, taught, and set forth among Christian people, according to the mere and pure truth of scripture; and that all erroneous and corrupt doctrine, and the teachers thereof, may be rejected and corrected accordingly.

The third point, wherein consisteth the jurisdiction committed unto priests and bishops by the authority of God's law, is to make and ordain certain rules or canons concerning holydays, fasting days, the manner and ceremonies to be used in the ministration of the sacraments, the manner of singing the psalms and spiritual hymns, (as St. Paul calleth them,) the diversity of degrees among the ministers, and the form and manner of their ornaments, and finally concerning such other rites, ceremonies, and observances as do tend and conduce to the preservation of quietness and decent order to be had and used among the people when they shall be assembled together in the temple (Eph 5; Col 3). For sith that scripture commandeth that all Christian people should at certain times assemble themselves, and convene together in some public or open place, there to invocate and call upon the name of God, there to hear his will and his word by our preachers, there to receive the sacraments, there to give laud and praise to God in psalmody, in prayers, in meditations, and in reading; and finally, with all humility and reverent order, to magnify, extol, and set forth the honour of God with all our possible power. And forasmuch also as great trouble, unquietness, and tumult might arise among the multitude so assembled, in case there were no certain rules, ordinances, and ceremonies prescribed unto them, whereby they should be contained in quietness, and not suffered to do every man after his own fashion or appetite; it belongeth unto the jurisdiction of priests or bishops to make certain rules or canons concerning all these things, and for the causes aforesaid. For like as in the governance of a private family, or in the governance of a school, it belongeth unto the good man or ruler of that house, or the schoolmaster, to prescribe the times when his children and servants shall work, when they shall rest, when they shall learn, when they shall pray, and such other things; so in the public and open temple or church, it appertaineth also unto them that have the governance of the church in those points, to devise and prescribe such necessary and convenient ceremonies and ordinances unto the people, for the causes above rehearsed, as shall tend to their profit and increase in Christ's religion, and shall also tend to the honour of God and good tranquillity of the said people. For surely St. Paul himself did prescribe and make such rules unto the Corinthians, and commanded also other bishops to do the semblable (1 Cor 11). And the holy fathers of the church, at the beginning, before there were any Christian princes, upon great and urgent considerations, did ordain the celebrating of the Sunday, of Easter-day, and certain other feasts, and the fasting of Lent, and also divers other such ceremonies in the church, whereof a great part is observed through all Christendom unto this day: the continual observation whereof was always thought unto the holy fathers very necessary; forasmuch as such traditions and ceremonies be as a certain necessary introduction or learning expedient to induce and teach the people reverently to use themselves in their outward worshipping of God, and be also (as you would say) certain painted histories, the often sight and contemplation whereof causeth the people the better to remember the things signified and represented in the same.

For the better declaration of which three points two things be to be noted. First, that although the whole jurisdiction appertaining (as is aforesaid) unto priests and bishops be committed unto them in general words, (as it appeareth by divers places of scripture, and specially in the 20th chapter of the Acts, where the apostle saith, Take diligent heed to yourselves, and to all your whole flock, among whom the Holy Ghost hath set, ordained, and made you bishops, to rule and govern the church of God,) yet there is also a particular order, form, and manner requisite to the due execution of the same; according to the saying of St. Paul, Look that all things be done in the church seemly and in a decent order (1 Cor 14:40). Now this particular manner and form is not expressly declared, determined, or prescribed in scripture; but was and is left to be declared from time to time, and from age to age, by certain positive rules and ordinances, to be made by the ministers of the church, with the consent of the people, before such time as princes were christened; and after they were christened, with the authority and consent of the said princes and their people. For like as the authority to preach and teach, and to administer the sacraments, although it be committed unto priests and bishops by express words of scripture, yet there is no express mention concerning the particular circumstances convenient to be used in the execution of the same: even so in the power of jurisdiction, although the same be by general words in scripture committed unto priests and bishops, yet there is no particular mention what form, order, or process should be used in the execution of any part thereof. As for an example, concerning the sentence of excommunication, although the cognition of crimes, for the which the said sentence is to be given, and the examination of the witness also necessary for the trial of the crimes, and for the instruction of him that shall give the said sentence, be committed by general words of scripture unto priests and bishops; yet there is no mention made in scripture how the parties offending or the witness shall be cited and called to appear before the priests or bishops; nor there is no mention made what process or pain shall be used against them, in case any of them shall disobey the calling or sentence of the priest or bishop; nor finally there is any mention made of any other circumstance of time, place, or person necessary to be used in the due execution of the said sentence of excommunication. But all these things were afterward devised and ordained by the church, and the ministers of the same, and by the consent of those people which professed the name of Christ. And that this is of truth, it appeareth by such ordinances as St. Paul himself, and other the apostles, devised and prescribed to be observed in certain churches, as well concerning the excommunicating of the Corinthian, and divers other (1 Cor 5); as also concerning that men should pray bareheaded (11:4); that women should keep silence, and not take upon them to teach in the church (14:34-35); that two prophets or preachers should not speak at one time in the church, but that one should give place to the other (14:31); that the alms of poor men should be gathered, and how, and by whom, after it was gathered, it should be distributed (16:1-2); with such other like things. And this thing also appeareth to be true, by the canons and rules devised and made by the bishops and councils, concerning the premises, during the time that the church was subject to infidel princes, and before any princes were christened. During all which time it is evident what constitutions and canons they, with the consent of the people, made, concerning the premises. Insomuch that kings and princes, after they had once received the faith of Christ, and were baptized, considering the same to tend to the furtherance of Christ's religion, did not only approve the said canons, then made by the church, but did also enact and make new laws of their own, concerning the good order of the church, and furthermore did also constrain their subjects, by corporal pain and punishment, to observe the same. For it is out of all doubt that the priests and bishops never had any authority by the gospel to punish any man by corporal violence; and therefore they were oftentimes moved of necessity to require Christian princes to interpone their authority, and by the same to constrain and reduce in obedient persons unto the obedience and good order of the church: which the Christian princes, as God's ministers in that part, and for the zeal they had to the establishing of Christ's religion, not only did gladly execute, but did also give unto priests and bishops further power and jurisdiction in certain other temporal and civil matters, like as by the laws, statutes, immunities, privileges, and grants of princes made in that behalf, and by the uses also and customs of sundry realms and regions, it doth manifestly appear. And therefore it was and shall be always lawful unto the said kings and princes, and their successors, with the consent of their parliaments, to revoke and call again into their own hands, or otherwise to restrain all the power and jurisdiction which was given and assigned unto priests and bishops by the license, consent, sufferance, and authority of the said kings and princes, and not by the authority of God and his gospel, whensoever they shall have such grounds and causes so to do, as shall be necessary, wholesome, and expedient for the weal of their realms, the repressing of vice, and the increase of Christ's faith and religion.

The second thing to be noted is, that like as it is the will and commandment of God that priests and bishops should, in the execution of all those things which appertain unto their jurisdiction by the authority of the gospel, (as is aforesaid,) attemper their doings and proceedings with all charity and mildness, and should foresee by their singular wisdom that they pronounce no sentence, nor prescribe or make any constitution or ordinance which may in any wise be prejudicial or hurtful unto their flock, but such as undoubtedly do tend as well to the good preservation and increase of Christ's true religion, as also of Christian charity and tranquillity to be had among them; even so and in like manner all the people being under their cure, and within the limits of their said jurisdiction, (of what estate or condition soever they be,) be also bound by the law of God, and by the order and bond of charity, humbly to obey them, and to fulfil all their said precepts and ordinances, duly and rightfully made by the authority of their said jurisdiction; specially being the same ones received by the common consent of the people, and authorized by the laws of the Christian princes; wherein nevertheless one rule or canon is necessary to be considered and observed concerning the obedience which is required in the third and last part of the said jurisdiction; that is to say, forasmuch as the greatest part thereof consisteth only in outward ceremonies, and such things as be of themselves but mean and indifferent things, (that is to say, neither commanded expressly in scripture, nor necessarily contained or implied therein, nor yet expressly repugnant or contrary thereunto,) surely there is no other obedience required in the said third part, but that men may lawfully omit or do otherwise than is prescribed by the said laws and commandments of the priests and bishops, so that they do it not in contempt or despite of the said power and jurisdiction, but have some good and reasonable cause so to do, and offend not nor slander not their neighbours in their so doing. For in these points Christian men must study to preserve that Christian liberty, whereunto they be called and brought by Christ's blood and his doctrine; that is to say, although men ought to repute and think that the observation of such things be expedient and necessary for such ends and intents as they be made for, (as holydays were instituted to the intent the people should know what time they should assemble themselves in the church, there to honour God, to hear and learn the word of God, and to receive the sacraments; and likewise fasting days, to the intent the people should be more sober, and apt to prayer, and also to hear and occupy their whole meditation in the word of God, and so forth, in other constitutions;) and although men ought to repute and think that all the said ends and intents be also very good, expedient, and necessary, as well for a common order and tranquillity to be had among the people, as also for the better instruction and inducement of the people unto the observation of those things, wherein consisteth indeed that spiritual justice, and that spiritual honour and service, which God requireth of us; yet surely men may not esteem them, but as things indifferent, and of no such necessity, but that men may, upon causes reasonable, well omit and leave the same undone, so that it be not in case of contempt or slander. This rule and canon men must diligently learn. For surely the want of the knowledge hereof hath been the occasion of many great abuses and superstitions among Christian people; while a great part of them regardeth and esteemeth more the observation, and contrary conceiveth more grudge and scruple in their conscience for the transgression of men's traditions, and such works as of their own wills and elections they have chosen and determined with themselves to do, than the observing or breaking of

God's own precepts, commanded of his own mouth. And that this is of truth, we see it by daily experience in divers countries of this realm, wherein many of the people believe surely, that they more highly merit by abstaining from eating of an egg upon the Friday, and more damnably sin in doing the contrary, although they should have good and reasonable cause so to do, and did it without contempt of the jurisdiction or slander of their neighbour, than by the exercising of any of the works of charity commanded by God, or committing of theft, or fornication, or such other like offences, contrary to the laws of God.

Finally, being thus declared, not only what is the virtue and efficacy, with the whole institution and use of the sacrament of holy orders, but also in what things consisteth the power and jurisdiction of priests and bishops, and unto what limits the same is extended by the authority of the gospel, and also what is added thereunto by the grants and sufferances, or permission of kings and princes: we think it convenient, that all bishops and preachers shall instruct and teach the people committed unto their spiritual charge, that whereas certain men do imagine and affirm that Christ should give unto the bishop of Rome power and authority, not only to be head and governor of all priests and bishops in Christ's church, but also to have and occupy the whole monarchy of the world in his hands, and that he may thereby lawfully depose kings and princes from their realms, dominions, and seigniories, and so transfer and give the same to such persons as him liketh; that is utterly false and untrue: for Christ never gave unto St. Peter, or unto any of the apostles, or their successors, any such authority. And the apostles St. Peter and St. Paul do teach and command that all Christian people, as well priests and bishops, as others, should be obedient and subject unto the princes and potentates of the world, although they were infidels (1 Pet 2; Rom 13). And as for the bishop of Rome, it was many hundred years after Christ before he could acquire or get any primacy or governance above any other bishops, out of his province in Italy. Sith the which time he hath ever usurped more and more. And though some part of his power was given unto him by the consent of the emperors, kings, and princes, and by the consent also of the clergy in general councils assembled; yet surely he attained the most part thereof by marvellous subtilty and craft, and specially by colluding with great kings and princes; sometime training them into his devotion by pretence and colour of holiness and sanctimony, and sometime constraining them by force and tyranny: whereby the said bishops of Rome aspired and arose at length unto such greatness in strength and authority, that they presumed and took upon them to be heads, and to put laws by their own authority, not only unto all other bishops within Christendom, but also unto the emperors, kings, and other the princes and lords of the world, and that under the pretence of the authority committed unto them by the gospel: wherein the said bishops of Rome do not only abuse and pervert the true sense and meaning of Christ's word, but they do also clean contrary to the use and custom of the primitive church, and also do manifestly violate as well the holy canons made in the church immediately after the time of the apostles, as also the decrees and constitutions made in that behalf by the holy fathers of the catholic church, assembled in the first general councils: and finally, they do transgress their own profession, made in their creation. For all the bishops of Rome always, when they be consecrated and made bishops of that see, do make a solemn profession and vow, that they shall inviolably observe and keep all the ordinances made in the eight first general councils, among the which it is specially provided and enacted, that all causes shall be finished and determined within the province where the same be begun, and that by the bishops of the same province; and that no bishop shall exercise any jurisdiction out of his own diocese or province. And divers such other canons were then made and confirmed by the said councils, to repress and take away out of the church all such primacy and jurisdiction over kings and bishops as the bishops of Rome pretend now to have over the same. And we find that divers good fathers, bishops of Rome, did greatly reprove, yea and abhor, (as a thing clean contrary to the gospel, and the decrees of the church,) that any bishop of Rome, or elsewhere, should presume, usurp, or take upon him the title and name of the universal bishop, or of the head of all priests, or of the highest priest, or any such like title.[3] For confirmation whereof, it is out of all doubt, that there is no mention made, neither in scripture, neither in the writings of any authentical doctor or author of the church, being within the time of the apostles, that Christ did ever make or institute any distinction or differ-ence to be in the preeminence of power, order, or jurisdiction between the

---

[3] Concilium tertium Carthaginense, cap. 26. Gregorius, lib. 4. epistolarum, indictione 13. epist. 23.

apostles themselves, or between the bishops themselves; but that they were all equal in power, order, authority, and jurisdiction. And that there is now, and sith the time of the apostles, any such diversity or difference among the bishops, it was devised by the ancient fathers of the primitive church, for the conservation of good order and unity of the catholic church; and that either by the consent and authority, or else at the least by the permission and sufferance of the princes and civil powers for the time ruling. For the said fathers, considering the great and infinite multitude of Christian men, so largely increased through the world, and taking examples of the Old Testament, thought it expedient to make an order of degrees, to be among bishops and spiritual governors of the church; and so ordained some to be patriarchs, some to be primates, some to be metropolitans, some to be archbishops, some to be bishops. And to them did limit severally, not only their certain dioceses or provinces, wherein they should exercise their power, and not exceed the same, but also certain bounds and limits of their jurisdiction and power. Insomuch, that whereas in the time of the apostles it was lawful indifferently to all bishops (certain of them assembling themselves together) to constitute and consecrate other bishops; the said fathers restrained the said power, and reserved the same in such wise, that without the consent and authority of the metropolitan or archbishop, no bishop should be consecrated within any province. And likewise in other cases their powers were also restrained, for such causes as were then thought unto them convenient. Which differences the said holy fathers thought necessary to enact and establish, by their decrees and constitutions, not for that any such differences were prescribed or established in the gospel, or mentioned in any canonical writings of the apostles, or testified by any ecclesiastical writer within the apostles' time; but to the intent that thereby contention, strife, variance, and schisms or division, should be avoided, and the church should be preserved in good order and concord.

And for the better confirmation of this part, we think it also convenient, that all bishops and preachers shall instruct and teach the people committed unto their spiritual charge, that Christ did by express words prohibit that none of his apostles, or any of their successors, should, under the pretence of the authority given unto them by Christ, take upon them the authority of the sword; that is to say, the authority of kings, or of any civil power in this world; yea or any authority to make laws or ordinances, in causes appertaining unto civil powers. Truth it is, that priests and bishops may execute all such temporal power and jurisdiction as is committed unto them by the ordinance and authority of kings, or other civil powers, and by the consent of the people, (as officers and ministers under the said kings and powers,) so long as it shall please the said kings and people to permit and suffer them so to use and execute the same. Notwithstanding, if any bishop, of what estate or dignity soever he be, be he bishop of Rome, or of any other city, province, or diocese, do presume, or take upon him authority or jurisdiction, in causes or matters which appertain unto kings and the civil powers, and their courts, and will maintain or think that he may so do by the authority of Christ and his gospel, although the kings and princes would not permit and suffer him so to do; no doubt that bishop is not worthy to be called a bishop, but rather a tyrant, and an usurper of other men's rights, contrary to the laws of God, and is worthy to be reputed none otherwise than he that goeth about to subvert the kingdom of Christ. For the kingdom of Christ in his church is a spiritual, and not a carnal kingdom of the world; that is to say, the very kingdom that Christ, by himself or by his apostles and disciples, sought here in this world, was to bring all nations from the carnal kingdom of the prince of darkness unto the light of his spiritual kingdom; and so to reign himself in the hearts of people by grace, faith, hope, and charity. And therefore, sith Christ did never seek nor exercise any worldly kingdom or dominion in this world, but rather, refusing and fleeing from the same, did leave the said worldly governance of kingdoms, realms, and nations, to be governed by princes and potentates, (in like manner as he did find them,) and commanded also his apostles and disciples to do the semblable, as it was said before; whatsoever priest or bishop will arrogate or presume upon him any such authority, and will pretend the authority of the gospel for his defence therein, he doth nothing else but (in manner as you would say) crowneth Christ again with a crown of thorn, and traduceth and bringeth him forth again, with his mantle of purpure upon his back, to be mocked and scorned of the world, as the Jews did, to their own damnation.

Moreover, the truth is, that God constituted and ordained the authority of Christian kings and princes to be the most high and supreme above all other powers and offices in the regiment and governance of his people; and committed unto them, as unto the chief heads of their commonwealths, the cure and oversight of all the people which be within their realms and dominions, without any exception. And unto them of right, and by God's commandment, belongeth, not only to prohibit unlawful violence, to correct offenders by corporal death or other punishment, to conserve moral honesty among their subjects, according to the laws of their realms, to defend justice, and to procure the public weal, and the common peace and tranquillity in outward and earthly things; but specially and principally to defend the faith of Christ and his religion, to conserve and maintain the true doctrine of Christ, and all such as be true preachers and setters forth thereof, and to abolish all abuses, heresies, and idolatries, which be brought in by heretics and evil preachers, and to punish with corporal pains such as of malice be occasioners of the same; and finally, to oversee and cause that the said priests and bishops do execute their said power, office, and jurisdiction truly, faithfully, and according in all points as it was given and committed unto them by Christ and his apostles: which notwithstanding, we may not think that it doth appertain unto the office of kings and princes to preach and teach, to administer the sacraments, to absolve, to excommunicate, and such other things belonging to the office and administration of bishops and priests; but we must think and believe, that God hath constituted and made Christian kings and princes to be as the chief heads and overlookers over the said priests and bishops, to cause them to administer their office and power committed unto them purely and sincerely; and in case they shall be negligent in any part thereof, to cause them to supply and repair the same again. And God hath also commanded the said priests and bishops to obey, with all humbleness and reverence, all the laws made by the said princes, being not contrary to the laws of God, whatsoever they be; and that not only *propter iram,* but also *propter conscientiam* (Rom 13). Whereby it appeareth well, that this pretended monarchy of the bishop of Rome is not founded upon the gospel, but it is repugnant thereunto. And therefore it appertaineth unto Christian kings and princes, for the discharge of their office and duty towards God, to endeavour themselves to reform and reduce the same again unto the old limits and pristine state of that power and jurisdiction which was given unto them by Christ, and used in the primitive church. For it is out of all doubt that Christ's faith was then most firm and pure, and the scriptures of God were then best understood, and virtue did then most abound and excel. And therefore it must needs follow, that the customs and ordinances then used and made must needs be more conform and agreeable unto the true doctrine of Christ, and more conducing to the edifying and benefit of the church of Christ, than any customs or laws used or made sith that time. And therefore, whereas the king's most royal majesty, considering of his most excellent wisdom, not only the notable decay of Christ's true and perfect religion among us, but also the intolerable thraldom, captivity, and bondage, with the infinite damages and prejudices which we and other his subjects continually sustained, by reason of that long usurped and abused power which the bishops of Rome were wont to exercise here in this realm, hath now, of his most godly disposition, and by the consent of his nobles spiritual and temporal, and by the authority of the whole parliament, determined no longer to suffer the bishop of Rome to execute any part of his jurisdiction here within this realm; but clearly to deliver us from the same, and restore us again to our old liberty: surely we have great cause most joyfully and thankfully to embrace and accept the same, considering that thereby no prejudice is done to God's word or his ordinances. For, as we have shewed and declared before, it was by princes' and men's ordinance and sufferances only that the bishop of Rome exercised any such jurisdiction within this realm, and not by any authority given unto him by Christ. And as for the bishop of Rome, he cannot pretend himself no more to be grieved or injured therewith, than the king's chancellor, or any other his officers, might worthily think that the king's highness should do him wrong, in case he should upon good causes remove him from his said room and office, and commit it unto another.

And as for us, and other the king's faithful subjects, we shall undoubtedly receive and have thereby singular wealth and commodity, as well spiritually, to the edifying of our souls, as corporally, to the increase of our substance and riches. The which, how much was impaired and decayed continually from time to time, by the great exactions of the bishops of Rome, and such treasure as went yearly out of this realm to his coffers, for annates and exemptions, dispensations, pardons, and such other unprofitable things, or rather very trifles; we doubt not but all men endued with any wit and zeal to the wealth of this our country do right well perceive and understand.

The Sacrament of Extreme Unction

As touching the sacrament of extreme unction, we think it convenient, that all bishops and preachers shall instruct and teach the people committed unto their spiritual charge, first, how that the twelve apostles, being sent out by Christ, and commanded to go two and two into the world to preach his word, among other miracles which they wrought by the power of God, they cured also and restored many sick men unto health, anointing them with oil.

Second, that although it be not expressed in scripture, that the said apostles had then any new commandment of Christ to anoint such as they had healed with oil; yet forasmuch as the holy apostle St. James, endued with the holy Spirit of Christ, prescribed a certain rule or doctrine, and gave in manner a commandment, that whensoever any person should fortune to fall sick, he should call or send for the priests or ancients of the church, and cause them to pray over him, anointing him with oil in the name of our Lord; and further added hereunto, as an assured promise, that by the said prayer of the priests and the sick person, made in right faith and confidence in God, the sick man should be restored unto his health, and God should set him on foot again, and if he were in sin, his sins should be forgiven him (James 5:13-16): it shall therefore be very necessary and expedient, that all true Christian people do use and observe this manner of anoiling of sick persons, with due reverence and honour, as it is prescribed by the holy apostle St. James. That is to say, whensoever any person among us shall fall into any dangerous sickness, let him call the priests of the church, with other good and ancient Christian people, and let them go unto the sick person, and there not only comfort him corporally, but also give him ghostly instructions, and exhortations to lament and be sorry for his sins, to persevere in the right faith of Christ and charity towards his neighbour; to bear and sustain patiently the griefs and pains of his malady for God's sake, reputing the same as the manifest token of the love and favour of God towards him; to contemn the world, and to desire to reign with Christ in heaven, and such other things: which done, then let the priests and the company there assembled, and the sick man himself also, (as his sickness will suffer him,) pray unto God with full hope and confidence, as well for the remission of his sins as for the recovery of his health, (if it shall so stand with God's pleasure;) let the priests anoint the sick man, according to the teaching of St. James, and no doubt the fervent and faithful prayer of the priests, and other persons aforesaid, joined with the due contrition and faith of the sick person, shall obtain of Almighty God all things which shall seem unto God necessary for the health and comfort, as well of the soul as of the bodily sickness of the said person.

Thirdly, how that the holy fathers of the church, considering this place of St. James, and the manner also of anointing of sick men, used by the apostles, (as was aforesaid,) thought it convenient to institute and ordain, that this manner of anoiling of sick men, prescribed by St. James, should be observed continually in the church of Christ, as a very godly and wholesome medicine or remedy to alleviate and mitigate the diseases and maladies, as well of the soul as of the body of Christian men (Jas 5:14-16). And to the intent the same should be had in more honour and veneration, the said holy fathers willed and taught, that all Christian men should repute and account the said manner of anoiling among the other sacraments of the church, forasmuch as it is a visible sign of an invisible grace: whereof the visible sign is the anoiling with oil in the name of God; which oil (for the natural properties belonging unto the same) is a very convenient thing to signify and figure the great mercy and grace of God, and the spiritual light, joy, comfort, and gladness which God poureth out upon all faithful people, calling upon him by the inward unction of the Holy Ghost. And the grace conferred in this sacrament is the relief and recovery of the disease and sickness wherewith the sick person is then diseased and troubled, and also the remission of his sins, if he be then in sin. This grace we be assured to obtain by the virtue and efficacy of the faithful and fervent prayer used in the ministration of this sacrament of anoiling, according to the saying of St. James, before rehearsed, and also according to the sundry promises made by Christ unto the faithful prayer of his church; as when Christ saith, Whatsoever ye shall ask and pray my Father to give unto you in my name, it shall be granted unto you (Matt 7:7; Mark 11:24). For the better understanding whereof, two things be here specially to be noted. The first is, that St. James calleth here the prayer to be used in the time of this inunction, the prayer of faith: whereby he meaneth, that this prayer ought to be made in that right faith, trust, and confidence, which we ought to have in God, to obtain the effect of our petitions made in the ministration of this sacrament; and that it ought to contain nothing but that shall stand with the pleasure, the honour, and glory of God; and that when we direct our prayers unto God for any bodily health or relief, or for any other temporal commodity, we ought always to temper our said prayer with this condition, that is to say, if it shall so stand with God's will and his pleasure. And that we ought to say, as Christ said in his prayer unto his Father, Father, if it shall please thee, I am content to die and suffer this shameful and cruel death of the cross. Thy will be fulfilled herein: let not my will and desire be followed, but let thy will and disposition be fulfilled, whereunto I wholly commit myself (Matt 26:39).

The second thing to be noted is, that to the attaining of the said grace, conferred in this sacrament of extreme unction, it is expedient also that the sick person himself shall knowledge his offences towards God and his neighbour, and ask forgiveness of them for the same; and likewise forgive all them that have offended him in word or deed: and so being in perfect love and charity, to pray himself (as he may) with faithful heart, and full hope and confidence in God, for the remission of his sins, and restoring unto his bodily health, if it shall so stand with God's pleasure. And therefore the said apostle addeth immediately unto this place these words following: Confess your faults and offences, which ye have trespassed one to another, and be you ready and glad to forgive the same for God's sake, and to ask forgiveness the one of the other; and so being reconciled, pray each for other: and then you shall attain perfect health of all your infirmities, as well spiritual as corporal (Jas 5:16). For if you be so affected in heart, and united and knit the one to the other in perfect charity, no doubt ye be justified in the sight of God, and without doubt your prayer shall be heard and accepted of God. For surely the prayer of the man justified is of marvellous virtue and efficacy in the acceptation of God, as it appeareth by the example of Elias the prophet; who, although he were but a man, and subject to affections as other men be, yet because he was a just man, when he prayed to God that neither rain nor dew should descend upon the land of Israel from heaven by the space of three years and six months, God granted his prayer, and would not suffer that any rain or dew should fall upon the said land by the said space; whereby arose an extreme dearth and famine among them of that country (1 Kgs 17; Luke 4). And afterward, when the said Elias prayed again to God to send rain and moisture upon the said land, God likewise heard his prayer, and sent down rain plentifully upon the earth, and so the earth brought forth all kinds of fruits again, in like manner as it was wont to do before, to the great comfort of the people.

Finally, we think it convenient, that all bishops and preachers shall instruct and teach the people committed to their spiritual charge, first, that no man ought to think, that by the receiving of this sacrament of anoiling the sick man's life shall be made shorter, but rather that the same shall be prolonged thereby; considering the same is instituted for recovery of health both of the soul and body. Second, that it is an evil custom to defer the administration of this sacrament unto such time as the sick persons be brought by sickness unto extreme peril and jeopardy of life, and be in manner in despair to live any longer. Thirdly, that it is lawful and expedient to administer this said sacrament unto every good Christian man in the manner and form before rehearsed, so oft and whensoever any great and perilous sickness and malady shall fortune unto them. For the truth is, that the holy fathers of the church did neither call this sacrament the extreme unction (that is to say, the last unction) because it should be ministered last and after all other sacraments; neither yet they did ordain that the same should be ministered only when sick men should be brought unto the extreme pangs of death; but they did call it by the said name of extreme unction, because it is the last in respect of the other inunctions which be ministered before in the other sacraments of baptism and confirmation. (In both which sacraments Christian men be also anoiled and anointed.) And the truth is also, that the sacrament of the altar, being duly received, is the very spiritual food and the very necessary sustentation, comfort, and preservation of all Christian men in all dangerous passages and adventures. And therefore it is expedient, that the said sacrament of the altar should be received after this anoiling, done in the time of sickness. For surely the receiving of the body of our Saviour Jesu Christ is the very perfection, not only of this, but also of all the other sacraments.

And as unto the ordinance of the holy fathers concerning the time when this sacrament of extreme unction should be ministered and received, it is out of all doubt that they willed and ordained that the same should be observed according to the institution of the apostle St. James; which was, that it should be ministered and received so oft and whensoever any man should fortune to be sick of any dangerous sickness; and also at such time as the sick man himself were of perfect remembrance, judgment, discretion, and knowledge in such things as do appertain unto the profession and office of a good Christian man. For (as it was said before) St. James requireth such judgment, such spiritual affections and motions, and also such desire and devotion to be in the sick man, that he himself in the time of his anoiling should not only heartily, faithfully, devoutly, and religiously praise God, and thank God for his visitation and punishment; but also, putting his whole confidence and trust in God, and so committing himself wholly into his hands and mercy, should invocate and call upon him for the remission of his sins and recovery of his health; and finally, should declare his charity, in forgiving and asking of forgiveness for all offences committed by him against his neighbour, or by his neighbour against him.

Thus being declared the virtue and efficacy of all the seven sacraments, we think it convenient, that all bishops and teachers shall instruct and teach the people committed to their spiritual charge, that although the sacraments of Matrimony, of Confirmation, of Holy Orders, and of Extreme Unction, have been of long time past received and approved by the common consent of the catholic church, to have the name and dignity of sacraments, as indeed they be well worthy to have; (forasmuch as they be holy and godly signs, whereby, and by the prayer of the minister, be not only signified and represented, but also given and conferred some certain and special gifts of the Holy Ghost, necessary for Christian men to have for one godly purpose or other, like as it hath been before declared;) yet there is a difference in dignity and necessity between them and the other three sacraments, that is to say, the sacraments of Baptism, of Penance, and of the Altar, and that for divers causes. First, because these three sacraments be instituted of Christ, to be as certain instruments or remedies necessary for our salvation, and the attaining of everlasting life. Second, because they be also commanded by Christ to be ministered and received in their outward visible signs. Thirdly, because they have annexed and conjoined unto their said visible signs such spiritual graces, as whereby our sins be remitted and forgiven, and we be perfectly renewed, regenerated, purified, justified, and made the very members of Christ's mystical body, so oft as we worthily and duly receive the same.

The Exposition or Declaration of the Ten Commandments

The Ten Commandments

1.   Thou shalt have none other gods but me.

2.   Thou shalt not make to thyself any graven thing, ne any similitude of any thing that is in heaven above, or in earth beneath, nor in the water under the earth. Thou shalt not bow down to them, ne worship them.

3.   Thou shalt not take the name of thy Lord God in vain.

4.   Remember that thou do sanctify and keep holy thy sabbath day.

5.   Honour thy father and mother.

6.   Thou shalt not kill.

7.   Thou shalt not commit adultery.

8.   Thou shalt not steal.

9.   Thou shalt not bear false witness against thy neighbour.

10. Thou shalt not desire thy neighbour's house, his wife, his servant, his maid, his ox, his ass, ne any other thing that is his.

The Exposition of the First Commandment

The first Commandment, like as it is first in order, so it is the most chief and principal among all the other precepts. For in this first commandment

God requireth of us those things in the which consisteth his chief and principal worship and honour, that is to say, perfect faith, sure hope, and unfeigned love and dread of God. And therefore, as concerning this commandment, we think it convenient that all bishops and preachers shall instruct and teach the people committed unto their spiritual charge, first, that to have God is not to have him as we have other outward things, as clothes upon our back, or treasure in our chests; nor also to name him with our mouth, or to worship him with kneeling, or such other gestures: but to have him our God is to conceive him in our hearts, to cleave fast and surely unto him with heart and mind, to put all our trust and confidence in him, to set all our thought and care upon him, and to hang wholly of him, taking him to be infinitely good and merciful unto us.

Thou shalt have none other gods but me.

Second, that God commandeth us thus to do unto him only, and to no creature, nor to no false and feigned god. For as a kind and loving man cannot be content that his wife should take any other husband, so cannot our most kind and most loving God and Creator be pleased if we should forsake him, and take any other feigned gods. And surely he is more present with us, and more ready to shew us all kindness and goodness, than any creature is or can be. And already of his gift we have all that we have, meat, drink, clothe, reason, wit, understanding, discretion, and all good things that we have, pertaining both to the soul and the body. And therefore he cannot bear so much ungratitude and unkindness at our hands, that we should forsake him, or else fix our faith and trust in any other things besides him.

Thirdly, that by this precept God commandeth us not only to trust thus in him, but also to give him the whole love of our hearts above all worldly things, yea and above ourselves. So that we may not love ourselves, nor any other thing, but for him, according as Moses saith in the Book of Deuteronomy, Thy Lord God is one God, and thou shalt love him with all thy heart, and with all thy life, and with all thy mind, and with all thy strength and power (6:5). And this love must bring with it a fear, that even for very pure love we ought to be much abashed and afraid to break the least of his commandments: like as the child, the more he loveth his father, the more he is loath and afraid to displease him in any manner of case.

Fourthly, that all they offend against this commandment, which set their hearts and minds upon any worldly thing above God. For whatsoever we love above God, so that we set our minds upon it more than we do upon God, or for it we will offend God, truly that we make our god. For, as St. Paul saith, The covetous man maketh his goods his god (Col 3:5), and the gluttonous man maketh his belly his god (Phil 3:19). For the one setteth his mind more upon his goods, the other more upon his belly, than they do upon God; and for them they will not stick to offend God: and all these break this commandment.

Item, That all they which have more confidence in the creatures of God than in God, do also make the creatures of God their god. And how grievously God is offended therewith we find in the Book of Paralipomenon, where it is written, That when Asa, king of Judah, being sore constrained by Baasha king of Israel, sent for help to Ben-hadad, king of Syria, and gave to him great treasure for to allure him to his aid, our Lord sent the prophet Hanani to Asa, the king of Judah, who said unto him in this manner; Because thou hast trusted in the king of Syria, and not in thy Lord God, therefore those of the king of Syria are escaped from thy hands. Were not they of Ethiopia and Libya of far greater power, both in chariots and horsemen, and in number or multitude, which was innumerable? And yet our Lord, as long as thou diddest put thy trust in him, did yield them into thy hands. The eyes of God do behold all the world, and do give strength to them that trust in him with all their heart (2 Chr 16:1-9). In which words it doth appear, that it is laid to Asa his charge, that he did not believe in our Lord, because he had more trust in Ben-hadad, an heathen prince, than in our Lord. It is noted also in the same chapter, that whereas Asa afterward had very great pain in his feet, he sought not to our Lord for remedy of his said disease, but trusted more in the art and remedy of physic; whereby we may learn, that it is one great part of perfect belief in our Lord God, to put our trust and confidence most principally and above all other in him: wherefore they that do otherwise, transgress this commandment, and make to them other gods.

Item, That all they transgress this commandment, which either so much presume upon the mercy of God that they fear not his justice, and by reason thereof do still continue in their sin; or else so much fear his justice, that they have no trust in his mercy, and by reason thereof fall into desperation. For both these ways they make him no God, taking from him either justice or mercy, without which he cannot be God. And so do they, that by superstition repute some days good, some dismal or unfortunate;

or think it a thing unlucky to meet in a morning with certain kind of beasts, or with men of certain professions. For such superstitious folk infame the creatures of God.

Item, That they be of the same sort, which by lots, astrology, divination, chattering of birds, physiognomy, and looking of men's hands, or other unlawful and superstitious crafts, take upon them certainly to tell, determine, and judge beforehand of men's acts and fortunes, which be to come afterward. For what do they but make themselves gods in this behalf? as the prophet Esai saith; Tell us afore what shall come, and we shall say that you be gods (Isa 41:23).

Item, That all they which by charms and witchcrafts do use any, prescribed letters, signs or characts, words, blessings, rods, crystal stones, sceptres, swords, measures, hanging of St. John's Gospel or any other thing about their necks or any other part of their bodies, or any other such vain observation, trusting thereby to continue long life, to drive away sickness, or preserve them from sickness, fires, water, or any other peril, otherwise than physic or surgery doth allow, do also offend against this commandment.

But most grievously of all, and above all other, they do offend against this commandment, which profess Christ, and contrary to their profession, made in their baptism, do make secret pacts or covenants with the devil, or do use any manner conjuration or raising up of devils for treasure, or any other thing hid or lost, or for any other manner of cause, whatsoever it be. For all such commit so high offence and treason to God, that there can be no greater. For they yield the honour due unto God to the devil, God's enemy. And not only all such as use charms, witchcrafts, and conjurations, transgress this high and chief commandment, but also all those that seek and resort unto them for any counsel or remedy, according to the saying of God, when he said, Let no man ask counsel of them that use false divinations, or such as take heed to dreams, or chattering of birds. Let there be no witch or enchanter among you, nor any that asketh counsel of them that have spirits, nor of soothsayers, nor that seek the truth of them that be dead; for God abhorreth all these things (Deut 18:10-12).

The Exposition of the Second Commandment

Thou shalt not make to thyself any graven thing, ne any similitude of any thing that is in heaven above, or in earth beneath, nor in the water under the earth. Thou shalt not bow down to them, ne worship them.

The second Commandment Moses declareth at good length in the Book of Deuteronomy, where he speaketh in this manner: In the day when our Lord spake to you in Horeb from the midst of the fire, you heard the voice, and the sound of his words, but you saw no form or similitude, lest peradventure you should have been thereby deceived, and should have made to yourself an engraved similitude or image of man or woman, or a similitude of any manner beast upon earth, or of fowl under heaven, or of any beast that creepeth upon the earth, or of fishes that tarry in the water under the earth; and lest peradventure lifting up your eyes to heaven, and there seeing the sun, and the moon, and the stars of heaven, you should by error be deceived, and bow down to them, and worship them, which the Lord hath created to serve all people under heaven (Deut 4:10-19).

By these words we be utterly forbidden to make or to have any similitude or image, to the intent to bow down to it, or to worship it. And therefore we think it convenient, that all bishops and preachers shall instruct and teach the people committed to their spiritual charge, first, that God in his substance cannot by any similitude or image be represented or expressed. For no wit ne understanding can comprehend his substance. And that the fathers of the church, considering the dulness of man's wit, and partly yielding to the custom of gentility, (which before their coming unto the faith of Christ had certain representations of their false gods,) suffered the picture or similitude of the Father of heaven to be had and set up in churches; not that he is any such thing as we in that image do behold, (for he is no corporal ne bodily substance,) but only to put us in remembrance that there is a Father in heaven, and that he is a distinct person from the Son and the Holy Ghost; which thing nevertheless, if the common people would duly conceive of the heavenly Father without any bodily representation, it were more seemly for Christian people to be without all such images of the Father, than to have any of them.

Second, that although all images, be they engraven, painted, or wrought in arras, or in any otherwise made, be so prohibited that they may neither be bowed down unto ne worshipped, (forasmuch as they be the works of man's hand only,) yet they be not so prohibited, but that they may be had and set up in churches, so it be for none other purpose but only to the intent that we (in beholding and looking upon them, as in certain books, and seeing represented in them the manifold examples of virtues, which were in the saints, represented by the said images) may the rather be provoked, kindled, and stirred to yield thanks to our Lord, and to praise him in his said saints, and to remember and lament our sins and offences, and to pray God that we may have grace to follow their goodness and holy living. As for an example: The image of our Saviour, as an open book, hangeth on the cross in the rood, or is painted in cloths, walls, or windows, to the intent that beside the examples of virtues which we may learn at Christ, we may be also many ways provoked to remember his painful and cruel passion, and also to consider ourselves, when we behold the said image, and to condemn and abhor our sin, which was the cause of his so cruel death, and thereby to profess that we will no more sin. And furthermore, considering what high charity was in him that would die for us his enemies, and what great dangers we have escaped, and what high benefits we receive by his redemption, we may be provoked in all our distresses and troubles to run for comfort unto him. All these lessons, with many mo, we may learn in this book of the rood, if we will entirely and earnestly look upon it. And as the life of our Saviour Christ is represented by this image, even so the lives of the holy saints which followed him be represented unto us by their images. And therefore the said images may well be set up in churches, to be as books for unlearned people, to learn therein examples of humility, charity, patience, temperance, contempt of the world, the flesh, and the devil, and to learn example of all other virtues, and for the other causes above rehearsed. For which causes only images be to be set in the churches, and not for any honour to be done unto them. For although we use to cense the said images, and to kneel before them, and to offer unto them, and to kiss their feet, and such other things; yet we must know and understand, that such things be not nor ought to be done to the images self, but only to God, and in his honour, or in the honour of the holy saint or saints which be represented by they said images.

Thirdly, we think it convenient, that all bishops and preachers shall instruct and teach the people committed unto their spiritual charge, that against this commandment did offend generally, before the coming of Christ, all Gentiles, and people that were not of the nation of Israel. For they worshipped images and false gods, some one, some another. Of the which sort there was a great number. For beside their common gods, every country, every city or town, every house and family, had their proper gods; whereof is much mention made in authors, both Christian and heathen. And these Gentiles, though they had knowledge of a very God, yet, as St. Paul saith, they had idle and vain phantasies, which led them from the truth; and where they counted themselves wise, they were indeed very fools (Rom 1:21-22).

Item, That against this commandment also offended the Jews many and sundry times, and almost continually. For notwithstanding that they professed the knowledge and worshipping of the very true God, yet they fell to worshipping of images, idols, and false gods, as the holy scripture in many places maketh mention.

Finally, we think it convenient, that all bishops and preachers shall instruct and teach the people committed unto their spiritual charge, that to set up images, as the heathen people and the Jews did, to bow to them, and to worship them, is forbidden in this second commandment.

Item, That all they do greatly err, which put difference between image and image, trusting more in one than in another; as though one could help or do more than another, when both do represent but one thing, and, saving by way of representation, neither of them is able to work or to do any thing. And they also that be more ready with their substance to deck dead images gorgeously and gloriously, than with the same to help poor Christian people, the quick and lively images of God, which is the necessary work of charity, commanded by God; and they also that so dote in this behalf, that they make vows, and go on pilgrimages even to the images, and there do call upon the same images for aid and help, phantasying that either the image will work, or else some other thing in the image, or God for the image's sake, as though God wrought by images carved, engraven, or painted, brought once into churches, as he doth work by other his creatures. In which things, if any person heretofore hath or yet doth offend, all good and well learned men have great cause to lament such error and rudeness, and to put their studies and diligence for the reformation of the same.

The Declaration of the Third Commandment

As touching the third Commandment, we think it convenient, that all bishops and preachers shall instruct and
teach the people committed unto their spiritual charge,
that in the said commandment, God requireth of us to
use his name with all honour and reverence.

*Thou shalt not
take the name of
thy Lord God in
vain.*

Item, That the right use of the name of God, and the outward honour
of the same, standeth chiefly in these things following, that is to say, in the
constant confession of his name, in the right invocation of the same, in
giving of due thanks unto God, as well in prosperity as in adversity, and in
the preaching and teaching of his word. For Christ saith, He that openly
confesseth me before men, I shall confess him before my Father in heaven;
and he that is ashamed of me, to confess my name before men, I will be
ashamed of him before my Father in heaven (Matt 10:32-33). In which
words Christ teacheth us not only to profess the name of God, but also
boldly and constantly to defend the same, and not to swerve from it, for
any manner of persecution or injury. We must also in all tribulation and
necessity, and in all temptations and assaults of the devil, invocate and call
upon the name of God. For God accounteth his name to be hallowed,
magnified, and worshipped, when we call upon him in our need. Call
upon me (saith he) in the time of trouble, and I will deliver thee; and thou
shalt honour me (Ps 50:15). And again, the Wise Man saith, The name of
God is the most strong tower: the righteous man runneth to it, and he shall
be holpen (Prov 18:10). Furthermore, we may not seek our own name,
laud, and fame; but utterly avoid and eschew the desire of all worldly honour, glory, and praise, and must give all laud, praise, and thanks unto God
for his benefits, which be so many in number, and so great, that we ought
never to cease from such lauds and thanks. Like as the prophet David admonisheth us, saying, Offer unto God the sacrifice of laud and praise (Ps
50:14). And St. Paul commandeth us, Whensoever we eat, drink, or do
any manner of business, to give honour, praise, and thanks unto God (1
Cor 10:31). And we must also preach the word of God truly and purely,
and set forth the name of God unto other, and reprove all false and erroneous doctrine and heresies. For although priests and bishops only be specially called and deputed as public ministers of God's word, yet every

Christian man is bound particularly to teach his family, and such as be under his governance within his house, when time and place requireth.

Second, we think it convenient, that all bishops and preachers shall instruct and teach the people committed unto their spiritual charge, that by this precept we be commanded to use the name of God unto all goodness and truth: and contrariwise we be forbid in the same to use his name to any manner of evil, as to lying, deceiving, or any untruth. And therefore against this commandment they offend that swear in vain. They swear in vain that swear without lawful and just cause: for then they take the name of God in vain, although the thing which they swear be true. And likewise do all they, which, for every light and vain thing, be ready to swear unprovoked, or provoked of light cause, or that do glory in outrageous oaths, or of custom do use to swear, or that do swear a false oath, and be forsworn wittingly. And such an oath it not only perjury, but also a kind of blasphemy, and is high dishonour and injury to God; because that such persons as make such oath do wittingly bring God for a false witness, which is all truth, and hateth all untruth. For if he could be false, he were not God. And so such perjured men, as much as is in them, make God no God. And if they believe that he will or can bear false witness, then above and besides blasphemy they run into heresy.

Item, That they also do swear in vain which swear any thing that is true or false, they being in doubt whether it be true or false, and do not afore well examine and discuss whether it be true or false; or that swear that thing to be false, which though indeed it be false, yet they think it to be true; or that swear that thing to be true, which though indeed it be true, yet they think it to be false.

Item, That they also do take the name of God in vain, which swear to do that thing which they intended not to do; or swear to forbear that which they intended not to forbear; or swear to do any thing, which to do is unlawful; or swear to leave undone any thing, which to omit or leave undone is unlawful. And such as so swear to do things unlawful, not only offend in such swearing, but also they much more offend, if they perform the thing that they do swear.

Item, That they also break this commandment, which swear to do or to observe any thing which to do and observe they know not whether it be lawful or unlawful; or that make any oath contrary to their lawful oath or promise made before, so long as their former oath or promise standeth in strength.

Item, That they also do take the name of God in vain, which by rewards or fair promises, or by power or fear, do induce or constrain any man to be perjured.

Item, That they also take the name of God in vain, which abuse the holy name of God to unlawful practices, as to charms, enchantments, divinations, conjurations, or such like. And that priests and ministers of Christ's church do also break this commandment, if, in the administration of the sacraments, they yield not the whole efficacy, virtue, and grace thereof to our Lord, as the very author of the same; but ascribe the said efficacy, virtue, and grace, or any part thereof, to themselves: or if any of them do use any of the sacraments to any conjurations, or any other strange practice, contrary to that holy use for the which they be ordained.

Item, That they also break this commandment, which either by teaching or preaching, or by pretence of holy living, do abuse this name to their own vainglory, or any other ungodly purpose. And generally that all evil Christian men, which profess the name of Christ, and live not according to their profession, do also take the name of God in vain, in words confessing Christ, and denying him in deeds. They also break this commandment, which in trouble do not call upon the name of God, nor do thank him in all things, both sweet and sour, good and evil, well fare and evil fare. For God doth send us many troubles and adversities, because we should run to him, cry to him for help, and call upon his holy name.

Thirdly, we think it convenient, that all bishops and preachers shall instruct and teach the people committed unto their spiritual charge, that (forasmuch as the gifts of health of body, health of soul, forgiveness of sins, the gift of grace, or life everlasting, and such other, be the gifts of God, and cannot be given but by God) whosoever maketh invocation to saints for these gifts, praying to them for any of the said gifts, or such like, (which cannot be given but by God only,) yieldeth the glory of God to his creature, contrary to this commandment. For God saith by his prophet, I will not yield my glory to any other (Isa 42:8). Therefore they that so pray to saints for these gifts, as though they could give them, or be the givers of them, transgress this commandment, yielding to a creature the honour of God. Nevertheless, to pray to saints to be intercessors with us and for us to our Lord for our suits which we make to him, and for such things as we can obtain of none but of him, so that we make no invocation of them, is lawful, and allowed by the catholic church.

And again, because no temple, ne church, ne altar, ought to be made but only to God, (for to whom we make temple, church, or altar, to him, as St. Austin saith, we may do sacrifice, and sacrifice we may do to none but to God,) we think it convenient, that all bishops and preachers shall instruct and teach the people committed unto their spiritual charge, that we abuse our English when we call the temples, churches, or altars by the name of any saint, as the church or altar of our lady, the church or altar of St. Michael, of St. Peter, of St. Paul, or such other. For we ought to call them no otherwise but the memories of our lady, of St. Michael, St. Peter, St. Paul, and so of other saints; and the churches or temples of God only, in which be the memorials of those saints. And likewise must the altars be dedicated to our Lord only, though it be for the memorial of any saint. Notwithstanding it is not necessary to alter the common speech which is used, nor there is any error therein; so that the sentence or meaning thereof be well and truly understanded, that is to say, that the said altars and churches be not dedicated to any saint, but to God only, and of the saints but a memorial, to put us in remembrance of them, that we may follow their example and living. And therefore, if we mean as the words do import, when we call them the churches or altars of saints, we yield the honour of God from him to the saints, and break this commandment. And likewise, if we honour them any otherwise than as the friends of God, dwelling with him, and established now in his glory everlasting, and as examples whom we must follow in holy life and conversation; or if we yield unto saints the adoration and honour which is due unto God alone, we do (no doubt) break this commandment, and do wrong unto our Lord God.

The Exposition of the Fourth Commandment

Remember that thou do sanctify and keep holy thy sabbath day.

As touching the fourth Commandment, we think it convenient, that all bishops and preachers shall instruct and teach the people committed unto their spiritual charge, first, that this word *sabbote* is an Hebrew word, and signifieth in English *rest*. So that the sabbath day is as much to say as the day of rest and quietness. And therefore there is a special and notable difference between this commandment and the other nine. For as St. Austin saith, All the other nine commandments be moral commandments, and belonged not only to the Jews, and all the other people of the world, in the time of the Old Testament, but also to all Christian people in the New Testament. But this precept of sabbath, as concerning rest from bodily labour the seventh day, pertained only unto the Jews in the Old Testament, before the coming of Christ, and not to us Christian people in the New Testament. Nevertheless, as concerning the spiritual rest, (which is figured and signified by this corporal rest,) that is to say, rest from carnal works of the flesh, and all manner of sin, this precept remaineth still, and bindeth them that belong to Christ, and not for every seventh day only, but for all days, hours, and times. For at all times we be bound to rest from fulfilling of our own carnal will and pleasure, from all sins and evil desires, from pride, disobedience, ire, hate, covetousness, and all such corrupt and carnal appetites, and to commit ourselves wholly to God, that he may work in us all things that be to his will and pleasure. And this is the true sabbath or rest of us that be christened, when we rest from our own carnal wills, and be not led thereby, but be guided alway by God and his holy Spirit. And this is the thing that we pray for in the Paternoster, when we say. Father, let thy kingdom come unto us. Thy will be done in earth, as it is in heaven. Reign thou with us. Make thy will to be wrought in us, that from our own corrupt will we may rest and cease. And for this purpose God hath ordained that we should fast, watch, and labour; to the end that by these remedies we might mortify and kill the evil and sensual desires of the flesh, and attain this spiritual rest and quietness, which is signified and figured in this commandment.

Second, we think it convenient, that all bishops and preachers shall instruct and teach the people committed unto their spiritual charge, that besides this spiritual rest, (which chiefly and principally is required of us,) we be bound by this precept at certain times to cease from all bodily labour, and to give our minds entirely and wholly unto God; to hear and learn his word; to knowledge our own sinfulness unto God, and his great mercy and goodness unto us; to give thanks unto him for all his benefits; to make public and common prayer for all things needful; to receive the sacraments; to visit the sick; to instruct every man his children and family in virtue and goodness, and such other like works: which things, although all Christian people be bound unto by this commandment, yet the sabbath day, which is called the Saturday, is not now prescribed and appointed thereto, as it was to the Jews; but instead of the sabbath day succeedeth the Sunday, and many other holy and feastful days, which the church hath ordained from time to time; which be called holydays, not because one day is more acceptable to God than another, or of itself is more holy than another, but because the church hath ordained that upon those days we should give ourselves wholly without any impediment unto such holy works as be before expressed; whereas upon other days we do apply ourselves to bodily labour, and be thereby much letted from such holy and spiritual works.

And to the intent the ignorant people may be the more clearly instructed what holy and spiritual works they ought to do upon the holyday, we think it convenient, that all bishops and preachers shall exhort and teach the people committed to their spiritual charge, to use themselves in this manner following; that is to say, at their first entry or coming into the church, let them make account with themselves how they have bestowed the week past, remembering what evil minds and purposes they have had, what words they have spoken, what things they have done or left undone, to the dishonour or displeasure of God, or to the hurt of their neighbour; or what example or occasion of evil they have given unto other. And when they have thus recollected and considered all these things in their minds, then let them humbly knowledge their defaults unto God, and ask forgiveness for the same, with unfeigned purpose in their hearts to convert and return from their naughty lives, and to amend the same. And when they have so done, then let them clearly and purely in their hearts remit and forgive all malice and displeasure which they bear to any creature. And after that, then let them fall unto prayer, according to the commandment of Christ, where he saith, When you begin to pray, forgive whatsoever displeasure you have against any man (Matt 5:23-24). And when they be weary of prayer, then let them use reading of the word of God, or some other good and heavenly doctrine, so that they do it quietly, without disturbance of other that be in the church; or else let them occupy their minds with some wholesome and godly meditations, whereby they may be the better. And they that can read may be well occupied upon the holy day, if they read unto other such good works which may be unto them instead of a sermon. For all things that edify man's soul in our Lord God be good and wholesome sermons.

And truly if men would occupy themselves upon the holydays, and spend the same days wholly after this form and manner, not only in the house of God, but also in their own houses, they should thereby eschew much vice, confound their ancient enemy the devil, much edify both themselves and other, and finally obtain much grace and high reward of Almighty God.

Thirdly, we think it convenient, that all bishops and preachers shall instruct and teach the people committed unto their spiritual charge, to have special regard that they be not over scrupulous, or rather superstitious, in abstaining from bodily labour upon the holy day. For notwithstanding all that is afore spoken, it is not meant but that in time of necessity we may upon the holyday give ourselves to labour, as for saving of our corn and cattle, when it is in danger, or likely to be destroyed, if remedy be not had in time. For this lesson our Saviour doth teach us in the gospel; and we need to have no scruple ne grudge in conscience, in such case of necessity, to labour on the holydays; but rather we should offend, if we should for scrupulosity not save that God hath sent for the sustenance and relief of his people.

Finally, we think it convenient, that all bishops and preachers shall instruct and teach the people committed unto their spiritual charge, how against this commandment generally do offend all they which will not cease and rest from their own carnal wills and pleasure, that God may work in them after his pleasure and will.

Item, All they, which, having no lawful impediment, do not give themselves upon the holyday to hear the word of God, to remember the benefits of God, to give thanks for the same, to pray, and to exercise such other holy works as be appointed for the same; but (as commonly is used) pass the time either in idleness, in gluttony, in riot, or in plays, or other vain and idle pastime. For surely, such keeping of the holyday is not according to the intent and meaning of this commandment, but after the usage and custom of the Jews, and doth not please God; but doth much more offend him, and provoke his indignation and wrath towards us. For, as St. Austin saith of the Jews, they should be better occupied labouring in their fields, and to be at the plough, than to be idle at home. And women should better bestow their time in spinning of wool, than upon the sabbath day to lose their time in leaping and dancing, and other idle, wanton, lose time.

Item, That all they do offend against this commandment, which do hear the word of God and give not good heed thereunto, that they may understand it and learn it; or if they do learn it, yet they endeavour not themselves to remember it; or if they remember it, yet they study not to follow it.

Item, That all they do break this commandment also, which in mass time do occupy their minds with other matters, and, like unkind people, remember not the passion and death of Christ, nor give thanks unto him; which things in the mass time they ought specially to do; for the mass is ordained to be a perpetual memory of the same. And likewise do all those, which in such time as the common prayers be made, or the word of God is taught, not only themselves do give none attendance thereto, but also, by walking, talking, and other evil demeanour, let other that would well use themselves. And likewise do all they, which do not observe but despise such laudable ceremonies of the church as set forth God's honour, or appertain to good order to be used in the church.

And therefore concerning such ceremonies of the church, we think it convenient, that all bishops and preachers shall instruct and teach the people committed unto their spiritual charge, that although the said ceremonies have no power to remit sin, yet they be very expedient things to stir and cause us to lift up our minds unto God, and to put us in continual remembrance of those spiritual things which be signified by them: as sprinkling of holy water doth put us in remembrance of our baptism, and the blood of Christ, sprinkled for our redemption upon the cross. Giving of holy bread doth put us in remembrance of the sacrament of the altar, which we ought to receive in right charity; and also that all Christian men be one body mystical of Christ, as the bread is made of many grains, and yet but one loaf. Bearing of candles on Candlemas-day doth put us in remembrance of Christ the spiritual light, of whom Simeon did prophesy, as is read in the church that day. Giving of ashes on Ash Wednesday doth put us in remembrance, that every Christian man, in the beginning of Lent and penance, should consider that he is but ashes and earth, and thereto shall return. Bearing of palms on Palm-Sunday doth put us in remembrance of the receiving of Christ into Jerusalem a little before his death, and that we must have the same desire to receive him into our hearts. Creeping to the cross, and humbling ourselves to Christ on Good Friday before the cross, and there offering unto Christ before the same, and kissing of it, putteth us in remembrance of our redemption by Christ made upon the cross. And so finally the setting up of the sepulture of Christ, whose body after his death was buried. The hallowing of the font, and other like exorcisms and benedictions done by the ministers of Christ's church, and all other like laudable customs, rites, and ceremonies, do put us in remembrance of some spiritual thing. And that therefore they be not to be contemned and cast away, but be to be used and continued as things good and laudable for the purposes abovesaid.

The Declaration of the Fifth Commandment

As touching the fifth Commandment, we think it convenient, that all bishops and preachers shall instruct and teach the people committed to their spiritual charge, first, that by this word *father* is understood here, not only the natural father and mother which did carnally beget us and brought us up, but also the spiritual father, by whom we be spiritually regenerated and nourished in Christ; and other governors and rulers under whom we be nourished and brought up, or ordered and guided. And although this commandment make express mention only of the children or inferiors to their parents and superiors, yet in the same is also understanded and comprised the office and duty of the parents and superiors again unto their children and inferiors.

Honour thy father and mother.

Second, that by this word *honour,* in this commandment, is not only meant a reverence and lowliness in words and outward gesture, which children and inferiors ought to exhibit unto their parents and superiors, but also a prompt and a ready obedience to their lawful commandments, a regard to their words, a forbearing and suffering of them, an inward love and veneration towards them, a reverent fear, and loathness to displease or offend them, and a good-will and gladness to assist them, aid them, succour them, and help them with our counsel, with our goods and substance, and by all other means to our possible power. This is the very honour and duty which not only the children do owe unto their parents, but also all subjects and inferiors to their heads and rulers. And that children owe this duty unto their fathers, it appeareth in many places of scripture. In the Proverbs it is written, Obey, my son, the chastising of thy father, and be not negligent in thy mother's commandments (1:8). In the Book of the Deuteronomy it is also written, Accursed be he that doth not honour his father and his mother (27:16). And in the Book of the Leviticus it is said, Let every man stand in awe of his father and mother (19:3). And, If any man have a stubborn and a disobedient son, which will not hear the voice of his father and mother, and for correction will not amend and follow them, then shall his father and mother take him, and bring him to the judges of the city, and say, This our son is stubborn and disobedient, and despiseth our monitions, and is a rioter and a drunkard. Then shall all the people stone him to death; and thou shalt put away the evil from thee, that all Israel may hear thereof, and be afraid (Deut 21:18-21). And in the Book of Exody it is also written, He that striketh his father or mother, he shall be put to death (21:15). And likewise, He that curseth his father or his mother shall suffer death (21:17). And in the Book of Proverbs the Wise Man also saith, He that stealeth any thing from his father or mother is to be taken as a murderer (28:24). And although that these great punishments of disobedient children by death be not now in the new law in force and strength, but left to the order of princes and governors, and their laws, yet it evidently appeareth how sore God is grieved and displeased with such disobedience of children towards their parents: for so much as in the old law he did appoint thereunto so grievous punishments.

And as Almighty God doth threaten these punishments unto those children which do break this commandment, so he doth promise great rewards to them that keep it. For he that honoureth his father, (saith the Wise Man,) his sins shall be forgiven him: and he that honoureth his mother is as one that gathereth treasure. Whosoever honoureth his father shall have joy of his own children: and when he maketh his prayer to God, he shall be heard. He that honoureth his father shall have a long and a prosperous life (Sir 3:4-6). And as the children by this commandment be bound to honour and obey their parents, (according as is before expressed,) so it is implied in the same precept that the parents should nourish and godly bring up their children; that is to say, that they must not only find them meat and drink in youth, and also set them forward in learning, labour, or some other good exercise, that they may eschew idleness, and have some craft and occupation, or some other lawful mean to get their living; but also they must learn and teach them to trust in God, to love him, to fear him, to love their neighbour, to hate no man, to hurt no man, to wish well to every man, and, so much as they may, to do good unto every man; not to curse, not to swear, not to be riotous, but to be sober and temperate in all things; not to be worldly, but to set their minds upon the love of God and heavenly things, more than upon temporal things of this world; and generally to do all that is good, and to eschew all that is evil. And this the parents ought to do, not by cruel entreating of their children, whereby they might discourage them, and provoke them to hate their parents; but by charitable rebuking, threatening, and reasonable chastising and correcting of them when they do evil, and cherishing, maintaining, and commending them when they do well.

This office and duty of the parents towards their children is witnessed in many places of scripture. First, St. Paul writeth thus: Fathers, provoke not your children unto anger, but bring them up in the correction and doctrine of God (Eph 6:4). And in Deuteronomy, Almighty God saith, Teach my laws and commandments to thy children (6:7). And the Wise Man saith, The rod of correction giveth wisdom. The child that is left to his own will shall be confusion to his mother (Prov 29:15). And in another place he saith, He that spareth the rod hateth his son: and he that loveth him will see him corrected (Prov 13:24). And in another place he saith, See thou withdraw not from thy child discipline and chastising. If thou strike him with the rod, he shall not die: thou shalt strike him with a rod, and shalt thereby deliver his soul from hell (Prov 23:13-14). And on the other side it is written, The son untaught and unchastised in the confusion of his father (Sir 22:3). And for this cause we find in the Book of Kings, how that our Lord conceived high indignation against Eli the chief priest, because he did not duly correct his two sons, Hophni and Phinehas, when he knew that they did grievously offend God: and how, in revenging of the father's negligence and remissness in correcting of his children, Almighty God took from Eli, and all his issue and household for ever, the office of the high priesthood: and how his two sons Hophni and Phinehas were slain both upon a day, and Eli their father brake his neck (1 Sam 4). This example of Eli is necessary for fathers to imprint in their hearts, that they may see their children well taught and corrected, lest they run into the great indignation of Almighty God, as Eli did, and not only in this world have confusion, but also in the world to come have damnation for the misorder of their children through their default. And they must not think that it is enough to speak somewhat unto them when they do amiss. (For so did Eli to his sons, and yet our Lord was not pleased, because he did not more sharply correct them, and see them reformed.) But when words will not serve, the fathers and mothers must put to correction, and by such discipline save their souls, or else they shall answer to God for them. And truly they greatly deserve the indignation of God, that, when they have received of him children, do not bring them up to his service, but, without regard what cometh of them, suffer them to run to the service of the devil.

Thirdly, we think it convenient, that all bishops and preachers shall instruct and teach the people committed unto their spiritual charge, that all Christian men be bound to exhibit and do unto them, which under God be their spiritual fathers and parents of their souls, the like and the selfsame honour, which (as is aforesaid) children of duty do owe unto their natural fathers (1 Cor 4:15).

Item, That these spiritual fathers be appointed by God to minister his sacraments unto them, to bring them up, and to feed them with the word of God, and to teach them his gospel and scripture (Acts 20:24, 28); and by the same to govern, to conduct, and to lead them in the straight way to the Father in heaven everlasting (Heb 13:7, 17).

Item, That our Saviour Christ, in the gospel, maketh mention as well of the obedience as also of the corporal sustenance which all Christian people do owe unto their spiritual fathers. Of the obedience he saith, that whosoever receiveth you receiveth me (Matt 10:40). And in another place he saith, He that heareth you heareth me; and he that despiseth you despiseth me (Luke 10:16). And in another place he saith, Whatsoever they bid you do, do it (Matt 23:3). And St. Paul saith, Obey your prelates, and give place unto them: for they have much charge and care for your souls, as they which must give an account therefore, that they may do it with joy and not with grief (Heb 13:17); that is to say, that they may gladly and with much comfort do their cure and charge, when they do perceive that the people be obedient to their teaching: like as on the contrariwise they have little joy or pleasure to do it, when they find the people disobedient and repugnant.

And for the sustenance of their living, which is comprised in this word *honour,* (as before is declared,) Christ saith in the gospel, The workman is worthy his wages (Luke 10:7). And St. Paul saith, Who goeth on warfare upon his own stipend? And who planteth the vine, and eateth no part of the fruit? And who feedeth the flock, and eateth no part of the milk? And after followeth, Even so hath the Lord ordained, that they which preach the gospel should live of the gospel (1 Cor 9:7, 14). And therefore in another place it is written, Priests or ancients that rule well be worthy of double honour, specially they that labour in the ministration of the word of God, and his doctrine (1 Tim 5:17). In which place the apostle meaneth by *double honour,* not only the reverence which is due unto the spiritual fathers, (as is aforesaid,) but also that all Christian people be bound to minister, find, and give unto their spiritual fathers sufficiency of all things necessary and requisite, as well for their sustenance and finding, as for the quiet and commodious exercising and executing of their said office.

Fourthly, we think it convenient, that all bishops and preachers shall instruct and teach the people committed unto their spiritual charge, that this commandment also containeth the honour and obedience which subjects owe unto their princes, and also the office of princes towards their subjects. For scripture taketh princes to be, as it were, fathers and nourices to their subjects. And by scripture it appeareth, that it appertaineth unto the office of princes to see that the right religion and true doctrine of Christ may be maintained and taught; and that their subjects may be well ruled and governed by good and just laws; and to provide and care for them, that all things necessary for them may be plenteous; and that the people and common weal may increase; and to defend them from oppression and invasion, as well within the realm as without; and to see that justice be ministered unto them indifferently; and to hear benignly all their complaints; and to shew towards them (although they offend) fatherly pity. And finally, so to correct them that be evil, that they had yet rather save them than lose them, if it were not for respect of justice, and maintenance of peace and good order in the common weal (Isa 49). And therefore all their subjects must again on their parts be bound by this commandment, not only to honour and obey their said princes, according as subjects be bound to do, and to owe their truth and fidelity unto them, as unto their natural lords; but they must also love them as children do love their fathers; yea they must more tender the surety of their prince's person and his estate than their own: even like as the health of the head is more to be tendered than the health of any other member.

And by this commandment also subjects be bound not to withdraw their said fealty, truth, love, and obedience towards their prince, for any cause whatsoever it be. Ne for any cause they may conspire against his person, ne do any thing towards the hinderance or hurt thereof, nor of his estate.

And furthermore, by this commandment they be bound also to obey all the laws, proclamations, precepts, and commandments made by their princes and governors; except they be against the commandments of God. And likewise they be bound to obey all such as be in authority under their prince, as far as he will have them obeyed. They must also give unto their prince aid, help, and assistance, whensoever he shall require the same, either for surety, preservation, or maintenance of his person and estate, or of the realm, or for the defence of any of the same, against all persons; and whensoever subjects be called by their prince unto privy council, or unto the parliament, which is the general council of this realm, then they be bound to give unto their prince (as their learning, wisdom, or experience can serve them) the most faithful counsel they can, and such as may be to the honour of God, to the honour and surety of his regal person and estate, and to the general wealth of all his whole realm.

And further, if any subject shall know of any thing which is or may be to the annoyance or damage of his prince's person or estate, he is bound by this commandment to disclose the same with all speed to the prince himself, or to some of his council. For it is the very law of nature, that every member shall employ himself to preserve and defend the head. And surely wisdom and policy will the same. For of conspiracy and treason cometh never no goodness; but infinite hurt, damage, and peril to the common weal. And that all subjects do owe unto their princes and governors such honour and obedience, (as is before said,) it appeareth evidently in sundry places of scripture; but specially in the Epistles of St. Paul and St. Peter. For St. Paul saith in this manner: Every man must be obedient unto the high powers; for the powers be of God. And therefore whosoever resisteth the powers resisteth the ordinance of God (Rom 13:1-2). And they that resist shall get to themselves damnation. And St. Peter saith, Obey unto all sorts of governors for God's sake, whether it be unto the king as unto the chief head, or unto rulers as unto them that be sent of God for to punish evil doers, and to cherish them that do well. And shortly after it followeth, Fear God, honour thy king (1 Pet 2:14, 17).

And there be many examples in scripture of the great vengeance of God that hath fallen upon rebels, and such as have been disobedient unto their princes. But one principal example to be noted is of Kore, Dathan, and Abiram, whom for their rebellion Almighty God so punished, that when they and two hundred and fifty captains mo, with other people, to a great number, were all together, the earth opened and swallowed them down, with their houses, their wives, and their children, and all their substance. And they went down quick into hell, with all that they had (Num 16).

Fifthly, we think it convenient, that all bishops and preachers shall instruct and teach the people committed unto their spiritual charge, that this commandment doth, also contain the honour and obedience that servants do owe unto their masters; and the office and duty again of the masters unto their servants.

Item, That the honour and obedience of the servants unto their masters is to love their master; to be reverent and lowly unto him in all their words and gesture; to suffer and forbear him; to be ready, and with a goodwill, without murmuration or grudging, to obey all his lawful or reasonable commandments; to fear him, and to be loath to displease him; to be faithful and true unto him; and to their power to procure and do that which is to their master's honesty and profit, and that as well in their master's absence, and out of his sight, as when he is present, and looketh upon them; according to the words of St. Paul, where he saith, Servants, be you obedient unto your masters with fear and trembling, with simple and plain hearts, as unto Christ, not serving only in their sight, as pleasers of men, but as the servants of Christ, doing the will of God from the heart, and with goodwill, thinking that you serve God, and not men. And be you sure, that of all your good service you shall receive reward of God (Eph 6:5-8). And again to Titus he writeth thus: Exhort the servants to be obedient unto their masters, to please them well in all things, not to be patterers and praters against them, nor pickers or privy conveyers of their masters' goods, but to shew all truth and faithfulness (Titus 2:9-10). St. Peter also biddeth servants to obey their masters with all fear, not only if they be good and gentle, but also though they be froward (1 Pet 2:18).

Item, That the office and duty of the masters unto their servants is to provide sufficiently for them of all things necessary; to see them instructed in the laws of God, and that they observe the same; not to be over rigorous unto them; to correct them when they do amiss; and to commend and cherish them when they do well; according to the saying of St. Paul, You that be masters do unto your servants that is right and reason; know that yourselves have also a Master in heaven (Col 4:1). And in another place he saith, Be not rigorous unto your servants, for you have a Master in heaven that regardeth all persons indifferently (Eph 6:9). And the Wise Man saith, Meat, correction, and work is due unto the servants. Set thy servant to labour, that he be not idle: for idleness bringeth much evil. Set him to work, for that belongeth unto him: if he be not obedient, correct him (Sir 33:24, 27-28).

Item, That in this commandment is also implied, that children and young folks should give due honour and reverence to old men, and to all such as be their masters and tutors, to bring them up in learning and virtue, which be in this behalf as fathers unto them; and so as fathers must be honoured and obeyed.

Finally, we think it convenient that all bishops and preachers shall instruct and teach the people committed unto their spiritual charge, that all fathers ought diligently to consider and 'remember how much and how grievously they do offend God, and of how many evils they be the cause, which either bring up their children in wantonness and idleness, and do not put them forth in time to some faculty, exercise, or labour, whereby they may after get their living, or occupy their life to the profit and commodity of the common weal; or else do suffer their children in youth to be corrupted for lack of good teaching and bringing up in the true knowledge of God, and of his will and commandments; or commit in word or deed such things in the presence of their children, whereof the young tender hearts of their said children (which, like a small twig, is inclinable every way, and by frailness of youth is inclined to evil) do take so evil example and corruption of vices and worldly affections, that hard it will be for them after to eschew the same.

The Declaration of the Sixth Commandment

Thou shalt not kill.

As touching the sixth Commandment, we think it convenient, that all bishops and preachers shall instruct and teach the people committed unto their spiritual charge, first, that in this commandment is forbidden not only bodily killing, and all manner of violent laying of hands upon any man, as striking, cutting, wounding, and all manner of bodily hurting by act and deed; but also all malice, anger, hate, envy, disdain, and all other evil affections of the heart; and also all slander, backbiting, chiding, banning, railing, scorning, or mocking, and all other evil behaviour of our tongue against our neighbour: which all be forbidden by this commandment. For they be roots and occasions of murder, or other bodily hurt.

Item, That the contrary of all these things be commanded by this commandment, that is to say, that we should with our hearts love our neighbours, and with our tongues speak well of them and to them, and in our acts and deeds do good unto them, shewing towards them in heart, word, and deed patience, meekness, mercy, and gentleness, yea though they be our adversaries and enemies. And that this is the true sense and meaning of this commandment, it appeareth by the exposition of our Saviour Christ in the gospel, where he declareth, That we should neither hurt any man in deed, nor speak of him or unto him maliciously or contemptuously with our tongues, nor bear malice or anger in our hearts (Matt 5); but that we should love them that hate us, say well by them that say evil by us, and do good to them that do evil to us (Rom 12:21). And according to the same saying of Christ St. John also saith, That he that hateth his neighbour is a mankiller (1 John 3:15).

Item, That it is not forbidden by this commandment, but that all rulers and governors, as princes, judges, fathers, masters, and such other, may for the correction of them which be under their governance, use such manner of punishment, either by rebukeful and sharp words, or by bodily chastising, as the laws of every realm do permit. And not only they may do thus, but also they be bound so to do, and offend God if they do it not, as is before declared in the fifth Commandment.

Item, That all rulers must beware and take heed, that in their corrections or punishments they do not proceed upon any private malice of their hearts, or displeasure towards any man, or for any lucre, favour, or fear of any person; but that they have their eye and consideration only upon the reformation and amendment of the person whom they do correct, or else upon the good order and quietness of the common weal; so that still there may remain in their hearts charity and love towards the person whom they punish. And like as the father loveth his child, even when he beateth him, even so a good judge, when he giveth sentence of death upon any guilty person, although he shew outwardly cruelness and rigour, yet inwardly he ought to love the person, and to be sorry and heavy for his offences, and for the death which he himself by the law doth and must needs condemn him unto.

Item, That although inferior rulers or governors may correct and punish such as be under their governance, yet they may not punish by death, mutilate, maim, or imprison them, or use any corporal violence towards them, otherwise than is permitted by the high governor, that is to say, by the prince and his laws, from whom all such authority doth come. For no man may kill, or use such bodily coercion, but only princes, and they which have authority from princes. Ne the said princes, ne any for them, may do the same, but by and according to the just order of their laws.

Item, That no subjects may draw the sword (saving for lawful defence) without their prince's license. And that it is their duty to draw their swords for the defence of their prince and the realm, whensoever the prince shall command them so to do. And that for no cause, whatsoever it be, they may draw their swords against their prince, nor against any other, without his consent or commandment, as is aforesaid. And although princes do otherwise than they ought to do, yet God hath assigned no judges over them in this world, but will have the judgment of them reserved to himself, and will punish when he seeth his time. And for amendment of such princes that do otherwise than they should do, the people must pray to God, (which hath the hearts of princes in his hands,) that he may so turn their hearts unto him, that they may use the sword which he hath given them unto his pleasure.

Second, we think it convenient, that all bishops and preachers shall diligently from time to time instruct and teach the people committed unto their spiritual charge, that against this commandment offend all they which do kill, maim, or hurt any man, without just order of the law, or giveth counsel, aid, favour, provocation, or consent thereunto.

Item, That all they which may, if they will, by their authority or lawful means, deliver a man from wrongful death, mutilation, hurt, or injury, and will not do it, but will wink thereat, and dissimule it, be transgressors of this commandment.

Item, That all judges, which, seeing no sufficient matter or cause of death; or that, upon a light trial, without sufficient examination and discussion, giveth sentence of death; or that, when the matter and cause of death is sufficient, and the trial good, yet delighteth in the death of the person, be transgressors of this commandment.

And likewise be all those, which, in the causes of life and death, being impannelled upon inquests, do lightly condemn or indict any person without sufficient evidence, examination, and discussion of the informations given unto them. And moreover all those which either in such causes do give false evidence or information, or wittingly, contrary to their own conscience, or doubting of the truth of those informations, or without sufficient examination, do promote, enforce, or maintain such evidences, informations, or indictments, do also break this commandment.

And likewise do all they which willingly do kill themselves for any manner of cause; for so to do there can be no pretence of lawful cause, ne of just order. And therefore he that so doth, killeth at once both body and soul.

And finally, all they which be in hatred and malice with their neighbours, and either speak words of contempt, despite, checking, cursing, and such other, or else publish their neighbours' offences, to their slander rather than to their amendment; and generally all they that live in ire, malice, envy, and murmuring at other men's wealth, or rejoicing at other men's trouble or hurt, or such other like; they offend all against this precept.

The Declaration of the Seventh Commandment

As touching the seventh Commandment, we think it convenient, that all bishops and preachers shall instruct and teach the people committed unto their spiritual *Thou shalt not commit adultery.* charge, first, that this word adultery doth in this commandment signify, not only the unlawful commixtion of a married man with any other woman than his own wife, or else of a married woman with any other man than her own husband; but also all manner of unlawful copulation between man and woman, married or unmarried, and all manner of unlawful use of those parts which be ordained for generation, whether it be by adultery, fornication, incest, or any other mean, although it be in lawful matrimony. For in lawful matrimony a man may commit adultery, and live unchaste even with his own wife, if they do unmeasurably serve their fleshly appetite and lust; and of such the devil hath power, as the angel Raphael said unto Tobit, They that marry in such wise that they exclude God out of their minds, and give themselves to their own carnal lusts, as it were a horse or a mule, which have no reason: upon such persons the devil hath power (Tob 6).

Item, That all Christian people ought highly to regard the observation of this commandment, considering how much God is displeased, and what vengeance he hath always taken, and ever will take, for the transgression of the same. For confirmation whereof, we think it convenient, that all bishops and preachers shall instruct and teach the people committed unto their spiritual charge, first, how that God, in the time of Moses' law, commanded, that whosoever committed adultery should be stoned to death.

Item, How Hamor king of Shechem, and Shechem his son, with all the men of the city, were slain, and their wives and children were taken captive, and all their goods within the city were robbed and spoiled, because the said Shechem lay with Dinah the daughter of Jacob, and defiled her (Gen 34).

Item, How that Almighty God, after the children of Israel had committed adultery with the women of Moab and Midian, commanded first that the heads and rulers of the people should be hanged, for that they suffered the people so to offend God. And afterward commanded also every man to slay his neighbour that had so offended. Insomuch that there was slain of that people the number of fourteen thousand. And many mo should have been slain, had not Phinehas, the son of Eleazar the high priest, turned the indignation of God from the children of Israel. For this Phinehas, when he saw Zimri, chief of the tribe of Simeon, in the presence of Moses and all the people, go unto Cozbi, a nobleman's daughter of the Midianites, to commit fornication with her, he arose from among all the multitude, and taking a sword in his hand, went into the house where they were, and thrust them both through the bellies: whose fervent mind and zeal God did so much allow, that he did therefore both cease from further punishment of the Israelites, and also granted to Phinehas, and his succession for ever, the dignity of the high priest (Num 25).

Item, How the tribe and stock of Benjamin was so punished for the maintenance of certain persons of the city of Gibeah, (which had, contrary to this commandment, shamefully abused a certain man's wife,) that of twenty-five thousand and seven hundred men of arms, there remained on life but six hundred (Judg 20).

Item, How Almighty God, for the transgression of this command-ment, caused brimstone and fire to rain down from heaven upon all the country of Sodom and Gomorrah; and so destroyed the whole region, both men and beasts, and all that grew upon the earth, reserving only Lot and his three daughters (Gen 19). These terrible examples, and many other like, Almighty God did shew in times past; to the intent we should have them in our continual remembrance, and so should ever stand in awe and fear to offend God. For though he do not so presently punish us here in this world as he did the persons before rehearsed; yet his long patience and forbearing is no allowance or forgiveness of our offences, if we continue still in them, but a sore accumulation and heaping together of God's wrath and indignation against the day of judgment. At which time, instead of this temporal pain, we shall receive everlasting pain; being, as St. Paul saith, excluded from the everlasting kingdom of heaven (Rom 2:8); and, as Christ saith in the Gospel, and St. John in the Apocalypse, we shall be cast into the brenning lake of hell, where is fire, brimstone, weeping, wailing, and gnashing of teeth without end (Matt 22, 25; Luke 13).

Second, we think it convenient, that all bishops and preachers shall instruct and teach the people committed unto their spiritual charge, how that in this commandment not only the vices before rehearsed be forbid-den and prohibited, but also the virtues contrary to them be required and commanded; that is to say, fidelity and true keeping of wedlock in them that be married, continence in them that be unmarried, and generally in all persons shamefastness and chasteness, not only of deeds, but of words and manners, countenance and thoughts; and moreover, fasting, temper-ance, watching, labour, and all lawful things that conduce and help to chastity. And that therefore against this commandment offend all they which do take any single woman, or other man's wife, or that in their hearts do covet and desire for to have them. For as Christ saith, Whosoever eyeth a woman, wishing to have her, hath already committed adultery with her in his heart (Matt 5:28).

They also offend this commandment, that take in marriage or out of marriage any of their own kindred or affinity, within the degrees forbid-den by the laws of God.

They also offend against this commandment, which abuse them-selves, or any other persons, against nature; or abuse their wives in the time of their menstrual purgation (Lev 18, 20).

They also that do nourish, stir up, and provoke themselves or any other to carnal lusts and pleasures of the body, by uncleanly and wanton words, tales, songs, sights, touchings, gay and wanton apparel, and lascivious decking of themselves, or any such other wanton behaviour and enticement; and also all those which procure any such act, or that minister house, license, or place thereto; and all counsellors, helpers, and consenters to the same, do grievously offend God, and do transgress this commandment.

Likewise, all they that avoid not the causes hereof so much as they conveniently may, as surfeiting, sloth, idleness, immoderate sleep, and company of such (both men and women) as be unchaste and evil disposed, be guilty of the transgression of this commandment.

The Declaration of the Eighth Commandment

Thou shalt not steal. As touching the eighth Commandment, we think it convenient, that all bishops and preachers shall instruct and teach the people committed unto their spiritual charge, first, that under the name of *theft* or *stealing,* in this commandment, is understanded all manner of unlawful taking away, occupying, or keeping of another man's goods, whether it be by force, extortion, oppression, bribery, usury, simony, unlawful chevisance, or else by false buying and selling, either by false weights, or by false measure, or by selling of a worse thing for a better, or a thing counterfeit for a true, as gilt copper for true gold, or glass for precious stones, and generally all manner of fraud or deceit.

Item, That like as the vices before rehearsed be by this precept forbidden, even so sundry virtues, contrary to the said vices, be by the same commanded; as, to deal truly and plainly with our neighbours in all things; to get our own goods truly; to spend them liberally upon them that have need; to feed the hungry; to give drink to the thirsty; to clothe the naked; to harbour the harbourless; to comfort the sick; to visit the prisoners; and finally, to help our neighbours with our learning, good counsel, and exhortation, and by all other good means that we can.

Second, we think it convenient, that all bishops and preachers shall instruct and teach the people committed unto their spiritual charge, that against this commandment offend all they, which by craft or by violence, upon sea or land, spoil, rob, or take away any other man's servant or child, land or inheritance, horse, sheep, or cattle, fish, fowl, conies, or deer, money, jewels, apparel, or any other thing which is not his own.

And likewise offend they against this commandment, which have goods given to an use, and put them not to the same use, but keep them to their own advantage. As masters of hospitals, and false executors, which convert the goods given to the sustentation of the poor folks, and other good and charitable uses, unto their own profit.

Item, That all they which receive rent or stipend for any office, spiritual or temporal, and yet do not their office belonging thereunto, be thieves, and transgressors of this commandment.

Item, That all they which take wages or fee, pretending to deserve it, and yet do not indeed, as labourers and hired servants, which loiter, and do not apply their business; and likewise advocates, proctors, attornies, counsellors in any of the laws, which sometime for little pain take much stipend, or in their default and negligence mar good causes, or do any thing to the hinderance of speedy justice for their own advantage, do transgress this commandment.

Item, That all they transgress this commandment which buy any stolen goods, knowing that they be stolen; or that buy things of them that have no authority to sell them, or alienate them, if they know the same. And likewise do they, that find things lost, and knowing the owner thereof, will not restore them, or will not do their diligence to know the owner.

They also which defraud their hired servants of their due wages; and they that borrow any thing, or receive any thing delivered unto them upon trust, and will not restore the same again; and they that use false weights or measures, or deceitful wares, or sell their own wares at unreasonable price, far above the just valour; and they that engross and buy up any kind of wares whole into their own hands, to the intent that they may make a scarceness thereof in other men's hands, and sell it again as they list; and generally all covetous men and bribers, which by any means unlawfully get or unmercifully keep from them that have need, be transgressors and breakers of this commandment.

The Declaration of the Ninth Commandment

Thou shalt not bear false witness against thy neighbour.

As concerning the ninth Commandment, we think it convenient, that all bishops and preachers shall instruct and teach the people committed unto their spiritual charge, first, that by this commandment is forbidden all manner of lying, slandering, backbiting, false reporting, false accusing, evil counselling, and all manner of misusing of our tongue, to the hurt of our neighbours, whether it be in their body and goods, or in their good name and fame. The apostle St. James likeneth the tongue of a man unto a bit in a horse's mouth, which turneth the whole horse every way, as pleaseth him that sitteth on the horse's back. And he compareth it also unto the helm of a ship, whereby all the whole ship is ruled at the pleasure of him that governeth the helm. And thirdly he compareth it unto a sparkle of fire, which (if it be suffered) will burn up a whole town or city (James 3:3-6). And surely all these comparisons be very apt and meet. For the tongue of a man (no doubt) is the chief stay of all the whole body, either to do much good, or else to do much hurt. The voice of the tongue pierceth the hearts of the hearers, and causeth them to conceive of other men good or evil opinion; it kindleth or quencheth contention; it disposeth men to war or peace; and moveth the hearers sundry ways to goodness or vice. And like as the great rageous flames, that go from house to house, come but of one sparkle, which in the beginning might have been easily quenched, but by negligence and sufferance increaseth and waxeth so great that no man can resist it; and like as fire is a great commodity many ways, (if it be well and wisely used,) and contrary, an utter destruction, if it be suffered, and no heed taken thereunto; even so of a man's tongue, (although it be but a very small member of the body,) yet there cometh exceeding great benefit, both to himself and others, if it be well and wisely governed. And contrariwise, if no heed be taken thereunto, but it be suffered to run at large, then it is not one single evil alone, but a root and occasion, or rather an heaping together of all evils. And because that of the tongue cometh so much good or so much evil, therefore by this commandment is not only forbid all evil use of the tongue, to the hurt of our neighbours, but also in the same is commanded all the good use of the tongue, to the benefit of our said neighbours. As, to be true and plain in our words; to be faithful in covenants, bargains, and promises; to testify the truth in all courts, judgments, and other places; to report well of them that be absent; to use gentle words to them that be present; to give good counsel and exhortation to all goodness; to dissuade from all evil; and when we know any man to do amiss, not to publish his fault to other men, to his hinderance and slander, but rather to admonish him privily between him and us, and to seek his reformation; to speak well by our enemies; to pacify and set at one them that be enemies; to excuse them and to answer for them that be unjustly slandered; and generally in all other things to use our tongues in truth to the wealth of our neighbours.

Second, we think it convenient, that all bishops and preachers shall instruct and teach the people committed unto their spiritual charge, that against this commandment offend all they, which, by lying and uttering of false speech, deceive and hurt any man; and such liars be the devil's children. For, as St. John saith in his Gospel, The devil is a liar, and the father of liars (John 8:44). And therefore biddeth St. Paul that we should put away lying, and speak truth every man to his neighbour (Eph 4:25).

Item, That all they offend against this commandment which be detracters, backbiters, and slanderers; whom the Wise Man doth liken unto serpents, that privily bite or sting men behind, when they be not aware thereof (Eccl 8:11). And surely such men (whatsoever they pretend) go not about to heal and amend them that do amiss, but rather to satisfy their own malice and slanderous tongues. For like as a surgeon that will heal a wound doth cover it and bind it that it take no open air; so if we intend the amendment of our neighbour's fault, we must not open it abroad to his hurt, but we must be sorry, and pray to God for him; and so taking him unto us, we must privily counsel and exhort him. And no doubt this loving correction will make him beware and take heed that he offend no more. But if we tell his defaults first to one and after to another, and charge every one to keep counsel, as though we had told it to no mo; this is no amendment of his fault, but a declaration of our own, and a reprehension of ourselves, in that we utter forth unto other that thing which we ourselves judge not to be uttered. And surely we condemn ourselves therein. For we should first have kept it secret ourselves, if we would that another man should not utter the same. And therefore the Wise Man saith, If thou hast heard any thing against thy neighbour, let it die within thee, and be sure it will not burst thee (Sir 19:10). And against backbiters speaketh the prophet David, Whosoever privily slandereth his neighbour, him will I destroy (Ps 101:5).

And they also offend this commandment which gladly give ears and be ready to hear such backbiters. For as St. Bernard saith, Like as the backbiter carrieth the devil in his mouth, so the hearer carrieth the devil in his ear. For the detracter is not glad to tell but to him that is glad to hear. And the Wise Man saith, That like as the wind driveth away the rain, even so doth an hard and a displeasant countenance drive away the tongue of the backbiters, and maketh them abashed (Prov 25:23).

They also break this commandment which with flattering and double tongues go about to please such as be glad to hear complaints.

Judges also which give sentence contrary to that which they know to be true; and they that in judgment do hide and suppress the truth; and they that make any false pleas, to the delay and hinderance of justice, or any otherwise do stop justice; and inquests, which upon light grounds, or upon grounds not well examined or discussed, give verdict, be transgressors and breakers of this commandment.

And above other they do transgress this commandment, which in preaching or otherwise do teach or maintain any false or erroneous doctrine, contrary to the word of God, or that do teach fables or men's fantasies and imaginations, affirming them to be the word of God. For such be not false witness of worldly matters, but false witness of God.

The Declaration of the Tenth Commandment

Thou shalt not desire thy neighbour's house, his wife, his servant, his maid, his ox, his ass, ne any other thing that is his.

As concerning the tenth Commandment, we think it convenient, that all bishops and preachers shall instruct and teach the people committed unto their spiritual charge, first, that whereas in the other commandments before rehearsed, be forbidden all words, deeds, and counsel which be against God's pleasure and the love of our neighbours; in this last precept be forbidden the inward affections of our hearts. For in this last precept is forbid all inward motion, desire, delight, inclination, and affection unto evil; which things be so rooted and planted in all us the children of Adam, even from the first hour of our birth, that although by the inspiration of the Holy Ghost, and the grace of

God given unto us, we do intend never so well, and would most gladly eschew all evil, yet there remaineth in us a disposition and readiness unto such things as be contrary to the will and commandment of God. Insomuch that if the grace of God did not help us to stay and resist our own naughtiness and delight unto sin, the same our concupiscence and naughtiness should be so much, that we should run headlong into all mischief, and that at every light occasion; our nature is so corrupt, and we be so far from the perfect obedience unto God's will, which we had in the state of innocency, and yet still ought to have. And of this corruption of our nature and readiness unto evil complaineth St. Paul, in his Epistle unto the Romans, where he declareth at length, that the nature of man is so full of concupiscence and evil affections, that no man doth or can of himself satisfy or fulfil the law of God; and that the law condemneth all men as transgressors; and that therefore every man for his salvation must have refuge unto the grace and mercy of God, obtained by our Saviour Jesu Christ. I know (saith St. Paul) that in me, that is to say in my flesh, dwelleth no goodness. For I have a good will, but I find not how to perform it. For I do not that good thing which I would, but I do that evil which I would not. And if I do that I would not, then it is not I that do it, but sin that dwelleth in me. Thus find I by the law, that when I would do good, evil is present with me; for delight in the law of God as concerning mine inward man: but I see another law in the parts of my body, which rebelleth continually against the law of my mind, and subdueth me unto the law of sin, which is in the parts of my body. O wretched man that I am! who shall deliver me from this body of death? The grace of God by Jesu Christ (Rom 7:18-25).

By these words of St. Paul it appeareth what concupiscence, corruption, and evil resteth continually in the nature of man; by reason whereof, though he be never so well minded, yet he is stayed, letted, and hindered from, the perfect accomplishment of God's will and commandments.

Second, we think it convenient, that all bishops and preachers shall instruct and teach the people committed unto their spiritual charge, that notwithstanding that this corruption and concupiscence be damnable in all them that be not baptized, although they never commit any actual offence, yet unto us that be renewed by baptism in the right faith of Christ, it is neither damnable nor yet culpable, if we by the Spirit and grace of God endeavour and apply ourselves to withstand and resist it, and do not give ourselves to live after the motions and desires thereof. And there-fore St. Paul (upon the words before rehearsed) inferreth and saith, That there is no damnation now unto them that be in Christ Jesu, which walk not after the flesh but after the Spirit (Rom 8:1). And anon after he saith, If you live after the flesh, you shall die; but if by the Spirit you mortify the deeds of the body, you shall live (8:13).

Thirdly, we think it convenient, that all bishops and preachers shall instruct and teach the people committed unto their spiritual charge, that like as in the fifth commandment, under the name of *father* and *mother,* is understand all superiors; and in the sixth commandment, under the name of *killing,* is understand all wrath and revenging; and in the seventh commandment, under the name of *adultery,* is understand all unchaste living; and in the eighth commandment, under the name of *theft,* is under-stand all deceitful dealing with our neighbours; and in the ninth com-mandment, under the name of *false witness,* is understand all misuse of the tongue: so in this last commandment, under the name of *desiring of an-other man's wife and goods,* is understand all manner of evil and unlawful desire of any thing. And like as in this precept is forbid all evil desires, even so in the same be commanded all good desires, good affections, good incli-nations to godly things, and the perfect obedience of our hearts unto God's will; which although we shall not fully and absolutely attain unto while we be in this life, yet this commandment doth bind us to enforce and endeavour ourselves thereunto by continual resisting and fighting against the said corruption, concupiscence, and evil desires. Forasmuch as they be the very root and spring from whence doth flow and grow all evil deeds and vicious living; as Christ saith in the Gospel, From the heart springeth all evil thoughts, murder, adultery, fornication, theft, false wit-ness, blasphemy (Matt 15:19). And the same is shewed daily by experience. For when a man desireth another man's goods, if he cannot have them, then he falleth into envy, and grudgeth against them that have such goods, and desireth evil towards them, and is glad when they have loss or hurt. All which evil affections proceed of the said unlawful desire. For, as St. Paul saith, Such as be not content, but desire to be rich, they fall into divers temptations and snares of the devil, and into many noisome and unprof-itable wishes and desires, which drowneth men into perdition and destruc-tion. For the root of all evil is cupidity, or unlawful desire of goods in this world. And such persons as have much followed this covetousness have erred from the faith, and wrapped themselves in many pangs and sorrows (1 Tim 6:9-10).

Fourthly, we think it convenient, that all bishops and preachers shall instruct and teach the people committed unto their spiritual charge, that all manner of men be in such wise culpable of the transgression of this commandment, that no man can justify himself in the sight of God. For God looketh through every man's heart, and findeth therein much corruption and concupiscence, although in some more, some less, according as they have more or less mortified their said fleshly and worldly concupiscence. And if there were no more commandments of God but this one, yet is there no man in this world, but (if he diligently ensearch his own heart, and confer it with this commandment) he shall anon perceive that he is many ways culpable and guilty before God, by transgressions of this commandment, if God should enter into strait judgment with him, and deal with him according to justice without mercy. But among all other, they chiefly be transgressors of this commandment, which, by deliberation and full consent, cast their minds and studies to accomplish the concupiscence and desire which they have to obtain and get another man's wife, child, servant, house, land, corn, cattle, or any thing or goods that be his.

And they also be transgressors of this commandment, which by envy be sorry of their neighbour's wealth and prosperity, or be glad of their sorrow, hinderance, or adversity; and also all they which do not set their minds and studies to preserve, maintain, and defend unto their neighbours (as much as lieth in them) their wives, children, servants, houses, lands, goods, and all that is theirs. For (as before is declared) this commandment not only forbiddeth us to desire from our neighbour any thing which is his, but by the same we be also commanded gladly to wish and will unto him that he may quietly possess and enjoy all that God hath sent him, be it never so great abundance. And this mind we ought to bear unto every man by this commandment, not only if they be our friends and lovers, but also if they be our enemies and adversaries.

Here followeth certain Notes necessary to be learned for the better understanding of the Ten Commandments.

First, it is to be noted, how that our Lord not only delivered unto Moses, when he was in the mount of Sinai, two tables of stone, wherein these Ten Commandments were written with God's own finger, and not by Moses, ne any other creature; but also how, in the same place, and at the same time, God threatened to punish all them grievously and extremely, yea to the third and fourth generation, which should transgress any of the said commandments: and contrary, how he promised to shew mercy and to give life everlasting to all them that should observe and keep the same (Exod 19, 20); which thing was afterward confirmed by our Saviour Christ. For when a certain great man asked him, what he should do to come unto the life everlasting, Christ answered him and said, If thou wilt come unto the kingdom of heaven, keep the commandments (Luke 18:20).

Second, it is to be noted, that all the works of mercy, and all good things which we be bound to do, and likewise all sins which we be bound to eschew and leave undone, be sufficiently contained and comprised in these two tables. For whereas our whole office and duty, as well to God as to our neighbour, standeth in heart, word, and deed; the first four precepts, which be the precepts of the first table, contain our said whole duty towards God. The six other precepts, which be precepts of the second table, contain our whole duty towards our neighbour. For the first commandment chiefly sheweth how we ought to order ourselves unto God in our hearts by pure faith, hope, love, and dread. The second and fourth sheweth how we ought to order ourselves unto him in our outward acts and deeds. The third sheweth how we ought to order ourselves unto him in our tongue and words. And likewise the fifth, the sixth, the seventh, and eighth do shew how we should order our outward acts and deeds unto our neighbours; the ninth, how we should order our words and tongues unto them; and the tenth, how we should be towards them in heart and mind.

Thirdly, it is to be noted, that forasmuch as out of a good heart, endued and replenished with the love of God and our neighbour, springeth forth all good words and works; and out of an evil heart, void of the love and dread of God, and replenished with hate and malice towards our neighbour, springeth forth all evil words and works, according to the saying of our Saviour in the Gospel, where he saith, That a good man out of the good treasure of his heart bringeth forth all those things that be good; and an evil man out of the evil treasure of his heart bringeth forth those things that be evil: therefore our Saviour Christ reduceth all these ten commandments unto two commandments, belonging to the heart, that is to say, to the love of God and our neighbour (Matt 12:35). For whereas the Pharisees came unto Christ and said, Master, which is the greatest commandment of the law? our Saviour answered them and said, The chief and greatest commandment is, that thou shalt love thy Lord God with all thy heart, with all thy soul, and with all thy mind. And the second, like to this, is, that thou shalt love thy neighbour even as thyself. And in these two commandments standeth and consisteth all the whole law and the prophets (Matt 22:37-40).

These be the words of Christ; wherein it is further to be noted, that to love our Lord God with all our heart, soul, and mind, is to set all our whole mind and thought to know him, to honour him, to please him, and to love him unfeignedly above all other things in the world. For he is a jealous God, and will not be content, unless we yield unto him our whole heart and love. And if we shall set or fix any part of our heart or love upon the world or the flesh, no doubt God will not be partaker of our love. For he requireth the whole love of our hearts, and that we shall love nothing but him or for him; and that so heartily, that (if case require) we shall not refuse to suffer any bodily punishment, nor yet death for his sake. And this love towards him we do declare, when we set our minds to observe and fulfil his commandments. For, as Christ saith in the Gospel, He that hath my commandments, and keepeth them, it is he that loveth me (John 14:21). And contrary, the love and charity of God and our neighbour (as St. Paul saith) is the fulfilling of all the whole law (Rom 13:10). For no doubt if we love God above all things, then we love him more than ourselves. And if we love him more than ourselves, then will we follow in all things his will, and not our own. And in like manner, if we love God above all things, then do we love him above our neighbour, and so we will for nothing fulfil the will of our neighbour against his will. And as the love of God above all things should so keep, direct, and guide us, that for no love or pleasure to ourselves or to our neighbour we should willingly transgress the least part of any of the ten commandments; in likewise the hearty and fervent love that we should bear to our neighbour as to ourselves, should preserve and keep us, that we should not kill him, nor commit adultery with his wife, nor steal his goods, nor bear false witness against him, nor by any means do, speak, or wish any manner of evil unto him; but we should with heart, tongue, and hands, wish, speak, and work all goodness towards him, as St. Paul saith, He that loveth his neighbour hath fulfilled the law. For these commandments—Thou shalt not commit adultery, Thou shalt not kill, Thou shalt not steal, Thou shalt not bear false witness, Thou shalt not desire, and such other commandments—be all comprised in this saying, Thou shalt love thy neighbour as thyself. For if we love our neighbour as ourselves, then must we use ourselves towards him as we would that he should use himself towards us; that is to say, we must do for him as we of reason will and desire that he should do for us, and desire and wish towards him as we of reason would that he should desire and wish towards us. This is the law of nature, this is the law of the gospel. And therefore let us keep these two commandments, and then we shall keep the whole law. For, as St. Paul saith, The fulfilling of the law is love and charity.

Fourthly, it is to be noted, that there be three considerations, for the which all true Christian men ought to employ their labour and diligence to know these ten commandments. The first consideration is, for that in these commandments God hath sufficiently declared unto us his will and pleasure, as well what he would have us to do, as what he would have us not to do. The second consideration is, for that we may know hereby our infirmity, sin, and damnation. For when we look earnestly upon these commandments of God, and consider what things God requireth of us in them, we shall see ourselves as in a mirror or glass, and shall easily perceive how far we be from the true and perfect observing of the same commandments, and so we shall perceive our own defaults, our own misery, naughtiness, and our own damnable estate, as St. Paul saith, By the law of the commandments we may know our sins (Rom 3:20). The third consideration is, for that by these commandments we may also attain the knowledge of God's mercy. For when we perceive that of ourselves we have no strength, goodness, or life eternal, but weakness, sin, and everlasting death; then we may evidently see how much need we have of the mercy of God, and to have a Saviour and Redeemer to pay a ransom for our sins, and to deliver us from everlasting captivity, damnation, and death, due unto us for the same. And therefore St. Paul saith, The law was our schoolmaster, conductor, and leader unto Christ, that we might be justified by faith, that is to say, by God's mercy, which Christ obtained for us (Gal 3:24).

Fifthly, it is to be noted, that although these laws and commandments of God teach us what is good, and what we should do to please God, yet they give not unto us strength and power to do the same; but all such strength cometh of God, by his singular grace and gift. And therefore, as Almighty God taught us by his prophet Moses what we should do, so he taught us by his Son Jesu Christ what we should ask. For as these Ten Commandments do teach us what is God's will, so the Paternoster teacheth us, that we should daily and continually pray to the Father of heaven, that it may please him to give us his help and grace to do all his will, that is to say, to do all that is good, and eschew that is evil. For surely God commandeth us things which we of ourselves cannot do, because we might learn what of him we should ask. And therefore, after the declaration of these Ten Commandments, in manner as is before expressed, we shall descend now unto the declaration of the Paternoster.

The Exposition of the Paternoster and the Ave Maria

The Paternoster Divided into Seven Petitions

1. Our Father that art in heaven, thy name be hallowed.
2. Thy kingdom come unto us.
3. Thy will be done and fulfilled in earth, as it is in heaven.
4. Give us this day our daily bread.
5. And forgive us our trespasses, as we forgive them that trespass against us.
6. And lead us not into temptation.
7. But deliver us from the evil. Amen.

The Sense and Interpretation of the First Petition

Our Father that art in heaven, thy name be hallowed.

O God Almighty, our most dear heavenly Father, which of thine infinite benevolence and only mercy hast taught and commanded us, by thy only and dear beloved Son Jesu Christ, to believe constantly that for his sake thou hast admitted us into the number of thy children, and made us the very inheritors of thy kingdom, (whereas in deed thou mightest of justice and good right have utterly renounced and refused us for thy children, and have been a strait and a grievous judge against us sinners, forasmuch, as we

166

have so oft and so abominably offended and transgressed thy godly and most holy will, and have given thee so just occasion of displeasure against us:) lo here we now thy children, having conceived in our hearts firm and steadfast trust of thy fatherly love towards us, and lamenting in our hearts to see how many ways thy godly name is dishonoured and blasphemed here in this vale of misery; we most humbly, and even from the root and bottom of our hearts, beseech and pray thee, that thy name may be hallowed, honoured, praised, and glorified among us here in this world. Make (we beseech thee) that all witchcrafts and false charms may be utterly abolished among us. Cause all conjurations, by the which Satan or other creatures be enchanted, to cease by thy blessed name. Make that all false faith, by the which men either mistrust thee, or put their confidence in any other thing than in thee, may be destroyed. Make that all heresies and false doctrines may vanish away, and that thy word may be truly taught and set forth unto all the world, and that all infidels may receive the same, and be converted unto the right catholic faith. Make that we be not deceived by hypocrisy, or counterfeiting of truth, of righteousness, or of holiness. Make that no man swear in vain by thy name, or abuse thy name to lie or to deceive his neighbour. Keep us from pride, and from the vain ambition and desire of worldly glory and fame. Keep us from all envy, malice, covetousness, adultery, gluttony, sloth, from backbiting and slandering of our neighbours, and from all other evil and wicked thoughts and deeds, whereby thy name may be dishonoured and blasphemed. Grant us, that in all perils and dangers we may run unto thee, as unto our only refuge, and call upon thy holy name. Grant that in our good words and works we may only please and magnify thee. Keep us from the most damnable sin of unkindness towards thee. Grant that we which do already profess thy right faith may still continue in the same, and may declare and express the same, as well in our outward conversation, as in professing the same with our mouth. Grant that by our good life and our good works all other may be moved to good; and that by our evil works and sins no man may take occasion to slander thy name, or diminish thy laud and praise. Keep us that we desire nothing which should not return to the honour and praise of thy name: and if we ask any such thing, hear not our foolishness. Make that our life be such, that we may be truly found thy children in deed, and that we shall not in vain call thee our Father; but that in all things we may study and seek for the honour and glory of thy name.

For the better and more ample declaration of this first petition, we think it convenient, that all bishops and preachers shall instruct and teach the people committed unto their spiritual charge, first, that our Saviour Jesu Christ was the author and maker of the Paternoster. And that therefore, like as he was of infinite wisdom and of infinite love and charity towards us, even so all Christian men ought to think and believe, that the same prayer is the most excellent, and the most sufficient, and most perfect of all others. And surely so it is in very deed. For neither there is any thing in this prayer superfluous, neither there wanteth any petition, suit, or request, which may be necessary for our journey and passage in this world, or for our furtherance to the attaining of the life and glory everlasting.

Second, that every good Christian man may be assured to attain his requests made in this prayer, if he shall enforce himself, and apply his whole heart and will to the will and grace of him unto whom this prayer is made, and also if he shall utter and offer the said petitions inwardly with his heart, and with such confidence and trust in God as he requireth. For surely no prayer is thankful unto God, but that which springeth from the heart. And therefore the prophet David crieth to our Lord with all his heart (Ps 9, 119, 138; Prov 3; Wisd 8; Matt 7). And Moses is noted to cry out aloud, when he spake no word with his mouth, but he spake aloud in his heart. And our Lord by his prophet noteth, that some pray with their lips, and, in their heart, mind nothing less than that which they pray for (Isa 29:13; Matt 15:8). And therefore whosoever intendeth by saying of this Paternoster to attain that he desireth in the same, he must first hear himself, and understand what he saith, and so conjoin the word of his mouth with the same word in his heart, and say, as the prophet David said, The hymns and praisings which I shall yield to the good Lord, shall issue out from the inward lips of my heart to the lips of my mouth, when I shall sing lauds and praises unto thee (Ps 71:23; 19:14).

Thirdly, that all Christian men ought to conceive great comfort and joy, in that they be taught and commanded in this prayer to take Almighty God for their Father, and so to call him. If our sovereign lord the king would say to any of us, Take me for your father, and so call me; what joy in heart, what comfort, what confidence would we conceive of so favourable and gracious words. Much more then incomparably have we cause to rejoice that the King and Prince of all princes sheweth unto us this grace and goodness, to make us his children. And surely, as the natural son may assuredly trust that his father will do for him all things that may be for his setting forth and advancement; even so we may undoubtedly assure ourselves, that having Almighty God to our Father, we shall lack nothing, neither in this world nor in the world to come, which may be profitable and expedient for us towards the everlasting inheritance which our heavenly Father hath prepared for us.

Fourthly, that like as this word *Father* declareth the great benevolence, mercy, and love of God towards us, so it admonisheth us again of our duty towards him, and how we be bound to shew again unto him our whole hearty love, and our obedience, and readiness to fulfil all his precepts and commandments with all gladness and humility. And therefore whosoever presumeth to come to God with this prayer, and to call him *Father*, and yet hath not full intent and purpose to use himself in all things like a kind and an obedient son, he cometh to him as Judas came to Christ with a kiss, pretending to be his friend and his servant in calling him Master, and yet he was indeed a traitor to him and a deadly enemy. And for this consideration every Christian man that intendeth to make this prayer, ought inwardly and throughoutly to ensearch and examine himself. And if he find in himself any notable crime, for the which he may be ashamed to call God his Father, let him accuse himself thereof to God, and recognise his unworthiness, saying, as the prodigal son said, Father, I have offended thee; I am not worthy to be called thy son (Luke 15:19). And with entire repentance, and with firm purpose and intent to amend his naughty life, let him lift up his heart unto his celestial Father, and let him call for his grace of reconciliation; and then let him boldly say this Paternoster.

Fifthly, that in these words, *Our Father,* is signified, that we ought to believe, not only that Almighty God is the common Father of all Christian people, and equally and indifferently regardeth the rich and the poor, the free and the bond, the lord and the subject, but also that all Christian people be Christ's own brethren, and the very coinheritors and compartioners with him in the kingdom of heaven; and finally, that all Christian men be brethren together, and have all one Father, which is God Almighty (Eph 4:6). And that therefore we ought not only to be of one spirit towards our said Father, and to employ and endeavour ourselves to the uttermost to please him and to keep his laws and commandments, but we ought also each to consent with other in perfect love and charity, and each to help and further other towards our said inheritance in heaven, and finally in all our prayers to God, each to comprise other, and to pray for other: like as in this Paternoster we be taught to say, *Our* Father, give *us our* bread, forgive *us our* sins, suffer *us* not to fall in temptation, and deliver *us* from evil.

Sixthly, by these words, *which art in heaven*, we be taught, that we ought to have, not only an inward desire and a great care and study to come to that place where our heavenly Father is, but also an inward sorrow and grief that we be so long kept from the presence of our heavenly Father, and be subject here unto so manifold cures and thoughts, to so many troubles and misery, and to so many and so grievous perils and dangers of the world, of sin, and of the devil. For like as a loving child is ever desirous to be where his father is, and if his father shall depart to any place, he will lament and be sorry, unless he may go with him, and in his absence he will mourn, and at his return he will be joyful; even so ought we desire ever to be with our heavenly Father; and to see that our conversation be all withdrawn from the world, the flesh, and the devil, and be set in heaven and heavenly things, as St. Paul saith (Eph 4:22; Phil 3:20). And we ought continually to wail and lament, because we be not with our heavenly Father, saying with the prophet, Woeful am I, that my dwelling upon the earth is so much prolonged (Ps 120:6).

The Sense and Interpretation of the Second Petition

Thy kingdom come unto us. O God Almighty, our most merciful Father, we thy wretched children most humbly beseech and pray thee, help us by thy grace, not only that we may attain and come to thy kingdom in heaven after this mortal life, but also that in this present life we may be delivered from the kingdom and power of the devil and sin, and that we may live under thy dominion and kingdom, which is the kingdom of innocency and grace. We confess and knowledge our folly, our blindness, yea and our extreme unkindness towards thee our most merciful Father, in that we have so willingly and gladly forsaken thee, so mighty and so gracious a King, and have given ourselves to serve the devil, which hath ever hated us, and like a most cruel and wicked tyrant hath ever vexed and troubled us, nor never goeth about any other thing but to destroy us:

whereas thou, our merciful Father, hast created and made us when we were nothing, hast redeemed us when we were damned, and hast ordained everlasting life for us, when for our sins we should have been judged to everlasting death. And therefore, considering now this our own madness and ingratitude, and being weary of this miserable thraldom and bondage which we sustain under this kingdom of the devil and sin; help us (we pray thee) most dear Father, that we may escape from out of this most wretched thraldom and captivity, and that we may be subject unto thy kingdom. Give us before all things true and constant faith in thee, and in thy Son Jesu Christ, and in the Holy Ghost. Give us pure love and charity towards thee and all men. Keep us from infidelity, desperation, and malice, which might be the cause of our destruction. Deliver us from dissensions, covetousness, lechery, and all evil desires and lusts of sin. Make the virtue of thy kingdom so to come and to reign within us, that all our heart, mind, and wits, with all our strength inward and outward, may suffer themselves to be ruled by thee, to serve thee, to observe thy commandments and thy will; not themselves, the flesh, the world, or the devil. Make that thy kingdom, once in us begun, may be daily increased, and go forward more and more. Suffer not the subtle and secret hate or sloth which we have to goodness to rule so in us, that it shall cause us to look back again, and to fall into sin. Give us a stable purpose and strength, not only to begin the life of innocency in thy kingdom, but also to proceed earnestly in it, and to perform it. Lighten our eyes, lest we sleep or be weary in good life once begun, and so suffer our enemy to bring us again under his power (Ps 13:3-4). Grant that we may continue in goodness; and that after this kingdom, which is begun in this life, we may come unto thy heavenly kingdom, which endureth ever.

For the better understanding of this second petition, we think it convenient, that all bishops and preachers shall instruct and teach the people committed unto their spiritual charge, that this second petition is very necessary. For no doubt our ancient enemy the devil goeth about continually by all craft and means to deceive us, and to bring us under his power and dominion. And surely, so long as pride or disobedience reigneth in us; so long as ire, envy, wrath, or covetousness reigneth in us; so long as sloth, gluttony, lechery, or any kind of sin reigneth in us; so long we be under the dominion and kingdom of the devil. For the devil (undoubtedly) is king over all the children of pride, that is to say, over all them that be sinners, rebels, and disobedient unto God. And forasmuch as it is not in our powers to deliver ourselves from under this tyranny of the devil, but only by God's help, (for our perdition and undoing is of ourselves, but our help and salvation is only of God, as saith the prophet Hosea,) therefore is it very necessary for all true Christian people to make this petition incessantly unto our heavenly Father, and to beseech him, according to this doctrine of Christ, that by his grace and help we may escape the dominion and power of the devil, and that we may be made subject unto his heavenly kingdom (Hos 13:9).

The Sense and Interpretation of the Third Petition

Thy will be done and fulfilled in earth, as it is in heaven.

Father, grant us, we beseech thee, that like as thy holy angels and saints in heaven, in whom thou reignest perfectly and holy, do never cease, ne shall cease to glorify thee, and praise thee, and to fulfil thy will and pleasure in all things, and that most readily and gladly, without any manner of grudging or resisting thereunto, knowing certainly and clearly that thy will is alway best; even so we thy children here on earth may daily and continually praise thee by our holy conversation in good works and good life, and that we may from time to time so mortify our own carnal affections and evil desires, and so renounce and deny our own corrupt and sinful appetite and will, that we may be ever ready, like loving children, humbly, lowly, and obediently to approve, allow, and accomplish thy will in all things, and to submit ourselves with all our heart unto the same; and to knowledge, that whatsoever is thy will, the same is most perfect, most just, most holy, and most expedient for the wealth and health of our souls. Give us true and stable patience, when our will is letten and broken. Grant us, that when any man speaketh or doth any thing contrary to our will, that therefore we be not out of patience, neither curse or murmur. Grant that we seek not vengeance against our adversaries, or them which let our will; but that we may say well of them, and do good to them. Endue us with thy grace, that we may gladly suffer all diseases, poverty, despisings, persecutions, and adversities, knowing that it is thy will that we should crucify and mortify our wills. Make us that we impute not to the devil or evil men, when any adversity chanceth unto us; but that we may attribute all unto thy godly will, and give thee thanks therefore, which dost ordain all such things for our weal and benefit. Give us grace, that whensoever it shall please thee to call us out of this transitory life, we may be willing to die, and that for thy will we may take our death gladly; so that by fear or infirmity we be not made disobedient unto thee. Make that all our members, eyes, tongue, heart, hand, and feet be not suffered to follow their desires; but that all may be used to thy will and pleasure. Give us grace, that we maliciously rejoice not in their troubles, which have resisted our will, or have hurted us; nor that we be enviously sorry when they prosper, and have welfare. And finally, that we may be contented and pleased with all thing that is thy will.

For the better understanding of this third petition, we think it convenient, that all bishops and preachers shall instruct and teach the people committed unto their spiritual charge, how that by the occasion and ever sith the disobedience and sin of our first father Adam, the will of man hath been so corrupted with original sin, that we be all utterly inclined to disobey the will and precepts of God, and so to love ourselves and our own wills, that without a special grace and a singular inspiration of God, we cannot heartily love neither God nor man, but in respect to ourselves, as we may have benefit and commodity by them.

Item, That we have this corruption in our nature, and this inordinate love of ourselves, from Adam, as it were by inheritance; and that it goeth from one to another, from the fathers and mothers unto the children, as soon as they be conceived within their mothers' wombs. For as the children take of their parents their original and natural qualities and conditions, even so they receive with the same this original corruption of nature, which cometh by original sin. And though the parents be never so clean purged and pardoned of their original sin, by baptism, and by the grace and mercy of God, and be drawn up from the love of themselves and of these worldly things unto the pure love of God; yet nevertheless the children of them begotten be conceived and born in original sin and corruption, loving themselves better than God or man. Like as corn, though it be never so clean winnowed and purged from chaff, yet if it be sown, the young seed is full of chaff again, until it be winnowed and made clean: even so be the children born full of chaff and corruption of original sin, until that by baptism in the blood of our Saviour Jesu Christ they be washed and purged, as their parents were.

Item, That so long as we be in this mortal life, we shall never be so clean purged from this concupiscence, and this inordinate love of ourselves and of this world, and of worldly things and pleasures, but some root will ever remain of this corrupt weed; which (if the grace of God help us not, and we also apply not all our forces to mortify and overcome the same) no doubt will so overgrow the whole garden of our heart, that there shall be left no good herb therein, but it shall be so overgrown with the love of ourselves and of this world, that the love of God and our neighbour shall continually decay from time to time, and at length it shall grow not only to a negligence and a small regarding, but also unto an utter contempt both of God and of our neighbour; and then we shall appertain wholly unto the city of the devil. For, as St. Austin saith, There be in this world two cities: the one builded by God, in the which he reigneth as a most gracious Lord and King: the other is builded by the devil, wherein the devil reigneth as a most merciless and cruel tyrant. The city of God consisteth and is inhabited of them which love God so much, that for to accomplish his will and commandments they be content to refuse their own wills and pleasures. The city of the devil hath inhabitants all such as love themselves so much, that (for to have their own wills and pleasures here in this world) they care not or little regard the will, pleasure, and commandments of God. And therefore surely we have great need continually to pray (according to Christ's doctrine in this third petition) for aid unto our heavenly Father, that being thus clothed and encumbered with this corruptible flesh here in this world, (which dulleth and draweth down man's mind, as the Wise Man saith,) it may please him to grant us the grace, that so long as we live here we may fulfil his will in all things, and not our own, and so to have a dwelling-place in his city. And contrary, that the devil may never have power to take us, and to bring us unto his city and possession.

The Sense and Interpretation of the Fourth Petition

Give us this day our daily bread. O our heavenly Father, we beseech thee give us this day our daily bread. Give us meat, drink, and clothing for our bodies. Send us increase of corn, fruit, and cattle. Give us health and strength, rest and peace, that we may lead a peaceable and a quiet life in all godliness and honesty. Grant us good success in all our business, and help in adversity and peril. Grant us, we beseech thee, all things convenient for our necessity in this temporal life. And to them, to whom thou dost vouchsafe to give more than their own portion necessary for their vocation and degree, give thy grace, that they may be thy diligent and true dispensators and stewards, to distribute that they have (over and above that is necessary, considering their estate and degree) to them that have need of it. For so (good Lord) thou dost provide for thy poor people that have nothing, by them which have of thy gift sufficient to relieve themselves and other. And give also thy grace to us, that we have not too much solicitude and care for these transitory and unstable things; but that our hearts may be fixed in things which be eternal, and in thy kingdom, which is everlasting. And yet moreover (good Lord) not only give us our necessaries, but also conserve that thou dost give us, and cause that it may come to our use, and by us to the poor people, for whom by us thou hast provided. Give us grace, that we may be fed and nourished with all the life of Christ, that is to say, both his words and works; and that they may be to us an effectual example and spectacle of all virtues. Grant that all they that preach thy word may profitably and godly preach thee and thy Son Jesu Christ through all the world; and that all we which hear thy word preached may so be fed therewith, that not only we may outwardly receive the same, but also digest it within our hearts; and that it may so work and feed every part of us, that it may appear in all the acts and deeds of our life. Grant that the holy sacrament of the altar, which is the bread of life, and the very flesh and blood of thy Son Jesu Christ, may be purely ministered and distributed, to the comfort and benefit of all us thy people; and that we also may receive the same with a right faith and perfect charity, at all times when we ought to receive the same; and specially against our death, and departing out of this world, so that we may be then spiritually fed with the same to our salvation, and thereby enjoy the life everlasting. Give us an inward hunger and thirst to have thy word, and the righteous living taught in the same. Grant this also, merciful Father, that all false doctrines contrary to thy word, which feedeth not, but poisoneth and killeth the soul, may be utterly extinct and cast away out of thy church, so that we may be fed as well with the true doctrine of thy word, as with all other things necessary for us in this life.

For the better understanding of this fourth petition, we think it convenient, that all bishops and preachers shall instruct and teach the people committed unto their spiritual charge, first, how that our Lord teacheth us not
in this petition to ask any superfluous things, or things of pleasure or delight, but only things sufficient. And therefore he biddeth us only ask
bread, wherein is not meant superfluous riches, or great substance, or
abundance of things above our estate and condition, but such things only
as be necessary and sufficient for every man in his degree. And that this is
the meaning of this word, St. Paul declareth at good length, where he saith,
We have brought nothing into this world, ne shall take any thing with us
when we shall depart hence. And therefore if we have meat and drink, and
clothes, that is to say, things sufficient, we ought to hold ourselves content. For they that set their minds on riches, and will have superfluities
more than needeth or is expedient to their vocation, they fall into dangerous temptations, and into the snares of the devil, and into many, and unprofitable, and noisome desires, which drown men into perdition and
everlasting damnation; for the spring and root of all evils is such superfluous desire (1 Tim 6:7-10). The Wise Man also, making his suit to our Lord,
saith, Give me neither poverty ne excess, but only things sufficient for my
living, lest that having too much, I be provoked to deny God, and to forget
who is the Lord: and, on the other side, lest that by poverty constrained, I
fall unto theft, and forswear the name of my God (Prov 30:8-9). These
two wise men, the one of the Old and the other of the New Testament,
agree with the lesson of our Saviour. Both ask bread, that is, things necessary, and both refuse and renounce superfluities, as things unprofitable,
dangerous, and noisome.

Second, that in these words of our Saviour Jesu Christ be reproved all
those persons which eat not their own bread, but devoureth other men's
bread. Of which sort be all those which live of ravin and spoils, of theft, of
extortion, of craft, and deceit.

Item, All they which neither labour with their hands, nor otherwise
apply their study, industry, and diligence to something which is good and
beneficial in the common weal, and to the honour of God, but live in ease,
rest, idleness, and wanton pleasures, without doing or caring for any such
thing.

Item, All they which being called in this world unto any room, office, or authority, do abuse the same, and do not employ themselves according to their vocation.

Thirdly, that although we be bound by labour or other lawful means to provide for ourselves from time to time a sufficient living, yet we must surely believe and trust that our Father in heaven provideth for us also, and that all our own provision and industry is in vain without his provision. For it is he that giveth unto us and taketh from us at his pleasure more or less. Therefore, notwithstanding all our own labour, industry, and diligence, yet we must thank him for all that we have; of him must we hang; in him must we cast our whole hope and trust that he shall send us sufficient, and in no wise mistrust him. For if he provide sufficiently for all fishes and birds, and other creatures, which labour not for their living as we do, how much more ought we, being his own children, and also using all labour and diligence to get our livings, to trust that our Father, which hath all things in his disposition, will see unto us that we shall lack nothing necessary! And as the husbandman tilleth and soweth his ground, weedeth it, and keepeth it from destroying, and yet he prayeth to God for the increase, and putteth all his trust in him to send him more or less at his pleasure; even so, besides our own diligence, policy, labour, and travail, we must also pray daily to God to send us sufficient; and we must take thankfully at his hands all that is sent; and be no further careful, but put our whole confidence and trust in him. For our Saviour Christ saith in the Gospel, I say to you, Be not careful for your living, what you shall eat, ne what clothes you shall wear. Is not life better than your meat, and your body better than your clothing? Look upon the birds of the air: they sow not, they reap not, they bring nothing into the barn; but your heavenly Father feedeth them. Be not you of more price than they? Look upon the lilies in the field: they labour not, they spin not; and yet I tell you, that Solomon, in all his precious and royal apparel, was not so clothed as one of them. Therefore care you not for these things. Leave this care to them that know not God. Your heavenly Father knoweth that you have need of all these things. But seek you first the kingdom of God and his righteousness, and then God shall cast all these things unto you (Matt 6:25-33).

These be the words of Christ, full of good and comfortable lessons, that we should not care ne set our hearts too much upon these worldly things, ne care so much for tomorrow, that we shall seem to mistrust our

Lord; and that we should sequester this care from us, and seek for the king-dom of God, and employ ourselves wholly to the getting thereof: and then he maketh a comfortable promise that we shall not lack things necessary for us. And although our Lord hath so provided for some, that they have already sufficient and plenty for many days or years, yet that notwith-standing they ought to make this petition to God, and say, Give us this day our daily bread. Forasmuch as their substance, (though it be never so great,) like as it could not have been gotten without God had sent it; so it cannot prosper and continue, except God preserve it. For how many great rich men have we known suddenly made poor, some by fire, some by wa-ter, some by theft, some by escheat, and many other ways? Was not Job the one day the richest man that was in all the east land, and the morrow after had utterly nothing? It is therefore as needful to pray our Lord to preserve that he hath given us, as to pray him to give it. For if he give it, and do not preserve it, we shall have no use of it.

Fourthly, that by this bread, which our Saviour teacheth us to ask in this petition, is principally meant the word of God, which is the spiritual bread that feedeth the soul (Matt 4:4). For as the body is nourished, brought up, groweth, and feedeth with bread and meat; so needeth the soul, even from our youth, to be nourished and brought up with the word of God, and to be fed daily with it. And like as the body will faint and decay, if it be not from time to time relieved and refreshed with bodily sustenance; even so the soul waxeth feeble and weak towards God, unless the same be continually cherished, refreshed, and kept up with the word of God, according to the saying of Christ, A man liveth not with meat only, but by every word that proceedeth from the mouth of God (Matt 4:4). And surely there is no other thing that can feed and comfort the soul, but only this bread of the word of God. For if we have adversity in this world, as poverty, sickness, imprisonment, and such other miseries, where should we seek for comfort but at God's word? If we think ourselves so holy, that we be without sin, where should we find a glass to see our sins in, but in the word of God? If we be so full of sins that we be like to fall into desperation, where can we have comfort, and learn to know the mercy of God, but only in God's word? Where shall we have armour to fight against our three great enemies, the world, the flesh, and the devil, where shall we have strength and power to withstand them, but only as Christ did, in and by the word of God? And finally, if we have any manner of sickness or disease in our souls, what medicine or remedy can we have, but only the word of God? So that the word of God is the very bread of the soul. And therefore, as well for this bread of the soul, as also for the bread and daily sustenance of the body, our Saviour Christ teacheth us to pray in this fourth petition.

The Sense and Interpretation of the Fifth Petition

Our heavenly Father, lo, we wretched sinners, knowledging and confessing unto thee, our most merciful Father, the great and manifold sins wherewith our conscience is continually cumbered, and having none other refuge but unto thy mercy, we most humbly beseech thee, comfort our conscience both now and in the hour of our death,

And forgive us our trespasses, as we forgive them that trespass against us.

which is now abashed and ashamed to look upon our sin and iniquity, and then also shall be more ashamed and afraid, remembering thy hard and strait judgment, which shall then be at hand. Give us thy peace in our hearts, that we to our comfort may look for thy judgment. Enter not into judgment against us with the strait extremity of thy justice; for in thy sight no man shall be found innocent or righteous, but manifold ways to have sinned against thee (Ps 143:2). Give us grace, dear Father, not to stick, stay, or ground ourselves in our own good works or deservings; but to give and submit ourselves plainly and faithfully to thine infinite and incomparable mercy. Help and comfort all men's conscience, which in point of death, or in any such other temptation, are vexed with desperation. Forgive both them and us our offences; comfort us, refresh us, and be reconciled unto us. Judge us not after the accusation of the devil, and our wretched consciences, neither hear the voice of our enemies, which accuse us day and night before thee. But like as we forgive them heartily which trespass against us, even so we beseech thee forgive us the manifold sins, whereby from our youth we have provoked thy displeasure and wrath against us, and daily do provoke it, by doing that is evil, and omitting that is good. And so wash our sins daily more and more, through the blood of thy Son and our Saviour Jesu Christ. And forasmuch as it is all repugnant and contrary unto our frail and corrupt nature to love them which hate us, or to forgive them (without revenging) which do hurt or offend us; give us (we beseech thee) this heavenly grace, and make thou our hearts so meek and gentle, that we may gladly and unfeignedly forgive them which have hated or hurted us in word or in deed, and that we may behave ourselves unto all men, friends and foes, with such mercy, gentleness, and kindness, as we would desire not only that they, but also that thou, good Lord, shouldest use unto us. For we cannot otherwise trust or look for any forgiveness or remission of our trespasses at thy hands, unless we shall, according to thy commandment, forgive all them that have trespassed in any wise against us.

For the better understanding of this fifth petition, we think it convenient, that all bishops and preachers shall instruct and teach the people committed unto their spiritual charge, that no man ought to glory in himself, as though he were innocent, and without sin; but rather that every good Christian man (without exception) ought to knowledge himself to be a sinner, and that he hath need to ask forgiveness of God for his sins, and to require him of his mercy. For doubtless he daily committeth sin, which is commanded daily to ask remission of his sins. And St. John saith, in his Epistle, If we say that we be without sin, we deceive ourselves, and truth is not in us (1 John 1:8).

Second, that God will not forgive us our sins, but upon condition that we shall likewise forgive all them which trespass against us; and that not in tongue only, but also in our hearts. And that this is a certain sure law and decree of God, Christ declareth in sundry places of the Gospel. For, first, by express words Christ saith, If you forgive men their offences done against you, your heavenly Father will forgive you your offences. And if you will not forgive them that offend you, be you assured your Father will not forgive you your offences (Matt 6:14-15). And in another place, when Peter came to our Lord, and demanded of him how oft he should forgive his brother which had offended him, and whether it were not sufficient to forgive him seven times; our Lord answered him and said, I tell thee, Peter, that thou oughtest to forgive him, not only seven times, but seventy times seven times; meaning thereby, that from time to time we must continually forgive our brother or neighbour, although he trespass against us never so often (Matt 18:21-22). And Christ also declareth the same by a parable. There was (saith Christ) a king, which calling his servants unto an account, and finding that one of them should owe unto him the sum of ten thousand talents; because he had it not to pay, commanded that the said debtor, his wife, and his children, and all that he had, should be sold. But when this debtor came unto the king, and prayed him on his knees to have patience with him, promising him to pay all, the king had pity of him, and forgave him the whole debt. It fortuned afterward, that this man being thus acquitted, met with another of his fellows that owed him but an hundred pence, and with violence almost strangled him, and said to him, Pay me my money. And the said servant his fellow fell upon his knees, and prayed him to have patience, promising to pay all. Albeit he would not, but cast him into prison until all was paid. And when the rest of their fellows, seeing this cruelty, had told the king thereof, the king forthwith sent for this cruel fellow, and said to him, wicked man, I forgave thee thy whole debt, at thy suit and request: it should therefore have beseemed thee to have shewed like compassion to thy fellow, as I had shewed to thee. And the king, being sore displeased with this cruelty, committed him to tormentors, that should roughly and straitly handle him in prison, till he had paid the whole debt. Upon this parable Christ inferreth and saith, Even so shall your heavenly Father do with you, if you will not forgive every one of you his brother, even from the heart (Matt 18:23-35).

Thus it appeareth plainly, that if we will be forgiven, if we will escape everlasting damnation, we must heartily forgive those which have trespassed and offended against us. No man can offend us so much as we offend God; and yet he is alway ready to forgive us. What ingratitude is it then, what hardness of heart, what cruelness is in us, if we for his sake will not forgive one another! There is none offence great that man doth to man, if it be compared to our offences against God. And therefore we may be well accounted to have little respect and consideration unto our own benefit, if we will not remit and forgive small faults done unto us, that we may have pardon and forgiveness of so many thousands of great offences which we have committed against God. And if any peradventure will think it to be a hard thing to suffer and forgive his enemy, which in word and deed hath done him many displeasures, let him consider again, how many hard storms our Saviour Christ suffered and abode for us. What were we, when he gave his most precious life and blood for us, but horrible sinners, and his enemies? How meekly took he for our sake all rebukes, mocks, binding, beating, crowning with thorn, and the most opprobrious death! Why do wo boast us to be Christian men, if we care not for Christ, of whom we be so named, if we endeavour not ourselves to take example at him? We be not worthy to have the name of the members, if we follow not the Head. And if any will say that his enemy is not worthy to be forgiven, let him consider and think that no more is he worthy to have forgiveness of God. And by what equity or justice can we require that God should be merciful unto us, if we will shew no mercy, but extremity unto our neighbour and brother? Is it a great matter for one sinner to forgive another, seeing that Christ forgave them that crucified him? And although thy enemy be not worthy to be forgiven, yet we be worthy to forgive: and Christ is worthy, that for his sake we should forgive. But surely it is above our frail and corrupt nature to love our enemies that do hate us, and to forgive them that do hurt and offend us. Thus to do is a greater grace than can come of ourselves. Therefore our Saviour Christ teacheth us to ask this heavenly gift of our heavenly Father, that we may forgive our enemies, and that he will forgive us our trespasses, even so as we forgive them that trespass against us.

Thirdly, that to forgive our brother his default is to pray to our Lord that he will forgive him, and will not impute his offence to him; and to wish to him the same grace and glory that we desire unto ourselves; and in no case to annoy him, but when occasion shall come, to help him as we be bound to help our Christian brother.

Fourthly, that none enemy can wish or desire more hurt unto us than we desire unto our own selves, when we offer unto God this fifth petition, if we will not remit and forgive our displeasure unto them which offend us. For what enemy was ever so malicious, or so far from all grace and humanity, that would desire and daily pray to God to send unto his enemy eternal damnation, and that God should withdraw his mercy from him for ever? And surely in this petition we ask continually these things of God for ourselves, if we will be merciless towards our enemies, and will not forgive them their trespasses. For none otherwise we do ask forgiveness of God, but upon this condition, that we shall forgive them which trespass against us. And in case we do not fulfil this condition, then we pray unto God that he shall never shew mercy unto us, nor never forgive us our sins, but suffer us to be damned perpetually.

The Sense and Interpretation of the Sixth Petition

O our heavenly Father, lo, we here thy most unworthy and miserable children, feeling and considering the great and violent assaults whereby not only the devil and his *And lead us not into temptation.* wicked spirits, but also our own flesh and concupiscence continually do tempt and provoke us to break and violate thy most holy will and commandments; and considering also our own ignorance and frailness, and how weak and unable we be to resist so mighty and so crafty enemies, without thy heavenly grace and help; we most humbly beseech thee, our most dear Father, help us, succour us, and defend us in all temptations of the devil, and of our own concupiscence, and suffer us not to be vanquished or overthrown by them. Endue us so with thy grace, that we may withstand the desires of the flesh. Make that we may resist and fight against all temptation, which proceedeth of superfluity of meat and drink, sleep, sloth, or idleness; and that by temperance in diet, by fasting, watch, and labour, we may be able to subdue the same, and be meet and apt to all good works. Make that we may overcome the evil desires of lechery, with all affections and instigations thereof. Keep us, that the false subtilty of this world, and the vain enticements of the same, bring us not to follow it. Keep us, that we be not drawn by the evils and adversities of this world, to impatience, avengement, wrath, or such other vices: and that we may not too much esteem the things that belong to the world, nor inordinately love them, but that we may renounce the same, according as we have promised in our baptism; and that we may continue in that same promise, going forward therein daily more and more. Keep us from the enticements of the devil, that we consent not to any of his temptations or persuasions. Keep us, that he by no suggestion bring us from the right faith, neither cause us to fall into desperation now nor in the point of death. Put thy helping hand, heavenly Father, to them that fight and labour against these hard and manifold temptations. Look, most dear Father, upon us thy children, which, in this most tempestuous and troublous sea of this world, be tossed on every side with the most perilous waves of temptation, and be compassed about both within and without with most dreadful and cruel enemies. Defend us, we beseech thee, of thy infinite goodness, and for thy Son Jesu Christ's sake, from all these enemies and dangers; and give us thy grace and help, that they never tempt us further, nor have greater power over us than we shall be able to bear, resist, and sustain; and that they may never overcome us, but that we may ever have the over hand upon them.

For the more plain declaration of this sixth petition, we think it convenient that all bishops and preachers shall instruct and teach the people committed unto their spiritual charge, first, that there be two manner of temptations, whereof one cometh and is sent unto us by God, who suffereth those that be his never to be without temptation, by one means or other, for their probation and trial: albeit he so assisteth and aideth them in all such temptations, that he turneth all at the end unto their profit and benefit. For as the Wise Man saith, Like as the oven trieth the potter's vessel, so doth temptation of trouble try the righteous man (Sir 27:5). And with this manner of temptation God tempted sundry wise our holy father Abraham. He tempted also Job with extreme poverty, horrible sickness, and sudden death of his children. And daily he tempteth and proveth all his chosen and elect children, whom he loveth. The other manner of temptation cometh chiefly of the devil, which, like a furious and a wode lion, runneth and rageth about perpetually, seeking how he may devour us (1 Pet 5:8). And secondly, it cometh also of our own concupiscence, which continually inclineth and stirreth us unto all evil, as St. James saith, Every man is tempted, led, and enticed by his own concupiscence (James 1:14). This concupiscence is an inclination and pronity, or readiness, and in manner a violent disposition of our own corrupt nature, to fall into all kind of sins, which, after the fall of Adam, all mankind hath naturally grafted in them: so that it is born, and groweth, and shall die with us, and not before. There is no man so mortified, so sequestered from the world, ne so ravished in spirit, in devotion, or in contemplation, but that this concupiscence is in him. Howbeit it reigneth only in them that yield unto it. It will never cease; but one way or other it will ever assault us. And if we do not fight with it, and resist it continually, it will overcome us, and bring us into bondage. So that between the devil and this our concupiscence all vice and sins be engendered; like as between man and woman children be engendered. According to the saying of St. James, where he saith, Concupiscence, when she doth conceive, she bringeth forth sin, and that of all sorts; that is to say, first acts and deeds contrary to the laws of God, and after that, use and custom of the same deeds, and at length blindness and contempt (James 1:15). For so the Wise Man saith, The wicked man, when he cometh to the bottom of sin, setteth nought thereby; but blinded with evil custom, either thinketh the sin which he useth to be no sin, or else if he take it for sin, yet he careth not for it, but either upon vain trust of the mercy of God, (which is indeed no right trust, but a very presumption,) he will continue still in purpose to sin, or else upon vain hope of long life, he will prolong, defer, and delay to do penance for the same, until the last end of his life. And so, oft-times prevented with sudden death, dieth without repentance. Wherefore, considering how dangerous it is to fall into sin, and how hard it is to arise, the chief and the best way is to resist with God's help the first suggestion unto sin, and not to suffer it to remain with us, but as soon as may be to put it clean out of our minds. For if we suffer it to have place in our hearts any while, it is great peril lest that consent and deed will follow shortly after.

Second, that our Saviour Jesu Christ teacheth us not in this sixth petition to pray unto God our Father that we should be clearly without all temptation, but that he will not suffer us to be led into temptation, that is to say, when we be tempted, that he suffer us not to be overcome therewith. For surely temptations be profitable, if they do not overcome us. And therefore St. Paul saith, The true and faithful God will not suffer us to be tempted above that we may bear; but he will turn temptation to our profit, that we may sustain it and overcome it (1 Cor 10:13). And St. James saith, Think that you have a great cause of joy when you be troubled with divers temptations (James 1:2). For the trying of your faith bringeth patience, and patience maketh perfect work, so that you may be perfect and sound, lacking nothing. And Almighty God also exhorteth us, and calleth upon us to fight against temptations, saying, He that hath the victory against them, I shall give him to eat of the tree of life (Rev 2:7). And again he saith, He that overcometh them shall not be hurt with the second death (Rev 2:11). And St. Paul saith, No man shall be crowned, except he fight, yea and that as he ought to fight; that is to say, except he defend himself, and resist his enemies at all points to his power (2 Tim 2:5). And our Saviour giveth us a good courage to fight in this battle, where he saith, Be of good comfort, for I have overcome the world; that is to say, I have had the victory of all sins and temptations: and so shall you have, if the default be not in yourselves (John 16:33). For you fight with an adversary which is already vanquished and overcome.

The Sense and Interpretation of the Seventh Petition

But deliver us from the evil. Amen.

O Father, keep us from the danger of water and fire, from thunder, lightning, and hail. Keep us from hunger and dearth. Keep us from war and manslaughter. Keep us from thy most grievous strokes, the pestilence, and all other diseases. Keep us from sudden death. Keep us from all evils and perils of the body, if it be thy pleasure so to do. But most specially keep us from sin, and all things that may displease thee. Deliver us from thy strait judgment at our death, and at the last day of doom. Turn never thy face from us, most loving Father. Look never away from us, lest we turn from thee unto the world, the flesh, and the devil. Good Lord, grant unto us all these our suits and petitions, according to our humble request and desire. Amen.

For the better understanding of this last petition, we think it convenient, that all bishops and preachers shall instruct and teach the people committed unto their spiritual charge, first, that like as in the sixth petition Christ taught us to desire of our heavenly Father that we should not be overcome with temptation, ne brought into sin, so now in this seventh and last petition he teacheth us to pray him, that if by frailness we fall into sin, he will soon deliver us from it, not to let us continue in it, not to let it take root in us, not to suffer sin to reign upon us; but to deliver us, and make us free from it. This sin is the exceeding evil, from the which in this petition we desire to be delivered. And though in this petition be also comprehended all evils in this world, as sickness, poverty, dearth, with other like adversities; yet chiefly it is to be understood of sin, which only of itself is evil, and ought ever without condition to be eschewed. And as for other adversities, neither we can ne ought to refuse, when God shall send them; neither we ought to pray for the eschewing of them, otherwise than with this condition, If God's pleasure so be.

Second, that nothing can be called properly and of itself evil, but only sin; and that all other things, whatsoever they be, be the works and creatures of God, which neither made any thing evil, nor can do any thing that is evil. Many things we suffer in this world, and take them for evil; but they be not evil of themselves. All afflictions, diseases, punishments, and torments of this body, all the trouble and anguishes of the soul, all the troubles of this world, and all adversities, be good and necessary instruments of God for our salvation. For God himself (who cannot say other than truth) saith, Those that I love I chastise (Rev 3:19; Prov 3:19). And again, the apostle saith, He receiveth none but whom he scourgeth (Heb 12:6). This is the time of scourging, purging, and scouring; and the time to come is the time of rest, ease, and bliss. And surely there is no better token that we be in the favour of God, than that he doth scourge us, and trieth and fineth us, like gold in the fire, whiles we be in this world. As contrary, there is no more certain token of his indignation towards us, than to suffer us still to live in prosperity, and to have all things after our will and pleasure, and never to nip us or touch us with adversity. Therefore our Saviour Christ Jesu (who knoweth what is best for us) teacheth us not chiefly to pray and desire to be delivered from worldly afflictions, trouble, and adversity, which God sendeth abundantly even to them whom he best loveth, and with whom he is best pleased; but the evil which we most chiefly should pray to be delivered from is sin, which of itself is so evil, that in no wise he can be pleased therewith. And because our whole study and endeavour in this world ought to be to please God, therefore our continual prayer should be, that we might specially above all things be preserved from sin and eternal punishment for the same.

The Ave Maria

Hail, Mary, full of grace, the Lord is with thee. Blessed art thou amongst women; and blessed is the fruit of thy womb.

For the better understanding of this Ave, or salutation of the angel, we think it convenient, that all bishops and preachers shall instruct and teach the people committed unto their spiritual charge, first, how that it was decreed in the high consistory of the whole Trinity, that after the fall of our first father Adam, by which mankind was so long in the great indignation of God, and exiled out of heaven, the second Person, the everlasting Son of the Father everlasting, should take upon him the nature of man, to redeem mankind from the power of the devil, and to reconcile the same again to his Lord God; and that he should be so perfect God, and also perfect man. And for this purpose, as St. Luke in his Gospel reporteth, In the sixth month after St. Elisabeth was conceived with St. John the Baptist, the angel Gabriel was sent from God into a city of Galilee named Nazareth, to a virgin, which was despoused or ensured to a man, whose name was Joseph, of the house of David, and the virgin's name was Mary. And when this angel came unto this said virgin, he said these words: *Hail, full of grace, the Lord is with thee: blessed art thou among women* (Luke 1:24-28).

And when the virgin hearing these words was much troubled with them, and mused with herself what manner of salutation it should be, the angel said to her, Fear not, Mary, be not abashed: for thou hast found favour and grace in the sight of God. Lo, thou shalt conceive in thy womb, and shalt bring forth a son, and thou shalt call his name Jesus. He shall be great, and shall be called the Son of the Highest: and the Lord God shall give to him the seat of David his father: and he shall reign over the house of Jacob for ever; and his kingdom shall have no end. Then said Mary to the angel, How can this be done, for I know no man? And the angel answering said unto her, The Holy Ghost shall come from above into thee, and the power of the Highest shall overshadow thee: and therefore that holy thing which shall be born of thee shall be called the Son of God. And, lo, thy cousin Elisabeth hath also conceived a son in her old age: and this is the sixth month sith she conceived, which was called the barren woman. For there is nothing impossible to God. To this Mary answered, Lo, I am the handmaid of our Lord; be it done unto me as thou hast spoken. And then forthwith, upon the departure of the angel, and being newly conceived with the most blessed child Jesus, Mary went up into the mountains with speed into a city of Judah; and came to the house of Zachary, and saluted Elisabeth. And as soon as Elisabeth heard the salutation of Mary, the child sprung in her belly. And forthwith Elisabeth was replenished with the Holy Ghost, and cried with a great voice, and said, *Blessed art thou among women, and blessed is the fruit of thy womb.* And whereof cometh this to me, that the mother of my Lord cometh to me? For, lo, as soon as the voice of thy salutation was in my ears, the child in my womb leapt for joy. And blessed art thou that diddest believe. For all things that have been spoken to thee from our Lord shall be performed.

Second, that the angel Gabriel, which spake to the virgin, was an high angel, and an high messenger. And truly it was convenient that he should be so. For he came with the highest message that ever was sent, which was the treaty and league of peace between God and man. And therefore the first word of his salutation (that is to say, Hail, or, Be joyful) was marvellous convenient for the same: for he came with the message of joy. And so said the other angel, which at the birth of our Saviour appeared to the shepherds. I shew to you (said he) great joy, that shall be to all the people (Luke 2:10). And surely, considering the effects that ensued upon this high message, all mankind had great cause to joy. For man being in the indignation and the displeasure of God, was hereby reconciled; man being in the bonds of the devil, was hereby delivered; man being exiled and banished out of heaven, was hereby restored thither again. These be such matters of joy and comfort to us, that there never was or shall be, nor can be any like. But not only for this purpose he began with this high word of comfort, but also for that he perceived that the virgin, being alone, would be much abashed and astonied at his marvellous and sudden coming unto her. And therefore he thought it expedient first of all to utter the word of joy and comfort, which might comfort and put away all fear from the blessed virgin. And he calleth not her by her proper name, but giveth her a new name, calling her *full of grace.* This is now her new name; and this is the highest name that can be in any creature. For her Son, the Son of God, was content with this name, where he is by the holy evangelist St. John called also *full of grace.* And yet she is not in this behalf equal with him. For that she is full of grace, she hath it of him. And how could it be otherwise but that she must needs be full of grace, that should conceive and bear him that was the very plenitude and fulness of grace, the Lord of grace, by whom is all grace, and without whom is no grace. Holy scripture calleth also St. Stephen *full of grace;* but he may not be compared with the blessed virgin, ne have communion in this name, *full of grace,* equal with her; for she conceived and bare him that is the Author of all grace: and this is the singular grace by which she is called, not only the mother of man, but also the mother of God (Acts 6:8).

Thirdly, that by these words, the *Lord is with thee,* is declared the name which the angel gave to her, calling her *full of grace:* and they signify, that she was full of God's favour, and full of his grace. For surely our Lord is not with them that be not in grace: he cannot tarry with them that be void of grace, and be in sin. For there is a separation and divorce between the sinful soul and our Lord, as the Wise Man saith, Perverse thoughts make a separation and divorce from God; much more perverse deeds (Wis 1:3).

Fourthly, that these words, *Blessed art thou among women*, was meant, that there was never woman so blessed. And truly she may well be called so, most blessed amongst all women: for she had great and high prerogatives, which none other woman ever had, hath, or shall have. Is not this an high prerogative, that of all women she was chosen to be mother to the Son of God? And what excellent honour was she put to, when, notwithstanding the decree was made of his nativity by the whole Trinity, yet the thing was not done and accomplished without or before her consent was granted, for the which so solemn a messenger was sent! And how high grace was this, that after the default made through the persuasion of the first woman, our mother Eve, (by whom Adam was brought into disobedience,) this blessed virgin was elect to be the instrument of our reparation, in that she was chosen to bear the Saviour and Redeemer of the world! And is not this a wonderful prerogative, to see a virgin to be a mother, and against the general sentence of the malediction of Eve, to conceive and bring forth her child without sin? And who can esteem that marvellous solace and comfort which was in her heart, when she embraced that child, and nourished it with her paps, and had continually company of such a son so many years together? Wherefore we may worthily say that she is the most blessed of all other women. And to the intent that all good Christian men should repute and take her so, behold the providence of God, that would by another witness confirm the same. For even the same words that the angel spake, the blessed matron St. Elisabeth spake also: and where the angel made an end, there she began. The angel made an end of his salutation with these words, *Blessed art thou among women*. The blessed matron began her salutation with the same words, declaring that she was inspired with the same Spirit that sent the angel; and that they were both ministers of the whole Trinity, the one from heaven, the other in earth. And afterward she added these words, and said, *And blessed is the fruit of thy womb*. These be not the words of the angel, but of St. Elisabeth. For when the virgin Mary came to salute her, the said Elisabeth being inspired with the Holy Ghost, and knowing that the virgin Mary was conceived, spake these words of the fruit that the virgin should bring forth. And here is also another wonderful thing to be noted: for, as it appeareth in the Gospel, the child in St. Elisabeth's womb, that is to say St. John, which yet had scant life, gave testimony to this fruit, that this fruit should save him and all the world; and as a prophet he leapt for joy in his mother's belly. And although he could not yet speak, yet nevertheless he declared by such signs and tokens as he could, that blessed was the fruit of that womb. This is the fruit that the angel spake of, saying, His name shall be Jesus, that is to say, a Saviour; for he shall save his people from their sins. And well he may be called the blessed fruit, which hath saved us and given us life, contrary to the cursed fruit, which Eve gave to Adam, by which we were destroyed and brought to death: but blessed is the fruit of this womb, which is the fruit of life everlasting.

Fifthly, we think it convenient, that all bishops and preachers shall instruct and teach the people committed unto their spiritual charge, that this Ave Maria is not properly a prayer, as the Paternoster is. For a prayer properly hath words of petition, supplication, request, and suit; but this Ave Maria hath no such. Nevertheless the church hath used to adjoin it to the end of the Paternoster, as an hymn, laud, and praise, partly of our Lord and Saviour Jesu Christ for our redemption, and partly of the blessed virgin for her humble consent given and expressed to the angel at this salutation. Lauds, praises, and thanks be in this Ave Maria principally given and yielded to our Lord, as to the author of our said redemption: but herewith also the virgin lacketh not her lauds, praise, and thanks for her excellent and singular virtues, and chiefly for that she humbly consented, according to the saying of the holy matron St. Elisabeth, when she said unto this virgin, Blessed art thou that diddest give trust and credence to the angel's words; for all things that have been spoken to thee shall be performed.

The Article of Justification

As touching the order and cause of our justification, we think it convenient, that all bishops and preachers shall instruct and teach the people committed unto their spiritual charge, that this word justification signifieth remission of our sins, and our acceptation or reconciliation into the grace and favour of God, that is to say, our perfect renovation in Christ.

Item, That sinners attain this justification by contrition and faith, joined with charity, after such sort and manner as is before mentioned and declared in the sacrament of penance. Not as though our contrition or faith, or any works proceeding thereof, can worthily merit or deserve to attain the said justification. For the only mercy and grace of the Father, promised freely unto us for his Son's sake Jesu Christ, and the merits of his blood and passion, be the only sufficient and worthy causes thereof. And yet that notwithstanding to the attaining of the same justification, God requireth to be in us not only inward contrition, perfect faith and charity, certain hope and confidence, with all other spiritual graces and motions, which, as was said before, must necessarily concur in remission of our sins, that is to say, our justification; but also he requireth and commandeth us, that after we be justified we must also have good works of charity and obedience towards God, in the observing and fulfilling outwardly of his laws and commandments. For although acceptation to everlasting life be conjoined with justification, yet our good works be necessarily required to the attaining of everlasting life. And we being justified, be necessarily bound, and it is our necessary duty, to do good works, according to the saying of

St. Paul, We be bound not to live according to the flesh and to fleshly appetites; for if we live so, we shall undoubtedly be damned. And contrary, if we will mortify the deeds of our flesh, and live according to the Spirit, we shall be saved (Rom 8:1). For whosoever be led by the Spirit of God, they be the children of God. And Christ saith, If you will come to heaven, keep the commandments (Matt 19:17). And St. Paul, speaking of evil works, saith, Whosoever commit sinful deeds, shall never come to heaven (Gal 5:21). Wherefore all good Christian people must understand and believe certainly, that God necessarily requireth of us to do good works commanded by him, and that not only outward and civil works, but also the inward spiritual motions and graces of the Holy Ghost, that is to say, to dread and fear God; to love God; to have firm confidence and trust in God; to invocate and call upon God; to have patience in all adversities; to hate sin; and to have certain purpose and will not to sin again; and such other like motions and virtues. For Christ saith, We must not only do outward civil good works, but we must also have these foresaid inward spiritual motions, consenting and agreeable to the law of God (Matt 5).

The Article of Purgatory

Forasmuch as due order of charity requireth, and the book of Maccabees and divers ancient doctors plainly shewen, that it is a very good and a charitable deed to pray for souls departed; and forasmuch also as such usage hath continued in the church so many years, even from the beginning; we think it convenient, that all bishops and preachers shall instruct and teach the people committed unto their spiritual charge, that no man ought to be grieved with the continuance of the same; and that it standeth with the very due order of charity, that Christian men should pray for the souls departed, and commit them in our prayers to God's mercy; and also to cause other to pray for them in masses and exequies; and to give alms to other to pray for them, whereby they may be relieved and holpen of some part of their pain. But forasmuch as the place where they be, the name thereof, and kind of pains there also be to us uncertain by scripture, therefore this with all other things be to be remitted to Almighty God, unto whose mercy it is meet and convenient for us to commend them, trusting that God accepteth our prayers for them, referring the rest wholly to God, to whom is known their estate and condition. Wherefore it is much necessary that such abuses be clearly put away, which under the name of purgatory hath been advanced; as to make men believe that through the bishop of Rome's pardons souls might clearly be delivered out of purgatory, and all the pains of it; or the masses said at *Scala coeli*, or other where, in any place, or before any image, might likewise deliver them from all their pain, and send them straight to heaven; and other like abuses.

————————————————

LONDINI IN AEDIBUS
THOMÆ BER-
THELETI REGII IMPRES-
SORIS.
AN. M.D.XXXVII.

CUM PRIVILEGIO.

The King's Book

Also Known As

A Necessary Doctrine and Erudition for Any Christian Man

Set Forth By

The King's Majesty of England, &c.

Lord preserve the king;
and hear us when we call upon thee.

PSALM 20:9

Lord, in thy strength the king shall rejoice,
and be marvellous glad through thy salvation.

PSALM 21:1

Henry the VIII by the grace of God king of England, France, and Ireland, defender of the faith, and in earth of the church of England and also of Ireland supreme head, unto all his faithful and loving subjects, sendeth greeting.

Like as in the time of darkness and ignorance, finding our people seduced and drawn from the truth by hypocrisy and superstition, we by the help of God and his word have travailed to purge and cleanse our realm from the apparent enormities of the same; wherein, by opening of God's truth, with setting forth and publishing of the scriptures, our labours (thanks be to God) have not been void and frustrate: so now, perceiving that in the time of knowledge the devil (who ceaseth not in all times to vex the world) hath attempted to return again (as the parable in the gospel sheweth) into the house purged and cleansed, accompanied with seven worse spirits, and hypocrisy and superstition being excluded and put away, we find entered into some of our people's hearts an inclination to sinister understanding of scripture, presumption, arrogancy, carnal liberty, and contention; we be therefore constrained, for the reformation of them in time, and for avoiding of such diversity in opinions as by the said evil spirits might be engendered, to set forth, with the advice of our clergy, such a doctrine and declaration of the true knowledge of God and his word, with the principal articles of our religion, as whereby all men may uniformly be led and taught the true understanding of that which is necessary for every Christian man to know, for the ordering of himself in this life, agreeably to the will and pleasure of Almighty God. Which doctrine also the lords both spiritual and temporal, with the nether house of our parliament, have both seen and like very well. And for knowledge of the order of the matter in this book contained, forasmuch as we know not perfectly God but by faith, the declaration of Faith occupieth in this treatise the first place; whereunto is next adjoined the declaration of the Articles of our Creed, containing what we should believe. And incontinently after them followeth the explication of the Seven Sacraments, wherein God ordinarily worketh, and whereby he participateth unto us his special gifts and graces in this life: which matters so digested and set forth with simplicity and plainness, as the capacities and understandings of the multitude of our people may easily receive and comprehend the same, there followeth conveniently the declaration of the Ten Commandments, being by God ordained the high way, wherein each man should walk in this life to finish fruitfully his journey here, and after to rest eternally in joy with him: which because we cannot do of ourselves, but have need always of the grace of God, as without whom we can neither continue in this life, ne without his special grace do any thing to his pleasure, whereby to attain the life to come; we have, after declaration of the Commandments, expounded the seven petitions of our Paternoster, wherein be contained requests and suits for all things necessary to a Christian man in this present life; with declaration of the Ave Maria, as a prayer containing a joyful rehearsal, and magnifying of God in the work of the incarnation of Christ, which is the ground of our salvation, wherein the blessed virgin our lady, for the abundance of grace wherewith God endued her, is also with this remembrance honoured and worshipped. And forasmuch as the heads and senses of our people have been embusied, and in these days travailed with the understanding of freewill, justification, good works, and praying for the souls departed; we have, by the advice of our clergy, for the purgation of erroneous doctrine, declared and set forth openly, plainly, and without ambiguity of speech, the mere and certain truth in them. So as we verily trust, that to know God, and how to live after his pleasure, to the attaining of everlasting life in the end, this book containeth a perfect and sufficient doctrine, grounded and established in holy scriptures: wherefore we heartily exhort our people of all degrees willingly and earnestly both to read and print in their hearts the doctrine of this book, considering that God (who, as St. Paul saith, distributeth and divideth to his church his graces distinctly) hath ordered some sort of men to teach other, and some to be taught, that all things should be done seemly and in order, and hath beautified and set forth by distinction of ministers and offices the same church. And considering also, that for the one part, which should teach other, is necessary, not only knowledge, but also learning and cunning in the same knowledge, whereby they may be able conveniently to dispense and distribute to their audience the truth of God, according to their cunning, for the edification of other, and by true exposition of the scriptures, according to the apostolical doctrine received and maintained from the beginning, and by conferring and declaration of them, to convince, refel, and reprove all errors and untruths set forth to the contrary; and finally be also able to give an account, as St. Peter saith, of that they profess: it must be agreed then, that for the instruction of this part of the church, whose office is to teach other, the having, reading, and studying of holy scripture, both of the Old and New Testament, is not only convenient, but also necessary: but for the other part of the church, ordained to be taught, it ought to be deemed certainly, that the reading of the Old and New Testament is not so necessary for all those folks, that of duty they ought and be bound to read it, but as the prince and the policy of the realm shall think convenient, so to be tolerated or taken from it. Consonant whereunto the politic law of our realm hath now restrained it from a great many, esteeming it sufficient for those so restrained to hear and truly bear away the doctrine of scripture taught by the preachers, and so imprint the lessons of the same, that they may observe and keep them inwardly in their heart, and as occasion serveth express them in their deeds outwardly, whereby they may be partakers of that bliss which the giver of blessedness, our Saviour Christ, spake of and promised to such, saying, *Beati qui audiunt verbum Dei, et custodiunt illud:* Blessed be they that hear the true doctrine of God, and keep it; which is the true sense of that text (Luke 11:28). Wherefore we exhort and desire all our loving subjects, that they, praying to God for the spirit of humility, do conform themselves, as good scholars and learners ought, to hear and bear away as afore, and willingly to observe such order as is by us and our laws prescribed, and to read and bear well away the true doctrine lately by us and our clergy set forth for their erudition; whereby presumption and arrogancy shall be withstanded, malice and contention expelled, and carnal liberty refrained and tempered, and disdain clearly removed and taken away. So as endeavouring ourselves to live quietly and charitably together, each one in his vocation, we shall be so replenished with manifold graces and gifts of God, that after this life we shall reign in joy everlasting, with the only Head of the universal catholic church, our Saviour and Redeemer Jesus Christ. Amen.

The Declaration of Faith

Forasmuch as in this book, which is set forth for the institution and erudition of the common people, the articles of our faith have the first place, it is very necessary, before we enter into the declaration of the said articles, something to entreat of faith, to the intent that it may be known what is meant properly by the word faith, as it is appertaining to a Christian man, who by faith is partaker of God's benefits by Christ. And although faith be diversely taken in scripture, it shall be sufficient to entreat here of two kinds or acceptions of the same.

Faith, in the first acception, is considered as it is a several gift of God by itself, distinct from hope and charity; and so taken, it signifieth a persuasion and belief wrought by God in man's heart, whereby he assenteth, granteth, and taketh for true, not only that God is, which knowledge is taught and declared by the marvellous works of the creation of the world, (as saith St. Paul in the Epistle to the Romans,) but also that all the words and sayings of God which be revealed and opened in the scripture be of most certain truth and infallible verity (Rom 1:20). And further also, that all those things which were taught by the apostles, and have been by an whole universal consent of the church of Christ ever sith that time taught continually, and taken always for true, ought to be received, accepted, and kept, as a perfect doctrine apostolic. And this is the first acception of faith which man hath of God, wherein man leaneth not to his own natural knowledge, which is by reason, but leaneth to the knowledge attained by faith; without the which faith we be ignorant and blind, and cannot understand, according as the prophet Esay saith, *Nisi credideritis, non intelligetis:* Unless ye believe, ye shall not understand (Isa 7:9). And this faith is the beginning, entry, and introduction unto all Christian religion and godliness. For, as St. Paul saith, He that cometh to God must believe that he is, and that he is a rewarder unto them which seek to please him (Heb 11:6). And this faith, although it be the necessary beginning of all righteousness, yet if it proceed not further to hope and charity, it is called in scripture a dead faith, because it is void and destitute of the life and efficacy of charity.

Faith, in the second acception, is considered as it hath hope and charity annexed and joined unto it: and faith so taken, signifieth not only the belief and persuasion before mentioned in the first acception, but also a sure confidence and hope to attain whatsoever God hath promised for Christ's sake, and an hearty love to God, and obedience to his commandments. And this faith is a lively faith, and worketh in man a ready submission of his will to God's will. And this is the effectual faith that worketh by charity, which St. Paul unto the Galatians affirmeth to be of value and strength in Christ Jesu (Gal 5:6). By this faith, Abraham, not knowing whither he should go, went out of his country, and dwelt in the land of behest, as in a strange land, looking and trusting for a city founded and builded by Almighty God. By this faith also he was ready to offer up his only begotten son Isaac, when he was tempted, in whom he looked for the promise, nothing doubting but that God was able to raise him up again from death. And this wise is faith taken in the most part of the examples which be recited of St. Paul, in the eleventh chapter of his Epistle to the Hebrews. And this faith every Christian man professeth and covenanteth to keep, when he receiveth the sacrament of baptism.

For declaration whereof it is to be noted, that all promises of God made to man after the fall of Adam, for Christ's sake, be made under this condition, that man should believe in God, and with the grace of God, given for Christ, endeavour himself to accomplish God's commandments. The church therefore (intending that man should always have in mind how the promises of God be made upon condition, and without keeping of the condition no man is partaker of God's promises) hath taught and ordained, that men before they receive baptism shall promise and covenant to fulfil the said condition, and to forsake the devil and the world, and to serve only God. And of this especial covenant, whereby man bindeth himself to God, he is called in Latin, *fidelis, faithful;* and he that never made the same covenant, or after he hath made it, renounceth and refuseth the same, is called amongst Christian men, *infidelis, unfaithful* or *heathen.* And because God hath made promise and covenant with man, (as is before declared,) which we must most assuredly believe that God will observe and keep, and is ever in his words and promises most true, most just, most constant; therefore God is called (as he is indeed) faithful to man, and keepeth and observeth his faith, that is to say, his promise to man, requiring that man should likewise keep his faith and promise towards him.

Now of that which is before said, it is manifest, that faith (as it is taken in the second acception) is the perfect faith of a true Christian man, and containeth the obedience to the whole doctrine and religion of Christ. And thus is faith taken of St. Paul, and in other places of scripture, where it is said, that we be justified by faith. In which places men may not think that we be justified by faith, as it is a several virtue separated from hope and charity, fear of God and repentance; but by it is meant faith neither only ne alone, but with the foresaid virtues coupled together, containing, as it is aforesaid, the obedience to the whole doctrine and religion of Christ.

And here is to be noted, that every man that doth offend God doth not lose his faith thereby. For they that sin by frailty and sudden motions, (which just men do not avoid,) and be taught therefore of Christ to say in their Paternoster, Forgive us our trespasses as we forgive them that trespass against us: yet those men so breaking their promise with God, and slacking in such care and desire as they should have to please God, nevertheless be not accounted to have lost their faith thereby; yea they also, who, after the knowledge of God, fall into deadly sin advisedly, as they that commit murder, adultery, and other abominations, and so fall from faith, as it is taken in the second acception, and be therefore out of the state of grace and favour of God for the time, yet do not those men fall from faith, as it is taken in the first acception, that is to say, from certain and assured knowledge of God and his doctrine. And therefore the gospel speaketh of a servant that knoweth the will of his lord, and doeth it not (Luke 12:47). And St. James, in his Epistle, saith, that faith may remain without charity: wherefore a transgressor of the law of Almighty God, after baptism, keepeth still a remorse of conscience, and the light of knowledge by faith, whereby he seeth the remedies how to attain remission of sin, and by a special gift of further grace is moved to use the same remedies, and so by faith walketh the ways ordained to attain remission of sins, as in the sacrament of penance shall be declared (James 2).

Thus we have shewed two acceptions of faith, and declared that the faith of knowledge may remain in him that hath fallen from faith after the second acception. But whether there be any special particular knowledge which man by faith hath certainly of himself, whereby he may testify to himself that he is of the predestinates, which shall to the end persevere in their calling, we have not spoken, ne cannot in scripture ne doctors find that any such faith can be taught or preached. Truth it is, that in the sacraments instituted by Christ we may constantly believe the works of God in them, to our present comfort, and application of his grace and favour, with assurance also that he will not fail us, if we fall not from him; wherefore so continuing in the state of grace with him, we may believe undoubtedly to be saved. But forasmuch as our own frailty and naughtiness ought ever to be feared in us, it is therefore expedient for us to live in continual watch and continual fight with our enemies the devil, the flesh, and the world, and not to presume too much of our perseverance and continuance in the state of grace, which on our behalf is uncertain and unstable. For although God's promises made in Christ be immutable, yet he maketh them not to us but with condition; so that his promise standing, we may yet fail of the promise, because we keep not our promise. And therefore if we assuredly reckon upon the state of our felicity, as grounded upon God's promise, and do not therewith remember that no man shall be crowned unless he lawfully fight, we shall triumph before the victory, and so look in vain for that which is not otherwise promised but under a condition. And this every Christian man must assuredly believe.

The Creed, or the Twelve Articles of the Christian Faith

The Apostles' Creed

1. I believe in God the Father Almighty, Maker of heaven and earth.

2. And in Jesu Christ, his only Son, our Lord.

3. Which was conceived by the Holy Ghost, born of the Virgin Mary.

4. Suffered under Ponce Pilate, was crucified, dead, buried, and descended into hell.

5. And the third day he rose again from death.

6. He ascended into heaven, and sitteth on the right hand of God the Father Almighty.

7. From thence he shall come to judge the quick and the dead.

8. I believe in the Holy Ghost.

9. The holy catholic church.

10. The communion of saints: The forgiveness of sins.

11. The resurrection of the body.

12. And the life everlasting. Amen.

Here follow certain notes for the better understanding of this Creed.

First, it is to be noted, that all and singular the twelve articles contained in this Creed be so necessary to be believed for man's salvation, that whosoever will not constantly believe them, or will obstinately affirm the contrary of them, cannot be the very members of Christ and his espouse the church, but are very infidels or heretics, and members of the devil, with whom they shall be perpetually damned.

Secondly, it is to be noted, that all true Christian men ought and must most constantly believe, maintain, and defend all those things to be true which be comprehended in this Creed, and in the other two Creeds, whereof the one is used to be said at mass, and is approved by the ancient general councils; and the other was made by the holy man Athanasius: and also all other things which be comprehended in the whole body and canon of the Bible.

Thirdly, that all true Christian men ought and must not only repute, take, and hold all the said things for the most holy, most sure, and most certain and infallible truths of God's word, and such as neither ought ne can be altered or convelled by any contrary opinion or authority; but also must take and interpretate all the same things according to the selfsame sentence and interpretation which the words of scripture do signify, and the holy approved doctors of the church do agreeably entreat and defend.

Fourthly, that all true Christian men ought and must utterly refuse and condemn all those opinions contrary to the said twelve articles of our Creed, which were of long time past condemned in the four holy councils, that is to say, in the council of Nice, Constantinople, Ephese, and Calcidonense.

The First Article

I believe in God the Father Almighty, Maker of Heaven and Earth.

For the plain understanding hereof, every material word of this article shall be declared hereafter. And first we must know, that God is a spiritual and an invisible substance or nature, of infinite power, and eternal, without beginning or ending, and of incomprehensible knowledge, wisdom, goodness, justice, and mercy; and that there is but one very God, three Persons, the Father, the Son, and the Holy Ghost, and that these three Persons be not three Gods, but all one God, one nature, one substance, all one everlasting essence or being, and all like and equal in might, power, wisdom, knowledge, righteousness, and all other things belonging unto the Deity. And that beside or without this God there is none other God.

Moreover we must know that God the Father is the first Person in Trinity, and Father of his only begotten Son, the second Person in Trinity; and that he did beget him of his own substance by eternal generation, that is to say, by generation that never had beginning.

And where this article containeth that God the Father is Almighty, it is as much to say as that he may do all things that he will in heaven and in earth, and nothing is to him impossible; and that his godly power and might excelleth infinitely and incomparably all other powers in heaven, earth, and hell: so that all other powers which be in heaven, earth, or hell, be nothing as of themselves, but have all their might, force, and strength of him, and be all subject unto his power, and cannot resist or let the same. And although God be omnipotent, and of infinite power, yet he is not author or worker of any sin; for whensoever any sin is done by any creature, the same is wrought by the malice of the devil, or free will of man, only by the sufferance and permission of God, and not by the working and power of God, in stirring up, furthering, or assisting the malice of the evil thought or deed.

This article containeth further, that God the Father Almighty did at the beginning create, form, and make of nought heaven and earth, and all things visible and invisible; and that he did give unto them all their power and might, and so he doth from time to time continually preserve, govern, sustain, and maintain the whole world and all creatures therein by his only goodness and high providence, insomuch that without his continual working nothing should be able any while to continue.

And for the more evident and plain understanding of the first part of this article, which is, *I believe in God,* it is to be noted, that we must not only believe steadfastly that God is, and that he is true in all his words and promises, and that he is omnipotent, and Creator of heaven and earth, and so forth; but we must also with this our belief love God, and cleave only unto him, and that with all our heart and power, and so continue and dwell still in him by love. It signifieth also, that we must obey unto his will, as well in all our inward thoughts and affections as also in all our outward acts and deeds; and that we must abhor all vice, and not wish or desire of God any evil or ungodly thing. It signifieth also, that we must constantly betake and commit ourselves and all ours wholly unto God, and fix all our whole hope, trust, and confidence in him, and quiet ourselves in him, believing perfectly and assuredly that he will indeed shew no less goodness, love, mercy, grace, and favour unto us, than he promiseth by his word to do with us, using ourselves as afore is said.

This manner of belief we ought to have in no creature of God, be it never so excellent, but in God only; and therefore in this Creed the said manner of speaking, *I believe in*, is used only in the three articles which concern the three Persons in Trinity, that is, the Father, the Son, and the Holy Ghost.

The Second Article

And in Jesu Christ, his only Son, our Lord. For the understanding of this second article, it is to be known, that Jesus Christ is the only begotten Son of Almighty God the Father, and that he was begotten of his godly nature and substance eternally, and that he is very God, the same substance with God the Father and the Holy Ghost, unto whom he is equal in all things of the Godhead. And although we Christian men may be called the children of God by adoption and grace, yet only our Saviour Jesus Christ is God the Father's Son by nature.

We must know also and believe, that Jesus Christ was eternally preordained and appointed by the decree of the whole Trinity to be our Lord, and to redeem and bring us from under the dominion of the devil and sin unto his kingdom, lordship, and governance; and therefore is worthily called *Jesus,* that is to say, Saviour; and *Christ,* that is to say, anointed King and Priest; and *Lord,* that is to say, Redeemer and Governor; for he hath done and fulfilled for all mankind the very office both of a Priest, and of a King and Lord. Of a Priest, forasmuch as he hath made sacrifice and oblation on the cross, in that he there willingly suffered his natural body to be slain and his blood to be shed for remission of sin, and so was both the priest and the sacrifice itself: and of a King and Lord, in that he hath, like a most mighty conqueror, overcome and utterly oppressed his enemies, and hath spoiled them of the possession of mankind, which they won before by fraud and deceit, by lying and blaspheming, and hath brought us now into his possession and dominion, to reign over us in mercy, like a most loving Lord and Governor. And therefore in this article we call him *our Lord*.

And although this word *Dominus* divers times is translated into our English tongue *the Lord,* and the place and circumstance of scripture oftentimes requireth the same, yet among us Christian men, in our common speech, when we speak of Christ, and call him *Lord,* it is most meet and convenient that we call him *our Lord*, to signify and admonish us that we be his peculiar people, redeemed by him, and delivered from the dominion and the captivity of the devil, and be made his own proper and obedient servants; after which sort the heathen people (because of their infidelity) be neither his servants ne partakers of his benefits, and therefore cannot say and call him (as Christian men do) *our Lord.*

The Third Article

For declaration of this article, ye shall understand, that when the time was come, in the which it was before ordained and appointed by the decree of the whole Trinity that mankind should be saved and redeemed, then the Son of God, the second Person in Trinity, and very God, *Which was conceived by the Holy Ghost, born of the virgin Mary.* descended from heaven into the world, to take upon him the very habit, form, and nature of man, and in the same nature to suffer his glorious passion for the redemption and salvation of all mankind.

And for further declaration hereof, it is to be considered, that before the coming of Christ mankind was so blinded and drowned in sin, that the true knowledge of God was every where in the world forgotten, and his laws broken, not only by the Gentiles in all other nations, but also by the Jews, the chosen people of God, to whom God had by his servant Moses given his laws, whereby they might know how to avoid sin, and please him; and where those laws given by God were often by them transgressed; yet Almighty God did from time to time send to them his prophets, inspired with his holy Spirit, both to admonish them of their sins, and to teach them how they should truly understand and observe the said laws given by his servant Moses. After the which admonitions, many times so given by the prophets, and nothing regarded, Almighty God of his infinite goodness and inestimable mercy, for the love that he bare to mankind, did send at the last into the world his only begotten Son, being his eternal wisdom, by whom in the beginning he did create heaven and earth, and all creatures in them, to take upon him man's nature, for to redeem mankind, and to teach the world the truth of his laws, and by what means the world might, by faith to be given to his words and doctrine, amend their lives, and attain to come to the life in heaven, following him in his doctrine, who was the *way,* to come to the Father, the *truth,* to attain the knowledge of the Father, and the *life* itself, wherein he should finally lead them, to come unto the Father, unto whom God the Father commanding the world to give full credence, said to all men, *Ipsum audite,* Hear him (Matt 17:5).

Wherefore the said Son of God, in the womb of the blessed virgin called Mary, did take upon him of her very flesh, nature, and substance, man's nature, and being conceived by the Holy Ghost, was born of her body, and did unite and conjoin together the same nature of man, taken of the substance of the said most blessed virgin, with his Godhead in one person, with such an indissoluble and inseparable knot and bond, that he being one person Jesus Christ, was, is, and ever shall be in the same person very perfect God and very perfect man; which holy work of the incarnation was not wrought by the seed of man, but by the Holy Ghost in the said most blessed virgin, without any motion of concupiscence or spot of sin, and was accomplished without any violation or detriment unto the virginity of that blessed virgin St. Mary, who, both in the conception and also in the birth and nativity of our Saviour Jesu Christ, her child, and ever after, retained still her virginity pure and immaculate, and as clear without blot as she was at the time that she was first born.

The Fourth Article

Suffered under Ponce Pilate, was crucified, dead, buried, and descended into hell.

For declaration of this article, it shall be expedient briefly to repeat the process of a great part of our Saviour Christ's life, from the beginning unto the time of his most glorious passion, with the same passion also, and the descense of his soul into hell: wherefore we must understand, that Christ, very God and man, after he was conceived and born of his blessed mother, waxed and lived forth here in the world until he came unto the thirty-third year of his age; and that in all this time of his life he suffered and endured for our sakes and our wealth, and also for our example, much bodily affliction, much labour, much travail, much hunger, thirst, and poverty, much injury and ignominy, and many other such miseries and infirmities, as all mortal men be subject unto, (sin and ignorance only except,) and so passed over all the whole course of his life, even from his nativity until his death, in such perfect obedience unto the laws of God and man, according to the will of his Father, and in such perfect innocency of living, that no fault or blame of living, ne any offence or transgression could justly and truly be laid against him: and yet the blind, ignorant, and obstinate Jews, replete with envy and malice, as the very members of the devil, by whom they were provoked and induced thereunto, laboured continually by all craft and means they could, to destroy him; and at length conspiring together, they took him, searching and procuring false witness to accuse him; and after they had beat him, and spit in his face, and used all the villainy they could unto him, they bound him, and brought him before Pontius Pilatus, being then the chief judge in Jerusalem, under the emperor of Rome, and there they most falsely accused him as a subverter of the laws of God, and as a person that seduced the people and moved sedition among them, and as a traitor against the emperor of Rome. After which accusations our said Saviour and Redeemer Jesus Christ was grievously scourged by the commandment of Pilate, and had a crown of thorn put upon his head by the soldiers of the garrison, and was by them not only most spitefully mocked and scorned, but also most cruelly tormented and afflicted, and after this he was at the last in public and open judgment condemned by the sentence of the said judge to be crucified, to the intent he should suffer that kind of death which among the Jews was ever most abhorred and detested, and accounted to be the most shameful and cursed of all other: and so, according to the said sentence, the soldiers of the garrison crucified him, that is to say, they nailed him through hands and feet to a cross, and hanged him upon the same between two thieves, upon a certain hill called Calvary, until he was dead; and after he was thus dead, one Joseph of Arimathea, being one of Christ's disciples, obtained license of the said judge to take down the blessed body of our Saviour Jesu Christ from the said cross; and that done, he and another of Christ's disciples, called Nicodemus, wrapped and folded the same body in a clean syndon, and so laid it and buried it in a new grave or sepulchre, which the said Joseph had made of stone, wherein here was never man buried before. And after he was thus crucified, and dead upon the cross, he descended in soul into hell, and loosed the pains or sorrows thereof, wherewith it was not possible that he should be holden, and conquered and oppressed both the devil and hell, and also death itself, whereunto all mankind was condemned by the fall of our forefather Adam into sin.

The process of our Saviour Jesu Christ's life, death, burial, and descense to hell, thus declared, it is specially to be noted, and to be believed for a certain truth, that our said Saviour, in all the time of his most bitter and grievous passion, and in suffering his most painful and cruel death, not only endured and sustained for our redemption all the pains and injuries, and all the opprobries and ignominies which were done to him, most patiently, without resistance, and like an innocent lamb, but also that he did willingly and gladly suffer this cross and this kind of death for our example, that we should follow the steps of him in patience and humility, and that we should bear our own cross, as he did bear his, and that we should also hate and abhor all sin, knowing for surety that whosoever doth not in his heart hate and abhor sin, but rather accounteth the breach and violation of God's commandment but as a light matter, and of small weight and importance, he esteemeth not the price and value of the passion and death of Christ according to the dignity and worthiness thereof.

The Fifth Article

And the third day he rose again from death.

By this article it appeareth, how our Saviour Jesus Christ, after he had conquered and spoiled the devil and hell, he returned again from thence, like a most mighty king and conqueror, in triumph and glory, and so resumed and took again his blessed natural body, the third day after his said death. And so doing, rose out of that sepulchre in his natural and perfect manhood, that is to say, in his soul and in the selfsame body which was born of the virgin Mary, and did hang upon the cross. After which resurrection he was conversant in the world by the space of forty days, and did eat and drink with his apostles and his disciples, and preached unto them, and authorized them to go forth into the world to manifest and declare that he was the very Christ, the very Messias, and the very God and man which was promised in scripture to come to save and to redeem all those that believing in him ordered themselves in obeying and following his precepts and commandments accordingly.

In this article of resurrection it is to be noted, that there is nothing that can in all adversity and trouble be more joyful and comfortable unto us than the belief of this article, that Christ rose again from corporal death to life, and that we shall also do the same. The faith and belief of this (if we do continue in living well) is our victory and triumph over the devil, hell, and death, and a special remedy to put away the horror and fear of them; forasmuch as hereby we be assured, that as death could not hold Christ, even so it cannot hold us, which are by a Christian faith the very members and body of Christ, but that we shall rise from death, and live again in glory with him everlastingly, if we order and conform our will in this world to his precepts. And the only hope hereof should make us not to fear the adversities in this world, because we, living as afore, be assured to have a better and more glorious life after this, as St. Paul writeth to the Corinthians, saying, If we Christian men had no hope of other life than this that is present, then were we the most miserable of all men (1 Cor 15:19). But now Christ is risen again from death, and hath declared thereby that there is a life after this life, which all Christian men hope to come to. According hereunto, saith St. Augustine, All the hope of our faith standeth in this point, that we shall rise again. This made the faithful and good men (of whom St. Paul speaketh to the Hebrews) to refuse to be preserved from bodily death, because they looked assuredly for a better resurrection (Heb 11).

Of this article the Epistles of St. Paul and the New Testament be full. To the Romans he writeth, Christ rose again for our justification (4:15): to Timothy he saith, Remember that Jesus Christ is risen again from death (2 Tim 2:8). The apostles, besides other names pertaining to their office, be specially called the witnesses of Christ's resurrection; the which resurrection, as it was by many and sundry apparitions, and other infallible arguments, declared and proved unto them, so they did in all places and at all times open and inculcate the same, as a special and a chief article of Christ's doctrine, wherein should depend and rest the great comfort and solace of all true and faithful believers in Christ (Acts 1, 2).

Moreover by this article it is not only confirmed unto us how the natural body of man shall, after the corporal death and departing out of this present life, arise again, as is before expressed, but also by this resurrection of our Saviour Christ we be admonished, that as Christ after his death rose again, so we, dying from sin, should rise again, and walk in a new life of spirit and grace.

The Sixth Article

He ascended into heaven, and sitteth on the right hand of God the Father Almighty.

This article containeth how our Saviour Jesus Christ, after that he had perfectly accomplished and performed the whole mystery of the redemption of mankind, by his incarnation, his birth, his passion, his death, his burial, his descending into hell, and rising again from death to life, and after he had been here in earth conversant with his apostles and disciples by the space of forty days after his resurrection, when he was among the apostles, he in their sight ascended up into heaven in the very same his natural body which was born of the blessed virgin his mother, and was crucified upon the cross, and so did withdraw his accustomed visible conversation from the presence of his apostles, and from the bodily sight of all other creatures. By remembrance whereof both they and we should here in earth elevate and lift up our whole hearts, minds, desires, and all affections from earthly things, and from all carnal and worldly cares, towards heaven and heavenly things, and so should by his grace prepare our hearts, and make ourselves meet and apt to receive his spiritual gifts, which he sendeth into the world.

In this article also is expressed how our Saviour Christ, being ascended into heaven, sitteth on the right hand of God the Father, that is to say, hath and shall ever have communicate unto him of God the Father glory, honour, felicity, power, and everlasting monarchy, governance, rule, and dominion over all the principates, potestates, powers, dominions, and over all creatures that can be named either in this world or in the world to come, to be ordained King of all kings, and Lord of all lords, and all things in heaven and earth to be cast under his feet, and made subject unto him, and he is appointed the only Head of the universal catholic church, which is his mystical body. And likewise as the head always excelleth all the other members, so Christ doth excel incomparably in honour and dignity all the members of his said body the church, whereof he is the only perfection and consummation, and is also the only eternal Priest and Bishop of his said church, that is to say, the only Mediator between God and mankind, the Redeemer, Intercessor, and Advocate for the remission of sins, as hereafter in this book it shall more at large appear.

And it is to be noted, that although the intercession and mediation by prayer of saints departed, and of such the members of the catholic church as be yet living on earth, be good, acceptable, and profitable unto us, yet that is only by the mediation and intercession of Christ our Head, in whom God the Father is pleased and contented, and through whom saints departed this life, and reigning in heaven with Christ, and such as truly confess Christ in the church catholic, yet living, may and do effectually pray for us; and therefore be of us also availably prayed unto, that is to say, desired to pray for us: according whereunto all common prayers of the church ought to be always finished and ended with a remembrance of our Saviour Jesu Christ; in whom, by whom, and for whom all is accepted of God, and without whom nothing can be effectually done or granted.

And therefore it is much to our comfort to remember the exaltation of man's nature in our Head, our Saviour, and Redeemer Jesu Christ, which, inseparably and indissolubly conjoined and united to the Deity in the person of him, sitteth on the right hand of God the Father Almighty, by communion of preeminence and power, as before is expressed, whereby we be certified how our Saviour Jesus Christ is God, equal to God the Father in Godhead, and therein not inferior unto him, and therefore to be honoured, worshipped, loved, and dread, feared and trusted on, believed and hoped on, as on very God Almighty, to whom nothing is impossible; and yet he is man also, which hath experience of our infirmities, and can and will mercifully have compassion on the same; who ascended unto heaven to send gifts unto men, whereby we might be able and strong to pass over this transitory life, to the pleasure of God, and the attaining of everlasting life.

The Seventh Article

From thence he shall come to judge the quick and the dead.

In this article it is declared how our Saviour and Redeemer Jesu Christ shall come from thence, that is to say, from heaven, to the which he ascended, and coming in his majesty and glory, shall then in the very visible form of his natural body, appear unto the bodily eyes of all the people of the world in his perfect manhood, and in the selfsame body wherein he ascended, to the inestimable comfort and rejoice of the good, and to the extreme terror and confusion of the wicked: where being accompanied with his holy angels, his ministers, waiting upon him, he shall sit openly in the clouds of the air, and shall judge all, quick and dead, according to truth and justice, and according to his holy word expressed in scripture, that is to say, according to every man's own works and deeds done by him in his lifetime, which works and deeds shall be then examined, discussed, and tried, not after men's own phantasy and invention, without authority and ground of scripture, but according to the commandment of God, and the teaching of Christ and his apostles: for at that day of judgment all the people of the world, quick and dead, that is to say, as well all those which shall be found on life in the world at that day, as also all those which ever sith the creation of Adam lived here in this world, and died before that day, shall come and appear afore the presence of Christ, in their very bodies and souls. And when they shall be so gathered and assembled together, our Saviour Jesus Christ shall pronounce the final sentence and judgment of everlasting salvation upon all those persons which in their lifetime obeyed and conformed themselves unto the will of God, and exercised the works of right belief and charity, and so persevering in well-doing, sought in their hearts and deeds honour, glory, and life immortal: and contrary, upon all those which in their lifetime were contentious, and did repugn against the will of God, and followed injustice and iniquity rather than truth and virtue, our Saviour Christ shall then and there pronounce the sentence of everlasting punishment and damnation. In which sentence there shall be made a perfect separation or division between these two sorts of people, that is to say, between the sheep and the goats, the corn and the chaff, the good and the bad, the blessed and the cursed, the members of his body and the members of the devil; and so the good and the blessed being upon his right hand, he shall clearly and perfectly deliver them for ever from the power and malice of the wicked, and from all the pains and evil, and so take them all up with him into heaven, there to be crowned and rewarded in body and soul with honour and glory, and everlasting joy and peace, which was prepared for them from the beginning of the world. And all the other, which shall be judged to everlasting pain and death, being upon his left hand, he shall send them down into hell, there to be punished in body and soul eternally with fire that never shall have end, which was prepared from the beginning of the world unto the devil and his angels (Matt 25).

And here it is especially to be remembered how this article was for great considerations added immediately and conjoined unto the former articles, and chiefly to the intent that no man should in this life time presume upon the said benefits of Christ, or take occasion of carnal liberty or security, and so live without fear to transgress, or without regard to observe the commandments of God; but rather that every good Christian man should, in every part of his life, have a continual remembrance and respect unto the last day of judgment, and so be in continual fear to commit any thing contrary to the will of God, for the which he might deserve to have the sentence of everlasting damnation pronounced upon him. For this is certainly true, that at that day every man shall be called to an account of his life, and shall be then finally judged according to his works, good or bad, done in his lifetime, that is, as St. Paul saith, to them that persevere in well-doing, and labour to attain glory, honour, and immortality, shall be given life everlasting; and to them that be contentious, and obey not the truth, but follow and do injustice, shall come indignation, ire, affliction, trouble, and pains everlasting (Rom 2).

In this article it is further to be noted, that like as there is nothing more certain unto us, than that we be all mortal, and shall once die, and yet no man living knoweth the time when he shall die; even so there is nothing more certain than that this day of judgment shall once come, and yet the hour and time when it shall be is hidden and kept secret from the knowledge of all men and angels, and is reserved to the only knowledge of God. Which thing proceedeth of his only goodness towards us, and is done to the intent we should always here in our lifetime flee from sin, and employ all our whole study and endeavour to walk in the ways of God, that is to say, in such faith, hope, and charity as God requireth of us, and so prepare ourselves, and order our living towards God, that we may be in a readiness at all times, whensoever it shall please God to call and summon us, to appear before him in the said general judgment, there, by his mercy and goodness, to receive the crown, which he promised unto all men that do fear him, and love him, and walk in his ways.

The Eighth Article

I believe in the Holy Ghost. The Holy Ghost is the third Person in Trinity, very God and Lord, Author and Former of all things created, and proceedeth both from God the Father and from God the Son, one with them in nature and substance, and of the same everlasting essence or being which the Father and the Son be of, and equal also unto them both in almightiness of power, and in the work of creation, and all other things pertaining unto the Deity or Godhead; wherefore he is also to be honoured and glorified equally with them both.

This Holy Ghost, which is the Spirit of God, is of his nature all holy, yea holiness itself, that is to say, he is the only Ghost or Spirit, which, with the Father and the Son, is, was, and ever shall be the author, causer, and worker of all holiness, purity, and sanctimony, and of all the grace, comfort, and spiritual life, which is wrought and cometh into the heart of any man, insomuch that no man can think well, or do any thing that good is, but by the motion, aid, and assistance of this Holy Spirit; neither it is possible that the devil, or any of those evil spirits which do possess and reign in such persons as be subject unto sin, can be expelled or put out of them but by the power of this Holy Spirit; neither it is possible that the heart of any man, being once corrupted and made as profane by sin, can be purged, purified, sanctified, or justified, without the work and operation of this Holy Spirit; neither it is possible for any man to be reconciled unto the favour of God, or to be made and adopted into the number of his children, or to obtain that incomparable treasure which our Saviour Jesus Christ hath purchased and laid up for mankind, unless this Holy Spirit shall first illumine and lighten his heart with the right knowledge and faith of Christ, and stir him by grace to have due contrition and penance for his sins, and shall also instruct him, govern him, aid him, direct him, and endue him with such spiritual gifts and graces, as shall be requisite and necessary to that end and purpose.

Moreover this Holy Spirit of God is of his own nature full of all goodness and benignity, yea goodness itself, from whom proceedeth all and singular graces and gifts of fear, wisdom, understanding, counsel, strength, faith, charity, hope, and all other, which be given, conferred, and distributed unto us mortal men here in the earth, at his own will and dispensation; and that no man can purchase or obtain, ne yet retain or use any one of them, without the special operation of this Holy Spirit; which gifts nevertheless he giveth not, nor dispenseth the same equally and unto every man in like, but he divideth them particularly and specially to every member of the church, as is most necessary for the whole body, and in such plenty and measure as unto his godly will and knowledge is thought to be most beneficial and expedient for the same. All which things he doth of his mere mercy and goodness freely and above our deserving.

Furthermore, this Holy Spirit is of his own nature full of charity and holy love, yea charity itself, from whom proceedeth all charity; and so, by his godly operation, is the bond and knot wherewith our Saviour Jesus Christ and his most dear espouse the church (which is also his mystical body) be united, knit, and conjoined together in such perfect and everlasting love and charity, that the same cannot be dissolved or separated: and over this is also the very bond and knot whereby all and every one of the very members of Christ's church and body be united, coupled, and conjoined the one of them with the other in mutual love and charity.

Also this Holy Spirit of God is the Spirit of truth, and the author of all holy scripture contained in the whole canon of the Bible; and did not only inspire and instruct all the holy patriarchs and prophets, with all the other members of the catholic church that ever was from the beginning of the world, in all the godly truths and verities that ever they did know, speak, or write, but also descended and appeared in the similitude and likeness of fiery tongues, and did light upon the apostles and disciples of Christ, and inspired them with the knowledge of all truth, and replenished them with heavenly gifts and graces; and shall be continually present in the catholic church, and shall teach and reveal unto the same church the secrets and mysteries of all truths which are necessary to be known; and shall also continually from time to time rule, direct, govern, and sanctify the same church, and give remission of sins, and all spiritual comfort, as well inwardly by secret operations, as also outwardly by the open ministration and efficacy of the word of God, and of the holy sacraments in the said church, and shall endue it with all such spiritual graces and gifts as shall be necessary for the same.

Finally, it is to be noted, that albeit holy scripture doth worthily attribute unto the Holy Ghost our sanctification, our justification, and all other benefits which Christ by his passion hath merited and deserved for us, yet nevertheless the same be also the works of the whole Trinity, and be not to be separated in any wise, although scripture commonly doth attribute them unto the Holy Ghost: for in like manner doth scripture attribute power unto the Father, and wisdom unto the Son, which nevertheless be common unto all three.

The Ninth Article

The holy catholic church.

After the eight articles of our belief, in which we knowledge God's might and power in the creation of the world, his mercy and goodness in our redemption, and his spiritual benefits exhibited and given to us by the Holy Ghost, followeth the ninth article, in which we declare, that we do believe and confess the manner of God's working, in calling us to have fruition of him, and to be made partakers of his said benefits.

Wherefore we must understand, that besides the inward and secret calling which God hath always used, and yet still doth use, he hath also ordained an outward calling of the people unto him, by preaching of his most holy word; upon which outward calling, the people yielding, assenting, and obeying to the same word of God, and receiving it also with true faith, and the sacrament of baptism, (as Christ's law requireth,) be named in scripture *ecclesia*, that is to say, an assembly of people called out from other, as from infidels or heathens, to one faith and confession of the name of Christ, which word *ecclesia* is in English called *church*.

And it is to be noted specially, that, in our English tongue, by the word *church* we understand, not only the whole multitude of people which be called of God to one faith, be they of the clergy or of the laymen, but also by the same word we signify the place wherein the word of God is commonly preached, and the sacraments ministered and used, and call that the church: to entreat whereof at this time, in this article, is no part of our intent, but only of the assembly and company called to profess Christ in one faith, which in this article is named the *holy church*.

For albeit in this assembly of men called by the word of God, and received by faith and baptism, be many evil men, many sinners, many that turn by true penance to grace, and sometime yet fall again, some after their turn by true penance still persevere and increase in goodness, many that fall and never rise again; so that spots, blots, and imperfections appear evidently in this church, and many times in the more part thereof; yet nevertheless because the calling is of itself holy, the caller also holy, and the end of the calling holiness, with this also, that the people so called profess holiness, and make a body, whereof the only Head our Saviour Christ is most holy and holiness itself, by the merits of whose passion they be relieved and nourished with divers holy sacraments, and be in their calling endued with most special holy gifts and graces of Almighty God, author thereof, and by his holy Spirit directed and governed in the same, so long as they, by following their concupiscence, the devil, or the world, fall not from that state. For these causes (although some members thereof be evil) the church is called *holy church*, taking the name of *holy* of that, that Christ the only Head is holy, the caller holy, the profession and calling holy, and the end holiness, which of very duty ought to be in all them that be called, and is indeed in such members as continue and persevere in that holy calling.

And forsomuch as God of his goodness calleth people, as afore, without exception of persons or privilege of place; therefore this holy church is also catholic, that is to say, not limited to any one place or region of the world, but is in every place universally through the world, where it pleaseth God to call people to him in the profession of Christ's name and faith, be it in Europe, Afric, or Asia. And all these churches, in divers countries severally called, although for knowledge of the one from the other among them they have divers additions of names, and for their most necessary government, as they be distinct in places, so they have distinct ministers and divers heads in earth, governors and rulers, yet be all these holy churches but one holy church catholic, invited and called by one God the Father to enjoy the benefit of redemption wrought by our only Lord and Saviour Jesu Christ, and governed by one Holy Spirit, which teacheth to this foresaid holy church one truth of God's holy word in one faith and baptism. And this church is relieved, nourished, and fortified by his holy and invincible word and his sacraments, which in all places have each of them their own proper force and strength, with gifts of graces also, distributed by the goodness of Almighty God in all places, as to his wisdom is seen convenient.

Whereby it appeareth, that the unity of these holy churches, in sundry places assembled, standeth not by knowledging of one governor in earth over all churches. For neither the whole church catholic together, nor any particular church apart, is bound to acknowledge any one universal gov-

ernor over the whole church other than Christ, although by sufferance of
some princes and potentates not being truly instructed in the word of God
by such as of duty both to God and them ought to have declared the truth
of scripture to them, and by hypocrisy and usurpation of the see and court
of Rome, the bishop of the same, giving himself more to worldly policy
than to the execution of his duty, hath long time gone about to obtain and
establish unto himself such an universal authority, and hath by abuses always compassed to cause other to uphold and maintain the same, contrary
to God's law, as more largely shall be declared in the sacrament of orders.

The unity therefore of the church is not conserved by the bishop of
Rome's authority or doctrine; but the unity of the catholic church, which
all Christian men in this article do profess, is conserved and kept by the
help and assistance of the Holy Spirit of God, in retaining and maintaining
of such doctrine and profession of Christian faith, and true observance of
the same, as is taught by the scripture and the doctrine apostolic. And particular churches ought not in the said doctrine so accepted and allowed, to
vary one from another for any lucre, arrogance, or any other worldly affection, but inviolably to observe the same, so that by reason of that doctrine each church that teacheth the same may be worthily called (as it is
indeed) an apostolic church, that is to say, following such teaching as the
apostles preached, with ministration of such sacraments as be approved by
the same.

And this unity of the holy church of Christ is not divided by distance
of place nor by diversity of traditions and ceremonies, diversely observed
in divers churches, for good order of the same. For the church of Corinth
and of Ephese were one church in God, though the one were far distant in
place from the other: and though also in traditions, opinions, and policies
there was some diversity among them, likewise as the church of England,
Spain, Italy, and Poole be not separate from the unity, but be one church
in God, notwithstanding that among them there is great distance of place,
diversity of traditions, not in all things unity of opinions, alteration in
rites, ceremonies, and ordinances, or estimation of the same, as one church
peradventure doth esteem their rites, traditions, laws, ordinances, and ceremonies to be of more virtue and efficacy than another church doth esteem the same. As the church of Rome doth affirm certain of their laws
and ordinances to be of such estimation that they be of equal force with
the word of God, and that whosoever disobeyeth or transgresseth the same

committeth deadly sin; yet we perceiving the same to be discrepant from the truth of scripture, must needs therein dissent from them. But such diversity in opinions, and other outward manners and customs of policy, doth not dissolve and break the unity which is in one God, one faith, one doctrine of Christ and his sacraments, preserved and kept in these several churches without any superiority or preeminence, that one church by God's law may or ought to challenge over another.

And therefore the church of Rome, being but a several church, challenging that name of *catholic* above all other, doeth great wrong to all other churches, and doeth only by force and maintenance support an unjust usurpation: for that church hath no more right to that name than the church of France, Spain, England, or Portugal, which be justly called catholic churches, in that they do profess, consent, and agree in one unity of true faith with other catholic churches. This usurpation, before rehearsed, well considered, it may appear, that the bishop of Rome doeth contrary to God's law in challenging superiority and preeminence by a cloke of God's law over all. And yet to make an appearance that it should be so, he hath and doth wrest scriptures for that purpose, contrary both to the true meaning of the same, and the interpretation of ancient doctors of the church; so that by that challenge he would not do wrong only to this church of England, but also to all other churches, in claiming this superiority without any authority by God so to him given; for God by his goodness hath called indifferently and equally all such churches in sundry places as his high wisdom hath thought good to assemble and call unto him.

Moreover the perfect belief of this article worketh in all true Christian people a love to continue in this unity, and a fear to be cast out of the same; and it worketh in them that be sinners and repentant great comfort and consolation to obtain remission of sin, by virtue of Christ's passion and administration of his sacraments at the minister's hands, ordained for that purpose, forasmuch as God doth not ordinarily give such things, but only within this church.

It is to be noted, that this church of England, and other known particular churches, in which Christ's name is truly honoured, called on, and professed in faith and baptism, be members of the whole catholic church, and each of them by himself is also worthily called a catholic church, when they merely profess and teach the faith and religion of Christ, according to the scripture and the apostolic doctrine. And so every Christian man ought to honour, give credence, and to follow the particular church of that region so ordered (as afore) wherein he is born or inhabiteth. And as all Christian people, as well spiritual as temporal, be bound to believe, honour, and obey our Saviour Jesus Christ, the only Head of the universal church, so likewise they be, by his commandment, bound to honour and obey, next unto himself, Christian kings and princes, which be the head governors under him in the particular churches, to whose office it appertaineth not only to provide for the tranquillity and wealth of their subjects in temporal and worldly things, to the conservation of their bodies, but also to foresee that within their dominions such ministers be ordained and appointed in their churches as can and will truly and purely set out the true doctrine of Christ, and teach the same, and to see the commandments of God well observed and kept, to the wealth and salvation of their souls.

The Tenth Article

The communion of saints, the forgiveness of sins. In this article be taught two special fruits and benefits, which all men called of God, and obeying to the same calling in their will and works, do obtain by God's grace in the said catholic church; which benefits be, the communion of saints and forgiveness of sins.

And here is to be noted, that although this word *saints,* in our English tongue, signifieth properly them that be departed this life, and be established in glory with Christ; yet the same word *saints,* whereby in this article we express the Latin word *sanctorum,* is here extended to signify not only these before mentioned, but also all such as be called into this holy assembly and church, and be sanctified in our Saviour Jesu Christ.

And as touching the communion, that is to say, the mutual participation of these saints, ye must understand, that like as all the parts and members which be living in the natural body of a man do naturally communicate and minister each to other the use, commodity, and benefit of all their forces, nutriments, and perfections; insomuch that it lieth not in the power of any man to say that the meat which he putteth into his own mouth shall nourish one particular member of his body and not another, but that all and every one particularly shall receive of the said nutriment, and of the virtue and benefit thereof, more or less, according to the natural disposition, portion, and place which it hath within the same body: even so, whatsoever spiritual gifts or treasure is given by God unto any one member of the holy church, although the same be given particularly unto one member, and not unto another, yet the fruits and merits thereof shall, by reason of their abiding together in the unity of the catholic church, redound unto the common profit, edifying, and increase of all the other members of the same catholic church. Insomuch that there shall need no man's authority to dispense and distribute the same, or to apply it unto this member or that, but each member shall be made participant of the said treasure, and shall have and enjoy the fruit and benefit of the same in such quantity and measure, as, for the rate and proportion of the faith and charity which he hath in the same body, shall be expedient and necessary for him to have.

And hereby is notified and declared unto us the utility and profit which all the members of the church do receive by the merits, suffrages, and prayers of the church.

And forasmuch as the most blessed sacrament of the altar, wherein, by the mighty operation of God's word, is really present, in form of bread, the natural living body and blood of our Saviour and Redeemer Jesu Christ, increaseth and worketh in them that worthily receive it the communion and conjunction in body and soul of them to Christ and Christ to them, with a mutual conjunction also in love and charity of each good man in Christ to other; therefore the said sacrament may worthily be called the communion of saints. And so the first part of this article hath been by good, devout, and learned men expounded, to signify the said blessed sacrament of the altar, which we must believe to be a real and effectual communion of all saints, that is to say, of all men which be called by the holy calling of God, and therewith willingly and obediently do knowledge and follow the same.

In the second part of this article we be taught to believe remission of sins, which is one of the effects and chief benefits of the most blessed passion of Christ, Head of the holy church, which is called and assembled in his name, in which church is applied the benefits of remission of sins, by the working of God in his sacraments, ministered in the same, as shall be hereafter declared in their place.

The Eleventh and Twelfth Article

The resurrection of the body, and the life everlasting.

At the day of the general doom or judgment, when Christ shall come, (as in the seventh article of this Creed is contained,) and sit to judge both quick and dead. Almighty God shall stir and raise up again the very flesh and bodies of all men, women, and children, both good and bad, christened and heathen, that ever lived here in this world, from the beginning of the same, and died before that day. And although the said flesh and bodies were dead and buried, yea and consumed, or by any means destroyed, yet God shall of his infinite power make them all at that day whole and perfect again. And so every man generally shall resume and take again the very selfsame body and flesh which he had whiles he lived here on earth, and so shall rise from death, and live again in the very selfsame body and soul which he had before.

At which time man, being thus made perfect in conjunction of body and soul, shall at that day appear before the high Judge, our Saviour Jesu Christ, and there shall make an account of his works and his deeds, such as he did, good or evil, while he lived here in this world. And such as have led their lives in obedience and observation of God's commandments, and die in true faith and charity, shall then be perfectly sanctified, purified, and delivered from all contagion of sin, and from all corruption and mortality of the flesh, and shall be perpetually glorified, and receive both in body and soul together everlasting life.

Which life everlasting, though it passeth all men's wits to express how pleasant and joyful it is, nor yet man's capacity can comprise and understand the same, as St. Paul witnesseth, saying, That which the eye hath not seen, nor the ear hath not heard, nor hath not entered into man's heart, God hath ordained for them that love him: yet holy scripture speaketh of it after our capacity and intelligence, but far under the worthiness and excellency thereof (1 Cor 2:9). The prophet Esay saith, Everlasting gladness shall be over their heads: they shall have joy and gladness, sorrow and wailing shall forsake them (Isa 35:10). And St. John saith, God that sitteth on his throne shall dwell over them. They shall not hunger or thirst any more, neither sun nor heat shall hurt them; for the Lamb that is in the midst of the throne shall feed them, and bring them to the fountains of the water of life: and God shall wipe away all weeping and tears from their eyes:

death shall endure no longer. There shall be no wailing, nor crying, nor sorrow any more: yea, there is no joy or comfort that can be wished for, but it is there most plentifully (Rev 7:15-17). There is true glory, where praise shall be without error or flattery. There is true honour, which shall be given to none, unless he be worthy. There is true peace, where no man shall be molested or grieved, neither by himself nor by others. There is true and pleasant fellowship, where is the company of blessed angels, and the elect and chosen saints of God. There is true and perfect love, that never shall fail. For all the heavenly company is linked and fastened together by the bond of perfect charity; whereby also they be united and knit to Almighty God everlastingly.

Finally, there is the true reward of all godliness, God himself: the sight and fruition of whom is the end and reward of all our belief, and all our good works, and of all those things which were purchased for us by Christ. He shall be our satiety, our fulness, and desire; he shall be our life, our health, our glory, our honour, our peace, our everlasting rest and joy. He is the end of all our desires, whom we shall see continually, whom we shall love most fervently, whom we shall praise and magnify world without end.

The Seven Sacraments

The Sacrament of Baptism

As touching the holy sacrament of baptism, it is to be noted, first, that this sacrament was instituted and ordained by our Saviour Jesu Christ in the New Testament, as it doth appear by Christ's own words unto his apostles, where he saith, Go ye abroad throughout all the world, and preach the gospel unto all people, and baptize them in the name of the Father, of the Son, and of the Holy Ghost (Matt 28:19).

Furthermore, that the effect and virtue of this sacrament is forgiveness of sin, and grace of the Holy Ghost, as is manifestly declared in the second chapter of the Acts of the Apostles, where it is said, Do penance, and be baptized every one of you, and ye shall have forgiveness of sin, and shall receive the gift of the Holy Ghost (Acts 2:38). Which effect of grace and forgiveness of sin this sacrament hath, by virtue and force of the working of Almighty God, according to his promise annexed and conjoined unto this sacrament, as is manifestly declared by the word of Christ, saying, Whosoever believeth and is baptized shall be saved (Mark 16:16). Which saying of our Saviour Christ is to be understand of all such persons which die in the grace conferred and given to them in baptism, and do not finally fall from the same by sin.

Moreover, because all men be born sinners, through the transgression of our father Adam, in whom, (as the apostle saith,) all have sinned, and cannot be saved without remission of their sin, which is given in baptism by the working of the Holy Ghost, therefore the sacrament of baptism is necessary for the attaining of salvation and everlasting life, according to the words of Christ, saying, No man can enter into the kingdom of God, except he be born again of water and the Holy Ghost (Rom 5:5; John 3:5). For which causes also it is offered and pertaineth to all men, not only such as have the use of reason, in whom the same, duly received, taketh away and purgeth all kind of sins, both original and actual, committed and done before their baptism; but also it appertaineth and is offered unto infants, which, because they be born in original sin, have need and ought to be christened: whereby they being offered in the faith of the church, receive forgiveness of their sin, and such grace of the Holy Ghost, that if they die in the state of their infancy they shall thereby undoubtedly be saved.

And here we must know, that as touching original sin in infants, like as they take of their parents their original and natural qualities, even so they receive from them original sin, by which they are made the children of the ire of God, and by the same have a natural inclination to sin, by lusts and desires, which, in further age and time, sensibly move and stir them to wickedness. For although the parents be never so clean purged, and pardoned of their original sin by baptism, and grace given in the same, yet nevertheless the children of them begotten be conceived and born in original sin. Example we may take of corn, which, though it be never so clean winnowed and purged from the chaff, yet if it be cast into the ground and sown, the new which springeth of it is full of chaff again, until it be also winnowed and cleansed; so likewise the children of Christian men be full of the chaff and corruption of original sin, until that by baptism they be washed, cleansed, and purged from the same, as their parents were.

And whereas we have before shewed that original sin is remitted and taken away by baptism, both in infants and all other which having the use of reason duly receive the same, yet further we think good to note a special virtue and efficacy of this sacrament of baptism: which is, that albeit there remain in us that be christened a certain infirmity or inclination of sin, called *concupiscence,* which by lusts and desires moveth us many times to sin and wickedness, yet Almighty God of his great mercy and goodness hath given us such grace in this his holy sacrament of baptism, that such carnal and fleshly lusts and desires shall or can in no wise hurt us, if we do not consent unto them. And by the same grace also conferred unto us in baptism, we be made more strong and able to resist and withstand the said concupiscence and carnal desires than is another man which never was christened.

Furthermore, forasmuch as in these days certain heresies have risen and sprung up against the christening of infants, it is to be noted, that (as the holy doctors of the church do testify) the universal consent of the churches in all places and of all times, using and frequenting the christening of infants, is a sufficient witness and proof that this custom of the church in baptizing of infants was used by Christ's apostles themselves, and by them given unto the church, and in the same hath been always continued even unto these days. And this custom and perpetual usage of the church, even from the beginning, is agreeable with the saying of St. Paul; Christ loved his church, and hath given himself to the death for his church's sake, to sanctify her, and make her holy, in cleansing her by the fountain of water in his word, &c. (Eph 5:25-26). So that no man is nor can be of this church but he which is cleansed by the sacrament of baptism: like as the text before alleged sheweth, where Christ saith, Whosoever is not born again of water and the Holy Ghost shall not enter into the kingdom of heaven (John 3:5). Wherefore seeing that out of the church neither infants nor no man else can be saved, they must needs be christened and cleansed by baptism, and so incorporated into the church. And as the infancy of the children of the Hebrews, in the Old Testament, did not let, but that they were made participant of the grace and benefit given in circumcision; even so, in the New Testament, the infancy of children doth not let, but that they may and ought to be baptized, and so receive the graces and virtues of the same.

In this part also it is to be noted, that children or men once baptized ought never to be baptized again. And all good Christian men ought and must repute and take all the anabaptists' and the Pelagians' opinions, which be contrary to the premises, and every other man's opinion agreeable unto the said anabaptists or the Pelagians in that behalf, for detestable heresies, and utterly to be condemned.

Moreover, for because as well this sacrament of baptism as all other sacraments instituted by Christ, have all their virtue, efficacy, and strength by the word of God, which by his holy Spirit worketh all the graces and virtues which be given by the sacraments to all those that worthily receive the same; we must understand and know, that although he which doth minister the sacrament be of a sinful and evil conversation, yet the virtue and effect of the sacrament is thereby nothing diminished or hurted, neither in infants, nor yet in them which being endued with the use of reason come thereunto truly contrite and penitent of all their sins done before, believing and confessing all the articles of the Creed, and having a sure faith and trust in the promises of God, of remission of their sins, and purposing ever after to live a Christian life.

Finally, this sacrament of baptism may well be called a covenant between God and us, whereby God testifieth, that he for his Son Christ's sake justifieth us, that is to say, forgiveth us our sins, and endueth us with his Holy Spirit, and giveth us such graces, that thereby we be made able to walk in the works of justice ordained by God to be exercised of us in this present life, to the glory and praise of God: and so persevering, to enjoy the fruit of the life everlasting. And we again, upon our part, ought most diligently to remember and keep the promise that we in baptism have made to Almighty God, that is, to believe only in him, only to serve and obey him, to forsake all sin, and the works of Satan, to mortify our affections of the flesh, and to live after the Spirit in a new life. Of which promise and covenant by us made to God, St. Paul putteth us in remembrance, saying, Know ye not that all we which are baptized in Jesu Christ are baptized to die with him? for we be buried with him by baptism to die, that likewise as Christ was raised up from death by the glory of his Father, even so we should walk in a new life (Rom 6:3-4). By the which words St. Paul giveth us to understand, that all we which be baptized in Christ, that is to say, which by baptism are incorporated into the mystical body of Christ, have professed and bound ourselves in baptism to die from sin, and utterly to abstain from the corruption of our old sinful life, and to walk and proceed in a new life of grace and the Spirit, into the which we are called by the word of God, and by faith and due receiving of this holy sacrament are brought and set into the same.

The Sacrament of Penance

For the clear understanding of this sacrament, it is to be considered what penance is, and also what is the sacrament of penance.

Penance is an inward sorrow and grief of the heart for the sins by us done and committed, and an hatred and detestation of the same, with an earnest desire to be purged from them, and to recover again the grace and favour of God by such means and remedies as God hath appointed for the obtaining thereof, with a steadfast purpose and mind never to offend again. For he that saith that he is sorry for his offences committed against the high majesty of God, and yet still continueth or intendeth to continue in the same, is no penitent person, but a dissembler, or rather a derider of penance. And thus is penance commonly taken in the scripture, as well in the New as in the Old Testament. And this penance is a thing so necessary for man's salvation, that without it no man that offendeth God can be saved, or attain everlasting life.

The sacrament of penance is properly the absolution pronounced by the priest upon such as be penitent for their sins, and so do knowledge and shew themselves to be. To the obtaining of the which absolution or sacrament of penance be required contrition, confession, and satisfaction, as ways and means expedient and necessary to obtain the said absolution. In all which ways and means faith is necessarily required as the ground and foundation of all things that are to be done, for to attain the benefit of the sacrament of penance. For who can have true penance, with hope to attain any grace of remission of sin thereby, unless he believe steadfastly that God is, and that in the New Testament, by the mean of our Saviour Jesu Christ, and by the force of his passion, there is promise made to his church to grant remission of sins by his ministers to such as falling from the grace received in baptism, do at his calling turn unto him by penance? And like as they which were not baptized, being infants, when they come to the years of discretion, and desire baptism, be taught first to believe in God, and to renounce the devil and his works, upon which ground of faith they desire baptism as a necessary sacrament for remission of sin; so every man, before he entereth into the ways of fruitful penance, must have for a ground and foundation such a belief as whereby he hopeth and looketh, by the sacrament of penance, to attain remission of all his sins, whereunto we do come (as is aforesaid) by contrition, confession, and satisfaction.

Contrition is an inward sorrow and grief for sin, which every true penitent, called by God's grace, hath by knowledge of the word of God, whereupon remembering his own sinful and vicious living, whereby he hath provoked the high indignation and wrath of God; and on the other side, considering the dignity and purity of that state whereunto he was called in baptism, and his promise made there to God, the manifold benefits also daily received of God; hereupon the said penitent, moved and stirred with the great love and goodness of God, shewed before towards him on the one party, and his own ingratitude or unkindness towards God on the other party, conceiveth an earnest sorrow for that he hath relinquished so loving a Lord, and an hateful displeasure that he hath followed sin, and thereby so grievously offended God, of whom he was before called to be in the state of a son, and inheritor with our Saviour Jesu Christ.

And thus being moved and troubled in spirit, and lamenting the miserable state which he is now in, by his own default, is pricked and stirred in his heart, according to the teaching of his mother, holy church, to repair to such a minister as God hath ordained to pronounce the sentence of remission of sin. And knowing him to occupy that place, as deputed of God, doth prostrate himself to God, and there humbly proceedeth to confession, wherein he, calling to his remembrance his sinful life past, doth knowledge to the priest all such sins in which his conscience telleth him that he hath grievously offended the goodness of God Almighty; and the same before the priest, God's minister, he declareth and uttereth with his mouth; and so blameth, accuseth, and condemneth himself for an unkind prodigal son to Almighty God his Father, for a naughty servant, that knew by light of grace the commandment of his Lord Jesu Christ, and did it not, was endued with many gifts of the Holy Ghost, and exercised them not (Luke 15; 12). And so detesting and abhorring sin, and desirous to be raised from that estate, confesseth in humility the cause of sin to have been of himself, by yielding to the concupiscence of the flesh, the world, and the devil. Wherefore he is glad to submit himself to such discipline and ways of reformation as the priest, hearing his sins and offences, shall by his discretion and wisdom, according to the word of God, think convenient. Which humble submission to the ghostly father, with consent and agreement to receive the said discipline, is a part of satisfaction, which is the third way or mean to the sacrament of penance, as is before rehearsed.

And this satisfaction declareth a desire to please and content God his Father, for the unkindness towards him, in falling from the estate of grace, wherein he was called to be his son and inheritor of heaven, unto the miserable condition of sin, whereby he hath made himself most vile bondman unto the devil.

But here ye must understand, that the satisfaction (which is here spoken of) is not so to be taken as though the penitent sinner could worthily merit or deserve remission of sins by any pain or punishment to be by him suffered, or to make to God any just or full recompense equivalent to the sin that he hath committed against him, and so to satisfy, which he can never do; for that satisfaction hath only our Saviour Christ wrought in his glorious passion: but to satisfy (as here is meant by satisfaction) is to please God with an humble, lowly heart, ready to bring forth the fruits of penance, and to bring them forth in deed, as in alms, prayer, and fasting, with all such means as may serve for the cutting away of the occasion of sin, as the minister shall think good, according to the word of God, and with such weeping, lamenting, and wailing, as do burst out of the heart, with a full purpose to lead a new life, and therewith to forgive all men their trespasses, to restore to all men that he hath unjustly taken or retained from them, to recompense all hurts and injuries done by him, according to his ability and power, and as he may; not only to will, but also to do thus to his neighbour indeed, wherein the neighbour ought to be satisfied.

And hereby appeareth how God esteemeth satisfaction, both to himself and to the neighbour, after the will and power, and not after the equivalence of that which is done. For to God no man can so satisfy for sin. And Christ therefore hath satisfied for all; by virtue whereof our satisfaction is accepted and allowed of God, who, of his infinite goodness, and for Christ's sake, is satisfied, that is to say, pleased with that little we do.

Whereupon, after this contrition had in heart, confession made with mouth, and satisfaction shewed and promised, the penitent may desire to hear of the minister the comfortable words of remission of sins. And the minister thereupon, according to Christ's gospel, pronounce the sentence of absolution; unto the which absolution the penitent must give credence, and believe with a perfect faith that his sins be now forgiven freely by the merits of Christ's passion, to the which forgiveness he hath recourse by the sacrament of penance, as he had at the first entry unto Christ's religion by the sacrament of baptism.

It is also to be noted, that confession to the priest is in the church profitably commanded to be used and frequented, for many other good causes, and especially for this cause, that they which by custom be drowned in sin, and see not the abomination and filthiness thereof, ne remember the goodness of God, and want therefore contrition, may, by a good ghostly father, be stirred and moved to detest and lament their sin, by declaring unto them the word of God in such scriptures as serve for that purpose, in such wise, that not only contrition shall arise in the heart to the pleasure of God, but also satisfaction ensue, wherewith God's merciful goodness shall be contented. So that the words of absolution may be effectually pronounced to the penitent of the remission of his sins.

Finally, it is to be remembered, that notwithstanding this way before described is the ordinary mean for penitent sinners to obtain remission of sins, and to be reconciled to the favour of God, yet in case there lack a minister to pronounce the words of absolution, or in time of necessity, when a sinner hath not sufficient leisure or opportunity to do the works of penance before declared, if he truly repent him of his sinful life, and with all his heart purpose through God's grace to change and amend the same, he shall undoubtedly have pardon and forgiveness of all his misdoings. For, as St. Cyprian saith, Even in the hour of death, when the soul is ready to depart out of the body, the great merciful goodness of God despiseth not penance: insomuch that then, neither the greatness of sin, nor the shortness of time, nor yet the enormity of life, excludeth from the mercy of God, if there be true contrition, and an unfeigned change of the heart from sinful conversation. The thief that hanged upon the cross asked mercy with a contrite heart, and forthwith was made a citizen of paradise; and whereas he deserved condemnation and punishment, this contrite heart changed his pain into martyrdom, and his blood into baptism: yet notwithstanding, no man ought, upon hope of God's mercy, still to continue in sinful living. Like as no man would be sick in his body upon hope to recover health. For such as will not forsake their wickedness, and yet think that God will forgive them, be oftentimes so prevented with the just plague of God, that neither they have time to convert nor grace to receive the benefit of forgiveness. Therefore scripture saith, Slack not to convert and turn to God; and linger not from day to day: for his anger will come suddenly; and in the time of vengeance he will destroy thee (Sir 5:8-9). Wherefore, embracing the mercy of God on the one side, and fearing the justice of God on the other side, let us at no time neither despair of forgiveness of our sins, nor yet presumptuously remain still in our sins, knowing that the justice of God will straitly exact and require the debts of all men which be not pardoned through his clemency and mercy.

The Sacrament of the Altar

The sacrament of the altar was institute by our Saviour Christ the night afore he suffered his passion, where he, sitting at supper with his apostles, after he had eaten of the paschal lamb, according to the ordinance of the law of Moses, and willing all such sacrifices and sacraments of the Old Testament to cease, and declaring that they were but shadows and signs to signify him, who (as St. Paul saith) is the end and perfection of the law, did then institute and ordain this most high and principal sacrament of the New Testament (Rom 10:4). Wherein is verily expressed and presented the most exceeding and inexplicable love of our Saviour Jesu Christ towards us, his church, with whom it hath pleased him to leave for our nourishment, strength, and comfort, so precious and glorious a sacrament: which among all the sacraments is of incomparable dignity and virtue, forasmuch as in the other sacraments the outward kind of the thing which is used in them remaineth still in their own nature and substance unchanged. But in this most high sacrament of the altar, the creatures which be taken to the use thereof, as bread and wine, do not remain still in their own substance, but by the virtue of Christ's word in the consecration be changed and turned to the very substance of the body and blood of our Saviour Jesu Christ. So that although there appear the form of bread and wine, after the consecration, as did before, and to the outward senses nothing seemeth to be changed, yet must we, forsaking and renouncing the persuasion of our senses in this behalf, give our assent only to faith, and to the plain word of Christ, which affirmeth that substance there offered, exhibited, and received, to be the very precious body and blood of our Lord, as it is plainly written by the evangelists, and also by St. Paul: where they, entreating of the institution of this sacrament, shew how our Saviour Christ, sitting at his last supper with his apostles, took bread and blessed it, and brake it, and gave it unto his disciples, and said, Take *Matt 26; Mark* ye and eat, this is my body. And also when he gave the cup, *14; Luke 22;* he said, This is my blood of the New Testament, which *1 Cor 11* shall be shed for many for the remission of sins.

By these words it is plain and evident to all them which with meek, humble, and sincere heart will believe Christ's words, and be obedient unto faith, that in the sacrament, the things that be therein be the very body and blood of Christ in very substance.

Which thing whosoever will deny, he denieth the very open and plain words of Christ, which cannot be but true: for he is truth itself, and cannot lie. Wherefore in this most high mystery no man ought to reason over-far, nor go about to compass the will and work of God by his weak sense and imagination: but we must without further searching give firm assent and credence unto Christ's almighty word, by the which heaven and earth were made, and not trouble our wits in labouring to comprehend the power and might of God, but rather (steadfastly giving faith to his word) apply our whole will and affection to attain the fruit and profit of this most holy sacrament towards our salvation, according to the intent of Christ's institution: who, of his inestimable mercy and love towards us, willing that we should have perfect hope, strength, comfort, and joy in him, and that we should have continual remembrance of his most dear charity shewed towards us in his death and passion, did institute this sacrament as a permanent memorial of his mercy and the wonderful work of our redemption, and a perpetual food and nourishment for our spiritual sustentation in this dangerous passage and travail of this wretched life. It is therefore necessary, that in the using, receiving, and beholding of this sacrament, we have hearty remembrance of our most loving and dear Saviour Jesu Christ, that is to say, that we think effectuously of his most bitter passion, which he, being the Lord of glory, suffered for us; and to bewail our sins, which were cause of the said death and passion, calling meekly for grace and the mercy of God, which most abundantly is obtained by the virtue and merit of the same passion: and thinking that our Lord, which gave himself in that manner for us, will not forsake us, or cast us away, but forgive us, if we truly repent, and will amend and become faithful servants to him which so dearly hath bought us, and payed for us neither gold ne yet silver, as St. Peter saith, but his own precious blood (1 Pet 1:19). Wherefore, seeing we be so bought, we must know that we be not our own, that is to say, we may not be at the liberty and wildness of our own flesh, nor we may not be servants to the world nor the devil; but we must be servants to our Lord and Master Jesu Christ in all obedience unto righteousness and godliness, according to his will and commandments.

Therefore, whensoever we shall receive or use this holy sacrament, we must take heed and have reverence to the majesty thereof, and beware that we come not unworthily thereunto. For as St. Paul saith, He that eateth of that heavenly food, or drinketh of the cup of our Lord unworthily, that is to say, without due reverence, faith, repentance, charity, and the fear of God, he eateth and drinketh his own damnation, because he putteth no difference between the body of our Lord and other meats (1 Cor 11:27). And further truly, since Christian men ought to have remembrance of God, whensoever they go to their bodily meat or drink, and receive it not without thanksgiving unto God, (as St. Paul saith, Whether ye eat or drink, or whatsoever ye do, do it in the name of our Lord Jesu Christ [1 Cor 10:31];) how much more ought all Christian men, when they come to be fed at the table of our Lord, and to receive this blessed and glorious sacrament, to have special and entire devotion, with most thankful remembrance to God for his goodness declared towards us in the benefit of our redemption? And therefore amongst other names, this sacrament is called *Eucharistia,* that is to say, the sacrament of thanks and blessing: forasmuch as it setteth before us and doth exhibit unto us the very price of our redemption and salvation, which is the body of our Lord that suffered and died for us.

Furthermore here is to be noted, as touching the receiving of this sacrament, that although our Saviour Jesus Christ, at the first institution thereof in his supper, did minister it unto his disciples then present under both the kinds of bread and wine, yet that fashion and manner of ministering is not so necessary to the receiver, except it be to the priest, when he consecrateth, that without the due observation of that way, man might not receive that blessed sacrament to his salvation. For the benefit or hurt that cometh to a Christian man by receiving of this sacrament, standeth not in the fashion or manner of receiving of it, under one or both kinds, but in the worthy or unworthy receiving of the same. For he that receiveth this sacrament worthily under the one kind, as under the form of bread only, receiveth the whole body and blood of Christ, and as many and great benefits of Christ as he that receiveth it in both kinds. And therefore if any man should teach that the lay people (which by the ordinance and ancient custom of the catholic church have used to receive this holy sacrament in form of bread only) be seduced, and so cause them to think that the whole body and blood of Christ were not comprehended in that only form of bread, as well as in both the kinds, this doctrine ought utterly to be refused and abjected, as a pestiferous and a devilish school. For surely scripture teacheth the contrary. And also natural reason, although it cannot comprehend the whole mystery of this sacrament, yet herein it teacheth us, agreeably with scripture, that the lively body cannot be without blood; and so men ought to be led from that fond opinion (if any such be) both by that faith and credit they owe to scripture, and in this point also by natural reason. Wherefore Christian men ought not to grudge at this form and manner of receiving of this sacrament under one kind, used and allowed by the catholic church, both to avoid that error afore rehearsed, and also for many other weighty considerations, concerning both the honour of the sacrament, and the liberty and commodity of the whole church, and not only laymen but also priests (saving when they consecrate) use to receive this sacrament none otherwise. Let Christian men, therefore, humbly apply themselves to put all erroneous fantasies (if any such arise) clean out of their hearts, and satisfy themselves with this, that when they receive this sacrament worthily, though it be but in one kind, they lose no part of the profit and benefit promised by virtue of the said sacrament.

Wherefore, considering (as is afore rehearsed) the dignity and excellency of this sacrament, we ought with all humbleness of heart and devotion to prepare ourselves, that we (using accordingly the same) may be partakers of such fruit and grace as undoubtedly is offered and given to all such as in due manner receive this sacrament. For they that so do, be made one with Christ, and dwell in him, and he in them, as he saith in the sixth chapter of St. John's Gospel, where he speaketh also of this sacrament: This is the bread which descended from heaven, that whosoever eateth thereof should not die. I am the lively bread, which have descended from heaven. If any shall eat of this bread, he shall live everlastingly. And then he declaring himself what he meaneth by the bread, saith, as incontinently followeth, And the bread which I shall give is my flesh, which I shall give for the life of the world (6:50-51). Which words be most comfortable for the perfect confirmation and establishment of our faith in this sacrament: forasmuch as they both certify us that his very flesh, blood, and body is that meat which we receive in the sacrament, and that also it preserveth from death, and conferreth life to all which duly receive it. For seeing it the very body of our Saviour Christ, which is united and knit to his godhead in one person, and by reason thereof hath the very virtue and substance of life in it, it must needs consequently, by the most holy and blessed participation of the same, give and communicate life also to them that worthily receive it. And it endueth them with grace, strength, and virtue against all temptation, sin, and death, and doth much ease and relieve all the troubles, diseases, and infirmities of their soul. For seeing the woman which was diseased with the flux of blood (as it is written in the Gospel) was healed by touching the hem of the garment of Christ, through the virtue which came from him, how much more shall they find remedy of the sickness and malady of their soul, which with due reverence and faith receive and eat the blessed body of Christ, and so be made lively temples of him dwelling in them, yea, made as one flesh and body with him (Matt 9)? For this heavenly meat is not turned into our substance, as other corporal meat is; but by the godly operation thereof we be turned towards the nature of it, that is to say, of earthly, corruptible, and sinful, we be made heavenly, spiritual, and strong against sin and all wickedness.

And further, it is to be remembered, that as in the receiving of this sacrament we have most entire communion with Christ, so be we also joined by the same in most perfect unity with his church, and all the members thereof. And for that cause amongst other this sacrament was instituted of our Saviour Christ, in the form of bread, to signify the unity, concord, and charity that is between Christ our head, and his mystical body the church, and every part and member thereof one with another. For as bread is made of many grains or corns, which all make but one loaf, so should all true Christian people, being many in number, yet be all one in faith and charity, as St. Paul saith, We be one bread and one body, all that be partakers of one bread, that is, of this blessed sacrament (1 Cor 10:17).

Finally, it is to be noted, that although Christ, at the first institution of this sacrament, did consecrate and give it to his disciples at supper, after they had eaten the paschal lamb, partly to declare that the sacraments and sacrifices of the old law should from thenceforth cease and take an end, and partly that by this sacrament, being the last thing that he next before his death left unto his disciples, the remembrance of him should be the more deeply and effectuously imprinted in the hearts of them, and of all other that after should receive the same; yet (as St. Augustine saith) it was thought good to the apostles, and the universal church, being moved with the Holy Ghost, for the more honour of so high a sacrament, and for the more reverence and devout receiving thereof, that it should always be received of Christian people when they be fasting, and before they receive any bodily sustenance, except it be in case of sickness or necessity.

Wherefore, considering the most excellent grace, efficacy, and virtue of this sacrament, it were greatly to be wished and prayed for, that all

Christian people had such devotion thereunto, that they would gladly dispose and prepare themselves to the more often worthy receiving of the same. But seeing that in these last days charity is waxed cold, and sin doth abound, (as Christ saith in the Gospel that it should,) yet if Christian men will avoid the great indignation of God, it shall be good for them, whensoever they receive this sacrament themselves, or be present where it is ministered or used, as specially in the time of mass, to behave themselves reverently, in pure devotion and prayer, and not to talk or walk up and down, or to offend their brethren by any evil example of unreverence to the said sacrament; except they will declare themselves to have small regard to our Saviour Christ, there bodily present, of which unreverence and contempt may ensue, not only spiritual punishments of God, by withdrawing his grace from such ungodly persons, but also bodily and open scourge, as St. Paul sheweth to the Corinthians, That for the unworthy entreating and using of this sacrament, many amongst them were weak, sick, and died (1 Cor 11:30).

The Sacrament of Matrimony

As touching the sacrament of matrimony, and the institution thereof, you shall understand, that Almighty God, at the first creation of man, considering of his infinite goodness and wisdom how necessary it was to couple and conjoin man and woman together in marriage, as well for their mutual aid and comfort, and for the preservation and continuance of mankind in lawful succession, as also that the same generation might, after the fall of man, be exercised perpetually unto the world's end, without sin and offence towards God, did conjoin Adam and Eve together in marriage: and then instituted matrimony, and consecrated and blessed it by his holy word, as appeareth in the Book of Genesis, where is also described the virtue and efficacy of the same, by these words following: Now this bone is of my bones, and this flesh is of my flesh; and therefore the man shall leave his father and mother, and adhere and cleave unto his wife, and they shall be two in one flesh and in one body (Gen 2:23). By which words it is meant, that by the virtue and efficacy of matrimony, rightfully and by the authority of God contracted, the man and woman, which were before two bodies, be now united and made one body during their lives: so that the husband hath no power of his own body, to use the same as him list, and with whom him liketh, but it is his wife's, and with her only he may use the act of matrimony: nor the wife hath any power of her own body, to use it as her list, or with whom her liketh, but her body is her husband's body, and with him only may she use the act of matrimony. And therefore the said two persons so conjoined may not after be divided for any affection to father or mother, or for any earthly thing in the world, but each must adhere and cleave to other, forasmuch as they be now two persons in one flesh and in one body.

Secondly, how that Almighty God, allowing and approving the said institution of matrimony, sanctified and blessed it with his holy word, immediately after Noe's flood, saying unto Noe and his children in this wise: Increase, and be ye multiplied, and replenish the earth (Gen 9:1). This institution of matrimony, thus allowed by God unto Noe and his children, although it was a sufficient instruction unto them and all their posterity how to use the same in all purity and cleanness, to God's pleasure and his contentation; yet God, considering the natural inclination of man to malice and sin, did afterward further explicate and establish the same by his other laws written, whereby God prohibited that any matrimony should be made in the degrees following, that is to say:

No man shall marry with his mother, his grandame, his great grandame, and so upward: neither may he marry with the wife of his father, his grandfather, or his great grandfather, and so upward: neither any man may marry with the sister of his father, or of his mother, his grandfather or his grandmother, and so upward: neither may any man marry with the wife of him that is brother to his father, his mother, his grandfather, his grandmother, and so upward. And likewise every woman is forbidden to marry any man within any degrees above rehearsed. It is also further forbidden that any man shall marry with his sister, whether she be his whole sister or his half sister, begotten in marriage or out of marriage: neither may he marry with his brother's wife, nor with his wife's sister. Which laws of prohibition in marriage, although they were not by express words of God declared at the first institution of matrimony, ne also when the same was allowed after Noe's flood, God did engrave and imprint the same laws in the heart of man before they were written by Moses. And forasmuch as the natural light and knowledge of man was not only by original sin obscured and blinded, but also, in the most part of men, by the increase of sin and malice, in long continuance and process of time almost perished and extinct; insomuch that they could not perceive nor judge what things were of their own nature nought and detestable in the sight of God, ne yet how far the natural honesty and reverence which we owe unto such persons as be near of our kin or alliance unto us was extended: God therefore, willing man to return from darkness, commanded his prophet Moses to promulgate and to declare by his word unto the people of Israel the said laws of prohibition of matrimony in certain degrees of consanguinity and affinity, as is before mentioned. In the declaration of the which laws of prohibition, Moses so tempered his words, that it may evidently appear thereby, that not only the Jews, but also all other the people of the world, were as much and as straitly bounden to the continual observation of the same laws, as they were to the other moral laws of the Ten Commandments.

Thirdly, that the conjunction between man and woman in matrimony doth not only signify and represent the perfect and indissoluble conjunction and union of the nature of God with the nature of man, which was fulfilled when the second Person in Trinity, descending from his Father, did take upon him the very form and substance of our nature, and so these two natures were united and knit together in one person; but also thereby is signified and represented the society and conjunction in perfect and indissoluble love and charity between Christ and his church, that is to say, the congregation of all Christian people. And this to be true, St. Paul himself affirmeth in the fifth chapter of the Epistle unto the Ephesians. In which place the apostle, minding to prove and persuade that all women, being married, ought to love, to reverence, to honour, to obey, to be subject unto their husbands in all things, even as the church is subject unto Christ; and likewise, that all husbands ought and be bound to love their wives even as they love their own selves and their own bodies, and even as Christ loveth the church his espouse; he bringeth in the first institution of matrimony, as it was ordained by God in paradise, and allegeth the words of God, as they be before rehearsed: upon which words the apostle inferreth and saith, This conjunction of man and woman together in marriage, whereby they are knitted, united, and made, all one flesh and one body, is the sacrament, that is to say, a mystery and signification of that great and marvellous conjunction which is between Christ and his church (Eph 5:31-32). For like as by virtue and efficacy of the first institution of matrimony, the husband and the wife be made to be but one body, whereof the husband is head; even so Christ doth knit and unite, conglutinate and make his church to be one body with him, whereof he is the very head. By the which words of St. Paul it appeareth not only what is the virtue and efficacy of matrimony, in the uniting and incorporating of two bodies in one, but also that it doth signify this other conjunction which is between Christ and his church: and that this conjunction between Christ and the church is the very self thing which is signified and represented by the other conjunction of man and woman in marriage. For though St. Paul used in this place other arguments and persuasions, taken of the law of nature, to induce married persons the one to love the other, saying, that men naturally do love and nourish their own bodies and their own flesh; yet he useth this as a reason of great efficacy to persuade his purpose, that is to say, that all husbands and wives ought so to use themselves the one to the other, that their matrimony, and all their works and affections in the same, might and should correspond, and be conformable and like unto that most holy thing which is signified and represented thereby, that is to say, unto that spiritual conjunction which is between Christ and his espouse the church. And that therefore especially the man ought and is bound to love his wife, and the wife to love and obey her husband in all things, lest by doing the contrary they should make their matrimony unlike to the thing that is signified thereby.

And thus was matrimony not only instituted by God, sanctified by his word, and dignified by his laws, even from the beginning of the world, but also Christ himself did accept, approve, and allow the same in the New Testament, as well by his word as also by his sundry works and deeds testifying the same: insomuch that he, being invited to a certain marriage made in Cana, a town of Galilee, did vouchsafe not only to come thither, and there to honour the said marriage with his corporal presence, and with the presence also of his blessed mother and his holy apostles; but there he began also, by turning of water into wine, first to work miracles, and to manifest his glory unto the world (John 2). And afterward, in one other place, when the Pharisees came unto him, and demanded whether a man might lawfully be divorced from his wife for every cause, Christ, putting the said Pharisees in remembrance of the first institution of matrimony, said unto them, Have you not read how that God, which created all things in the beginning, did also form and create man and woman, and said these words, Therefore the man shall leave his father and mother, and shall adhere and cleave unto his wife, and they shall be two in one flesh and one body? Wherefore understand you (saith he) that sith man and woman conjoined in matrimony be by God's ordinance but one flesh and one body, they should not afterward be separated or divorced one from the other. And understand you also, that it is not lawful for any man to separate and divide those persons asunder, which by God's word and his will and power be conjoined together. And when the Pharisees, replying thereunto, said, Why then did Moses command us to make a libel of divorce, and so to depart and separate ourselves from our wives? Christ answered them and said, Moses, considering the hardness and obstinacy of your hearts, did permit and suffer you so to do; howbeit I say unto you that it was not so at the beginning: that is to say, it is clean contrary to the godly institution and natural order of the laws of matrimony, as it was instituted by God at the beginning, that any man married should be divorced from his lawful wife, and be set at liberty to marry. And therefore I say again unto you, that whosoever doth forsake his lawful wife, unless it be for adultery committed by her, and marry another, I say he committeth adultery in so doing. And likewise what woman soever doth forsake her lawful husband, and marrieth another, she also committeth adultery; and the man also that marrieth her offendeth in like manner (Matt 19:1-12).

These words of Christ evidently declare his sentence in the approbation of the institution of matrimony, made at the beginning of the world, and that it is Christ's will and commandment that the people of God should follow and conform their doings unto the laws of matrimony then made, and should observe the same in such purity and sanctimony as it was first ordained, without separation or divorce, and that under the pain of damnation.

And here also is one thing specially to be noted, that in these words of Christ (That which God hath conjoined man may not separate) is declared the infinite benignity and goodness of God towards us, in that he hath not only conjoined our first progenitors, Adam and Eve, together in marriage, whereby he gave unto us the original beginning of our procreation, but that he doth also ever sith that time continually assist man and woman, and worketh with them in this conjunction of marriage, and is the very author of all matrimonies which be lawfully made between man and woman. And therefore St. Paul saith, *Honorabile conjugium in omnibus, et thorus immaculatus;* that is to say, Matrimony is honourable in all, and the bed undefiled (Heb 13:4).

Another thing also is to be noted, that not only the act and procreation, which else of itself were unlawful, is by the sacrament made lawful, but also that the good bringing up of children born in matrimony is so well accepted of God, that unto it, as unto other good works done in faith by grace, is promised life everlasting, according to the words of St. Paul, where he saith, The woman was seduced and blinded by the serpent, and so sinned deadly; but she shall be saved by procreation and bringing forth of children, if the same do persevere and continue in faith and love towards God, and in holiness and temperance in their acts and deeds (1 Tim 2:15). And as this is spoken of the woman, so it is also verified in the man, doing his duty likewise as is required of the woman.

Finally it is to be considered, how in matrimony be commended specially three good things, all which they that contract matrimony ought to remember and regard. First of all, the thing itself which is signified thereby, which, as is said before, is the high, the mighty, and incomprehensible work of God, in the conjunction of Christ and the church together, wrought by him to our singular benefit and everlasting salvation: and that therefore the man and wife ought to live together in perfect unity and concord, and to love each other as their own bodies, and to use the same in all cleanness, purity, and honour, even as Christ himself loved his espouse the church, and suffered all afflictions and pains to make her glorious, and void from all manner of spot or wrinkle of uncleanness (Eph 5:27). Which matter St. Paul most godly declareth, in his Epistle to the Thessalonians, where he writeth in this manner: I pray you, brethren, and instantly desire you, for our Lord Jesu Christ's sake, that like as ye have heard heretofore of us, how and in what manner you should go forward, and please God, so ye do proceed in the same, and that after such sort and manner that you may continually profit and increase therein. You remember, I doubt not, what precepts and commandments I have given unto you in times past, in the name of our Lord Jesu Christ. And now in like manner, and in his name also, I say again unto you, that the will and commandment of God is, that you should sanctify yourselves, that is to say, that you should abstain from all manner of fornication, and that every one of you should use and keep the vessel of his body in holiness and honour, and not in desire of carnal concupiscence, like as the Gentiles do, which know not God: and that no man should craftily compass and circumvent his brother to obtain his fleshly lusts: for Almighty God taketh vengeance upon all such people as do commit any of those things. Know you also, that God hath not called us to uncleanness and filthiness of life, but unto holiness and sanctimony. And therefore I do exhort you all, and in the name of God command you, to eschew all fornication and adultery, all uncleanness and carnal concupiscence, all filthiness and unpure living in fleshly lusts of the body. And I say further, that whosoever despiseth and breaketh these my commandments doth not despise me, but despiseth God: for they be his commandments, whose Spirit ye have received (1 Thess 4:1-8).

The second good thing which ought to be remembered in the said sacrament, is the faith and mutual promise made between the husband and the wife conjoined in lawful matrimony, whereby, and by the virtue of the said sacrament, the persons so lawfully conjoined be bound each one to keep promise with the other, according to such trust and confidence as each had in the other, and expressed by words in the same contract; which promise God did assist and ratify, and is now party thereunto: so that the breach of that promise and faith is now a high and displeasant offence unto Almighty God, like as the observation and keeping thereof is in the sight of God pleasant, acceptable, and meritorious, and the knot also and bond of matrimony contracted between the said persons is made thereby to be indissoluble. Truth it is, that if in any marriage it may appear and be duly proved that there is such insufficient impediment, by the laws of God or by the laws of the realm, that the same matrimony was at the beginning unlawful and of none effect; in that case the church may and ought to divorce the same persons so unlawfully contracted, and declare that such matrimony is unlawful, and the bond thereof to be of no strength or efficacy, because it was never good from the beginning. Notwithstanding, in marriages lawfully made, and according to the ordinance of matrimony prescribed by God and the laws of every realm, the bond thereof cannot be dissolved during the lives of the parties between whom such matrimony is made.

The third good thing to be considered and observed in matrimony is the child that cometh of marriage, and the good and virtuous education and bringing up of the same. Whereunto all married men and women ought to have a special regard, and to follow therein the example of Tobit, which taught his son from his infancy to love and dread God, and to flee and abstain from all manner of sin for God's sake (Tob 4). For surely, if the fathers and mothers be negligent in good bringing up of their children in their youth, and suffer them to fall into follies, and sin, in default of due correction and chastisement of them for the same, no doubt they shall answer unto God for it, as it appeareth by the great stroke and punishment of God, when he did suddenly strike Ely unto death, because that he, knowing his children to do amiss, did not punish them therefore (1 Sam 2, 4).

And therefore let all parents employ their diligence and busy care to educate and instruct their children by all means in virtue and goodness, and to restrain them from vices by convenient discipline and castigation, according to the saying of the Wise Man: Withdraw not thy just discipline from thy child; for if thou do so, he will fall into sundry inconveniences, and so finally shall be lost and undone. Wherefore spare not to chastise thy child with the rod; and so doing, thou shalt deliver his soul from hell (Prov 23:13-14). And concerning the child's duty towards the father, it shall be declared hereafter in the Commandments.

The Sacrament of Orders

As concerning the sacrament of orders, it is to be understand, that order is a gift or grace of ministration in Christ's church, given of God to Christian men, by the consecration and imposition of the bishop's hands upon them; and this sacrament was conferred and given by the apostles, as it appeareth in the Epistle of St. Paul to Timothy, whom he had ordered and consecrate priest; where he saith thus: I do exhort thee that thou do stir up the grace of God, the which is given thee by the imposition of my hands (2 Tim 1:6). And in another place he doth monish the same Timothy, and put him in remembrance of the room and ministry that he was called unto, in these words: Do not neglect the grace which thou hast in thee, and the which is given thee through prophecy and with imposition of hands, by the authority of priesthood (1 Tim 4:14). Whereby it appeareth that St. Paul did consecrate and order priests and bishops by the imposition of his hands. And as the apostles themselves, in the beginning of the church, did order priests and bishops, so they appointed and willed the other bishops after them to do the like, as St. Paul manifestly sheweth in his Epistle to

Titus, saying thus: For this cause I left thee at Crete, that thou shouldest ordain priests in every city, according as I have appointed thee (Titus 1:5). And to Timothy he saith, See that thou be not hasty to put thy hands upon any man (1 Tim 5:22).

And here is to be noted, that although this form before declared is to be observed in giving orders, yet there is no certain rule prescribed or limited by the word of God for the nomination, election, presentation, or appointing of any such ecclesiastical ministers; but the same is wholly left unto the positive laws and ordinances of every Christian region, provided and made or to be made in that behalf, with the assent of the prince and ruler. And as concerning the office and duty of the said ecclesiastical ministers, the same consisteth in true preaching and teaching the word of God unto the people, in dispensing and ministering the sacraments of Christ, in consecrating and offering the blessed body and blood of Christ in the sacrament of the altar, in loosing and assoiling from sin such persons as be sorry and truly penitent for the same, and excommunicating such as be guilty in manifest crimes, and will not be reformed otherwise; and finally, in praying for the whole church of Christ, and specially for the flock committed unto them. And although the office and ministry of priests and bishops stand chiefly in these things before rehearsed, yet neither they nor any of them may exercise and execute any of the same offices, but with such sort and such limitation as the ordinances and laws of every Christian realm do permit and suffer.

And because it is not meet that this so chargeable a cure should be committed to every man that peradventure ambitiously would desire it; therefore St. Paul doth diligently set out to his disciples, Timothy and Titus, the conversation, learning, conditions, and qualities of them that should be admitted to the ministry of priesthood; writing in this manner: A bishop or a priest ought to be blameless, as the steward of God, not wilful, not angry, no drunkard, no fighter, not greedy of filthy lucre, but given to hospitality, liberal, discreet, sober, righteous, devout, temperate, and continent, and such one as holdeth the true word of doctrine, that he may be able to exhort with wholesome learning, and to reprove them that say against it (1 Tim 3; Titus 3). Thus we have shortly touched, first the ordering of priests and bishops; secondly, their ministry, office, and duty, with the charge and cure belonging thereunto; and finally, the qualities and conditions required in the same.

And forasmuch as it is an old heresy of the Donatists, condemned in the general councils, to think that the word of God and his sacraments should be of no efficacy, strength, or virtue, when they be ministered by evil men, it is to be remembered, that according to the saying of St. Gregory Nazianzene, Like as there is no difference between the selfsame image or figure of any thing imprinted with a signet of gold and a signet made of iron or of wood, or any other viler matter, even so the word of God and the sacraments of God, ministered by an evil and naughty man, be of the selfsame vigour, strength, and efficacy, as when they be ministered by a man of excellent virtue and goodness. The cause and reason whereof is, for that the priests and bishops, although in the execution of their office and administration they do use and exercise the power and authority of God committed unto them, yet they be not the principal causers, nor the sufficient, or of themselves the efficient causers or givers of grace, or of any other spiritual gift which proceedeth and is given of God by his word and his sacraments; but God is the only principal, sufficient, and perfect cause of all the efficacy of his word and his sacraments; and by his only power, grace, and benefits it is that we receive the Holy Ghost and his graces, by the office and administration of the said priests and bishops: and the said priests and bishops be but only as officers to execute and minister with their hands and tongues the outward and corporal things wherein God worketh and giveth grace inward, according to his pact and covenant made with and to his espouse the church. And this also Chrysostom affirmeth, the eighty-fifth Homily upon St. John, where he saith in this manner: What speak I of priests? I say that neither angel nor archangel can give us any of these things which be given unto us of God; but it is the Father, the Son, and the Holy Ghost, which is the effectual cause of all these things; the priest doth only put to his hands and his tongue. And in this point St. Ambrose also agreeth with the said sayings of Chrysostom, writing thus: The priest layeth his hands upon us, but it is God that giveth the grace; the priest layeth upon us his beseeching hands, but God blesseth us with his mighty hand; the bishop consecrateth another bishop, but it is God that giveth the worthiness. Wherefore we must always think and believe that the virtue and efficacy of the word of God and his sacraments consisteth and dependeth in and upon the commandment, ordinance, power, and authority of God only, and that neither the merits or worthiness of the ministers, be they never of such excellency, do give them their authority, strength, or efficacy; neither yet the malice nor corrupt living of them, be it never so evil, can frustrate or take away from the said word or sacraments their said power, authority, strength, or virtue.

Moreover, as touching the order of deacons, we read in the Acts of the Apostles, that they were ordered and instituted by the same apostles by prayer and imposition of their hands upon them (Acts 6). And as for the qualities and virtuous conversation which be required in them, St. Paul setteth them out, in his Epistle to Timothy, in these words: Deacons ought to be chaste, not double-tongued, no drunkards, not greedy of filthy lucre, having the mystery of faith in a pure conscience (1 Tim 3). And their office in the primitive church was partly in ministering meat and drink and other necessaries to poor people found of the church, partly also in ministering to the bishops and priests, and in doing their duty in the church. And of these two orders only, that is to say, priests and deacons, scripture maketh express mention, and how they were conferred of the apostles by prayer and imposition of their hands. And to these two the primitive church did add and conjoin certain other inferior and lower degrees, as sub-deacons, acolytes, exorcists, with divers other, of the which mention is made of, both of the most ancient writers that we have in the church of Christ, after the apostles, and also in divers old councils, and namely, in the fourth council of Africa, in which St. Augustine was present, whereas all the kinds of orders which were then in the church be rehearsed, and also with what rites and ceremonies they were conferred and given at that time. And thus by succession from the apostles hath order continued in the church, and hath ever been called and counted for a sacrament, as it may appear by divers other ancient writers, and specially by St. Augustine, where he writeth thus, speaking both of the sacrament of baptism and of order: Either of them (saith he) is a sacrament, and either of them is given to men by a certain consecration, the one when a man is baptized, and the other when he is ordered: and therefore neither of them both may be iterate or repeated in the catholic church of Christ.

And whereas we have thus summarily declared what is the office and ministration which in holy scriptures hath been committed to bishops and priests, and in what things it consisteth, as is afore rehearsed, lest peradventure it might be thought to some persons that such authorities, powers, and jurisdictions, as patriarchs, primates, archbishops, and metropolitans, now have, or heretofore at any time have had justly and lawfully over other bishops, were given them by God in holy scripture: we think it expedient and necessary, that all men should be advertised and taught, that all such lawful powers and authorities of one bishop over another were and be given to them by the consent, ordinance, and positive laws of men only, and not by any ordinance of God in holy scripture. And all other power and authority which any bishop hath used or exercised over another, which hath not been given to him by such consent and ordinance of men, (as is aforesaid,) is in very deed no lawful power, but plain usurpation and tyranny.

And therefore whereas the bishop of Rome hath heretofore claimed and usurped to be head and governor of all priests and bishops of the whole catholic church of Christ, by the laws of God; it is evident, that the same power is utterly feigned and untrue, and was neither given to him by God in his holy scripture, nor allowed by the holy fathers in the ancient general councils, nor yet by the consent of the whole catholic church. For it is plain that Christ never gave unto St. Peter, or to any of the apostles or their successors, any such universal authority over all the other. But he set them all indifferently, and in like power, dignity, and authority, as it doth evidently appear in all such places where any authority is given to them by Christ. And also by St. Paul, in his Epistle to the Galatians, where he compareth himself to James, Peter, and John, which were the most notable among the apostles, affirming himself to be equal in authority with them (Gal 2:9).

And as concerning the most ancient and most famous holy general councils, it is evident that they gave the bishops of Rome no such authority; for in them be divers acts and decrees plainly testifying the contrary.

As first, in the former council of Nice, among other, there is one decree, that the patriarchs of Alexandria and Antiochia should have like power over the countries about those cities, as the bishops of Rome have had over the countries about Rome.

Also in the council Milevitan, in which council St. Augustine was present, and subscribed to the same, it was decreed, that if any clerk of the countries of Africa would appeal out of Africa unto any bishops beyond the sea, that such a one should be taken throughout all the countries of Africa as a person excommunicate.

Moreover in the general council Constantinopolitan the first, it was likewise decreed, that every cause and controversy between any persons should be determined within the provinces where the matters did lie, and that by the bishops of the same provinces; and also that no bishops should exercise any power out of his own diocese or province. And this was also the mind of the holy doctor and martyr St. Cyprian, and of the other holy fathers of Africa, before the time of any general council.

And for the better and more plain and assured confirmation that the bishop of Rome hath no such universal authority, neither by God's law, ne yet by any ordinances of any ancient catholic council; it is to be considered, that in the sixth great council Carthaginense, the bishop of Rome sent his legates to that council to allege and vindicate his usurped primacy, and by title of the same to defend and maintain the receiving of appeals made unto him of causes and controversies commenced in Africa, because the whole council had by their decree prohibited and forbidden before all such appeals to any foreign bishop. In the entreating and debating of which matter, the bishop of Rome for his title alleged only a canon, made (as he pretended) in the first Nicene council; the bishops of Africa denying any such canon to be made. For trial whereof, messengers were sent to the patriarchs' sees of the Orient, to make search for the whole canons of that council. And finally, after long and diligent search, when the whole canons were brought forth from thence, there was no such canon amongst them as the bishop of Rome for his said title had alleged.

Whereupon two things are to be noted, as evident by the premises. First, that the bishop of Rome hath no such primacy, nor any such can challenge by any words in scripture: for then the bishop of Rome would at that time by his legates have alleged it, and the great multitude of so many fathers, as were assembled in that African council, (of whom St. Augustine was one,) were so well and profoundly learned in holy scripture, that no such thing (if it were there) could have been hid unto them. And also they were so good and virtuous, that if they had known it there, they then would have made no act before to the contrary, nor yet at that time so earnestly and extremely refused it.

The second thing to be noted, as evident by the premises, is, that the bishops of Rome have no such power given them by any ancient general council. For they at that time of this African council would then have alleged it, where indeed they alleged none but a pretensed canon of the first Nicene council; which, after great trial and search, as is aforesaid, could never be found in the authentics. And that chapter authentic, which of all the canons of that council most concerneth the bishop of Rome, maketh directly and plainly against the said pretensed universal primacy, giving (as is said before) to other patriarchs like and equal authority in their countries, as bishops of Rome had and used then in the countries about Rome.

Thirdly, that the bishops of Rome had no such universal primacy given unto them by the common consent of the whole catholic church, it well appeareth in that, that divers patriarchs and archbishops have of ancient time refused to owe unto them any such subjection as they, by colour of an universal primacy, challenged and required over them; as the patriarchs of Constantinople, and other of the east, and the archbishops of Ravenna, Milan, and such other. And also Agatho himself, being bishop of Rome, long after the four first universal councils, in his letters sent unto the emperor, concerning a general council to be holden at Constantinople, plainly declareth and confesseth his primacy to extend only to the bishops of the west and north parts; and that in such wise, as it is evident, that at that time the bishops of Rome, neither by the words of scripture, nor by any decree of ancient general councils, nor by the consent of the whole catholic church, had any such universal primacy as he now requireth.

And if the bishops of Rome will allege any later councils for their pretensed universal primacy, as the councils of Constance, Basil, and Florence; it is manifest and open that the councils of Basil and Constance were in the time of schisms, and they which were there, divided into factions, after the favour of their princes, which princes were also divided, some favouring the one part of the schism, some the other. And the great part of the learned men that were there were of this later institute religious, and therefore obsequent to the pleasure and will of the bishops of Rome, and brought up only in this later scholastical doctrine, and little exercised or learned in the holy scriptures, or in the old ancient doctors and writers. And both of those councils were dissolved and broken up, without any perfect end or conclusion. And sith that time the canons pragmatical of these two councils be no where used nor yet alleged as to be of effect by the authority of those councils. And as to the council Florentine, over and besides that the greatest part of learned men there were such as we spake of before, the consent also in this matter of the Orientals and Grecians that were there seemed to the whole countries that sent them so far both against scripture and general councils, and their ancient holy writers, that they forthwith shewed themselves so much discontent with that consent of their ambassadors, that they then neither would receive the determination concerning the universal primacy of the bishop of Rome, neither sith that time could be induced to agree to the same.

And thus by all those things before rehearsed, it plainly appeareth that the bishops of Rome claiming this pretensed universal primacy, do yet not only without any ground of holy scripture, and without any consent of the whole catholic church, but also contrary to the determination and decrees of such general councils as the bishops of Rome these many hundred years unto this day in their creation do solemnly and expressly profess to keep and observe. For, as it appeareth by their own laws and acts from time to time, every bishop of Rome, when he is created, doth openly and solemnly profess that he shall inviolably observe and keep all the canons of the first eight general councils, among the which be the canons before rehearsed, plainly repugnant and contrary to his said pretensed universal primacy.

Finally, this being manifestly declared and proved, that the bishops of Rome hath not justly and lawfully any such universal power over the bishops and clergy, all wise men may easily perceive and see that they may much less claim to have the whole monarchy of the world, and such authority over all princes and kings, that they may thereby depose them from their realms, dominions, and seigniories, and transfer and give the same unto such persons as them liketh: whereas the scripture doth teach and command the contrary, that is to say, that all Christian people, as well priests and bishops as all other, should be obedient unto princes and potestates of the world. For the truth is, that God constituted and ordained the authority of Christian kings and princes to be the most high and supreme above all other powers and officers in this world, in the regiment and government of their people, and committed unto them, as unto the chief heads of their commonwealths, the cure and oversight of all the people which be in their realms and dominions, without any exception and to them of right, and by God's commandment, belongeth not only to prohibit unlawful violence, to correct offenders by corporal death, or other punishment, to conserve moral honesty among their subjects, according to the laws of their realms, to defend justice, and to procure the public weal and common peace and tranquillity in outward and earthly things; but specially and principally to defend the faith of Christ and his religion, to conserve and maintain the true doctrine of Christ, and all such

as be true preachers and setters forth thereof, and to abolish abuses, heresies, and idolatries, and to punish with corporal pains such as of malice be
the occasion of the same. And finally, to oversee and cause that the said
bishops and priests do execute their pastoral office truly and faithfully, and
specially in those points which by Christ and his apostles was given and
committed unto them: and in case they shall be negligent in any part
thereof, or would not diligently execute the same, to cause them to redou-
ble and supply their lack: and if they obstinately withstand their prince's
kind monition, and will not amend their faults, then and in such case to
put other in their rooms and places. And God hath also commanded the
said bishops and priests to obey with all humbleness and reverence both
kings and princes and governors, and all their laws, not being contrary to
the laws of God, whatsoever they be, and that not only *propter iram,* but
also *propter conscientiam*, that is to say, not only for fear of punishment,
but also for discharge of conscience. Whereby it appeareth well that this
pretended monarchy of the bishop of Rome is not founded upon the gospel, but it is repugnant thereunto.

And therefore it appertaineth to Christian kings and princes, for the
discharge of their office and duty toward God, to endeavour themselves to
reform and reduce the same again unto the old limits and pristine estate of
that power which was given to them by Christ, and used in the primitive
church. For it is out of doubt that Christ's faith was then most firm and
pure, and the scriptures of God were then best understand, and virtue did
then most abound and excel. And therefore it must needs follow, that the
customs and ordinances then used and made be more conform and agreeable unto the true doctrine of Christ, and more conducing unto the edifying and benefit of the church of Christ, than any customs or laws used or
made by the bishop of Rome, or any other addicted to that see and
usurped power sith that time.

And therefore whereas the king's most royal majesty, considering of
his most excellent wisdom, not only the notable decay of Christ's true and
perfect religion amongst us, but also the intolerable thraldom, captivity,
and bondage, with the infinite dangers and prejudices which we his subjects continually sustained by reason of that long usurped and abused
power which the bishops of Rome were wont to exercise here in this realm;
hath now, of his most godly disposition, and by the consent of his nobles
spiritual and temporal, by authority of the whole parliament, determined

no longer to suffer the bishop of Rome to exercise any part of his usurped jurisdiction here within this realm, but clearly to deliver us from the same, and restore us again unto our liberty.

Surely we have great cause most joyfully and thankfully to embrace and accept the same, considering that thereby no prejudice is done to God's word or his ordinances. For, as we have shewed and declared before, it was by princes' sufferance only that the bishop of Rome exercised any such jurisdiction within this realm, and not by the authority given unto him by Christ. And as for the bishop of Rome, he cannot pretend himself no more to be grieved or injured therewith, than any of the king's officers might worthily think that the king's highness should do him wrong in case he should upon good cause remove him from his room and office, and commit it to another. And as for us the king's faithful subjects, we shall undoubtedly receive and have thereby singular wealth and commodity, as well spiritually to the edifying of our souls, as corporally to the increase of our substance and riches. The which how much it was impaired and decayed continually from time to time, by the great exactions of the bishops of Rome, and such treasures as went yearly out of this realm to his coffers for annates, annuities, and exemptions, pardons, and such other unlawful exactions; we doubt not but all men, endued with any wit and zeal to the wealth of this our country, do right well perceive and understand, and accordingly with heart and mind will not only pray for the king's highness and his preservation, by whose occasion this light came first unto us, but also firmly and constantly stick to those laws, whereby we have so much ease of wrongful exactions and abuses, and also our prince and king now enjoyeth most rightfully his just title, with restitution of his royal and imperial dignity and princely governance.

The Sacrament of Confirmation

We read in holy scripture how the apostles, in the beginning of the church, although they did certainly know and believe that all such as had duly received the sacrament of baptism were by virtue and efficacy thereof perfectly regenerated in Christ, perfectly incorporated and made the very members of his body, and had received full remission of their sins, and were endued with graces and gifts of the Holy Ghost; yet they went unto the people after they were baptized, and so by their prayer and imposition of their hands upon them, the Holy Ghost was given and conferred unto them. And the said people did speak divers languages, and prophesied: whereby not only they which had received baptism, and professed Christ, were the better confirmed and established in Christ's religion, and made more constant to confess the same; but also other which were out of the church, and infidels, might the sooner be reduced by such gift and miracle from their errors, and be brought into the right belief of Christ and his gospel.

Whereupon the holy fathers of the primitive church, taking occasion, and founding themselves upon the said acts and deeds of the apostles, and considering also that such as had once received the gifts and benefits of the Holy Ghost by the sacrament of baptism might, and oftentimes did indeed, by temptation, frailty, or otherwise by their own sin and malice, lose and fall from the same again; did use and observe (as it hath been hitherto by succession of ages continued) that all Christian people should, after their baptism, be presented to their bishops, to the intent that by their prayers and imposition of their hands upon them, and consigning them with the holy chrism, they should be confirmed, that is to say, they should receive such gifts of the Holy Ghost, as whereby they should be so corroborated and established in the gifts and graces before received in baptism, that they should not lightly fall again from the same, but should constantly retain them, and persevere therein, and should also be made stronger and hardier, as well to confess boldly and manfully their faith before all the persecutors of the same, and to resist and fight against their ghostly enemies, the world, the devil, and the flesh, as also to bear the cross of Christ, that is, to suffer and sustain patiently all the afflictions and adversities of this world, and finally that they should attain increase and abundance of virtues and graces of the Holy Ghost.

And although men ought not to contemn this sacrament, but should present their children unto the bishop to receive at his hands the sacrament of confirmation, yet it is not to be thought that there is any such necessity of confirmation of infants, but that they being baptized, and dying innocents before they be confirmed, shall be assured to attain everlasting life and salvation by the effect of the sacrament of baptism received.

The Sacrament of Extreme Unction

As touching extreme unction, we must understand, how according to scripture, and the rule and order prescribed by the holy apostle St. James, the catholic church of Christ hath observed and ministered this sacrament to such as have required it in their sickness and disease of body, to the intent that by the working of God in ministration thereof the sick man, through prayer of the priest the minister, and such as assist him, might be relieved of his bodily disease, and also attain pardon and remission of his sins. For St. James saith, If any be sick among you, let him call for the priests of the church, and let them pray over him, anointing him with oil in the name of our Lord; and the prayer of faith shall save the sick man; and if he be in sins, they shall be forgiven him (Jas 5:14-15).

By which words, like as the use of the sacrament is confirmed and proved, so that the church may well use the same, with assurance that God assisteth the ministration thereof; so we must also remember, that although health of body, which here is prayed for, doth not always follow, yet we should not doubt but God ordereth man's prayer therein always to the best, as he doth of his infinite goodness all other prayers that men make, who indeed know not what they should ask, ne what is best or most profitable for them. Wherefore albeit we be taught to make all our prayers in a most certain faith, to attain our desires, according to the general promise made by God through Christ, Ask and you shall receive (Matt 7:8); which promise cannot fail, for God's word cannot be frustrate, but taketh ever effect; yet may we not trust our own determination and our judgment so precisely in our prayers and requests, but committing ourselves wholly to God's governance, we ought to take, esteem, and judge for the best whatsoever God shall order and dispose for us, although it be contrary to our prayer and desire, which must ever have direction and submission to God's pleasure, who knoweth our necessities, and can and will dispose all things sweetly and pleasantly, to the attaining of everlasting comfort, which all good men chiefly desire and pray for.

And whereas St. James speaketh of remission of sin, to be obtained in this sacrament, inasmuch as the remission of sin is a necessary petition to be made of and for all men, considering the frailty of man's nature, which continually sinneth, and therefore continually is taught to say, *Dimitte nobis debita nostra*, Lord, forgive us our trespasses (Matt 6:12); we ought assuredly to trust that God, working in the ministration of his sacrament, doth by the prayer of the minister, and of such as assist him, forgive those sins of the sick man, which, by the frailness of his nature, in sudden motions and vehement agonies, he doth commit and fall into.

And yet we ought not thereupon to conceive a vain false hope of the effect of this sacrament, that, living in filthy and abominable sin, and not caring to be delivered from it by true penance, we should, by the ministration of extreme unction, have all our sins forgiven; for this sacrament is ministered fruitfully only to those that be members of Christ's church, and such as, being fallen out of the state of grace by deadly sin, have been by penance restored to the same; which men, by this sacrament, be strengthened and comforted in their agony and fight against the devil, who, in the time of sickness and vexation of the body, is very busy to assault them.

And where it is called the extreme unction, that is to say, the last unction, we must not so understand it, as though this sacrament might never be ministered but once, that is to say, in extreme peril of death, when men be without hope of life; for it should rather be ministered in the entry of sickness, and so oftener, whensoever any great and perilous sickness and malady shall come to any man. But the fathers of the church did call it by the said name of extreme unction, because it is the last in the respect of the other unctions, which be ministered before, in the other sacraments of baptism, confirmation, and order, in which sacraments Christian men be also anointed.

And forasmuch as the sacrament of the altar (being duly received) is the very spiritual food and the very sustentation, comfort, and preservation of all Christian men in all dangerous passages and adventures; therefore it is expedient that the said sacrament of the altar should be received after this anoiling done, in the time of sickness. For surely the receiving of the body of our Saviour Jesu Christ is the very consummation, not only of this, but also of all other sacraments.

The seven sacraments thus declared, the use and effect of them doth manifestly appear. For by baptism we be incorporated into the body of Christ's church, obtaining in that sacrament remission of sin, and grace, wherewith we be able to lead a new life.

By the sacrament of penance, they that be fallen into deadly sin may be restored unto the state of grace received in baptism, and so made again the lively members of Christ's mystical body.

In the most blessed sacrament of the altar is the most precious body and blood of our Saviour and Redeemer Jesu Christ, both in form of bread and wine, by whom, for whom, and in whom all sacraments take effect; and therefore is this the most worthy sacrament, and of highest dignity.

The sacrament of matrimony is a necessary thing for due generation of man to God's pleasure, which, although it be honourable and acceptable to God, and therefore the lawful conjunction of man and woman is assisted by God in this holy sacrament, yet this estate is not commanded as necessary to any particular man, but left at liberty to all men, saving priests, and to other, which, of their free liberty, by vow advisedly made, have chosen the state of continency, who, according to their free choice, must freely and willingly continue in the same.

The sacrament of order, although it be not commanded to any particular man as necessary for the attaining of everlasting life, yet in the church, which is the mystical body of Christ, it hath a necessity, to the intent that by ministers duly placed there may be due spiritual fathers for spiritual generation. So that both the estates of matrimony and order be for the whole church necessary, but yet not so necessarily commanded to any particular man.

The other two sacraments of confirmation and extreme unction, although they be not of such necessity but that without them men may be saved, yet, forasmuch as in the ministration of them, if they be worthily taken, men receive more abundantly ghostly strength, aid, and comfort, they be very wholesome and profitable, and to be desired and reverently received.

The Ten Commandments of Almighty God

The Ten Commandments

1. Thou shalt have none other gods but me.

2. Thou shalt not have any graven image, nor any likeness of any thing that is in heaven above, or in the earth beneath, or in the water under the earth, to the intent to do any godly honour and worship unto them.

3. Thou shalt not take the name of thy Lord God in vain.

4. Remember that thou keep holy the sabbath day.

5. Honour thy father and thy mother.

6. Thou shalt do no murder.

7. Thou shalt not commit adultery.

8. Thou shalt not steal.

9. Thou shalt not bear false witness against thy neighbour.

10. Thou shalt not unjustly desire thy neighbour's house, nor thy neighbour's wife, nor his servant, nor his maid, nor his ox, nor his ass, nor any thing that is thy neighbour's.

The Exposition of the First Commandment of God

This first commandment, like as it is first in order, so it is the most chief and principal among all the other precepts. For in this first commandment God requireth of us those things, in the which consisteth his chief and principal worship and honour, that is to say, perfect faith, sure hope, and unfeigned love and dread of God.

Thou shalt have none other gods but me.

And therefore it is to be noted, that to have God, is not to have him as we have other outward things, as clothes upon our back, or treasure in our chests, nor also to have him in our mouth outwardly, or to worship him with kneeling, or such other gestures only: but to have him our God, is to conceive him in our hearts, to cleave fast and surely unto him with heart and mind, to put all our trust and confidence in him, to set all our thoughts and care above all things to please him, and to depend wholly of him, taking him to be infinitely good and merciful unto us, being his creatures, and continuing in his flock.

Secondly, God commandeth us thus to do to him only, and to no creature, nor to no false and feigned god. For as a kind and loving man cannot be content that his wife should take any other husband; so cannot our most kind and most loving God and Creator be pleased if we should forsake him, and take any other gods. And surely he is more present with us, and more ready to shew us all kindness and goodness, than any creature is or can be. And already of his gift we have all that we have, meat, drink, clothe, reason, wit, understanding, discretion, and all good things that we have pertaining both to the soul and the body. And therefore he will not suffer unpunished so much ingratitude and unkindness at our hands, that we should forsake him, and fix our faith and godly trust in any other thing besides him.

Thirdly, by this precept God commandeth us not only to trust thus in him, but also to give him the whole love of our hearts above all worldly things, yea and above ourselves, so that we may not love ourselves, ne any other thing but for him, according as Moses saith in the book of Deuteronomy, Thy Lord God is one God, and thou shalt love him with all thy heart, and with all thy soul, and with all thy mind, and with all thy strength and power (Deut 6:4). And this love must bring with it a fear that even for very pure love we ought to be much ashamed and afraid to break the least of his commandments. Like as the child, the more he loveth his father, the more he is loath and afraid to displease him in any manner of case.

Fourthly, all they offend against this commandment, which set their hearts and minds upon any worldly thing above God. For whatsoever we love above God, so that we set our minds upon it more than we do upon God, or for it we will offend God, truly we make that for the time our god. For, as St. Paul saith, The covetous man maketh his goods his god (Col 3:5). And, The gluttonous man maketh his belly his god (Phil 3:19). For the one setteth his mind upon his goods, the other upon his belly, more than they do upon God; and for them they will not stick to offend God.

Also, all they which have more confidence in the creatures of God than in God, do make the creatures of God their god. And how grievously God is offended therewith, we find in the book of Paralipomenon, where it is written, that when Asa king of Judah, being sore constrained by Baasha king of Israel, sent for help to Ben-hadad king of Syria, and gave him great treasure for to allure him to his aid, our Lord sent the prophet Hanani to Asa the king of Judah, who said unto him on this manner: Because thou hast trusted in the king of Syria, and not in thy Lord God, therefore the host of the king of Syria is escaped from thy hands. Were not they of Ethiopia and Libya of far greater power, both in chariots and horsemen, and in number and multitude, which were innumerable? and yet our Lord (as long as thou diddest put thy trust in him) did yield them into thy hands. The eyes of God do behold all the world, and giveth strength to them that trust in him with all their heart. In which words it doth appear, that it is laid to Asa's charge that he did not believe in our Lord, because he did more trust in Ben-hadad, the heathen prince, than in our Lord (2 Chr 16:1-9).

It is noted also in the same chapter, that whereas Asa had very great pain in his feet, he sought not to our Lord for remedy of his disease, but trusted more in the art and remedy of physic. Whereby we may learn, that it is one great part of perfect belief in our Lord God to put our trust and confidence most principally and above all other in him. Wherefore they that do otherwise do transgress this commandment, and make to them other gods.

Also, all they transgress this commandment, which either presume so much upon the mercy of God, that they fear not his justice, and by reason thereof do still continue in their sin, or else so much fear his justice that they have no trust in his mercy. Also they be of the same sort, which by lots, divination, chattering of birds, and looking of men's hands, or other unlawful or superstitious crafts, take upon them certainly to tell, determine, and judge beforehand of men's acts and fortunes, which be to come afterward. For what do they but make themselves gods in this behalf? As the prophet Esay saith, Tell us afore what shall come, and we shall say that ye be gods (Isa 41:23).

Also, all they which by charms and witchcrafts do use any prescribed letters, signs or characts, words, blessings, rods, crystal stones, sceptres, swords, measures, or for any superstitious intent, charms or witchcrafts, hang St. John's Gospel, or any other thing about their necks, or any other parts of their bodies, or use to drink holy water, or any other such vain observation, trusting thereby to continue in long life, to drive away sickness, to preserve them from sickness, fire, water, or any other peril, otherwise than physic or surgery doth allow, do also offend against this commandment.

But most grievously of all, and above all other, they do offend against this commandment, which profess Christ, and, contrary to their profession made at their baptism, do make secret pacts and covenants with the Devil; or do use any manner of conjurations to raise up devils for treasure, or any other thing hid or lost, or for any manner of cause, whatsoever it be; for all such commit so high offence and treason to God, that there can be no greater. For they yield the honour due unto God to the Devil, God's enemy. And not only all such as use charms, witchcrafts, and conjurations, transgress this chief and high commandment, but also all those that seek and resort unto them for any counsel or remedy, according to the saying of God, when he said, Let no man ask counsel of them that use false divinations, or such as take heed to dreams, or chattering of birds. Let there be no witch or enchanter amongst you, or any that asketh counsel of them that have spirits, nor of soothsayers, nor that seek the truth of them that be dead; for God abhorreth all these things (Deut 18:10-12).

The Exposition of the Second Commandment of God

By these words we be not forbidden to make or to have similitudes or images, but only we be forbidden to make or to have them to the intent to do godly honour unto them, as it appeareth in the 26th chapter of Leviticus.

Thou shall not have any graven image, nor any likeness of any thing that is in heaven above, or in earth beneath, or in the water under the earth, to the intent to do any godly honour and worship unto them.

And therefore, although images of Christ and his saints be the works of men's hands only, yet they be not so prohibited but that they may be had and set up both in churches and in other places, to the intent that we (in beholding and looking upon them, as in certain books and signs) may call to remembrance the manifold examples of virtues which were in the saints whom they do represent. And so may they rather be provoked, kindled, and stirred, to yield thanks to our Lord, and to praise him and his said saints, and to remember and lament our sins and offences, and to pray God that we may have grace to follow their goodness and holy living.

As for an example, the image of our Saviour hangeth on the cross in the rood, or is painted in clothes, walls, or windows, as an open book, to the intent, that besides the examples of virtues which we may learn at Christ, we may be also many ways provoked to remember his painful and cruel passion, and also to consider ourselves, when we behold the same image, and to condemn and abhor our sin, which was the cause of his so cruel death. And furthermore, considering what high charity was in him, that would die for us his enemies, and what great dangers we have escaped, and what high benefits we receive by his redemption, we may be provoked in all our distresses and troubles to run for comfort unto him. All these lessons, with many more, be brought to our remembrance by the book of the rood, if we being first well instruct and taught what is represented and meant thereby, do diligently behold and look upon it. And as our Saviour Christ is represented by this image of the rood, even so the holy saints which followed him be represented unto us by their images: and therefore the said images may well be set up in churches, to be as books for unlearned people, to put them in remembrance of those saints, of whom they may learn examples of faith, humility, charity, patience, temperance, and of all other their virtues and gifts of God, which were in them: for which causes images may be set in the church, and ought not to be despised, but to be used reverently, although we be forbidden to do any godly honour unto them. These lessons should be taught by every curate to their parish. And whereas we use to cense the said images, and to kneel before them, and to creep to the cross, with such other things; yet we must know and understand, that such things be not nor ought to be done to the image itself, but to God, and in his honour, although it be done afore the image, whether it be of Christ, of the cross, or of our lady, or of any other saint.

Against this commandment did offend generally, before the coming of Christ, all Gentiles and people that were of the nation of Israel. For they did godly honour unto images, and worshipped false gods, some one, some another, of the which sort there was a great number. For besides their common gods, every country, every city or town, every house and family, had their proper gods; whereof is much mention made in authors, both Christian and heathen. And these Gentiles, though they had knowledge of a very God, yet (as St. Paul saith) they had idle and vain phantasies, which led them from the truth; and where they counted themselves wise, they became fools.

And against this commandment offended the Jews many and sundry times, and almost continually. For notwithstanding that they professed the knowledge and worshipping of the very true God, yet they fell to the adoration of images, idols, and false gods; as the holy scripture maketh mention in many places.

Also all they do greatly err, which put difference between image and image, trusting more in one than in another, as though one could help or do more than another, when both do represent but one thing, and, saving by way of representation, neither of them is able to work or do any thing.

And they also do err that be more ready with their substance to deck images gorgeously, than with the same to help poor Christian people, the quick and living images of God, which is the necessary work of charity commanded by God. And they also offend, that so dote in this behalf that they make vows and go on pilgrimages even to the images, and there do call upon the same images for aid and help, phantasying that either the image will work the same, or else some other thing in the image, or God for the image sake, as though God supernaturally wrought by images carved, engraven, or painted, brought once into churches, as he doth naturally work by other his creatures. In which things, if any person heretofore hath or yet doth offend, all good and learned men have great cause to lament such error and rudeness, and to put their studies and diligences for the reformation of the same.

The Exposition of the Third Commandment of God

Thou shalt not take the name of thy Lord God in vain. In this commandment God requireth of us to use his name with all honour and reverence. Whereupon you shall understand, that the right use of the name of God, and the true honour of the same, standeth chiefly in these things following; that is to say, in the constant confession of his name, and maintaining of his doctrine, in the right invocation of him, in the giving of due thanks unto him, as well in adversity as in prosperity. For Christ saith, He that openly confesseth me before men, I shall confess him before my Father in heaven; and he that is ashamed of me, to confess my name before men, I will be ashamed of him before my Father in heaven (Matt 10:32-33). In which words Christ teacheth us not only to profess the name of God, but also boldly and constantly to defend the same, and not to swerve from it for any manner of persecution or injury.

We must also, in our tribulation and necessity, and in all temptations and assaults of the Devil, invocate and call upon the name of God. For God accounteth his name to be hallowed, magnified, and worshipped, when we call upon him in our need. Call upon me, saith he, in the time of trouble, and I will deliver thee, and thou shalt honour me (Ps 50:15). And again the Wise Man saith, The name of God is the most strong tower; the righteous man runneth to it, and he shall be holpen (Prov 18:10).

Furthermore, we may not seek our own name, laud, and fame, but utterly avoid and eschew the desire of all worldly honours, glory, and praise, and must give all laud, praise, and thanks unto God for his benefits, which be so many in number, and so great, that we ought never to cease from such lauds and thanks, like as the prophet David admonisheth us, saying, Offer unto God the sacrifice of laud and praise (Ps 50:14). And St. Paul commandeth us, whensoever we eat, drink, or do any manner business, to give honour, praise, and thanks unto God (1 Cor 10:31).

And finally, they that be appointed to be ministers of God's word, must also preach the word of God truly and purely, and set forth the name of God unto other, and reprove all false and erroneous doctrine, heresies, and idolatries. And although the bishops and priests only be specially called and deputed to be public ministers of God's Word, teachers, preachers, and interpreters of the same; yet every Christian man is bound particularly by good example of living, and according to the godly knowledge that he hath learned, to teach and order his family, and such as be under his governance within his house, when time and place requireth. So that as much as in him lieth, he suffer not sin to be used in his rule and family, but virtue to be used and exercised.

Secondly, by this precept we be commanded to use the name of God to all goodness and truth. And contrariwise, we be forbidden in the same to use his name to any manner of evil, as to lying, deceiving, or any untruth. And therefore against this commandment they do offend that swear in vain. They swear in vain that swear without lawful or just cause; for that they take the name of God in vain, although the thing which they swear be true. And likewise do all they which for every light and vain thing be ready to swear unprovoked, or provoked of light cause; and they that do glory in outrageous oaths, or of custom do use to swear, or that do swear a false oath, and be forsworn wittingly. And such an oath is not only perjury, but also a kind of blasphemy, and is high dishonour and injury to God, because such persons as make such oaths do wittingly bring God for a false witness, who is all truth, and hateth all untruth.

They also do take the name of God in vain, which swear any thing that is true or false, they being in doubt whether it be true or false, and do not afore well examine and discuss whether it be true or false; or that swear that thing to be false, which though indeed it be false, yet they think it to be true; or swear that thing to be true, which though indeed it be true, yet they think it to be false.

They also do swear in vain, which swear to do that thing which they intend not to do, or swear to forbear that which they intend not to forbear, or swear to do any thing which to do is unlawful, or swear to leave any thing undone which to omit or leave undone is neither right nor reasonable. And all such as swear to do things unlawful, not only offend in such swearing, but also they much more offend, if they perform the thing which they do swear.

They also break this commandment which make any oath contrary to their lawful oath or promise made before, so long as their promise standeth in strength, which in no wise it doth, if it be contrary to the laws of God, or to the due obedience to the princes and their laws.

They also break this commandment, which by rewards or fair promises, or by power or fear, do induce or constrain any man to be perjured.

They also break this commandment, which either by preaching or teaching, or by pretence of holy living, do abuse this holy name to their own vain glory, or to any other ungodly purpose. And generally all evil Christian men, which profess the name of Christ, and live not according to their profession, do also take the name of God in vain, in words confessing Christ, and denying him in deeds.

They also break this commandment, which in trouble do murmur or grudge, and do not call upon the name of God, nor do thank him in all things, both sweet and sour, good and evil, welfare and evil fare. For God doth send us many troubles and adversities, because we should run to him, cry to him for help, and call upon his holy name.

Thirdly, forasmuch as the gifts of health of body, health of soul, forgiveness of sins, the gift of grace or life everlasting, and such other, be the gifts of God, and cannot be given but by God; whosoever maketh invocation to saints for these gifts, praying to them for any of the said gifts, or any such like, which cannot be given but by God only, yieldeth the glory of God to his creature, contrary to this commandment. For God saith to his prophet, I will not yield my glory to any other (Isa 42:8). Therefore they that so pray to saints for these gifts, as though they could give them, or be givers of them, transgress this commandment; yielding to a creature the honour of God. Nevertheless, to pray unto saints to be intercessors with us and for us to our Lord in our suits which we make unto him, and for such things as we can obtain of none but of him, so that we esteem not or worship not them as givers of those gifts, but as intercessors for the same, is lawful, and allowed by the catholic church: and if we honour them any other ways than as the friends of God, dwelling with him, and established now in his glory everlasting, and as examples which were requisite for us to follow in holy life and conversation; or if we yield unto saints the adoration and honour which is due unto God alone, we do (no doubt) break this commandment.

Finally, it is to be considered, that because no temple, ne church, nor altar ought to be made but only to God, (for to whom we make temple, church, or altar, to him, as St. Augustine saith, we do sacrifice; and sacrifice we may do to none but to God;) therefore where we use in our English tongue to call the temples, churches, or altars by the name of any saint, as the church or altar of our lady, the church or altar of St. Michael, of St. Peter, of St. Paul, and so of other saints, the true meaning thereof is, and ought to be taken, that the said altars and churches be not dedicate to any saints, but to God only, and be of the saints but a memorial to put us in remembrance of them, that we may follow their example and living, and also to make a knowledge of diversity between one church or altar and another. And therefore, if we mean otherwise than here is declared when we call them churches or altars of saints, we yield the honour of God from him to the saints, and break this commandment.

The Exposition of the Fourth Commandment of God

As touching this commandment, it is to be noted, that this word *sabbote* is an Hebrew word, and signifieth in English *rest*: so that the sabbath day is as much to say as the day of rest and quietness. And there is specially a notable difference between this commandment and the other nine commandments. For, as St. Austin saith, All the other nine be merely moral commandments, and belonged not only to the Jews, and all other people of the world in the time of the Old Testament, but also belong now to all Christian people in the New Testament. But this precept of the sabbath, as concerning rest from bodily labour the seventh day, is ceremonial, and pertained only unto the Jews in the Old Testament, before the coming of Christ, and pertaineth not unto us Christian people in the New Testament. Nevertheless, as concerning the spiritual rest which is figured and signified by this corporal rest, that is to say, rest from the carnal works of the flesh, and all manner of sin, this precept is moral, and remaineth still, and bindeth them that belong unto Christ; and not for every seventh day only, but for all days, hours, and times. For at all times we be bound to rest from fulfilling of our own carnal will and pleasure, and from all sins and evil desires, from pride, disobedience, ire, hate, covetousness, and all such corrupt and carnal appetites, and to commit ourselves wholly unto God, that he may work in us all things that be to his will and pleasure. And this is the true sabbath or rest of us that be christened, when we rest from our own carnal wills, and be not led thereby, but be guided by God and his Holy Spirit. And this is the thing that we pray for in the Paternoster, when we say, Father, let thy kingdom come to us. Thy will be done in earth as it is in heaven. Reign thou in us. Make that we may do thy will, and from

Remember that thou keep holy the sabbath day.

our corrupt will we may rest and cease. And for this purpose God hath
ordained fast, watch, and labour, to the end that by these and such other
exercises we might mortify and kill the evil and sinful desires of the flesh,
and attain this spiritual rest and quietness which is figured and signified in
this commandment.

Furthermore, besides this spiritual rest, which chiefly and principally
is required of us, we be bound by this precept at certain times to cease from
bodily labour, and to give our minds entirely and wholly unto God, to hear
the divine service approved, used, and observed in the church, and also the
word of God, to acknowledge our own sinfulness unto God, and his great
mercy and goodness unto us, to give thanks unto him for his benefits, to
make public and common prayer for all things needful, to visit the sick, to
instruct every man his children and family in virtue and goodness, and
such other like works. Which things, although all Christian people be
bound unto by this commandment, yet the sabbath day, which is called
the Saturday, is not now prescribed and appointed thereunto as it was to
the Jews; but instead of the sabbath day succeedeth the Sunday, in the
memory of Christ's resurrection. And also many other holy and festival
days, which the church hath ordained from time to time, which be called
holy days, not because that one day is more acceptable to God than another, or of itself more holy than another, but because the church hath
ordained that upon those days we should give ourselves wholly without
any impediment unto such holy works as be before expressed, whereas
upon other days we may do and apply ourselves to bodily labour, and be
thereby much letted from such holy and spiritual works.

And to the intent the ignorant people may be the more clearly instructed what holy and spiritual works they ought to do upon the holy
day, here followeth a brief declaration thereof. First, let them make an account with themselves how they have bestowed the week past, remembering what evil minds and purposes they have had, what words they have
spoken, what things they have done or left undone, to the dishonour and
displeasure of God, and to the hurt of their neighbour, and what example
or occasion of evil they have given unto other. And when they have thus
recollected and considered all these things in their minds, then let them
humbly knowledge their faults unto God, and ask forgiveness for the
same, with unfeigned purpose in their hearts to convert and return from
their naughty lives, and to amend the same; and let them also clearly and

purely in their hearts remit and forgive all malice and displeasure which they bear to any creature. Then let them fall unto prayer, according to the commandment of Christ, where he saith, When you begin to pray, forgive whatsoever displeasure you have against any man (Matt 5:23-24). And when they be weary of prayer, then let them use reading of the word of God, or some other good or heavenly doctrine, so that they do it quietly, without disturbance of other that be in the church; or else let them occupy their minds with wholesome and godly meditations, whereby they may be the better; and they that can read may be well occupied upon the holy day, if, in time and place convenient, they read soberly and quietly unto other, such as they have charge of, such good books as be allowed, which may be unto them instead of a sermon: for all things that edify man's soul in our Lord God be good and wholesome sermons.

And truly if men would occupy themselves upon the holy days, and spend the same days holily after this form and manner, not only in the house of God, but also in their own houses, they should eschew thereby much vice, confound their ancient enemy the Devil, much edify both themselves and other, and finally attain much grace and high reward of Almighty God.

Also men must have special regard that they be not over scrupulous or rather superstitious in abstaining from bodily labour upon the holy day. For notwithstanding all that is afore spoken, it is not meant but we may upon the holy day give ourselves to labour for the speedy performance of the necessary affairs of the prince and the commonwealth, at the commandment of them that have rule and authority therein. And also in all other times of necessity, as for saving of our corn and cattle, when it is like to be in danger, or like to be destroyed, if remedy be not had in time. For this lesson our Saviour teacheth us in the gospel; and we need not to have any scruple or grudge in conscience, in such case of necessity, to labour on the holy days; but rather we should offend if we should for scrupulosity not save that God hath sent for the sustenance and relief of his people. And yet in such times of necessity (if their business be not very great and urgent) men ought to have such regard to the holy day that they do bestow some convenient time in hearing divine service, as is aforesaid.

Against this commandment generally do offend all they which will not cease from their own carnal wills and pleasures.

Also they, which, having no lawful impediment, do not give themselves upon the holy day to hear mass, to hear the word of God, to remember the benefits of God, to give thanks for the same, to pray, to exercise such holy works as be appointed for such days, but (as commonly is used) pass the time either in idleness, in gluttony, in riot, or other vain or idle pastime, do break this commandment. For surely such keeping of holy day is not according to the intent and meaning of this commandment, but after the usage and custom of the Jews, and doth not please God, but doth much more offend him, and provoke his indignation and wrath towards us. For, as St. Austin saith of the Jews, they should be better occupied labouring in their fields, and to be at plough, than to be idle at home. And women should better bestow their time in spinning of wool, than upon the sabbath day to lose their time in leaping or dancing, and other idle wantonness.

All they do also offend against this commandment, which do hear the word of God, and give not good heed thereunto that they may understand it, or if they do understand it, yet they endeavour not theirselves to remember it, or if they remember it, yet they study not to follow it.

And all they break this commandment which in mass time do occupy their minds with other matters, and like unkind people remember not the passion and death of Christ, nor give thanks unto him: which things in the mass time they ought specially to do. For the mass, wherein after the consecration is really present the very blessed body and blood of Christ, is celebrate in the church for a perpetual memory of his death and passion.

And likewise do all those, which in such time as the common prayers be made, or the word of God is taught, not only themselves do give none attendance thereunto, but also by reading, walking, talking, and other evil demeanour, let other that would well use themselves.

And likewise do all they which do not observe, but despise such laudable ceremonies of the church, as set forth God's honour, and appertain to good order to be used in the church. And therefore concerning such ceremonies of the church as have been institute by our forefathers, and be allowed by the princes or kings of the dominions, which next to God be the chief heads of the churches, although men ought not to have so fond opinion of the said ceremonies to think that they have power to remit sin, yet they be very expedient things, either to excite or stir up men's devotion, and to cause them to have the more reverence toward the sacraments; as the hallowing of the font, of the chalice, of the corporace, of the altar, and other like exorcisms and benedictions done by the ministers of Christ's church; or else to put us in continual remembrance of those spiritual things which be signified by them. As sprinkling of holy water doth put us in remembrance of our baptism, and of the blood of Christ, sprinkled for our redemption upon the cross. Giving of holy bread doth put us in remembrance of the sacrament of the altar, which we ought to receive in right charity; and also that all Christian men be one body mystical of Christ, as the bread is made of many grains, and yet but one loaf. Bearing the candles on Candlemas day doth put us in remembrance of Christ, the spiritual light, of whom Simeon did prophesy, as is read in the church that day. Giving ashes on Ash-Wednesday doth put us in remembrance that every Christian man should consider that he is but ashes and earth, and thereunto he shall return. Bearing of palms on Palm-Sunday doth put us in remembrance of the receiving of Christ into Jerusalem a little before his death, and that we must have the same desire to receive him in our hearts. Creeping to the cross on Good Friday, and there offering unto Christ before the same, and kissing of it, declareth our humble submission and thanksgiving to Christ for our redemption, which he hath wrought for us upon the cross. And so finally the setting up of the sepulchre of Christ, whose body after his death was buried. And all other like laudable customs, rites, and ceremonies do put us in remembrance of some spiritual thing. And therefore they be not to be contemned and cast away, but obediently to be used and continued, as things good and laudable for the purposes abovesaid.

The Exposition of the Fifth Commandment of God

In this commandment, by these words *father and mother*, is understand not only the natural father and mother which did carnally beget us, and brought us up, but also princes and all other governors, rulers, and pastors, under whom we be nourished and brought up, ordered and guided.

Honour thy father and mother.

And by this word *honour*, in this commandment, is not only meant a reverence and lowliness in words and outward gesture, which children and inferiors ought to exhibit unto their parents and superiors, but also a prompt and a ready obedience to their lawful commandments, a regard to their words, a forbearing and suffering of them, an inward love and veneration towards them, reverence, fear, and loathness to displease or offend them, and a good will or gladness to assist them, aid them, succour them, and help them with their counsel, with their goods and substance, and by all other means to their power, as hereafter is declared. This is the very honour and duty which not only the children do owe unto their parents, but also all subjects and inferiors to their heads and rulers.

And that children owe this duty to their fathers, it appeareth in many places of scripture. In the Proverbs it is written, Obey, my son, the chastisement of thy father, and be not negligent in thy mother's commandments (1:8). In the Book of Deuteronomy it is also written, Accursed be he that doth not honour his father and his mother (27:16). And in the Book of Leviticus it is said, Let every man stand in awe of his father and mother (19:3). And if any man have a stubborn and a disobedient son, which will not hear the voice of his father and mother, and for correction will not amend and follow them, then shall his father and mother take him and bring him to the judge of the city, and say, This our son is stubborn and disobedient, and despiseth our admonitions, and is a rioter and a drunkard. Then shall all the people stone him to death; and thou shalt put away the evil from thee, that all Israel may hear thereof, and be afraid (Deut 21:18-21). And in the Book of Exodus it is also written, He that striketh his father or mother, he shall be put to death (21:15). And likewise, He that curseth his father and mother shall be put to death (Exod 21:17). And in the Book of Proverbs the Wise Man also saith, He that stealeth any thing from his father or mother is to be taken as a murderer (28:24). And although these great punishments of disobedient children by death be not now in the new law in force and strength, but left to the order of princes and governors, and their laws; yet it evidently appeareth how sore God is aggrieved and displeased with such disobedience of children towards their parents, forasmuch as in the old law he did appoint thereunto so grievous punishments. And as Almighty God doth threaten these punishments unto those children which do break this commandment, so he doth promise great rewards to them that keep it. For he that honoureth his father (saith the Wise Man) his sins shall be forgiven him; and he that honoureth his mother is as one that gathereth treasures. Whosoever honoureth his father shall have joy in his own children; and when he maketh his prayer unto God, he is heard. He that honoureth his father shall have a long and a prosperous life (Sir 3:4-6).

And as the children by this commandment be bound to honour and obey their parents, according as is afore expressed, so it is implied in the same precept that the parents should nourish and godly bring up their children; that is to say, that they must not only find them meat and drink in youth, and also set them forward in learning, labour, and some other good exercise, that they may eschew idleness, and have some craft or occupation, or some other lawful mean to get their living; but also they must learn them to believe and trust in God, to love him, to fear him, to love their neighbours, to hate no man, to hurt no man, to wish well to every man, and, so much as they may, do good to every man; not to curse, not to swear, not to be riotous, but to be sober and temperate in all things; not to be worldly, but to set their minds upon the love of God and heavenly things more than upon temporal things of the world; and generally to do all that is good, and to eschew all that is evil. And this the parents ought to do, not by cruel entreating of their children, whereby they might discourage them, and provoke them to hate their parents, but by charitable rebuking, threatening, and charitable chastising and correcting of them when they do evil, and cherishing, maintaining, and commending them when they do well. This office and duty of the parents towards their children is witnessed in many places of scripture. First, St. Paul writeth thus, Fathers provoke not your children unto anger, but bring them up in the correction and doctrine of God (Eph 6:4). And in Deuteronomy Almighty God saith, Teach my laws and commandments to thy children (6:7). And the Wise Man saith, The rod of correction giveth wisdom: the child that is left to his own will shall be confusion to his mother (Prov 29:15). And in another place he saith, He that spareth the rod hateth his son; and he that loveth him will see him corrected (Prov 13:24). And in another place he saith, See thou withdraw not from thy child discipline and chastising; if thou strike him with the rod, he shall not die: thou shalt strike him with a rod, and shalt thereby deliver his soul from hell (Prov 23:13-14). And on the other side it is written, The son untaught and unchastised is the confusion of his father (Sir 22:3). And for this cause we find in the Book of the Kings, how that our Lord conceived great indignation against Eli the chief priest, because he did not duly correct his two sons, Hophni and Phinehas, when he knew that they did grievously offend God; and how, in revenging of their father's negligence and remissness in correcting of his children, Almighty God took from Eli and all his issue and household for ever, the office of the high priesthood; and how his two sons Hophni and Phinehas were slain both upon a day, and Eli their father brake his neck (1 Sam 4). This example of Eli is necessary for fathers to imprint in their hearts, that they may see their children well taught and corrected, lest they run into the great indignation of Almighty God, as Eli did; and not only in this world have confusion, but also in the world to come have damnation for the misorder of their children through their default: and they must not think that it is enough to speak somewhat to them when they do amiss; for so did Eli to his sons, and yet our Lord was not pleased because he did not much more sharply correct them, and see them reformed: but when words will not serve, the fathers and mothers must put to sharper correction, and by such discipline save their souls, or else they shall answer to God for them. And truly they greatly deserve the indignation of God, that when they have received of him children do not bring them up to his service, but, without regard what cometh of them, suffer them to run into the service of the Devil. Wherefore all fathers ought diligently to consider and remember how much and how grievously they offend God, and of how many evils they be the cause, which either bring up their children in wantonness and idleness, and do not put them forth betime to some faculty, exercise, or labour, whereby they may after get their living, or occupy their life to the profit and commodity of the common weal; or else do suffer their children in youth to be corrupted for lack of good teaching and good bringing up in the true knowledge of God and of his will and commandments; or commit in word or deed such things in the presence of their children, whereof the young tender hearts of the said children (which like a small twig be inclinable every way, and by frailness of youth be inclined to evil) do take so evil example, and corruption of vices, and worldly affections, that hard it will be for them after to eschew the same.

This commandment also containeth the honour and obedience which subjects owe unto their princes; and also the office of princes towards their subjects. For scripture taketh princes to be as it were fathers and nurses to their subjects. And by scripture it appeareth, that it appertaineth unto the office of princes to see that the right religion and true doctrine of Christ be maintained and taught, and that their subjects be well ruled and governed by good and just laws, and to provide and care

THE TEN COMMANDMENTS | 281

that the people and common weal may increase, and to defend them from oppression and invasion, as well within the realm as without, their subjects aiding them thereunto and to see that justice be ministered unto them indifferently; and to hear by themselves or by their ministers benignly all their complaints, and to shew toward them (although they offend) fatherly pity. And finally so to correct them that be evil, that they had yet rather save them than lose them, if it were not for respect of justice and maintenance of peace and good order in the common weal. And therefore all their subjects must again on their parts, and be bound by this commandment, not only to honour and obey the said princes, according as subjects be bound to do, and to owe their truth and fidelity unto them as unto their natural lords; but they must also love them as children do love their fathers, yea they must more tender the surety of their prince's person and his estate than their own or any others: even like as the health of the head is more to be tendered than the health of any other member.

And by this commandment also subjects be bound not to withdraw their said fealty, truth, love, and obedience towards their princes for any cause whatsoever it be, ne for any cause they may conspire against his person, ne do any thing towards the hinderance or hurt, thereof, nor of his estate.

And furthermore by this commandment they be bound to obey also all the laws, proclamations, precepts, and commandments, made by their princes and governors, except they be against the commandments of God. And likewise they be bound to obey all such as be in authority under their prince, as far as he will have them obeyed. They must also give unto their prince aid, help, and assistance, whensoever he shall require the same, either for surety, preservation, or maintenance of his person and estate, or of the realm, or of the defence of any of the same against all persons. And whensoever subjects be called by their prince unto privy-council, or unto the parliament, where is the general council of this realm, then they be bound to give unto their prince, as their learning, wisdom, or experience can serve them, the most faithful counsel they can, and such as may be to the honour of God, to the honour and surety of his regal person and state, and to the general wealth of this his whole realm.

And further, if any subject shall know of any thing which is or may be to the noyance or damage of his prince's person or estate, he is bound by this commandment to disclose the same with all speed to the prince himself, or to some of his council. For it is the very law of nature that every member shall employ himself to preserve and defend the head. And surely wisdom and policy will the same: for of conspiracy and treason cometh no goodness, but infinite hurt, damage, and peril to the common weal.

And that all subjects do owe unto their princes and governors such honour and obedience as is aforesaid, it appeareth evidently in sundry places of scripture, but specially in the Epistles of St. Paul and St. Peter. For St. Paul saith in this manner: Every man must be obedient unto the high powers, for the powers be of God (Rom 13:1-2). And therefore whosoever resisteth the powers, resisteth the ordinance of God; and they that resist the ordinance of God shall get to themselves damnation: for rulers are not fearful to them that be good, but to them that do evil. Wilt not thou fear the power? Do well, and thou shalt have praise of the same; for he is the minister of God for thy wealth. But if thou do evil, then fear, for he beareth not the sword without cause; for he is the minister of God to punish the evil doer: therefore you must obey, not only for the fear of punishment, but also because of conscience. And for this cause ye pay tributes; for they be God's ministers, serving for the same purpose. Give therefore to all men that is due; tribute to whom tribute is due, custom to whom custom is due, fear to whom fear is due, and honour to whom honour is due. And St. Peter saith, Obey unto all sorts of governors for God's sake, whether it be unto the king as unto the chief head, or unto rulers as unto them that be sent of him to punish evil doers, and to cherish them that do well. And shortly after it followeth, Fear God, honour the king (1 Pet 2:14, 17).

And there be many examples in scripture of the great vengeance of God that hath fallen upon rulers, and such as have been disobedient unto their princes. But one principal example to be noted is of the rebellion which Kore, Dathan, and Abiram made against their governors Moses and Aaron. For punishment of which rebels God not only caused the earth to open and to swallow them down, and a great number of other people with them, with their houses and all their substance, but caused also the fire to descend from heaven, and to burn up two hundred and fifty captains, which conspired with them in the said rebellion (Num 16).

Moreover all Christian men be bound by this commandment to exhibit due honour and reverence unto the spiritual fathers and parents which have cure and charge of their souls, as unto those who be appointed by God to minister his sacraments unto the people, and to feed them with his word, and by the same to conduct and to lead them the straight way to the Father in heaven everlasting.

And our Saviour Christ in the gospel maketh mention as well of the obedience as of the corporal sustenance which all Christian people do owe unto their spiritual fathers. Of the obedience he saith, That whosoever receiveth you receiveth me (Matt 10:40). And in another place he saith, He that heareth you heareth me; and he that despiseth you despiseth me (Luke 10:16). And St. Paul saith, Obey your prelates, and give place unto them: for they have much charge and much care for your souls, as they which must give an account therefore, that they may do it with joy and not with grief (Heb 13:17); that is to say, that they may gladly and with much comfort do their cure and charge when they do perceive that the people be obedient to their teaching. Like as contrariwise, although they be bound to do it, yet the people give them little comfort to do it, when they find them disobedient and repugnant.

And for the sustenance of their living, which is comprised in this word *honour,* as is before declared, Christ saith in the gospel, The workman is worthy his wages (Luke 10:7). And St. Paul saith, Who goeth on warfare upon his own stipend? And who planteth the vine, and eateth no part of the fruit? And who feedeth the flock, and eateth no part of the milk? And after followeth, Even so hath the Lord ordained, that they which preach the gospel should live of the gospel (1 Cor 9:7, 14). And therefore in another place it is written, Priests that rule well be worthy of double honour, specially they that labour in the ministration of the word of God and his doctrine (1 Tim 5:17). In which place the apostle meaneth by double honour, not only the reverence which is due unto the spiritual fathers, as is aforesaid, but also sufficiency of all things necessary and requisite, as well for their sustenance and finding, as for the quiet and commodious exercising and executing of their said office.

Finally, in this commandment is contained the honour and obedience of the servant unto his master, that is, to love his master, to be reverent and lowly to him in all his words and gesture, to suffer and forbear him, to be ready with a good will, without murmuration or grudging, to obey all his lawful and reasonable commandments, to fear him, and to be loath to displease him, to be faithful and true unto him, and to his power to procure and do that which is for his master's honesty and profit; and that as well in his master's absence and out of his sight, as when he is present and looketh upon him; according to the words of St. Paul, where he saith, Servants, be you obedient unto your masters with fear and trembling, with simple and plain hearts, as unto Christ, not serving only in their sight, as pleasers of men, but as the servants of Christ, doing the will of God from the heart, and with good will, thinking that ye serve God, and not men: and be you sure that of all your good service you shall receive reward of God (Eph 6:5-8). And again to Titus he writeth thus: Exhort the servants to be obedient unto their masters, to please them well in all things, not to be patterers and praters against them, nor pickers, nor privy conveyers of their masters' goods; but to shew all truth and faithfulness (Titus 2:9-10). St. Peter also biddeth servants to obey their masters with all fear, not only if they be good and gentle, but also though they be froward (1 Pet 2:18).

And of the other side, the office and duty of masters to their servants is to provide sufficiently for them of all things necessary, to see them instructed in the knowledge of the commandments of God, and that they observe the same, and not be over rigorous unto them, but with discretion to correct them when they do amiss, and to commend and cherish them when they do well; according to the saying of St. Paul, You that be masters, do unto your servants that is right and reason, knowing that yourselves have also a master in heaven (Col 4:1). And in another place he saith, Be not rigorous unto your servants; for you have a master in heaven that regardeth all persons indifferently (Eph 6:9). And the Wise Man saith, Meat, correction, and work is due unto servants. Set thy servant unto labour, that he be not idle, for idleness bringeth much evil: set him to work, for that belongeth to him: if he be not obedient, correct him (Sir 33:24, 27-28).

And in this commandment is also implied, that children and young folks should give due honour and reverence to old men, and to all such as be their masters and tutors to bring them up in learning and virtue, which be in this behalf as fathers unto them, and so as fathers must be honoured and obeyed.

The Exposition of the Sixth Commandment of God

In this commandment is forbidden not only bodily kill-
ing, and all manner of violent laying of hands upon any *Thou shalt do*
no murder.
man, as striking, cutting, wounding, and all manner of
bodily hurting, by act or deed; but also all malice, anger, hate, envy, disdain, and all other evil affections of heart, and also all slander, backbiting,
scolding, banning, railing, scorning, or mocking, and all other evil behaviour of our tongue against our neighbours, which all be forbidden by this
commandment, for they be roots and occasions of murder and other bodily hurt.

The contrary of all these things be commanded by this commandment, that is to say, that we should with our hearts love our neighbours,
and with our tongues speak well of them and to them, and in our acts and
deeds do good unto them, shewing towards them in heart, word, and deed,
patience, meekness, mercy, and gentleness, yea though they be our adversaries and enemies. And that this is the true sense and meaning of this commandment, it appeareth by the exposition of our Saviour Christ in the
Gospel, where he declareth that we should neither hurt any man in deed,
nor speak of him or unto him maliciously or contemptuously with our
tongues, nor bear malice or anger in our hearts (Matt 5); but that we
should love them that hate us, say well by them that say evil by us, and do
good unto them that do evil unto us (Rom 12:21). And according to the
same saying of Christ, St. John saith also, that he that hateth his brother is
a mankiller (1 John 3:15).

It is not forbidden by this commandment but that all rulers and governors, as princes, judges, fathers, masters, and such other, may, for the
correction of them which be under their governance, use such manner of
punishment, either by rebukeful or sharp words, or by bodily chastising,
as the laws of every realm do permit. And not only they may do thus, but
also they be bound so to do, (unless they see reasonable cause to the contrary,) and offend God if they do it not, as is before declared in the fifth
commandment.

All rulers also must beware and take heed that in their corrections and
punishments they do not proceed upon any private malice of their hearts,
or displeasure towards any man, or for any lucre, favour, or fear of any
person; but that they have their eye and consideration only upon the

reformation and amendment of the person whom they do correct, or else upon the good order and quietness of the common weal, so that still there may remain in their hearts charity and love towards the person they punish. And like as the father loveth his child even when he beateth him, even so a good judge, when he giveth sentence of death upon any guilty person, although he shew outwardly sharpness and rigour, yet inwardly he ought to love the person, and to be sorry and heavy for his offences, and for the death which he himself by the law doth and must needs condemn him unto. And although inferior rulers and governors may correct and punish such as be under their governance, yet they may not punish by death, nor mutilate, maim, or imprison them, or use any corporal violence towards them, otherwise than is permitted by the high governor, that is to say, by the prince and his laws, from whom all such authority doth come. For no man may kill, or use such bodily coercion, but only princes, and they which have authority from princes; ne the said princes, nor any for them, may do the same, but by and according to the just order of their laws and ordinances.

Moreover no subjects may draw their swords against their prince for any cause, whatsoever it be, nor against any other (saving for lawful defence) without their prince's licence: and it is their duty to draw their swords for the defence of their prince and realm, whensoever the prince shall command them so to do. And although princes, which be the chief and supreme heads of their realms, do otherwise than they ought to do, yet God hath assigned no judges over them in this world, but will have the judgment of them reserved to himself, and will punish them when he seeth his time. And for amendment of such princes that do otherwise than they should do, the subjects may not rebel, but must pray to God, which hath the hearts of princes in his hands, that he so turn their hearts unto him, that they may use the sword which he hath given them unto his pleasure.

Against this commandment offend all they which do kill, maim, or hurt any man without just order of the law, and giveth counsel, aid, favour, provocation, or consent thereto.

And also all they which may (if they will) by their authority or lawful means deliver a man from wrongful death, mutilation, hurt, or injury, and will not do it, but will wink thereat, and dissemble it, be transgressors of this commandment.

And all judges, which, seeing no sufficient matter or cause of death, or upon light trial, without sufficient examination and discussion, give sentence of death; or when the matter or cause of death is sufficient, and the trial good, yet delight in the death of the person, be transgressors of this commandment.

And likewise, be all those which in causes of life and death being impannelled upon inquests, do lightly condemn or indict any person, without sufficient evidence, examination, and discussion of the informations given unto them. And moreover all those which either in such causes do give false evidence or information, either wittingly, contrary to their own conscience, or doubting of the truth of those informations, or without sufficient examination do promote, enforce, or maintain such evidences, informations, or indictments, do also break this commandment.

So do all they which willingly do kill themselves for any manner of cause: for so to do there can be no pretence of lawful cause ne of just order. And therefore he that so doth, killeth at once both body and soul.

Finally, all they which bear hatred and malice against their neighbours, and either maliciously speak words of contempt, despite, checking, cursing, and such other, or else publish their neighbours' offences to their slander rather than to their amendment: and generally all they that live in ire, malice, envy, and murmuring at other men's wealth, or rejoicing at other men's trouble or hurt, or such other like, they offend all against this precept.

The Exposition of the Seventh Commandment of God

As touching this word, *adultery* doth signify properly the unlawful commixtion of a married man with any other woman than with his own wife, or else of a married woman with any other man than her own husband; yet *Thou shalt not commit adultery.* in this commandment it is taken not only for that, but also for all manner unlawful copulation between man and woman, married and unmarried, and all manner of unlawful use of those parts which be ordained for generation, whether it be by adultery, fornication, incest, or any other mean.

And in lawful matrimony a man may break this commandment, and live unchaste with his own wife, if he do immeasurably or inordinately serve his or her fleshly appetite or lust. And of such the Devil hath power, as the angel Raphael said unto Thobit, They that marry in such wise that they exclude God out of their hearts, and give themselves unto their own carnal lusts, as it were an horse or a mule, which have no reason; upon such persons the Devil hath power (Tob 6).

Also all Christian people ought highly to regard the observation of this commandment, considering how much God is displeased, and what vengeance he hath always taken and ever will take for the transgression of the same. For confirmation whereof you shall understand, that God, in the time of Moses' law, commanded, that whosoever committed adultery should be stoned to death.

And that Almighty God, after the children of Israel had committed adultery with the women of Moab and Midian, commanded first that the heads and rulers of the people should be hanged, for that they suffered the people so to offend God; and afterward commanded also every man to slay his neighbour that had so offended. Insomuch that there was slain of that people the number of twenty-four thousand; and many mo should have been slain, had not Phinehas, the son of Eleazar the high priest, turned the indignation of God from the children of Israel. For this Phinehas, when he saw Zimri, chief of the tribe of Simeon, in the presence of Moses and all the people, go unto a nobleman's daughter of the Midianites, to commit fornication with her, he rose from among all the multitude, and taking a sword in his hand, went into the house where they were, and thrust them both through the bellies: whose fervent mind and zeal God did so much allow, that he did therefore both cease from the farther punishment of the Israelites, and also granted to Phinehas and his successors for ever the dignity of the high priesthood.

Also the tribe and stock of Benjamin was punished for the maintenance of certain persons of the city of Gibeah, which had, contrary to this commandment, shamefully abused a certain man's wife, that of twenty-five thousand and seven hundred men of arms, there remained on life but six hundred (Judg 20).

Moreover Almighty God, for the transgression of this commandment, caused brimstone and fire to rain down from heaven upon all the country of Sodom and Gomorrah, and so destroyed the whole region, both men, women, and beasts, and all that grew upon the earth, reserving only Lot and his two daughters (Gen 19).

These terrible examples, and many other like, Almighty God did shew in times past, to the intent we should have them in our continual remembrance, and should ever stand in awe and fear so to offend God. For though he doth not presently punish us here in this world, as he did the persons afore rehearsed, yet his long patience and forbearing is no allowance or forgiveness of our offences, if we continue still in them, but a sore accumulation and heaping together of God's wrath and indignation against the day of judgment: at which time, instead of this temporal pain, we shall receive everlasting pain; being (as St. Paul saith) excluded from the everlasting kingdom of heaven (Rom 2:8); and, as Christ saith in the Gospel, and St. John in the Apocalypse, We shall be cast into the burning lake of hell, where is fire, brimstone, weeping, wailing, and gnashing of teeth without end (Matt 22, 25; Luke 13).

Furthermore, in this commandment not only the vices before rehearsed be forbidden and prohibited, but also the virtues contrary to them be required and commanded; that is to say, fidelity, and true keeping of wedlock in them that be married, continence in them that be unmarried, and generally in all persons shamefastness and chasteness, not only of deeds, but of words and manners, countenance and thought; and moreover fasting, temperance, watching, labour, and all lawful things that conduce and help to chastity.

And therefore against this commandment offend all they which take any single woman, or other man's wife, or that in their hearts do covet or desire unlawfully to have them.

For, as Christ saith, Whosoever beholdeth a woman, coveting her unlawfully, hath already committed adultery with her in his heart (Matt 5:28).

They also offend this commandment that take in marriage or out of marriage any of their own kindred or affinity, within the degrees forbidden by the law of God (Lev 28, 20).

They also offend this commandment which abuse themselves or any other persons against nature, or abuse their wives in the time of their menstrual purgation.

They also that do nourish, stir up, and provoke themselves or any other to carnal lusts and pleasures of the body, by uncleanly and wanton words, tales, songs, sights, touchings, gay and wanton apparel, and lascivious decking of themselves, or any such wanton behaviour and enticement;

and also all those which procure any such act, or that minister house, licence, or place thereunto; and all counsellors, helpers, and consenters to the same, do grievously offend and transgress this commandment. Likewise all they that avoid not the causes hereof so much as they conveniently may, as surfeiting, sloth, idleness, immoderate sleep, and company of such, both men and women, as be unchaste and evil disposed, be guilty of the transgression of this commandment.

The Exposition of the Eighth Commandment of God

Thou shalt not steal. Under the name of *theft* or *stealing*, in this commandment, is understand all manner of unlawful taking away, occupying, or keeping of another man's goods, whether it be by force, extortion, oppression, bribery, usury, simony, unlawful chevisance or shifts, or else by false buying and selling, either by false weights, or by false measures, or by selling of a thing counterfeit for a true, as gilt copper for true gold, or glass for precious stones; and generally all manner of fraud and deceit.

And like as the vices before rehearsed be forbidden by this precept, even so sundry virtues, contrary to the said vices, be commanded by the same; as, to deal truly and plainly with our neighbours in all things, to get our own goods truly, to spend them liberally upon them that have need, to feed the hungry, to give drink to the thirsty, to clothe the naked, to harborough the harbourless, to comfort the sick, to visit the prisoners; and, finally, to help our neighbours with our learning, good counsel, and exhortation, and by all other good mean that we can.

Against this commandment offend all they which by craft or violence, upon the sea or land, spoil, rob, or take away any other man's servant or child, land or inheritance, horse, sheep, or cattle, fish, fowl, conies, or deer, money, jewels, apparel, or any other thing which is not their own.

Likewise offend all they against this commandment which have goods given to an use, and put them not to the same use, but keep them to their own advantage, as masters of hospitals and false executors, which convert the goods given to the sustentation of the poor folks, and to other good and charitable uses, unto their own profit; and also all they which receive rent or stipend for any office, spiritual or temporal, and yet do not their office belonging thereunto, be transgressors of this commandment.

And so all they which take wages or fee, pretending to deserve it, and yet do not indeed, as labourers and hired servants, which loiter, and do not apply their business; and likewise advocates, proctors, attorneys, counsellors in any of the laws, which sometime for little pain take much stipend, or by their default and negligence mar good causes, or do any thing to the hinderance of speedy justice for their advantages, do transgress this commandment.

Also all idle vagabonds and sturdy beggars, which, being able to get their living by labour, take such alms wherewith the poor and impotent folks should be relieved and sustained, do offend against this commandment.

Moreover all they transgress this commandment which buy any stolen goods, knowing that they be stolen, or that buy things of them that have none authority to sell them, or alienate them, if they know the same: and likewise do they which withhold goods stolen, or that find things lost, and knowing the owner thereof, will not restore them, or will not do their diligence to know the owner.

They also which defraud their hired servants of their due wages, and they that borrow any thing, or retain any thing delivered unto them upon trust, and will not restore the same again; and they that use false weights or measures, or deceitful wares, or sell their own wares at an unreasonable price far above the just value.

And they that engross and buy up any kind of wares wholly into their own hands, to the intent that they may make a scarceness thereof in other men's hands, and sell it again as they list.

And generally all covetous men, which by any means unlawfully get or unmercifully keep their goods from them that have need, be transgressors and breakers of this commandment.

The Exposition of the Ninth Commandment of God

By this commandment is forbidden all manner of lying, slandering, backbiting, false reporting, false accusing, evil counselling, and all such misusing of our tongue to the hurt of our neighbours, whether it be in

Thou shalt not bear false witness against thy neighbour.

their body or goods, or in their good name and fame. The apostle St. James likeneth the tongue of a man unto the bit of an horse mouth, which turneth the whole horse every way, as pleaseth him that sitteth on the horse back. And he compareth it also to the helm of a ship, whereby all the whole ship is ruled at the pleasure of him that governeth the helm. And, thirdly, he compareth it unto a spark of fire, which, if it be suffered, will burn up an whole town or city (James 3:3-6). And surely all these comparisons be very apt and meet. For the tongue of a man no doubt is the chief stay of all the whole body, either to do much good or to do much hurt. The voice of the tongue pierceth the hearts of hearers, and causeth them to conceive of other men good or evil opinion. It kindleth or quencheth contention. It disposeth men to war or peace, and moveth the hearers sundry ways to goodness or vice. And like as the great rageous flames that go from house to house come but of one sparkle, which in the beginning might have been easily quenched, but by negligence and sufferance increaseth and waxeth so great, that no man can resist it; and like as fire is a great commodity many ways, if it be well and wisely used, and contrary an utter destruction, if it be suffered and not taken heed unto; even so of man's tongue, although it be a very small member of the body, yet there cometh exceeding great benefits both to himself and to others, if it be well and wisely governed. And contrariwise, if no heed be taken thereunto, but be suffered to run at large, then it is not one evil alone, but a root and occasion, or rather a heaping together of all evils.

And because that of the tongue cometh so much good or so much evil; therefore by this commandment is not only forbidden all evil use of the tongue, to the hurt of our neighbours, but also in the same is commanded all the good use of the tongue, to the benefit of our neighbours; as, to be true and plain in our words, to be faithful in covenants, bargains, and promises, to testify the truth in all courts, judgments, and other places, to report well of them that be absent, to give good counsel and exhortation to all goodness, to dissuade from all evil: and when we know any man to do amiss, not to publish his fault to other men to his slander, but rather to admonish him privily between him and us, and to seek his reformation; to speak well by our enemies, to pacify and set at one them that be enemies, to excuse them and to answer for them that be unjustly slandered; and generally in all other things to use our tongues in truth, to the wealth of our neighbours.

Against this commandment offend all they which by lying and uttering of false speech deceive and hurt any man: and such liars be the Devil's children. For, as St. John saith in his Gospel, the Devil is a liar, and father of liars (John 8:44). And therefore biddeth St. Paul, that we should put away lying, and speak truth every man to his neighbour (Eph 4:25).

They also offend against this commandment which be detracters, backbiters, and slanderers, whom the Wise Man doth liken unto serpents, that privily bite or sting men behind, when they be not ware thereof (Eccl 8:11). And surely such men (whatsoever they pretend) go not about to heal and amend them that do amiss, but rather do satisfy their own malice and slanderous tongues. For like as the surgeon that will heal a wound doth cover it and bind it, that it take no open air, so if we intend the amendment of our neighbour's fault, we must not open it abroad to his hurt, but we must be sorry, and pray to God for him, and so taking him to us, we must privily counsel and exhort him. And this loving correction will make him beware and take heed that he offend no more. But if we tell his faults first to one and after to another, and charge every one to keep counsel, as though we had told it to no mo, this is no amendment of his fault, but a declaration of our own, and a reprehension of ourselves, in that we utter forth unto other that thing which we ourselves judge not to be uttered. And surely we condemn ourselves therein, for we should first have kept it secret to ourselves, if we would not another man should utter the same. And therefore the Wise Man saith, If thou have heard any thing against thy neighbour, let it die within thee, and be sure it will not burst thee (Sir 19:10). And in another place, As evil is he that backbiteth privily, as the serpent which stingeth unawares (Eccl 10:11).

And they also offend against this commandment which gladly give ears and be ready to hear such backbiters. For, as St. Bernard saith, Like as the backbiter carrieth the Devil in his mouth, so the hearer carrieth the Devil in his ear: for the detracter is not glad to tell but to him that is glad to hear. And the Wise Man saith, that like as the wind driveth away the rain, even so doth a sad and a displeasant countenance drive away the tongue of the backbiters, and maketh them abashed (Prov 25:23).

They also break this commandment which with flattering and double tongues go about to please such as be glad to hear complaints. Judges also which give sentence contrary to that which they know to be true, and they that in judgment do hide and suppress the truth, and they that make false pleas to the delay and hinderance of justice, or any otherwise do stop justice. And inquests which upon light grounds, or upon grounds not well examined or discussed, give verdict, be transgressors and breakers of this commandment. And above other, they do transgress this commandment, which in preaching or other ways do teach or maintain any false or erroneous doctrine, contrary to the word of God, or that do teach fables, or men's phantasies and imaginations, affirming them to be the word of God: and such be worse than false witnesses of worldly matters, for they bear false witness against God and his truth.

The Exposition of the Tenth Commandment of God

Thou shalt not unjustly desire thy neighbour's house, nor thy neighbour's wife, nor his servant, nor his maid, nor his ox, nor his ass, nor any thing that is thy neighbour's.

Whereas in the other commandments before rehearsed be forbidden all words and deeds which be against God's pleasure and the love of our neighbours; in this last precept is forbidden the inward consent of the heart to all unlawful motions, desires, delights, inclinations, and affections unto evil; which things be so rooted and planted in all us the children of Adam, even from the first hour of our birth, that although, by the inspiration of the Holy Ghost, and the grace of God given unto us, we do intend never so well, and would most gladly eschew all evil, yet there remaineth in us a disposition and readiness unto such things as be contrary to the will and commandment of God: insomuch that if the grace of God did not help us to stay and resist our naughty thoughts and delight unto sin, the same our concupiscence and naughtiness should be so much, that we should run headlong into sin and mischief, our nature is so corrupt, and we be so far from the perfect obedience unto God's will, which obedience Adam had in the state of innocency. And of this corruption of our nature, and readiness unto evil, complaineth St. Paul, in his Epistle unto the Romans, where he declareth at length, that the nature of man is so full of concupiscence and evil affections, that no man doth or can of himself satisfy or fulfil the law of God: and that the law condemneth all men as transgressors;

and that therefore every man for his salvation must have refuge unto the grace and mercy of God, obtained by our Saviour Jesu Christ (Rom 7).

Furthermore, like as in the fifth commandment, under the name of *father* and *mother*, is understand all superiors; and in the sixth commandment, under the name of *killing*, is understand all wrath and revenging; and in the seventh commandment, under the name of *adultery*, is understand all unchaste living; and in the eighth commandment, under the name of *theft*, is understand all deceitful dealing with our neighbours; and in the ninth commandment, under the name of *false witness*, is understand all misreport and untrue use of our tongue; so in this last commandment, under the name of *desiring of another man's wife and goods*, is understand all manner of evil and unlawful desire of any thing.

And like as in this precept be forbidden evil desires, even so in the same be commanded good desires, good affections, good inclinations to godly things, and the perfect obedience of our hearts unto God's will, which, although we shall not fully and absolutely attain unto whiles we be in this life; yet this commandment doth bind us to enforce and endeavour ourselves thereunto by continual fighting and resisting against the said corruption, concupiscence, and evil desires; forasmuch as by them man is continually tempted to evil deeds and vicious living; according whereunto St. James writeth, Let no man say, when he is tempted to evil, that he is tempted of God. For as God cannot be tempted to evil, so he tempteth no man to evil; but every man is tempted, drawn, and allured by his own concupiscence: then concupiscence, when she hath conceived, bringeth forth sin (Jas 1:13-15).

All they be transgressors of this commandment which by deliberation and full consent cast their minds and lusts to accomplish the concupiscence and desire which they have to obtain and get unlawfully another man's wife, child, servant, house, land, cattle, or any thing or goods that be his.

And they also be transgressors of this commandment, which by envy be sorry of their neighbours' wealth and prosperity, or be glad of their sorrow, hinderance, and adversity. And also all they which do not set their minds and studies to preserve, maintain, and defend unto their neighbours (as much as it is in them) their wives, children, servants, houses, lands, goods, and all that is theirs. For (as before is declared) this commandment not only forbiddeth us to desire unlawfully from our neighbour any thing that is his; but by the same we be also commanded gladly to wish and will unto him that he may quietly possess and enjoy all that God hath sent him, be it never so great abundance. And this mind we ought to bear unto every man by this commandment, not only if they be our friends and lovers, but also if they be our enemies and adversaries.

The Exposition of
the Prayer of Our Lord

Here followeth the Exposition of the Prayer of our Lord, called the Paternoster, divided into seven Petitions.

1. Our father, which art in heaven: hallowed be thy name.

2. Thy kingdom come.

3. Thy will be done in earth, as it is in heaven.

4. Give us this day our daily bread.

5. And forgive us our trespasses; as we forgive them that trespass against us.

6. And let us not be led into temptation.

7. But deliver us from evil. Amen.

The Notes

For the better and more ample declaration of this prayer, ye shall understand, first, that our Saviour Jesu Christ was the author and maker thereof; and that therefore, like as he is of infinite wisdom and of infinite love and charity towards us, even so all Christian men ought to think and believe that this same prayer is the most excellent, and most sufficient, and most perfect of all others. For neither there is any thing in this prayer superfluous, neither there wanteth any petition, suit, or request for such things as be necessary for our journey and passage in this world, or for our furtherance to the attaining of the life and glory everlasting.

Secondly, that every good Christian man may be assured to attain the requests made in this prayer, if he shall enforce himself, and apply his whole heart and will to the will and grace of him unto whom this prayer is made, and also if he shall utter and offer the said petitions inwardly with his heart, and with such faith, confidence, and trust in God as he requireth. For surely no prayer is thankful unto God, but that which is made with the heart. And therefore the prophet David crieth to our Lord with all his heart (Ps 118). And Moses is noted to cry out aloud, when he spake no word with his mouth, but he spake aloud with his heart. And our Lord by his prophet noteth, that some pray with their lips, and in their hearts mind nothing less than that which they pray for (Isa 29:13; Matt 15:8). And therefore whosoever intendeth, by saying his Paternoster, to attain his desire, he must have with faith a good and earnest devotion, and his heart, as nigh as he can, void of vain thoughts, and applied to God, so that the intent and desire of his heart may be joined always with the prayer of his mouth.

And for this purpose it is meet and much requisite that the unlearned people should use to make their prayers in their mother tongue, which they best understand, whereby they may be the more moved and stirred unto devotion, and the more earnestly mind the thing that they pray for.

The First Petition

Our Father, which art in heaven, hallowed be thy name.

Of these words *Our Father*, placed in the beginning of this petition, all true Christian men ought to conceive a great comfort and joy, in that they be taught and commanded in this prayer to take Almighty God for their Father, and so to call him; as for example, if our sovereign lord the king would say to any of us, Take me for your father, and so call me, what joy in heart, what comfort, what confidence would we conceive of so favourable and gracious words! Then much more incomparably have we cause to rejoice that the King and Prince of all princes sheweth unto us this grace and goodness, to make us his children. And surely as the natural son may assuredly trust that his father will do for him all things that may be for his setting forth and advancement; even so we may undoubtedly assure ourselves, that having Almighty God to our Father, using ourselves as obedient children, we shall lack nothing which may be profitable for us, toward the everlasting inheritance prepared for us.

And here is to be noted a lesson, that as this word *Father* declareth the great benevolence, mercy, and love of God towards us, as well in the creation as also in the redemption of man; so it admonisheth us again of our duty towards him, and how we be bound to shew again unto him our whole heart, love, and our obedience and readiness to fulfil all his precepts and commandments with all gladness and humility. And therefore whosoever presumeth to come to God with this prayer, and to call him Father, and yet hath not full intent and purpose to use himself in all things like a kind and an obedient son, he cometh to him, as Judas came to Christ, with a kiss, pretending to be his friend and his servant, in calling him master, and yet he was indeed a traitor to him, and a deadly enemy (Luke 22:47). And for this consideration every Christian man that intendeth to make this prayer, ought inwardly and throughly to ensearch and examine himself; and if he find in himself any notable crime, for the which he ought to be ashamed to call God his Father, let him accuse himself thereof to God, and recognise his unworthiness; saying as the prodigal son said, Father, I have offended thee; I am not worthy to be called thy son (Luke 15:19). And with due repentance and firm purpose and intent to amend his naughty life, let him lift up his heart to God, and calling for his grace of reconciliation, humbly say, Our Father, &c.

Moreover, by these words *our Father,* is signified, that we ought to believe that Almighty God is the common Father of all true Christian people, and fatherly regardeth all, through and by the mean of our Saviour Jesu Christ, unto whom all faithful and obedient Christian men be brethren by grace and adoption, and called to inherit with him the kingdom of heaven. And they be also brethren each one to other, having all one Father, which is God Almighty. And therefore we ought not only to be of one spirit towards our said Father, and to employ and endeavour ourselves to the uttermost to please him, and to keep his laws and commandments, but we ought also each to consent with other in perfect love and charity, and each to help and further other towards the said inheritance of heaven. And finally, in all our prayers to God, each to comprise other, and to pray for other, like as in this prayer we be taught to say, *Our* Father, give *us* our bread: forgive *us* our sins: suffer *us* not to fall into temptation: and deliver *us* from evil.

By these words, *Which art in heaven,* we be taught, that we ought to have an inward desire and a great care and study to come to the place where our heavenly Father is, and much covet his sight and presence. For like as a loving child is ever desirous to be where his Father is; even so ought we ever desire to be with our heavenly Father, and to endeavour ourselves that our conversation be all withdrawn from the world, the flesh, and the devil, and be set in heaven and heavenly things, as St. Paul saith (Eph 4:22; Phil 3:20). And we ought continually to wail and lament, because we be not with our heavenly Father, saying with the prophet, Woeful am I, that my dwelling upon the earth is so much prolonged (Ps 120:6).

In these words, *Hallowed be thy name,* it is to be noted, that by the name of God is understand God himself, the power of God, the might, the majesty, the glory, the wisdom, the providence, the mercy and goodness of God, and all such other good things as in scripture be attributed unto God. And this name is hallowed when it is praised, glorified, set forth, honoured, and magnified of us both in word and deed.

And where in this petition we pray that his name might be hallowed, it is not to be taken or thought that this name of God, which in itself is evermore most holy, most glorious, most marvellous, and full of majesty, can be either advanced or diminished by us, or any thing that we can do, but we desire here that this most holy name may (according as it is in itself most holy) be so taken, used, honoured, and hallowed of us and of all others, as well heathen as christened, like as on the contrary part this name is said to be polluted and defiled, when we do, either in word or deed, contumeliously and contemptuously or otherwise dishonour the same.

We desire therefore in this petition, that all false faith, by the which men either mistrust God, or put their confidence in any other thing more than in him, may be destroyed: and that all witchcrafts, and false charms and conjurations, by the which Satan and other creatures be enchanted, may cease and give place to God's holy name: and so likewise that all heresies and false doctrines may vanish away, so that God's holy word may be truly interpreted, and purely taught and set forth unto all the world, and that all infidels may receive the same, and be converted to the right catholic faith, whereby all deceit, hypocrisy, and counterfeiting of truth, of righteousness, or of holiness, might clearly be extinct.

Furthermore, we beseech and pray God here that his name may be hallowed, so that no man should swear in vain by it, or otherwise abuse the same, to lie or to deceive his neighbour: and generally that none should fall into pride or ambition, into desire of worldly glory and fame, into envy, malice, covetousness, adultery, gluttony, sloth, backbiting, slandering of his neighbours, ne into any other evil or wicked thoughts and deeds, whereby the name of God may be dishonoured and blasphemed.

In this prayer also we require God to grant us that in all perils and dangers we run unto him as unto our only refuge, and call upon his holy name, and that in our good words and works we may please and magnify him, and be by him preserved from the most damnable sin of unkindness towards him; and also that we which do already profess the right faith may still continue therein, and may do and express the same as well in our outward conversation as in confessing it with our mouth, so that by our good life and our good works all other may be moved to good, and that by our evil works and sins no man may take occasion to slander the name or diminish the laud and praise of God, but that all our works and doings might return to the honour and praise of God's name.

The Second Petition

This second petition is very necessary; for no doubt our ancient enemy the devil goeth about continually by all crafty means to deceive us, and bring us under his power

Thy kingdom come.

and dominion. And surely so long as pride and disobedience reigneth in us; so long as ire, envy, wrath, or covetousness reigneth in us; so long as gluttony, lechery, or any kind of sin reigneth in us; so long we be under the dominion and kingdom of the devil. For the devil undoubtedly is king over all the children of pride, that is to say, over all them that be sinners, rebels, and disobedient unto God.

And forasmuch as it is not in our power to deliver ourselves from under this tyranny of the devil, but only by God's help, (for our perdition and undoing is of ourselves, but our help and salvation is of God, as saith the prophet Osee [Hos 13:9],) therefore it is very necessary for all true Christian people to make this petition incessantly unto our heavenly Father, and to beseech him, according to this doctrine of Christ, that by his grace and help we may escape the dominion and power of the devil, and that we may be made subject unto his heavenly kingdom. Therefore in this petition we desire God to give us, afore all things, true and constant faith in him, and in his Son Jesu Christ, and in the Holy Ghost, with pure love and charity towards him and all men; to keep us also from infidelity, desperation, and malice, which might be the cause of our destruction; to deliver us from dissensions, covetousness, lechery, and evil desires and lusts of sin, and so the virtue of his kingdom to come, and to reign within us, that all our heart, mind, and wits, with all our strength, inward and outward, may be ordered and directed to serve God, to observe his commandments and his will, and not to serve ourselves, the flesh, the world, or the devil.

We desire also that this kingdom, once in us begun, may be daily increased, and go forward more and more, so that all subtle and secret hate or sloth which we have to goodness, be not suffered to rule so in us that it shall cause us to look back again, and to fall into sin, but that we may have a stable purpose and strength, not only to begin the life of innocency, but also to proceed earnestly further in it, and to perform it, according to the saying of St. Paul, where he prayeth that we may walk worthily, pleasing God in all things, being fruitful in all good works, and growing and increasing in the knowledge of God (Col 1:10). Also in another place he saith, Work and do the truth in charity, and increase and go forward in Christ (Eph 4:15).

Therefore in this prayer, desiring the kingdom of God to come, we require also, that we being already received and entered into the kingdom of grace and mercy of God, may so continue and persevere therein, that after this life we may come to the kingdom of glory, which endureth for ever. And this is that great and fervent desire wherewith good men, being mortified from worldly affections, have been and be always kindled and inflamed, as appeareth by St. Paul, when he said, I would be loosed from this body, and be with Christ (Phil 1:23). And in another place he saith, We that have received the first-fruits of the Spirit, wail and mourn in ourselves, wishing and looking to be delivered from the mortality and miseries of this body into the glory of the children of God (Rom 8:23).

The Third Petition

For the better understanding of this third petition, we must know that, by disobedience and sin of our first father Adam, we be as of our nature only without the grace of God, unable to fulfil the will and precepts of God, and *Thy will be done in earth as it is in heaven.* so inclined to love ourselves and our own wills, that we cannot heartily love neither God nor man as we ought to do. And therefore we being once Christian men, it is requisite for us to pray, that like as the holy angels and saints in heaven (in whom God reigneth perfectly and wholly) do never cease ne shall cease to glorify him, to praise him, and to fulfil his will and pleasure in all things, and that most readily and gladly, without any manner of grudging or resisting thereunto, knowing certainly and clearly that his will is alway the best; even so that we, the children of God in earth, may daily and continually praise God, and by our holy conversation in good works and good life, honour and glorify him: and that we may from time to time so mortify our own natural corrupt and sinful appetite and will, that we may be ever ready, like loving children, humbly, lowly, and obediently to approve, allow, and accomplish the will of God our Father in all things, and to submit ourselves with all our heart unto the same, and to acknowledge that whatsoever is the will of God, the same is most perfect, most just, most holy, and most expedient for the wealth and health of our souls.

Wherefore in this petition also we desire of God true and stable patience when our will is letted or broken; and that when any man speaketh or doth contrary to our will, yet therefore we be not out of patience, neither curse or murmur, or seek vengeance against our adversaries, or them which let our will, but that we may say well of them, and do well to them (1 Tim 6:17-18). We pray also, that by God's grace we may gladly suffer all diseases, poverty, despisings, persecutions, and adversities, knowing that it is the will of God that we should crucify and mortify our wills; and when any such adversity chanceth unto us, attribute all unto the will or sufferance of God, and give him thanks therefore, who doth order all such things for our weal and benefit, either for the exercise and the trial of the good, to make them stronger in goodness and virtue, or else for the chastisement and amendment of the evil, to suppress their evil motions and desires.

And also we pray, that whensoever it shall please God to call us out of this transitory life, we may be willing to die; and that, conforming our will to the will of God, we may take our death gladly, so that by fear or infirmity we be not made disobedient unto him.

We desire furthermore, that all our members, eyes, tongue, heart, hands, and feet be not suffered to follow the desires of the flesh, but that all may be used to the will and pleasure of God; and that maliciously we rejoice not in their troubles which have resisted our will, or have hurt us; nor that we be enviously sorry when that they prosper and have welfare, but that we may be contented and pleased with all thing that is God's will.

The Fourth Petition

Give us this day our daily bread. For the better declaration of this fourth petition, ye shall understand, first, that our Lord teacheth us not in this petition to ask any superfluous thing of pleasure or delight, but only things necessary and sufficient, and therefore he biddeth us only ask bread: wherein is not meant superfluous riches, or great substance, or abundance of things above our estate or condition, but such things only as be necessary and sufficient for every man in his degree; and according thereunto St. Paul saith, We have brought nothing into this world, ne shall take any thing with us when we depart hence (1 Tim 6:7). And therefore if we Christian men have meat, and drink, and clothes, that is to say, things sufficient, let us hold ourselves content; for they that set their minds on riches, and will have superfluities more than needeth, or is expedient to their vocation, they fall into dangerous temptations, and into snares of the devil, and into many unprofitable and noisome desires, which drown men into perdition, and everlasting damnation: for the spring and root of all evils is such superfluous desire. The Wise Man also, making his petition to our Lord, saith, Give me neither poverty nor excess, but only things sufficient for my living, lest that having too much, I be provoked to deny God, and to forget who is the Lord: and on the other side, lest that, by poverty constrained, I fall into theft, and forswear the name of my God (Prov 30:8). These two wise men, the one of the Old and the other of the New Testament, agree with the lesson of our Saviour; for both declare that they desire only things necessary, signified here by bread, and both renounce superfluities, unprofitable, dangerous, and noisome.

Secondly, in these words of our Saviour Jesu Christ be reproved all those persons which eat not their own bread, and devour other men's bread; of which sort be all those that live of raven and spoils, of theft, of extortion, of craft, and deceit: and they also which neither labour with their hands, nor otherwise apply their study, industry, and diligence to something that is good and beneficial to the common weal and the honour of God, but live in ease, rest, idleness, and wanton pleasure, without doing or caring for any such thing. Also all they be reproved, which being called in this world to any office or authority, do abuse the same, and do not employ themselves according to their vocation.

Thirdly, as the husbandman tilleth and soweth his ground, weedeth it, and keepeth it from destroying, praying therewith to God for the increase, and putteth all his trust in him, to send him more or less at his pleasure; even so, besides our own diligence, policy, labour, and travail, we must also pray daily to God to send us sufficient; and we must take thankfully at his hands all that is sent, and be no further careful than needeth, but putting to our endeavour, set our whole confidence and trust in him: for our Saviour Christ saith in the Gospel, I say to you, Be not careful for your living, what ye shall eat, ne what clothes ye shall wear. Is not life better than your meat, and your body better than your clothing? Look upon the birds of the air: they sow not, they reap not, they bring nothing into the barn; and yet your heavenly Father feedeth them. Be not you of more price than they? Look upon the lilies of the field: they labour not, they spin not: and yet I tell you, Solomon, in all his precious and royal apparel, was not so clothed as one of them. Therefore care you not for these things. Leave this care to them that know not God. Your heavenly Father knoweth that you have need of all these things. But seek you first the kingdom of God and his righteousness, and the ways justly and truly to live, and then God shall cast all these things unto you (Matt 6:25-33). These be the words of Christ, full of good and comfortable lessons, that we should not care ne set our hearts too much upon these worldly things, ne care so much for tomorrow, that we shall seem to mistrust our Lord. And here is a thing greatly to be noted, in comfort of the true labouring man. For surely be he craftsman or be he labourer, doing truly his office whereunto he is called, he may in that state and kind of life please God and attain salvation as surely as in any other state or kind of living. And although our Lord hath so provided for some, that they have already sufficient and plenty for many days and years, yet that notwithstanding, they ought to make this petition to God, and say, Give us this day our daily bread; forasmuch as their substance, (though it be never so great,) like as it could not have been gotten without God had sent it, so it cannot prosper and continue except God preserve it. For how many great rich men have we known suddenly made poor, some by fire, some by water, some by theft, and many other ways? Was not Job the one day the richest man that was in all the east land, and the morrow after had utterly nothing? It is therefore as needful to pray our Lord to preserve that he hath given us, as to pray him to give it: for if he give, and do not preserve it, we shall have no use of it.

Fourthly, by this bread, which we be taught to ask in this petition, may be understand the holy sacrament of the altar, the very flesh and blood of our Saviour Jesu Christ, as it is written in the sixth chapter of St. John, I am the bread of life which came down from heaven. And the bread which I will give is my flesh, which I will give for the life of the world (John 6:35). And in this prayer we desire that the same may be purely ministered and distributed, to the comfort and benefit of all us the true children of God; and that we also may receive the same with a right faith and perfect charity at all times when we do and ought to receive the same, so that we may be spiritually fed therewith to our salvation, and thereby enjoy the life everlasting.

Finally, by the bread which our Saviour teacheth us to ask in this petition is meant also the true doctrine of the word of God, which is the spiritual bread that feedeth the soul. For as the body is nourished and brought up, groweth and feedeth with bread and meat, so need the soul, even from our youth, to be nourished and brought up with the word of God, and to be fed with it. And like as the body will faint and decay, if it be not from time to time relieved and refreshed with bodily sustenance; even so the soul waxeth feeble and weak towards God, unless the same be cherished and kept up with the word of God, according to the saying of Christ: A man liveth not with meat only, but with every word that proceedeth from the mouth of God (Matt 4:4). And surely the word of God is the very comfort, remedy, and health of the soul. For if we have adversity in this world, as poverty, sickness, imprisonment, and such other miseries, where should we seek for comfort but at God's word? If we think ourselves so holy that we be without sin, where should we find a glass to see our sins in but in the word of God? If we be so full of sins, that we be like to fall into desperation, where can we have comfort, and learn to know the mercy of God, but only in God's word? Where shall we have armour to fight against our three great enemies, the world, the flesh, and the devil? Where shall we have strength and power to withstand them, but as Christ did, in and by the word of God? And finally, if we have any manner of sickness or disease in our souls, what medicine or remedy can we have, but that is declared in God's word? So that the word of God is the very bread of the soul; and therefore, as well for this bread of the soul as for the blessed sacrament of the altar, also for the bread and daily sustenance of the body, our Saviour Christ teacheth us to pray in this fourth petition.

The Fifth Petition

In this petition we be taught a fruitful advertisement of man's estate in this present life, which considered, no man ought to glory in himself, as though he were innocent and without sin, but rather that every good Christian man, without exception, ought to knowledge *And forgive us our trespasses, as we forgive them that trespass against us.*
himself to be a sinner, and that he hath need to ask forgiveness of God for his sins, and to require him of his mercy: for doubtless we daily commit sin, which be commanded daily to ask remission for our sins. And St. John saith in his Epistle, If we say that we be without sin, we deceive ourselves, and truth is not in us (1 John 1:8).

Moreover it is to be noted, that we be taught to desire God to forgive us our sins, like as we forgive them that trespass against us: so that if we forgive in heart, God will forgive, and not otherwise; as by many places of scripture may appear. First, by express words Christ saith, If you forgive men their offences done against you, your heavenly Father will forgive you your offences: and if you will not forgive them that offend you, be you assured your Father will not forgive you your offences (Matt 6:14-15). And in another place, when Peter came to our Lord, and demanded of him how oft he should forgive his brother which had offended him, and whether it was not sufficient to forgive him seven times, our Lord answered him and said, I tell thee, Peter, that thou oughtest to forgive him not only seven times, but seventy times seven times: meaning thereby, that from time to time we must continually forgive our brother or neighbour, although he trespasseth against us never so often (Matt 18:21-22).

And Christ also declareth the same by a parable. There was (saith Christ) a king, which calling his servants unto account, and finding that one of them should owe unto him the sum of ten thousand talents, because he had it not to pay, commanded that the said debtor, his wife, and his children, and all that he had, should be sold. But when the debtor came unto the king, and prayed him on his knees to have patience with him, promising him to pay all, the king had pity of him, and forgave him the whole debt. It fortuned afterward, that this man, being thus acquitted, met with another of his fellows, that ought him but one hundred pence, and with violence almost strangled him, and said unto him, Pay that thou owest. And the said servant his fellow fell upon his knees, and prayed him to have patience, promising to pay all; which would not, but cast him into prison, until all was paid. And when the rest of his fellows, seeing this cruelty, had told the king thereof, the king forthwith sent for this cruel fellow, and said to him, O wicked man, I forgave thee thy whole debt at thy suit and request; it should therefore have beseemed thee to have shewed like compassion unto thy fellow, as I shewed to thee. And the king, sore displeased with this cruelty, committed him to tormentors, that should roughly and straitly handle him in prison, till he had paid the whole debt (Matt 18:23-34).

Upon this parable Christ inferreth and saith, Even so shall your heavenly Father do with you, if you will not forgive every one of you his brother even from the heart (Matt 18:35). Thus it appeareth plainly, that if we will be forgiven, if we will scape everlasting damnation, we must put out of our heart all rancour, malice, and will to revenge, and to satisfy our own carnal affections, referring the punishment of the offenders, which in their offences have transgressed the laws of God or of the prince, to the order of justice, whereof under God the princes and rulers be ministers in earth. In which doing we please God, so that we utterly forgive our own private grudge and displeasure.

And if any peradventure will think it to be an hard thing to suffer and forgive his enemy, which in word and deed hath done him many displeasures, let him consider again how many hard storms our Saviour Christ suffered and abode for us. What were we, when he gave his most precious life for us, but horrible sinners, and his enemies? How meekly took he for our sake all rebukes, mocks, binding, beating, crowning with thorn, and the most opprobrious death! It is undoubtedly above our frail and corrupt nature to love our enemies that do hate us, and to forgive them that do hurt and offend us; and it is a deed of greater perfection than man hath of himself; but God, that requireth it, will give grace that we may do it, if we ask and seek for it. And therefore in this petition our Saviour Christ teacheth us to ask this grace of our heavenly Father, that we may forgive our enemies, and that he will forgive us our trespasses, even so as we forgive them that trespass against us.

It is farther to be noted, that to forgive our brother his default is also to pray to God that he will forgive him, and will not impute his offence to him; and to wish to him the same grace and glory that we desire unto ourselves: and also ourselves, when occasion shall come, to help him, as we be bound to help our Christian brother.

And finally, forasmuch as in the expounding and declaration of scripture it is convenient and requisite to observe and follow this rule, that whensoever scripture speaketh of any duty to be done of one Christian man to another, that then the same duty be so plainly and fully opened and set forth, that each man may hear his own duty touched so that both parties, (that is to say,) as well he that is bound to forgive, as he which receiveth forgiveness, may indifferently know their duty and behaviour, and according thereunto endeavour themselves to do the same. For these causes it is expedient, that like as in the former part of this petition we have declared the part and duty of him which should for charity's sake forgive, so to declare the part and duty of them to whom forgiveness should be made, lest evil doers and naughty minded people might by the former declaration take occasion still to persevere in their naughty minds and doings, and yet claim forgiveness of their neighbour.

Wherefore ye shall understand, that forgiveness, afore spoken of, is not so meant in scripture, that by it justice or laws of princes should be broken, contemned, or not executed. For although our Saviour Christ, in this petition, doth teach us to remit and forgive all injuries and trespasses done against us, yet he which hath done the injury or trespass is nevertheless bound to acknowledge his fault, and to ask forgiveness therefore, not only of God, but of him also whom he hath offended, and to intend to do no more so: and furthermore to recompense and make amends unto the parties against whom he hath trespassed, according to his ability and power, and as the grievousness and greatness of the offence requireth. And in case he which hath committed the offence or trespass be obstinate, and will not do these things before rehearsed, which he is bound to do by the law of God, then may the party which findeth himself grieved, notwithstanding any thing that is said before in this petition, lawfully, and without offence of God's commandments, ask and seek recompense of such injuries as be done to him, according unto the order and provision of the laws of the realm, made in that behalf, so that he alway have an eye and respect unto charity, and do nothing for rancour or malice, or for sinister affection, neither bear any hatred in his heart towards him whom he sueth, but only upon a zeal and love of the maintenance of justice, correction of vice, and reformation of the party that hath offended, remembering always that he exceed not nor go beyond the limits and bounds of this general rule taught by our Saviour Christ in his Gospel, As ye would that other men should do unto you, even so do you unto them: for this is the law and the prophets (Matt 7:12). And thus we Christian folk, weighing forgiveness on the one party, and the duty of him that is forgiven on the other party, (as here now we be taught,) shall the better know how to endeavour ourselves to observe both ways; and by these means see and understand more perfectly the agreement and intent of scriptures, which we be bound to observe and follow.

The Sixth Petition

And let us not be led into temptation. It is to be noted, first, that there be two manner of temptations, whereof one cometh and is sent to us by God, who suffereth those that be his to be tempted by one means or other for their probation or trial, albeit he so assisteth and aideth them in all such temptations, that he turneth all at the end unto their profit and benefit. For, as the Wise Man saith, Like as the oven trieth the potter's vessel, so doth temptation of trouble try the righteous man (Sir 27:5). And with this manner of temptation God tempted sundrywise our holy father Abraham. He tempted also Job with extreme poverty, horrible sickness, and sudden death of his children. And daily he tempteth and proveth all such as he loveth.

The other manner of temptation cometh chiefly of the devil, which, like a furious and a wood lion, rageth and runneth about perpetually, seeking how he may devour us; and cometh also of our own concupiscence, which continually inclineth and stirreth us to evil, as St. James saith, Every man is tempted, drawn, and enticed by his own concupiscence (James 1:14). This concupiscence is an inclination and pronity of our inordinate nature to sin, which imperfection man hath by the fall of Adam; so that although original sin is taken away by baptism, and the displeasure appeased betwixt God and man, yet remaineth the disorder and debate between the soul and the flesh, which shall not be extinct but only by bodily death. For there is no man so mortified, so sequestered from the world, and so ravished in spirit, in devotion, or in contemplation, but that some concupiscence is in him, howbeit by God's grace and mercy it reigneth not, nor is of God accounted for sin, nor is hurtful but only to them that by consent yield unto it. It will never cease, but one way or another it will ever assault us; and if we do not fight with it, and resist it continually, it will overcome us, and bring us into bondage, so that the devil, by this our concupiscence and our consent, all vice and sins be engendered, like as between man and woman children be engendered: according to the saying of St. James, where he saith, Concupiscence, when she doth conceive, she bringeth forth sin, and that of all sorts, that is to say, first, acts and deeds contrary to the laws of God, and after that, use and custom of the same deeds, and at length blindness and contempt (James 1:15). For so the Wise Man saith, The wicked man, when he cometh to the bottom of sin, setteth nought thereby (Prov 18:3), but, blinded with evil custom, either thinketh the sin that he useth to be no sin, or else if he take it for sin, yet he careth not for it, but either upon vain trust of the mercy of God, (which is indeed no right trust, but a very presumption,) he will continue still in purpose to sin, or else, upon vain hope of long life, he will prolong, defer, and delay to do penance for the same, until the last end of his life; and so, ofttimes prevented with sudden death, dieth without repentance. Wherefore, considering how dangerous it is to fall into sin, and how hard it is to arise, the chief and the best way is to resist with God's help the first suggestion unto sin, and not to suffer it to prevail with us, but as soon as may be to put it out of our minds. For if we suffer it to tarry any while in our hearts, it is great peril lest that consent and deed will follow shortly after.

Secondly, that our Saviour Jesus Christ teacheth not us in this sixth petition to pray unto God our Father that we should be clearly without all temptation, but that he will not suffer us to be led into temptation, that is to say, that when we be tempted, he will give us grace to withstand it, and not to suffer us to be overcome therewith. According whereunto St. Paul saith, God is true and faithful, and will not suffer us to be tempted above that we may bear, but he will so moderate the temptation, that we may sustain and overcome it (1 Cor 10:13). And St. James saith, Think that you have a great cause to joy when you be troubled with divers temptations. For the trying of your faith bringeth patience, and patience maketh perfect works: so that you may be perfect and sound, lacking in nothing (James 1:2). And Almighty God also exhorteth us and calleth upon us to fight against temptations, saying, He that getteth the victory against them, I shall give him to eat of the tree of life (Rev 2:7). And again he saith, He that overcometh them shall not be hurt with the second death (Rev 2:11). And St. Paul saith, No man shall be crowned except he fight lawfully; that is to say, except he defend himself, and resist his enemies at all points to his power (2 Tim 2:5). And our Saviour giveth us a good courage to fight in this battle, where he saith, Be of good comfort, for I have overcome the world (John 16:33); that is to say, I have had the victory of all sins and temptations; and so shall you have, if the fault be not in yourselves: for ye fight with an adversary which is already vanquished and overcome.

The Seventh Petition

But deliver us from evil.

It is first to be noted, that like as in the sixth petition Christ taught us to desire of our heavenly Father that we should not be overcome with temptation, ne brought into sin, so now in this seventh and last petition he teacheth us to pray him, that if by frailness we fall into the captivity of the devil by sin, he will soon deliver us from it; not to let us continue in it; not to let it take root in us; not to suffer sin to reign upon us; but to deliver us, and make us free from it.

Sin is the exceeding evil from the which, in this petition we desire to be delivered. And though in this petition be also comprehended all evils in the world, as sickness, poverty, dearth, with other like adversities, yet chiefly it is to be understand of sin, which only of itself is evil, and ought ever without condition to be eschewed.

And as for other adversities, neither we can ne ought to refuse, when God shall send them, neither we ought to pray for the eschewing of them, otherwise than with this condition, if God's pleasure so be. Many things we suffer in this world, and take them for evil, but they be not evil of themselves. All affections, diseases, punishments, and torments of the body, all the troubles of this world, and all adversities, be good and necessary instruments of God for our salvation. For God himself, who cannot say other than truth, saith, Those that I love I chastise (Rev 3:19; Prov 3:19). And again, the apostle saith, He receiveth none but whom he scourgeth (Heb 12:6). This is time of scourging, and the time to come is the time of rest, ease, and bliss. And surely it is a great token that we be in the favour of God, when he doth scourge us, and trieth and fineth us like gold in the fire, whiles we be in this world: as contrary, it is a great token of his indignation towards us, to suffer us, living evil, to continue in prosperity, and to have all things after our will and pleasure, and never to trouble us or punish us with adversity. Therefore our Saviour Christ Jesus (who knoweth what is best for us) teacheth us to pray and desire to be delivered, not chiefly from worldly afflictions, trouble, and adversity, which God sendeth abundantly even to them whom he best loveth, and with whom he is best pleased; but the evil which we most chiefly should pray to be delivered from is sin, which of itself is so evil, that in no wise God can be pleased therewith.

And because our ancient enemy the devil, who is the well and spring of iniquity, and is not only himself an homicide, a liar, and an hater of the truth from the beginning, but also is the very root and occasion of all sin, and the common provoker and stirrer of man to the same, and the letter and hinderer of all virtue and goodness; because this enemy never ceaseth, but continually searcheth by all crafts and wiles to induce us to sin, and so to devour us, and to bring us thereby to everlasting damnation: therefore like as we desire here to be delivered from sin, so also we desire that our heavenly Father will save us, and defend us from this evil, the causer of sin, that is to say, the devil, and from his power and tyranny, so that he should not by his malice and guiles entice us and draw us into sin, whereby we might finally be brought unto everlasting damnation. From the which also we pray here to be delivered.

The Salutation of the Angel to the Blessed Virgin Mary

Hail, Mary, full of grace, the Lord is with thee. Blessed art thou among women; and blessed is the fruit of thy womb.

For the better understanding of this salutation of the angel, made to the blessed Virgin Mary, ye shall first consider, how it was decreed of the whole Trinity, that after the fall of our first father Adam, (by which mankind was so long in the great indignation of God, and exiled out of heaven,) the second Person, the everlasting Son of the Father everlasting, should take upon him the nature of man; and so as he was perfect God, should be perfect man, to redeem mankind from the power of the devil, and to reconcile the same again to his Lord God. And for this purpose, (as St. Luke in his Gospel declareth,) in the sixth month after St. Elisabeth was conceived with St. John the Baptist, the angel Gabriel was sent from God into a city of Galilee, named Nazareth, to a virgin, which was despoused or ensured to a man, whose name was Joseph, of the house of David, and the virgin's name was Mary. And when this angel came unto this said virgin, he said these words: Hail, full of grace, the Lord is with thee. Blessed art thou among women. And when the virgin, hearing these words, was troubled with them, and mused with herself what manner of salutation it should be, the angel said to her, Fear not, Mary, be not abashed, for thou hast found favour in the sight of God. Lo, thou shalt conceive in thy womb, and shalt bring forth a son, and thou shalt call his name JESUS. He shall be great, and shall be called the Son of the Highest: and the Lord shall give unto him the seat of David his father: and he shall reign over the house of Jacob for ever; and his kingdom shall have no end. Then said Mary to the angel, How can this be done, for I have not knowledge of man? And the angel answering said unto her, The Holy Ghost shall come from above into thee, and the power of the Highest shall overshadow thee: and therefore that holy one that shall be born of thee shall be called the Son of God. And, lo, thy cousin Elisabeth hath also conceived a son in her old age; and this is the sixth month sith she conceived, which was called the barren woman: for there is nothing unpossible to God. To this Mary answered, Lo, I am the handmaid of our Lord; be it done unto me as thou hast spoken. And then forthwith, upon the departure of the angel, Mary, being newly conceived with the most blessed child Jesus, went up into the mountains with speed into a city of Juda; and came to the house of Zachary, and saluted Elisabeth. And as soon as Elisabeth heard the salutation of Mary, the child sprang in her womb, and forthwith Elisabeth was replenished with the Holy Ghost, and cried with a great voice, and said, Blessed art thou among women; and blessed is the fruit of thy womb. And whereof cometh this, that the mother of my Lord cometh to me? For, lo, as soon as the voice of thy salutation was in mine ears, the child in my womb leaped for joy. And blessed art thou that diddest believe: for all things that have been spoken to thee from our Lord shall be performed.

Secondly, it is to be noted, that the angel Gabriel, which spake to the virgin, was an high angel, and an high messenger. And truly it was convenient that he should be so: for he came with the highest message that ever was sent, which was the entreaty and league of peace between God and man. And therefore the first word of his salutation, that is to say, *Hail,* or, *Be joyful,* was very convenient for the same: for he came with the message of joy. And so said the other angel, which at the birth of our Saviour appeared to the shepherds. I shew to you (said he) great joy that shall be to all the people. And surely considering the effects that ensued upon his high message, all mankind had great cause to joy. For man, being in the indignation and displeasure of God, was hereby reconciled. Man, being in the bonds of the devil, was hereby delivered. Man, being exiled and banished out of heaven, was hereby restored thither again.

These be such matters of joy and comfort to us, that there never was or shall be nor can be any like. And not only for this purpose he began with this high word of comfort, but also for he perceived that the virgin being alone, would be much abashed and astonied at his marvellous and sudden coming unto her. And therefore he thought it expedient, first of all to utter the word of joy and comfort, which might put away all fear from the blessed virgin. And he called her *full of grace*; by God endued so plenteously, because she should conceive and bear him that was the very plenitude and fulness of grace, the Lord of grace, by whom is all grace, and without whom is no grace. And this is the singular grace by which she is called, not only the mother of man, but also the mother of God (Acts 6:8).

Thirdly, by these words, *the Lord is with thee*, is declared why the angel called her *full of grace*: for surely our Lord is not with them that be not in grace, nor tarrieth with them that be void of grace, and be in sin. For there is a separation and divorce between the sinful soul and our Lord; as the

Wise Man saith, Perverse thoughts make a separation and a divorce from God (Wis 1:3).

Fourthly, by these words, *Blessed art thou among women,* was meant, that there was never woman so blessed. And truly she may well be called so, most blessed among all women: for she had great and high prerogatives, which none other woman ever had, hath, or shall have. Is not this an high prerogative, that of all women she was chosen to be mother to the Son of God? And what excellent honour was she put to, when, notwithstanding the decree was made of his nativity by the whole Trinity, yet the thing was not done and accomplished without or before her consent was granted, for the which so solemn a messenger was sent? And also how high grace was this, that after the default made through the persuasion of the first woman, our mother Eve, by whom Adam was brought into disobedience, this blessed virgin was elect to be the instrument of our reparation, in that she was chosen to bear the Saviour and Redeemer of the world? And is not this a wonderful prerogative, to see a virgin to be a mother, and conceive her child without sin? We may worthily say that she is the most blessed of all other women. And to the intent that all good Christian men should repute and take her so, behold the providence of God, that would by another witness confirm the same: for even the very same words that the angel spake, the blessed matron St. Elisabeth spake also; and where the angel made an end, there she began.

The angel made an end of his salutation with these words: *Blessed art thou among women.* The blessed matron began her salutation with the same words, declaring that she was inspired with the same Spirit that sent the angel, and that they were both ministers to the holy Trinity, the one from heaven, the other in earth. And afterward she added these words, saying, *And blessed is the fruit of thy womb.* These be not the words of the angel, but of St. Elisabeth: for when the virgin Mary came to salute her, the said Elisabeth, being inspired with the Holy Ghost, and knowing that the virgin Mary was conceived, spake these words of the fruit that the virgin should bring forth.

And there is also another wonderful thing to be noted. For, as it appeareth in the Gospel, the child in St. Elisabeth's womb, that is to say, St. John Baptist, (which yet had scant life,) gave testimony to this fruit, that this fruit should save him and all the world, and as a prophet he leaped for joy in his mother's womb; and although he could not then speak, yet nevertheless he declared by such signs and tokens as he could, that blessed was the fruit of that womb: and worthily called the fruit of her womb, in that the substance of the nature of man, which our Saviour Christ took upon him, was taken of the substance and nature of the most blessed virgin, and in her womb; and so is called the fruit of her womb. And well he may be called the blessed fruit, which hath saved us, and given us life, contrary to the cursed fruit which Eve gave to Adam, by which we were destroyed and brought to death. But blessed is the fruit of this womb, which is the fruit of life everlasting.

And it is to be noted, that although this salutation be not a prayer of petition, supplication, or request or suit; yet nevertheless the church hath used to adjoin it to the end of the Paternoster, as an hymn or a prayer of laud and praise, partly of our Lord and Saviour Jesu Christ, for our redemption, and partly of the blessed virgin, for her humble consent given and expressed to the angel at this salutation. Lauds, praise, and thanks are in this Ave Maria principally given and yielded to our Lord, as to the author of our redemption: but therewithal the virgin lacketh not her lauds, praise, and thanks for her excellent and singular virtues, and chiefly for that she believed and humbly consented, according to the saying of the holy matron St. Elisabeth, when she said unto this virgin, Blessed art thou that diddest give trust and credence to the angel's words: for all things that have been spoken unto thee shall be performed.

The Article of Freewill

The commandments and threatenings of Almighty God in scripture, whereby man is called upon and put in remembrance what God would have him to do, most evidently do express and declare that man hath freewill also now after the fall of our first father Adam, as plainly appeareth in these places following: Be not overcome of evil (Rom 12:21). Neglect not the grace that is in thee (1 Tim 4:14). Love not the world, &c (1 John 2:15-17). If thou wilt enter into life, keep the commandments (Matt 19:17). Which undoubtedly should be said in vain, unless there were some faculty or power left in man whereby he may, by the help and grace of God, (if he will receive it when it is offered unto him,) understand his commandments, and freely consent and obey unto them: which thing of the catholic fathers is called freewill; which if we will describe, we may call it conveniently in all men, a certain power of the will joined with reason, whereby a reasonable creature, without constraint in things of reason, discerneth and willeth good and evil; but it willeth not that good which is acceptable to God, except it be holpen with grace; but that which is ill it willeth of itself: and therefore other men defined freewill in this wise: Freewill is a power of reason and will, by which good is chosen by the assistance of grace, or evil is chosen without the assistance of the same.

Howbeit the state and condition of freewill was otherwise in our first parents before they sinned, than it was either in them or in their posterity after they had sinned. For our first parents Adam and Eve, until they wounded and overthrew themselves by sin, had so in possession the said power of freewill, by the most liberal gift and grace of God their Maker, that not only they might eschew all manner of sin, but also know God, and love him, and fulfil all things appertaining to their felicity and wealth. For they were made righteous, and to the image and similitude of God, having power of freewill (as Chrysostom saith) to obey or disobey: so that by obedience they might live, and by disobedience they should worthily deserve to die. For the Wise Man affirmeth, that the state of them was of that sort in the beginning; saying thus: God in the beginning did create man, and left him in the hands of his own counsel. He gave unto him his precepts and commandments, saying, If thou wilt keep the commandments, they shall preserve thee. He hath set afore thee fire and water: put forth thy hands to whether thou wilt. Before man is life and death, good and evil: what him liketh that shall he have (Sir 15:14-17). From this most happy estate our first parents falling by disobedience, most grievously hurted themselves and their posterity. For besides many other evils that came by that transgression, the high power of man's reason and freedom of will were wounded and corrupted, and all men thereby brought into such blindness and infirmity, that they cannot eschew sin, except they be illumined and made free by an especial grace, that is to say, by a supernatural help and working of the Holy Ghost, which, although the goodness of God offereth to all men, yet they only enjoy it which by their freewill do accept and embrace the same. Nor they also that be holpen by the said grace can accomplish and perform things that be for their wealth, but with much labour and endeavour; so great is in our nature the corruption of the first sin, and the heavy burden bearing us down to evil. For truly albeit the light of reason doth abide, yet it is much darkened, and with much difficulty doth discern things that be inferior, and pertain to this present life: but to understand and perceive things that be spiritual, and pertain to the everlasting life, it is of itself unable. And so likewise, although there remain a certain freedom of will in those things which do pertain unto the desires and works of this present life, yet to perform spiritual and heavenly things, freewill of itself is insufficient: and therefore the power of man's freewill being thus wounded and decayed, hath need of a physician to heal it, and an help to repair it, that it may receive light and strength, whereby it may see and have power to do those godly and spiritual things, which before the fall of Adam it was able and might have done.

To this blindness and infirmity of man's nature, proceeding of original sin, the prophet David had regard, when he desired his eyes to be lightened of Almighty God, that he might consider the marvellous things that be in his law (Ps 118:23). And also the prophet Jeremy, saying, Heal me, O Lord, and I shall be made whole (Jer 17:14). St. Augustine also plainly declareth the same, saying, We conclude that freewill is in man after his fall; which thing whoso denieth is not a catholic man: but in spiritual desires and works to please God, it is so weak and feeble, that it cannot either begin or perform them, unless by the grace and help of God it be prevented and holpen. And hereby it appeareth, that man's strength and will in all things which be healthful to the soul, and shall please God, hath need of grace of the Holy Ghost, by which such spiritual things be inspired to men, and strength and constance given to perform them, if men do not wilfully refuse the said grace offered unto them.

And likewise as many things be in the scripture which do shew freewill to be in man; so there be no fewer places in scripture which do declare the grace of God to be so necessary, that if by it freewill be not prevented and holpen, it can neither do nor will any thing good and godly. Of which sort be these scriptures following: Without me ye can do nothing (John 15:5). No man cometh to me, except it be given him of my Father (John 6:44). We be not sufficient of ourselves, as of ourselves, to think any good thing (2 Cor 3:5). According unto which scriptures, and such other like, it followeth, that freewill, before it may will or think any godly thing, must be holpen by the grace of Christ, and by his Spirit be prevented and inspired, that it may be able thereto: and being so made able, may from thenceforth work together with grace, and by the same sustained, holpen, and maintained, may do and accomplish good works, and avoid sin, and persevere also and increase in grace. It is surely of the grace of God only that first we be inspired and moved to any good thing: but to resist temptations, and to persist in goodness and go forward, it is both of the grace of God and of our freewill and endeavour. And finally, after we have persevered to the end, to be crowned with glory therefore is the gift and mercy of God, who of his bountiful goodness hath ordained that reward to be given after this life, according to such good works as be done in this life by his grace.

Therefore men ought with much diligence and gratitude of mind to consider and regard the inspirations and wholesome motions of the Holy Ghost, and to embrace the grace of God, which is offered unto them in

Christ, and moveth them to good things: and furthermore to go about by all means to shew themselves such as unto whom the grace of God is not given in vain. And when they do feel that notwithstanding their diligence, yet through their own infirmity they be not able to do that they desire, then they ought earnestly, and with a fervent devotion and steadfast faith, to ask of him, which gave the beginning, that he would vouchsafe to perform it: which thing God will undoubtedly grant, according to his promise, to such as persevere in calling upon him. For he is naturally good, and willeth all men to be saved, and careth for them, and provideth all thing by which they may be saved, except by their own malice they will be evil, and so by righteous judgment of God perish and be lost. For truly men be to themselves the authors of sin and damnation. God is neither author of sin nor the cause of damnation. And yet doth he most righteously damn those men that do with vices corrupt their nature, which he made good, and do abuse the same to evil desires, against his most holy will. Wherefore men be to be warned that they do not impute to God their vice or their damnation, but to themselves, which by freewill have abused the grace and benefits of God.

All men be also to be monished, and chiefly preachers, that in this high matter they looking on both sides, so attemper and moderate themselves, that neither they so preach the grace of God, that they take away thereby freewill, nor on the other side so extol freewill, that injury be done to the grace of God.

The Article of Justification

For the more clear understanding of this article following, it is to be noted, that all men after the fall of Adam, naturally descending and coming of him, be born in original sin, that is to say, they lack that original justice and innocency, wherewith Adam in his creation was endued, and which also all his posterity should have had, if he, through his disobedience and breaking of the commandment of God, had not lost the same from himself and all his posterity. And further also, they be born with concupiscence, whereof spring unlawful desires, repugnant and contrary unto the laws of God, and be guilty to everlasting death and damnation, from the which they can in no wise be delivered by any strength or power that is in them, but rather fall daily into further displeasure of God, by committing and adding of many actual sins.

Wherefore, to the intent that man might be delivered out of this wretched and miserable state, whereunto he had brought himself, and might recover again the same things that were given unto him in his first creation, and thereby attain the everlasting bliss in heaven, it pleased Almighty God, of his great and infinite mercy and goodness, to send his own only begotten Son, the second Person in Trinity, to take upon him the nature of man, and therein to work the mystery of our redemption, that is to say, to deliver us from the captivity of the devil, sin, and damnation, and to be the very mean of our reconciliation to God, and of our justification. And surely this reconciliation of mortal man to the favour of God immortal did necessarily require such a mediator between them as had in himself the perfect nature of them both, which is the very property of a mean between two, to be partner with both them between whom he taketh upon him to be a mean. For if he be wholly joined with the one, and clearly separated from the other, then he is not meet to be a mean or mediator between two which be at debate and enmity. Wherefore our Saviour Christ, being naturally God, took upon him the nature of man, that he might thereby be conversant among men, and by his death redeem them, and yet he still retained and kept his Godhead, and was both God and man together. For if he had been man only, and not God, then his death could not have been a worthy and sufficient satisfaction for sin, to the justice of God. And if he had been only God, and not man, then he by his bodily conversation could not have called us again to God, nor suffered and died bodily for us. And this property of a mediator St. Paul considering, writeth to Timothy, That there is but one mediator between God and man, which is Christ Jesus (1 Tim 2:5); meaning thereby, that because he only had both the natures in him, therefore he only, and none other but he, was able to be a sufficient mediator and mean of our reconciliation to God, and of our justification.

And for a further declaration how and by what means we be made partakers of this benefit of justification, it is to be noted, that this word *justification*, as it is taken in scripture, signifieth the making of us righteous afore God, where before we were unrighteous, as when by his grace we convert unto him, and be reconciled into his favour, and of the children of ire and damnation, we be made the children of God, and inheritors of everlasting life, that by his grace we may walk so in his ways, that finally we may be reputed and taken as just and righteous in the day of judgment, and so receive the everlasting possession of the kingdom of heaven. And albeit God is the principal cause and chief worker of this justification in us, without whose grace no man can do no good thing, but following his freewill in the state of a sinner, increaseth his own injustice, and multiplieth his sin; yet so it pleaseth the high wisdom of God, that man, prevented by his grace, (which being offered, man may if he will refuse or receive,) shall be also a worker by his free consent and obedience to the same, in the attaining of his own justification, and by God's grace and help shall walk in such works as be requisite to his justification, and so continuing, come to the perfect end thereof by such means and ways as God hath ordained.

Wherein it is to be considered, that although our Saviour Christ hath offered himself upon the cross a sufficient redemption and satisfaction for the sins of all the world, and hath made himself an open way and entry unto God the Father for all mankind, only by his worthy merit and deserving, and willing all men to be saved, calleth upon all the world, without respect of persons, to come and be partakers of the righteousness, peace, and glory which is in him; yet for all this benignity and grace, shewed universally to the whole world, none shall have the effect of this benefit of our Saviour Christ, and enjoy everlasting salvation by him, but they that take such ways to attain the same as he hath taught and appointed by his holy word, in such order, manner, and form as here followeth; that is to say, first, as touching all them which be of age, and have the use of natural reason afore they be christened, the will of God is, that all such (if they will be saved) shall, at the hearing of his blessed word, give steadfast faith and assent thereunto, as St. Paul saith, He that cometh to God must believe (Heb 11:6); and by that faith, grounded on the truth of the word of God, being taught both of the threatenings of God against sinners, and also of the great goodness and mercy of God offered to mankind in our Saviour and Redeemer Christ Jesu, they must conceive an hearty sorrow and repentance for their sins, with a sure trust to have forgiveness of them by the merits and passion of our Saviour Christ. And joining thereunto a full purpose to amend their life, and to commit sin no more, but to serve God all their life after, they must then receive the sacrament of baptism. And this is the very plain ordinary way, by the which God hath determined that man, being of age, and coming to Christendom, should be justified. For as for infants, it is to be believed that their justification is wrought by the secret operation of the Holy Ghost in their baptism, they being offered in the faith of the church.

And this justification, whereof we have hitherto spoken, may be called the first justification, that is to say, our first coming into God's house, which is the church of Christ; at which coming we be received and admitted to be of the flock and family of our Saviour Christ, and be professed and sworn to be the servants of God, and to be soldiers under Christ, to fight against our enemies, the devil, the world, and the flesh: of which enemies, if it chance us, after our baptism, to be overthrown, and cast into mortal sin, then is there no remedy, but for the recovering of our former estate of justification which we have lost, to arise by penance, wherein proceeding in sorrow and much lamentation for our sins, with fasting, alms, prayer, and doing all such things, at the least in true purpose and will, as God requireth of us, we must have a sure trust and confidence in the mercy of God, that for his Son our Saviour Christ's sake he will yet forgive us our sins, and receive us unto his favour again; and so being thus restored to our justification, we must go forward in our battle aforesaid, in mortifying our concupiscence, and in our daily spiritual renovation, in following the motions of the Spirit of Christ, in doing good works, and abstaining from sin and all occasions thereof, being armed with faith, hope, and charity, to the intent we may attain our final justification, and so be glorified in the day of judgment with the reward of everlasting life.

Wherefore it is necessary, for the keeping and holding of this justification, once conferred and given in baptism, or recovered again by penance, through the mercy of our Saviour Christ, and also for the increasing of the same justification, and final consummation thereof, to take good heed, and to watch, that we be not deceived by the false suggestion and temptation of our ghostly enemy the devil, who, as St. Peter saith, goeth about like a roaring lion, seeking whom he may devour (1 Pet 5:8).

And it is no doubt, but although we be once justified, yet we may fall therefrom by our own freewill and consenting unto sin, and following the desires thereof; for albeit the house of our conscience be once made clean, and the foul spirit be expelled from us in baptism or penance, yet if we wax idle, and take not heed, he will return with seven worse spirits, and possess us again. And although we be illuminate, and have tasted the heavenly gift, and be made partakers of the Holy Ghost, yet may we fall, and displease God. Wherefore, as St. Paul saith, He that standeth, let him take heed that he fall not (1 Cor 10:12).

And here all phantastical imagination, curious reasoning, and vain trust of predestination, is to be laid apart. And according to the plain manner of speaking and teaching of scripture, in innumerable places, we ought evermore to be in dread of our own frailty and natural pronity to fall to sin, and not to assure ourselves that we be elected, any otherwise than by feeling of spiritual motions in our heart, and by the tokens of good and virtuous living, in following the grace of God, and persevering in the same to the end. And this St. Peter exhorteth us to make our vocation and election sure and stable (2 Pet 1:10). And Christ saith, He that persevereth unto the end shall be saved (Matt 24:13). And in Revelation of St. John,

Be faithful unto death, and I shall give thee the crown of life (Rev 2:10). Wherefore when we be once elected and admitted unto God's service, (as is aforesaid,) and have received our justification in baptism, or be restored thereunto by true penance, then must we continually walk after Christ, bearing our cross, and increasing in his grace by good works; and so doing, proceed, go forward, and increase in our justification, according to the saying of St. John, He that is just, let him be more justified (Rev 22:11). For as the grace of God, and the gifts thereof, that is to say, faith, repentance, dread, hope, charity, with other fruits of the Holy Ghost, do increase in us, so do we wax and increase in our justification.

And therefore it is plain, that not only faith, as it is a distinct virtue or gift by itself, is required to our justification, but also the other gifts of the grace of God, with a desire to do good works, proceeding of the same grace. And whereas in certain places of scripture our justification is ascribed to faith, without any further addition or mention of any other virtue or gift of God, it is to be understand of faith, in the second acception, as before is declared in the article of faith, wherein the fear of God, repentance, hope, and charity be included and comprised, all which must be joined together in our justification: so that no faith is sufficient to justification or salvation, but such a faith as worketh by charity (Gal 5:6), as is plainly expressed by St. Paul, in his Epistle to the Galatians: and that also our good works which we do, being once justified, by faith and charity, avail both to the conservation and perfection of the said virtues in us, and also to the increase and end of our justification and everlasting salvation.

And although we can never be justified without these gifts of the Holy Ghost, faith, repentance, hope, charity, with desire and study to bring forth good works; yet it is to be understand that nevertheless we be justified gratis, that is to say, freely, forasmuch as all gifts or works, whereby our justification is wrought and accomplished, come of the free mercy and grace of God, and not of our deserving: so that our pride and glory in ourselves, and our own worthiness, is utterly excluded. For we be not able of ourselves, as of ourselves, not as much as to think any good thing; but our ableness and our sufficiency is of God, which giveth us the said gifts of his own inestimable goodness, and doth also assist us with his holy Spirit, and strength us, to keep his commandments.

And further, where our keeping of them is unperfect, and even in the best men wanteth a great deal of that duty to God which they ought and

be bound to do; yet Almighty God of his mere mercy and goodness accepteth the same as a perfect fulfilling of them, for our Saviour Christ's
sake, which hath fulfilled the law for us, and is the end and perfection of
the law to all that truly believe in him. And so we have all gratis, that is to
say, of his grace, and not of our worthiness, or any merit going before
grace, but receiving all of God, as St. Paul saith, What hast thou that thou
hast not received (1 Cor 4:7)? We refer all unto his goodness and mercy,
by the which we both come unto the beginning of our justification, and
do proceed and go forward in the same, and finally attain the end thereof,
and be brought to everlasting life, unto the which the very way appointed
by Christ (whose word no man may change) is to keep and observe the
commandments of God; for he saith expressly, If thou wilt enter into life,
keep the commandments; that is, apply thy whole study and affection to
walk in the law of God, wherein if thou persevere, thou shalt be saved
(Matt 19:17). And so, after thy justification, thou shalt be glorified, according to the order of God, which St. Paul speaketh of, when he saith,
Quos justificavit, illos glorificavit (Rom 8:30).[1]

---

[1] [Those whom he justified he also glorified.]

The Article of Good Works

All preaching and learning of the word of God in Christ's church ought to tend to this end, that men may be induced, not only to know God, and to believe and trust in him, but also to honour and serve him with good works, wrought in faith and charity, and utterly to forsake the works of sin and the flesh, which whosoever do commit (except they repent and amend by penance) they shall not (as St. Paul saith) inherit the kingdom of God.

And that holy scripture goeth to this point, to persuade men to live well, and to do good works, St. Paul testifieth, saying unto Timothy, All scripture, written by the inspiration of God, is profitable to teach, to reprove, to correct, to instruct, that the servant of God may be perfect, and made apt unto every good work (2 Tim 3:16). And whereas we speak of good works, it is to be understand, that we mean not only of outward corporal acts and deeds, but also and rather of all inward spiritual works, motions, and desires, as the love and fear of God, joy in God, godly meditations and thoughts, patience, humility, and such like. And also it is to be understand, that by good works we mean not the superstitious works of men's own invention, which be not commanded of God, nor approved by his word, in which kind of works many Christian men, and specially of them that were lately called religious, (as monks, friars, nuns, and such other,) have in times past put their great trust and confidence: nor yet we mean not of such moral acts as be done by the power of reason and natural will of man, without faith in Christ, which albeit of their own kind they be good, and by the law and light of nature man is taught to do them, and God also many times doth temporally reward men for doing the same, yet they be not meritorious, nor available to the attaining of everlasting life, when they be not done in the faith of Christ, and therefore be not accounted among the good works whereof we do here entreat: but we speak of such outward and inward works as God hath prepared for us to walk in, and be done in the faith of Christ, for love and respect to God, and cannot be brought forth only by man's power, but he must be prevented and holpen thereto by a special grace.

And these works be of two sorts: for some be such as men truly justified, and so continuing, do work in charity of a pure heart, and a good conscience, and an unfeigned faith: which works, although they be of themselves unworthy, unperfect, and unsufficient; yet forasmuch as they be done in the faith of Christ, and by the virtue and merits of his passion, their unperfectness is supplied; the merciful goodness of God accepteth them, as an observation and fulfilling of his law, and they be the very service of God, and be meritorious towards the attaining of everlasting life. And these be called the works and fruits of righteousness.

Other works there be, which be not so perfect as these, and yet they be done by the grace of God in faith and good affection of heart towards God, as those be which men that have been in deadly sin, and by grace turn to God, do work and bring forth upon respect and remorse that they have for their offences done against God. And these may be called properly the works of penance. As for example, when a sinner, hearing or remembering the law of God, is moved by grace to be contrite and sorry for his offences, and beginneth to lament his estate, and to fall to prayer, and other good deeds, seeking to avoid the indignation of God, and to be reconciled into his favour: these works come of grace; but yet this man is not to be accounted a justified man, but he is yet in seeking remission of his sins and his justification, which the anguish of his own conscience telleth him that he yet wanteth; but he is in a good way, and by these means doth enter into justification: and if he do proceed, and with hearty devotion seek for further grace, he shall be assured of remission of his sins, and attain his justification, and so be made able and meet to walk in the very pure service of God with a clean conscience, and to bring forth the foresaid works of righteousness in Christ, which he cannot do afore he be justified.

And that such works of penance as we have spoken of be required to the attaining of remission of sins and justification, it is very evident and plain by scripture; as when our Saviour Christ saith, Be penitent, and believe the gospel; that is to say, First be contrite, and knowledge your sins, and then receive the glad tidings of remission of your sins (Mark 1:15). And St. John Baptist preached penance, and made a way unto Christ, and taught men which came unto him what they should do to come unto Christ, and to have remission of sins by him, as it is written in the third chapter of Luke: and specially that they which be once christened, and afterward fall from the grace of God by mortal sin, cannot recover their justification without penance, it is plain by the saying of St. Peter unto Simon Magus, where he saith, Do penance for this thy wickedness, and pray God, if peradventure this thought of thy heart may be forgiven unto thee (Acts 8:22).

And truly this way and form of doctrine is to be observed, which is the very trade of scripture, wherein men be taught first to leave sins, and to return by works of penance unto God, and that then they shall receive remission of sins and justification. And although such works of penance be required in us towards the attaining of remission of sins and justification, yet the same justification and remission of sins is the free gift of God, and conferred unto us gratis, that is to say, of the grace of God, whereby we doing such things, and having such motions and works of penance, be prepared and made more apt to receive further grace of remission of our sins and justification.

And it is not inconvenient that such things should through grace be done by us first, and yet it should be said that we receive the said gift freely. For Christ saith in the Revelation of St. John, *Qui sitit, veniat, et qui vult, accipiat aquam vitæ gratis*; He that is thirsty, let him come, and he that will, let him take the water of life freely (Rev 22:17). Where he affirmeth this gift of God to be freely given and conferred, and yet there is required some labour before, as, to have a will and desire to come, which coming cannot be without arising by faith and penance, and proceeding in the same, and so to take the water of life, that is to say, justification, through our Saviour Christ, which, once received in baptism, or after baptism being recovered by penance, although man daily do offend and fall into divers venial sins, by reason of his infirmity and weakness, and therefore hath need of continual and daily repentance, yet as long as he consenteth not to deadly sin, he leeseth not the state of his justification, but remaineth still the child of God: and being in that state, hath power, by God's grace dwelling in him, to do such works as by acceptation of God through Christ be counted works of righteousness, and do serve for the preservation and increase of his farther justification, and be appointed by God's most gracious promise to have everlasting reward in heaven. Which both inward and outward works be not only the declaring of our faith and confidence in God, and of the grace which we have received, but also a continual exercise, nourishment, preservation, increase, and perfection of the same. For if we should not, after that we have professed Christ, apply our will to work well, according to our said profession, then should we fall from the grace of God and the estate of righteousness and justification which we were once set in, and become again the servants of sin. And as St. Peter saith, We should be in worse case than we were before we received the knowledge of Christ (2 Pet 2:20).

And that we increase in grace by working in the grace of God once received, it appeareth by the word of our Saviour Christ, where he saith, *Omni habenti dabitur, et abundabit* (Matt 25:29);[1] meaning thereby, that whosoever useth well the grace of God which is offered unto him already, he shall have more, and wax plentiful in grace. Wherefore as we continue and persevere in good works, so more and more we go forward and proceed in our justification, and in increasing the same; whereunto St. Peter exhorteth us, saying, Fall not from the sure estate wherein ye be set, but increase and grow in grace, and in the knowledge of our Lord and Saviour Jesu Christ (2 Pet 3:18).

And to ascribe this dignity unto good works, it is no derogation to the grace of God: forasmuch as it is to be confessed that all good works come of the grace of God. And our merits, as St. Augustine saith, be but the gifts of God; and so in ourselves we may not glory, nor look back on our own worthiness or dignity, which is naught as of ourselves, but of the only acceptation of God's mercy. And therefore we must, as St. Paul saith, extend ourselves to that which is afore us, to the reward of the heavenly calling which is in Christ, and still proceed in good works, knowing ourselves to be evermore greater debtors to God for his grace (Phil 3:14). And when we have done all which we be bidden do, the scripture teacheth us to say

---

[1] [For to every one who has will more be given, and he will have abundance . . .]

that we be unprofitable servants, because that whatsoever we have done it is but our duty, nor we have done nothing but that we have received of his gift to do, and that to our profit, and not to his (Luke 17:10). But yet must we take heed, that seeing we have received the grace of God, we be not found unprofitable servants in this wise, that is to say, idle servants, to whom it shall be said, Cast out the unprofitable servants into the outward darkness, where shall be weeping and gnashing of teeth (Matt 25:30). And St. Paul also exhorteth, saying, Receive not the grace of God in vain; that is to say, Work well: for the grace of God is given you to that intent (2 Cor 6:1); and to that end we are redeemed by Christ, and delivered from the thraldom of sin and captivity of the devil, that we should serve God, as Zachary saith, in holiness and righteousness afore him all our life (Luke 1:75). And in another place St. Paul saith, The grace of God hath appeared to bring salvation unto all men, teaching us, that we, renouncing all ungodliness and worldly desires, should live in this present world soberly, justly, and devoutly, looking for the blessed hope and appearance of the glory of the great God, and our Saviour Jesu Christ, which gave himself for us, to redeem us from all wickedness, and to cleanse unto himself a special people, which should be studious followers of good works (Titus 2:11). In which godly sentence of St. Paul, besides other great plenty of fruitful learning and edifying, he toucheth in three words all the good works of a true Christian man, where he saith, *soberly, justly,* and *devoutly.* For in this word *soberly* he comprehendeth all abstinence and temperance, and our duty touching our body: and in saying *justly,* he containeth all works of charity towards our neighbour, with due obedience to our princes, heads, and governors: and in this word *devoutly,* he concludeth all our works spiritual, which be done immediately unto God, as prayer, thinking of God, desiring of his glory, &c.

And unto all these works ought we most diligently, with all labour and care, to apply our will for these effects and ends, that is to say, the glory of God, the profit of our neighbour, and our own merit, that we may shew ourselves thankful servants to our Saviour Jesu Christ, and to be the very people of God, and that he may be glorified in us; that his church may be edified by our example; that we may avoid falling into temptation and sin; that we may scape the scourge of God; that the grace of God and the gifts thereof may increase and be made perfect in us; that we may make our election stable and sure; that we may attain everlasting life, being found fruitful in the day of judgment, where every man shall receive according to his works (Matt 25).

Of Prayer for Souls Departed

Forasmuch as due order of charity requireth, and the Book of Maccabees and divers ancient doctors plainly shew, that it is a very good and charitable deed to pray for souls departed; and forasmuch as such usage hath continued in the church so many years, even from the beginning, men ought to judge and think the same to be well and profitably done. And truly it standeth with the very order of charity, a Christian man to pray for another, both quick and dead, and to commend one another in their prayers to God's mercy, and to cause other to pray for them also, as well in masses and exequies, as at other times, and to give alms for them, according to the usage of the church and ancient opinion of the old fathers; trusting that these things do not only profit and avail them, but also declare us to be charitable folk, because we have mind and desire to profit them, which, notwithstanding they be departed this present life, yet remain they still members of the same mystical body of Christ whereunto we pertain.

And here is specially to be noted, that it is not in the power or knowledge of any man to limit and dispense how much, and in what space of time, or to what person particularly the said masses, exequies, and suffrages do profit and avail: therefore charity requireth that whosoever causeth any such masses, exequies, or suffrages to be done, should yet (though their intent be more for one than for another) cause them also to be done for the universal congregation of Christian people, quick and dead; for that power and knowledge afore rehearsed pertaineth only unto

God, which alone knoweth the measures and times of his own judgment and mercies.

Furthermore, because the place where the souls remain, the name thereof, the state and condition which they be in, be to us uncertain, therefore these, with all other such things, must also be left to Almighty God, unto whose mercy it is meet and convenient for us to commend them, trusting that God accepteth our prayers for them; reserving the rest wholly to God, unto whom is known their estate and condition; and not we to take upon us, neither in the one part ne yet in the other, to give any fond and temerarious judgment in so high things so far passing our knowledge.

Finally, it is much necessary that all such abuses as heretofore have been brought in by supporters and maintainers of the papacy of Rome, and their complices, concerning this matter, be clearly put away; and that we therefore abstain from the name of purgatory, and no more dispute or reason thereof. Under colour of which have been advanced many fond and great abuses, to make men believe that through the bishop of Rome's pardons souls might clearly be delivered out of it, and released out of the bondage of sin; and that masses said at Scala cœli, and other prescribed places, phantasied by men, did there in those places more profit the souls than in another; and also that a prescribed number of prayers sooner than other (though as devoutly said) should further their petition sooner, yea specially if they were said before one image more than another which they phantasied. All these, and such like abuses, be necessary utterly to be abolished and extinguished.

IMPRINTED AT LONDON IN
FLETESTRETE BY THOMAS BERTHELET
PRINTER TO THE KYNGES HYGHNES
THE XXIX DATE OF MAYE
THE YERE OF OUR LORDE
M.D.XLIII.

CUM PRIVILEGIO AD IMPRI-
MENDUM SOLUM

Appendices

Appendix A

Extract from the King's Injunctions.
Wilkins, Conc. M.B. 3.813.

In the name of God, Amen. In the year of our Lord God M.D. XXXVI, and of the most noble reign of our sovereign lord Henry VIII, king of England and of France, the 28th year, and the day of —— I Thomas Cromwell, knight, lord Cromwell, keeper of the privy seal of our said sovereign lord the king, and vicegerent unto the same, for and concerning all his jurisdiction ecclesiastical within this realm, visiting by the king's highness supreme authority ecclesiastical the people and clergy of this deanery of —— by my trusty commissary —— lawfully deputed and constitute for this part, have, to the glory of Almighty God, to the king's highness honour, the public weal of this his realm, and encrease of virtue in the same, appointed and assigned these injunctions ensuing, to be kept and observed of the dean, parsons, vicars, curates, and stipendiaries resiant, or having cure of soul, or any other spiritual administration within this deanery, under the pains hereafter limited and appointed.

The first is, that the dean, parsons, vicars, and other having cure of souls any where within the deanery, shall faithfully keep and observe, and, as far as in them may lie, shall cause to be observed and kept of other, all and singular laws and statutes of this realm made for the abolishing and extirpation of the bishops of Rome's pretensed and usurped power and jurisdiction within this realm, and for th'establishment and confirmation

339

of the king's authority and jurisdiction within the same; as of the supreme head of the Church of England, &c.

Item, Whereas certain articles were lately devised and put forth by the king's highness authority, and condescended upon by the prelates and clergy of this his realm in convocation, whereof part are necessary to be holden and believed for our salvation, and th'other part do concern and touch certain laudable ceremonies, rites, and usages of the church, mete and convenient to be kept and used for a decent and a politic order in the same; the said dean, parsons, vicars, and other curates, shall so open and declare in their said sermons and other collations the said articles unto them that be under their cure, that they may plainly know and discern, which of them be necessary to be believed and observed for their salvation; and which be not necessary, but only do concern the decent and politic order of the said church, according to such commandment and admonition as hath been given unto them heretofore by authority of the king's highness in that behalf.

See also the king's Letter to his bishops. Wilkins, 3. 825.

Appendix B

Extract from the Injunctions Given by John Bishop of Exeter A.D. 1538.
Wilk. Conc. M.B. 3. 844.

Injunctions of John bishop of Exeter, made and given to the clergy of his diocese, upon his late ordinary visitation there had and finished in the month of May, the 30th year of the reign of our sovereign lord Henry the Eight, by the grace of God king of England and of France, defender of the faith, lord of Ireland, and supreme head in earth next under God of the Church of England. All and singular which injunctions, by authority given to me of God, and of our said sovereign lord the king, I exhort and command all parsons, vicars, curates, chantry priests, and all other of the clergy, to observe, keep, and perform, as severally concerneth them in virtue of obedience, and upon pain of laws and statutes, as they be hereafter objected against them for breaking and violating the same. *First, That all such of the clergy, having cure of soul within my diocese, do every Sunday declare sincerely in time and place accustomed, in the English tongue, or in the Cornish tongue where the English tongue is not used, all or part of the Epistle or Gospel of that day, or else the Paternoster, Ave Maria, Creed, and the Ten Commandments, or part of them, as the time shall require, as the said Paternoster, Ave Maria, Creed, and Ten Commandments been interpretate in the book called "The Institution of a Christian Man." Also that every curate in the declaration of the premises, set forth and declare in especial the second and the fourth commandments, as they been declared and interpretate in the said book; for want of the true knowledge whereof it is thought many of the unlearned people in my diocese been much blinded, following many times their own superstitious fantasies, and omitting to do the works of mercy, and other meritorious acts commanded by God in his holy scripture.*

Extract from the Injunctions Given by Edmund Bonner, Bishop of London, to His Clergy.
Wilkins, Conc. M.B. 3.864

Injunctions made by the consent and authority of me Edmund Bonner, bishop of London, in the year of our Lord God M.D.XLII, and in the 35th year of the reign of our sovereign lord king Henry the VIIIth, by the grace of God king of England, France, and Ireland, defender of the faith, and supreme head here in earth next under God of the Church of England and Ireland; all which and singular injunctions by the authority given to me of God, and by our said sovereign lord the king's majesty, I exhort, require, and also command all and singular parsons, vicars, curates, and chantry priests, with other of the clergy whatsoever they be, of my diocese and jurisdiction of London, to observe, keep, and perform accordingly, as it concerneth every one of them, in virtue of their obedience, and also upon pains expressed in all such laws, statutes, and ordinances of this realm, as they may incur and be objected against them, now or at any time hereafter, for breaking and violating of the same, or any of them.

First, That you and every of you shall with all diligence and faithful obedience observe and keep, and cause to be observed and kept, to the uttermost of your powers, all and singular the contents of the king's highness most gracious and godly ordinances and injunctions, given and set forth by his grace's authority, and that ye, and every of you, for the better performance thereof, shall provide to have a copy of the same in writing, or imprinted, and so to declare them accordingly.

Item, That every parson, vicar, and curate shall read over and diligently study, every day, one chapter of the Bible, and that with the gloss, ordinary, or some other doctor or expositor, approved and allowed in this Church of England, proceeding from chapter to chapter, from the beginning of the Gospel of St. Matthew to the end of the New Testament; and the same so diligently studied, to keep still, and retain in memory; and to come to the rehearsal and recital thereof, at all such time and times as they or any of them shall be commanded thereunto by me, or any of my officers or deputies.

Item, That every of you do procure, and provide of your own, a book called "The Institution of a Christian Man," otherwise called "The Bishops Book," and that ye and every of you do exercise yourselves in the same, according to such precepts as hath been given heretofore, or hereafter to be given.

Appendix C

First paragraph of the Necessary Doctrine and Erudition, as it is given in the three different copies printed by Thomas Berthelet on the 29th of May, 1543.

I. 4to.   *Faithe.*

Forasmoche as in this *boke, whiche* is *sette furthe* for the institution and er-udition of the common people, the articles of our *faith* have the *first* place, it is very *necessarye,* before we entre into the declaration of the *said* articles, some *thynge* to entreate of *faith,* to the intent that it *may* be knowen what is *ment* proprely by the worde *Faith,* as it is *apperteynyng* to a Christen man, who by *fayth* is partaker of Goddis benefites by *Chryste.*

II. 4to.   *Faithe.*

Forasmoche as in this *boke* whiche is sette furthe for the institution and erudition of the common people, the articles of our *faith* have the *fyrste* place, it is very *necessarye* before we entre into the declaration of the *sayde* articles, some *thyng* to entreate of *fayth,* to the intent that it *may* be knowen, what is *ment* proprely by the worde *Faythe* as it is *apperteynyng* to a Christen man, who by *faythe* is partaker of Goddis benefites by *Chryste.*

III. 8vo. *Faythe.*

For as moche as in this *booke whyche* is sette *furth* for the institution and erudition of the com̄on people, the articles of our *faythe* have the *fyrste* place, it is very *necessary,* before we entre into the declaration of the *sayd* articles, *somethyng* to entreate of *faith* to the intent that it *maye* be knowen what is *mente* proprely by the worde *Faithe* as it is *apperteyning* to a Christen man, who by faith is partaker of Goddis benefites by *Christe.*

A Note on the Text

When Charles Lloyd originally published *Formularies of Faith* with the University Press of Oxford in 1825, his aim was to provide readers with the chance to compare the different doctrinal statements of the Church of England during the reign of Henry VIII, and he did this by providing texts that were as close as possible to the original manuscripts themselves, albeit with a modernization of spelling and syntax. Lloyd's critical edition has been surpassed by that of Gerald Bray's *Institution of a Christian Man* (James Clarke & Co., 2018), which consolidates *The Bishops' Book* and *The King's Book* into a single reconstructed text and which provides other historically pertinent primary sources. Yet with its complex system of bold and italicized font denoting the differences between the two books, Bray's edition can prove overwhelming for students just beginning to get their feet wet in the headwaters of the English Reformation. As helpful and masterful as Bray's reconstructed text is, there is still something to be said for simply being able to read *The Bishops' Book* or *The King's Book* straight through. Our edition hopes to create just such a reading experience.

Yet, credit where credit is due, the idea of republishing these texts did not come from us. Rather, in the Fall of 2021, the Rev. Dr. Katherine Sonderegger requested that Seminary Street Press republish *The King's Book*, a text she uses regularly in her Anglican Thought class at Virginia Theological Seminary. She and her students were forging ahead with digitized facsimiles and a few stalwart but crumbling library copies from the 1800s. We were only too happy to undertake the project of republishing *Formularies of Faith*, knowing that Dr. Sonderegger would use the text to introduce a new generation of clergy, scholars, and lay leaders to one of the earliest attempts at systematic theology in the reformed Church of England.

With this audience in mind, we departed from Lloyd's edition only when it seemed that readability could be improved. While Lloyd used marginal scriptural citations, we moved these citations into the body of the text. Since these citations originally only referred to book and chapter, we have also supplied verse numbers where this seemed appropriate. Moreover, any Latin quotations that went untranslated in Lloyd's edition are now accompanied by a bracketed footnote with an English translation. Although we realize this is a departure from Lloyd's original intention to present the texts as he found them in manuscript, we hope that students will nevertheless benefit from these extra aids.

It is sometimes said that Anglicans do not write systematic theology. It would be better to say that Anglicans often do not read the systematic theology which their tradition has produced. We hope to begin reversing that trend through the publication of these formularies. While *The Bishops' Book* and *The King's Book* may have no binding dogmatic authority, they nevertheless preserved a medieval tradition of systematic thought and catechesis, one which never entirely died out in the reformed Church of England. We at Seminary Street Press look forward to proving this point as we continue to unearth texts which all too carelessly have been forgotten and neglected.

Andrew Raines and Christopher Poore
The Feast of St. Bartholomew
August 24, 2022

The Library of Anglican Theology

About the Editors

Charles Lloyd (1784-1829) was the Bishop of Oxford from 1827 until 1829. As Regius Professor of Divinity at the University of Oxford, Lloyd mentored many students who would go on to be part of the Oxford Movement, including John Henry Newman and Edward Bouverie Pusey.

Andrew Raines, from Olanta, SC, is a student pursuing ordination in the Episcopal Church at Duke Divinity School.

Printed in Great Britain
by Amazon